CRITICAL CONVERSATIONS IN PHILOSOPHY OF EDUCATION

CRITICAL CONVERSATIONS

IN PHILOSOPHY OF

EDUCATION

&

EDITED BY

WENDY KOHLI

ROUTLEDGE   NEW YORK   LONDON

Published in 1995 by

Routledge
29 West 35th Street
New York, NY 10001

Published in Great Britain in 1995 by

Routledge
11 New Fetter Lane
London EC4P 4EE

Library of Congress Cataloging-in-Publication Data

Critical conversations in philosophy of education / edited by Wendy
   Kohli.
      p.   cm.
   Includes bibliographical references.
   ISBN 0-415-90693-8. — ISBN 0-415-90694-6 (pbk.)
   1. Education—Philosophy.   I. Kohli, Wendy.
LB14.7.C75   1995
370'.1—dc20   94-44782
                                         CIP
                                       r95

To my hard-working,
ever-loving parents,
Barbara and Mike Kohli.

Contents

Rationality and Reason

Educating for Moral and Ethical Life

Knowledge and Certainty in Uncertain Times

Educating for Public Life

PART III EXPANDING/EXPLODING THE "CANON"

Culture, Art, and Representation

Acknowledgments

There are many people who deserve appreciation for their help and encouragement as I saw this volume through to completion. First and foremost is Philip for his sterling support from beginning to end. His intelligent editing suggestions, his marvelous sense of humor, and his loving reminders made the process almost a breeze.

A special thanks goes to Maxine Greene, whose work and being have been an inspiration to me ever since I took my first course with her over twenty years ago. It is she who demonstrated through word and deed the power of, and necessity for, seeing from multiple perspectives, speaking with multiple voices, and listening to multiple intelligences.

All of the other contributors deserve my thanks as well. They agreed to engage in respectful dialogue, write short original essays, and get their work in on time. All did their very best and made the complicated design for this book a reality.

And finally to Jayne Fargnoli and Anne Sanow at Routledge for believing in the idea from the start.

Contextualizing the Conversation

Wendy Kohli

Philosophy in Transition/Transformation

This collection brings together in dialogue, established philosophers of education along with emerging young scholars who represent, albeit partially, our field at this contested time in the history of ideas. Philosophy of Education, not unlike its "parent" discipline, Philosophy, has undergone several "turns" in recent decades: the linguistic, the analytic, and now the postmodern.[1] Just as philosophers in general are coming to terms with "end of philosophy" pronouncements and the implications of this development for their work,[2] so too are we who call ourselves philosophers of education faced with similar challenges: challenges to our long-held moral, political, aesthetic, and epistemological commitments. For example, no longer can we invoke generalizations about "rational man" without coming up against the particular effects of race, gender, and class on our concepts. Nor can we make claims about the "we" who is doing the conceptualizing without risking the question: *who* is the *we* about whom we are talking?

Why a "Conversation?"

Such challenges often reveal our professional/personal investments, investments we sometimes choose to defend at the expense of our intellectual openness, curiosity, and mutual respect. As editor, I was committed from the start to encouraging all three of these qualities from the contributors as they engaged each other in a dialogical format across their differences. In fact, it was a condition of their involvement in the project. Each author had to make a good faith effort to resist "going for the jugular," to avoid immediately "finding the flaw in the argument," to overcome their training in philosophy to "get it right." This is not to say they were expected to "lessen their standards," give up their integrity, or abandon critical reflection. But they *were expected* to try to see other points of view and be open to the possible contributions these differing perspectives could make to the field. Obviously in my commitment to dialogue, I was revealing some of my own investments and beliefs, particularly a belief in the possibility for *understanding,* if not agreement. This was not easy, for often at the heart of these different positions were competing and contradictory notions of what Philosophy and Philosophy of Education *are.*

Enter another of my commitments/investments: the issue of inclusion/exclusion in the field of Philosophy of Education. At any given time in our professional history, particular perspectives have dominated the discourse and identity of our discipline. Although multiple perspectives have always co-existed, they often suffered the hegemonic influence of the prevailing discourse. For too long, too many of us have felt left out of the conversation, or have been made to feel that we weren't "part of the club." This was particularly true for women, especially feminists whose work questioned some of the fundamental assumptions of much of Western philosophy.

But even as women philosophers of education struggled for their rightful place, the effects of the various feminisms and critical theories on Philosophy of Education became visible. The field is no longer identified with any one school of thought, whether Aristotelian, pragmatic or analytic. There is more slippage, more opportunity, perhaps more confusion.

Philosophers of education reflecting on the parameters of our field are faced not only with such perplexing and disruptive questions as: What counts as Philosophy of Education and why?; but also *Who* counts as a philosopher of education and why?; and What need is there for Philosophy of Education in a postmodern context? Embedded in these queries we find other no less provocative ones: What knowledge, if any, can or should be privileged and why?; and Who is in a position to privilege particular discursive practices over others and why?

Although such questions are disruptive, they offer the opportunity to take a fresh look at the nature and purposes of our work and, as we do, to expand the number and kinds of voices participating in the conversation. No guarantees for consensus are expected from these conversations. Instead, what is desired is a lively intellectual exchange that reveals different points of view on recurring philosophical themes. Through this kind of dialogue, the health and vitality of educational theorizing is more likely to be nurtured and strengthened.

Who is Talking in this Dialogue?

In an effort to discourage univocity, the volume includes voices representing several generations, countries and cultures, as well as a range of intellectual and political standpoints. Women and people of color are present in larger numbers and in greater proportion than is typical for the field. At the same time, I resisted pigeon-holing people and topics by correlating identities with points of view. There is no "feminist" slot; nor is there a prescribed "Marxist" position. I asked a variety of thoughtful people to speak their mind and share their thinking about particular themes that have engaged philosophers of education for some time.

This volume provides a forum for an *ongoing* conversation, one that is partial and incomplete. To prevent our field from becoming "moribund,"[3] we need to insure that conditions for dialogue encourage growth and renewal. We must ask ourselves what is at stake, individually and collectively, if we are not more inclusive; if we do not become more educated about and understanding of our differences; if we do not attend to the pressing problems of a diverse world.

The Structure of the Book

The book is divided into three sections. Part I addresses the question: What Counts as Philosophy of Education? Part II, Variations From/On the Canon, focuses on five perennial themes important to philosophers of education: the aims of education, rationality and reason, moral and ethical education, knowledge, and politics. Part III expands and explodes the canon by exploring current ideas that are moving in from the margins to center stage in philosophical and educational discourse. These include: culture, art and representation; difference, identity and "otherness"; ecology; sex, gender and the body; and power and interests.

Within each section one or two authors take on a theme knowing that another contributor will engage them in dialogue. All of the essays in this collection were written especially for this volume and with this dialogical intention.

Now it is up to the reader to enter into this dialogue, to continue it, to keep it open, to add your own voices to it.

NOTES

1. Clive Beck, in *Educational Theory*, Summer 1991 41(3), suggests it may not be a *turn* but instead a (re)turn.

2. See for example Kenneth Baynes, et al., *After Philosophy: End or Transformation,* Cambridge: MIT Press, 1987.

3. This is a reference to an oft-cited article in curriculum theory: "The Practical: A Language for Curriculum," by Joseph Schwab in which he declares in his opening paragraph that "the field of curriculum is moribund." See *School Review,* 1969–70, 78:1–23.

PART ONE

WHAT COUNTS AS PHILOSOPHY OF EDUCATION?

1

What Counts as Philosophy of Education?

Maxine Greene

When Hélène Cixous, critic and philosopher, was asked to deliver an Oxford Amnesty Lecture in 1992, she thought immediately of the millions deprived of liberty over the world; of the tortured ones, and of the forgotten men and women for whom Amnesty International was organized. Like many philosophers in the West, she was aware of the loss of legitimation of what used to be taken for granted about human subjects: freedom, social justice, and equality; and she found herself in tension with regard to a desire for the old standards and an acknowledgment of postmodern scepticism and questioning. She accepted the invitation and then recalled the questions being posed today about traditional norms and principles.

Is there such a thing as an inalienable self? Is the Western conception of the person "as a bounded, unique, more or less integrated motivational and cognitive universe, a dynamic center of awareness . . ." defensible in this time of multiple perspectives and multiple realities? (Geertz, 1983). If the self, as defined by an eighteenth century ideology of rights, does not exist, whose freedom are we trying so hard to protect? In any case, are "self" and "freedom" what they used to be?

> And I asked myself who these questions were meant for. For a "philosopher"? If they were meant for me, for "myself," what have I to say about freedom and the self?

I wondered whether I should not point out that *all* the components of the philosophy of the self in the West have, on the one hand, had a liberating effect, since the values of freedom of expression, of opinion, and so on, have been associated with them; but point out too that this philosophy was undermined by aspects unforeseen and at the time unforeseeable, repressive aspects having to do with phallocentric and colonial patterns of speech. And so, if I were to work towards this philosophy, might it not be necessary to do two things at once: to emphasize both the permanent value of the philosophy of rights and, simultaneously, the inadequacy, the limits of the breakthrough it represented; to construct and deconstruct, to praise and criticize, at one and the same time. [(Cixous 1993, pp. 201–2)]

The definitions of human rights have often assumed the existence of an autonomous, somehow disembodied self who *possesses* rights. The very notion of possession implies a type of power and, at once, a repression of any kind of dependency. The self, in such definitions, seemed to be identified against or in exclusion of an *other,* either feminine or in some sense subordinate. Not everyone agrees that the repressive aspects of Western philosophy derive primarily from phallocentrism and colonialism. There is little question, however, that power has effects on the ways in which discourse practices are organized. As Michel Foucault has pointed out, much of what we are able to say at any given moment is controlled by rules and conventions embedded in our social institutions, along with what he called a "régime of truth" (Foucault 1980, pp. 131–3). These rules and conventions also control discussions of the "philosophy of rights"—for so long embodying exclusions few people dared name—so it may well be with talk of growth, inquiry, development, and habits of mind in the discourse of education and the schools.

Educational philosophers also are drawn to assertions of the "permanent value" of Western philosophy when it comes to articulation of their beliefs, even at a time when multiculturalism has become the focus of so much attention. At once, many are impelled to indicate its shortcomings, its blind spots, its insufficiencies. The tension Cixous experienced, the consciousness of being required to "construct and deconstruct," the recollections of the "liberating effect" of so much now called canonical or "Eurocentric": all these relate to the question of "what counts as Philosophy of Education" today. We have, most of us would admit, come a long way from the conception of philosophy as "the mirror of nature" (Rorty 1979), from notions of objectivism, from confidence in authoritative foundations of what we consider knowledge to be. Whatever our philosophical specialty, most of us are very concerned about communication, intersubjectivity, and the role of language in providing social bonds. We work, in some dimension, from Ludwig Wittgenstein's conception of language games and the "forms of life." (1968). We understand that they are governed by different rules; but in their intersections, they seem to compose a fabric that may replace the encompassing and transcendent matrix that assured *a priori* truths.

This differs considerably from a conception of objectively existing frameworks in which we can somehow ground a normative order of consequence for young people in our schools. Yet it remains difficult to set aside our commitments to theoretically-grasped principles like freedom, justice, and equality. Similarly, for all our familiarity with the problematic of the "Enlightenment Project" (Horkheimer and Adorno 1972), we are still drawn to idealistic renderings of reason linked to progress and to humanism. They continue to draw us towards them, either as regulatory norms or unrealized possibilities. In a moment of shattered frameworks and alternations between scepticism and hopelessness, they seem to glow in the dark as reminders of what might be, and of what is still to be achieved.

Cixous, like many writers and artists of our time, chose to argue against unwarranted imprisonments as if they offended what everyone knew were universal principles of justice. Many of us oppose what we think of as "reason" to terror in the case of the *fatma* issued against the novelist Salmon Rushdie. A number of educational philosophers are committed to the Deweyan vision of education "as a freeing of individual capacity in a progressive growth directed to social aims" (Dewey, 1916, p. 115). The view may not be ascribed a universality; but many will say, along with Dewey, that the meaning of the idea of education has not been adequately grasped if educators do not believe it feasible to instill "as a working disposition of mind" a confidence in a "fuller, freer, and more fruitful association and intercourse of all human beings with one another. . . ." Dewey went on to say that the end of such intercourse might be the overcoming of international jealousy and animosity.

This confidence in the uses of intelligence and the possibility of social harmony is very much in the Enlightenment tradition. It even evokes the so-called "metanarrative"—or the grand narrative—associated with the all-encompassing world view of the Age of Reason, a view of ongoing progress that anticipated all questions and offered a range of predetermined answers (Lyotard 1984). Even as we are moved by it and often motivated by that narrative, we are bound to recall the repressive ends it—along with the discourse of rationality—came to serve. Reason, like science itself, can be dominating and oppressive, especially when it claims under all circumstances to have the "best answer" to social problems. Stephen Toulmin, looking back to the eighteenth and nineteenth centuries, has written about calculation being "enthroned as the distinctive virtue of the human reason," while the life of emotions "was repudiated as distracting one from the demands of clear-headed deliberation" (1990, p. 134). Dewey himself once warned against the "monopolistic jurisdiction" of true-and-false meanings with the reminder that "the realm of meaning is wider . . . it is more urgent and more fertile" (1958, p. 410).

More serious than that jurisdiction, of course, was the transformation of rationality in so many places into instrumental rationality; with all its linkages to technology, its neglect of self-reflectiveness, its setting aside of value considerations. We are all familiar with the ways in which instrumental rationality has been used to legitimate not merely bureaucracies and social engineering, but Hiroshima, the Holocaust, the massacres in Vietnam, and even (from a different point of view) Stalin's Gulag. We are aware that science and scientific method cannot be subsumed under the rubric of instrumental rationality; and we are equally aware that reflection on the relations between theoretical science and its applications must be part of what "counts as Philosophy of Education." D. C. Phillips, discussing the diversity of methods and theories in the spheres of the sciences, has written that contemporary Philosophy of Science "does emphasize the importance of research programs progressively opening up new phenomena, the exposing of assumptions; and the giving and receiving of strong criticism." (1981, p. 255). As critiques diversify, even within educational theory and research, it is important to hold this in mind. The contributions made by the sciences to medicine, psychology, the environment, and (on occasion) social policy decisions cannot be set aside. Educational philosophers also need to attend to feminist approaches to the sciences (Keller 1985): "feminist empiricism" and "feminist standpoint epistemologies" (Harding 1986, pp. 136–162). There is also a persistent dissonance between the predictability and organization of the sciences and the multiplicity, heteroglossia, contingency, relationality, and what Mikhail Bakhtin called "carnival" of social life (1981). We may wonder whether languages and methods enriched and expanded by feminist and humanistic ideas may become less tainted as we plead for freedom, human expression, and the growth of compassionate communities.

While wondering, we cannot set aside the texts that compose so much of our tradition and provide so many of our references and allusions, texts by: Jean-Jacques Rousseau, Immanuel Kant, Thomas Jefferson, John Stuart Mill, George Herbert Mead, William James, John Dewey, Paulo Freire. Can we prevent such texts from being undermined by the "unforeseen" and the "unforeseeable"? How can we expose the inadequacies (and the racism, and the sexism) in so much of the discourse without disposing of the texts—and our own intertextuality—as well? Must they be shredded? Must we start again? Nathaniel Hawthorne's story, "Earth's Holocaust," comes to mind. It tells of a great bonfire built on the American prairie to burn the world's accumulation of "worn-out trumpery." People toss in everything from thrones to uniforms, to guns, to vats of wine. At length, they begin throwing in books and pamphlets: "the weight of dead men's thought which hitherto has pressed so heavily on the living intellect that has been incompetent to any effectual self-exertion" (1969, p. 200). At the end, Hawthorne reminds us that the human heart must first be purified if crime and misery are to disappear; but "if we go no deeper than the intellect and strive, with merely that feeble instrument, to discern and rectify what is wrong, our whole accomplishment will be a dream" (p. 209).

The story communicates the weight of dead authorities, as it holds intimations of later positivism and reaches forward to the days of multiple language games. It also suggests that "self-exertion" on the part of the "living intellect" is a far more reliable panacea against "trumpery" than a vast fire on the prairie. Hawthorne renders obvious the degree of conceptual mastery that makes people feel entitled to destroy, or exclude, or ignore. At once, he makes clear the notion that formal reason, in disembodied form, cannot cure human ills nor solve existential problems. If free and enriching dialogues are to take place in the spheres of education, among teachers or learners; if serious efforts to deconstruct and to redescribe are to be undertaken; people must reach out from their own lived situations in as many directions as seem feasible. Educational philosophers, in their turn, must identify themselves as situated in the same fashion and actively participant in a community—stretching back in time and forward towards the unexplored. This means engaging with the canonical texts so as to make them our own, enlarging and diversifying the canon even while consulting the texts that have defined us to this point: the analytic and logical texts, the experiential, the linguistic, the phenomenological (Archambault 1965, Green 1971, Hirst 1965, Peters and Hirst 1970, Phillips 1981, Scheffler 1943, Soltis 1981). No list can be more than suggestive. To create "what counts," educational philosophers have to discover their own intertextuality, extend their minds towards the horizons, shape and reshape their traditions. In the shaping, in the interpretation, in the reflection, the questions will multiply. Posing the questions, loving the questions, philosophers may open whatever doors there are.

Elizabeth Bishop, in the poem "January First," wrote about the year's doors opening and about having to invent "once more, the reality of this world." At the end, she says:

> When you open your eyes
> we'll walk, once more,
> among the hours and their inventions.
> We'll walk among appearances
> and bear witness to time and its conjugations.
> Perhaps we'll open the day's doors.
> And then we shall enter the unknown. (1983, p. 274)

Taking this seriously, we may have to explore our own *bildung,* our self-formation as persons and as educational philosophers. For many, the authors listed previously evoke speakers and writers who are models—or thinkers against whom we may have chosen to rebel. In absorbing them as models or in refusing their ideas, we define and continue to redefine ourselves. When many of us began, we were not conscious of the "patriarchal" (what Cixous called "phallocentric") at the core of what we read. Often, as we now know, the adjective has been used to make us aware of a core, a kind of center in many philosophical pronouncements, sometimes even in the most rigorous analysis. As many feminist critics view it, it is a mode of communication tightly constrained by rules of logic, linearity, and (on occasion) a range of largely technical rules. Valuing distance and autonomy, such thinkers are "more exclusionary," unlikely to pay heed to the interdependence of "they" and "we" (Belenky et al. 1986, p. 4). It is at least likely that this mode of knowing and way of being prepared the ground and origin of what is described as instrumental rationality. This is another open question to be pondered in educational philosophy. We may find it to be of considerable moment that people who think in that manner are prone to assert that the rule-governed, "neutral" cognition of which they are capable can be relied upon for realistic representations of the world. (Judith Butler, seeking a paradigm for this mode of cognition, turns to the Gulf War and the celebration of the "phantasmatic subject, the one who determines its world unilaterally, and which is in some measure typified by the looming heads of retired generals framed against the map of the Middle East, where the speaking head of the subject is shown to be the same size, or larger than the area it seeks to dominate. This is, in a sense, the graphics of the imperialist subject, a visual allegory of the action itself" [1992, p. 10].)

We might think of the interplay in Virginia Woolf's *To the Lighthouse*. (Novels, of course, do not argue. They set forth; they present; they offer metaphors; in some indirect fashion, they illustrate.) At the beginning, Mrs. Ramsay is talking to her little son about going to the lighthouse.

> "Yes, of course, if it's fine tomorrow," said Mrs. Ramsay. "But you'll have to be up with the lark," she added. To her son these words conveyed an extraordinary joy, as if it were settled the expedition were bound to take place. . . . "But", said his father, stopping in front of the drawing-room window "it won't be fine". . . . What he said was true. It was always true. He was incapable of untruth. (1962, pp. 3–4)

Mr. Ramsay, usually thinking with the aid of abstract symbols (sometimes, the letters of the alphabet) is convinced (as is his irate little son) that he represents reality accurately, in contrast to his wife. When Andrew tries to explain to the artist Lily what his father does, he says: "'Think of a kitchen table then, . . . when you're not there.' So she always saw, when she thought of Mr. Ramsay's work, a scrubbed kitchen table . . . lodged now in the fork of a pear tree . . ." (p. 26). In truth, his is the kind of mind that constructs what is believed to be real; it excludes almost on principle his wife's sad hesitancies, his young son's despair, the length of the shadows in the garden, the feel of his own organic life. Whether or not we choose to see Mr. Ramsay as representing some masculine "essence," it is clear enough that the mode of thinking described excludes and subordinates intuition, imagination, feeling, and metaphoricality. Narrowing in on a particular type of cognition, the person favoring this way of sense-making has only a partial view of things. The rigor, the exclusiveness, the abstractness cannot but affect the discourse used in speaking about freedom, human rights, and education as well.

So it is with what Cixous calls the "colonial." Identifying with and making dominant a "First World" type of rationality and technicality, colonial thinking has not only imposed a "right" way, with a "right" pay-off; it has, in many cases, deformed, belittled, or exoticized what has been considered "undeveloped," "primitive," and implicitly regressive. We have only to recall the treatment of Native American cultures in this country. We have only to review our conception of those cultures Edward Said has grouped under the rubric of "orientalism" (1978). Said, among others, has written many times about the dependence "of what appeared to be detached and apolitical cultural disciplines upon a quite sordid history of imperialist ideology and colonialist practice" (1992, p. 41). The apparently detached has been assumed to be objective, unbiased, analytical, and rational. Using such perspectives, we have simply been unaware of oppositional habits of speech and thought: rendering people in the Middle East *other*, excluding them from what some of us might still call "the family of man."

We do recognize, of course, that our slow acknowledgement of our long confinement to a "Eurocentric" canon has made some of us sensitive to the traces of colonialism in practice and in our thought. It is still difficult for many of us to conceive of, much less sympathize with what Gayatri Spivak speaks of as "alternative histories" (1990, p. 269). Willing to revise our own history, we find it hard to acquiesce to Toni Morrison's view with regard to the growth of individualism. Fused with "the prototype of Americans as solitary alienated, and malcontent," she writes, "individualism was a response to "the potent and ego-reinforcing presence of an Africanist population" (1992, p. 45). A sense of absolute power, Morrison writes, was elicited by the presence of slavery, or "a bound and unfree, rebellious, black population" against which white men could measure their difference. For her, the new white man (the "American Adam") was a deliberate construction with regard to the "other, along with such associated qualities as autonomy, self-reliance, and what is often taken to be liberty." Again, if these qualities constitute a paradigm of what it takes to be an American, most of the world's people—along with many newcomers to the United States—are forever marginalized.

When we ponder curriculum, or questions as to what knowledge is worth communicating (and in what forms), we might ask whether we can construct and deconstruct at the same time. There is some agreement among educational philosophers that knowledge is a social construct, emergent from reciprocal relations among people inhabiting a shared world. Not only may it derive from transactions among individuals and their histories; at the same time, it may come from engagements with what are thought to be public knowledge systems. Many of us are aware that what is called *social reality*—Toni Morrison's, Virginia Woolf's, John Dewey's—is also constructed, even as we are atuned to the likelihood that what is called *reality* may also be understood to be interpreted experience.

As Alfred Schutz saw it, the interpretations that feed into our knowledge may begin in subjective common-sense modes of understanding. These are gradually structured or patterned by *schemata* made available by those who may be called our predecessors and contemporaries (1967, pp. 22–23). What we often take for granted as given, as merely normal for all onlookers and knowers, has actually been translated or constructed. It is or has been contingent on particular meaning systems, conversations, locations in the social world. To recognize this is often to have a shock experience. This has been the case for many educators when they have been made to see the influences of patriarchal or colonial (or nationalist, or imperial, or provincial) language on our formulations of what we believe to be true—or even good and right. At the same time, it has been very difficult to deal with the challenges to the referentiality of language in a world that once seemed to stand still and to be susceptible to representation. Now we too frequently find ourselves simply playing a range of often incommensurable language games (Wittgenstein 1968). Where, we ask ourselves, are the intersections of the languages associated with the form of life called history and those identified with the arts, or chemistry, or ethics, or economics? And how does this all relate to a notion of human consciousness thrusting into the world around, grasping the appearances of things? What (again) does it signify to utter words like "freedom", "growth", "learning", "meaning", "quest"? How do we move from games and texts and discourse to the material actualities of lived lives?

We are only now becoming used to the possibility that what is called the *signifier* (either a meaningful spoken sound or a meaningful mark inscribed on a page) is what we can be sure of, while the *signified* remains a possible or an open question (Barthes 1967, Lacan 1977, Gates 1988). We are becoming slowly aware of the signifiers in our discourse and our thinking; each one being what it is because it is different from another. Once we give priority to the signifier and realize that words refer and relate to other words, not to some objective world beyond, meanings proliferate and become richer. Hierarchies of meaning, like hierarchies in general, become more and more absurd. If culture can be partially understood as a discursive meshwork, a corpus of intersecting texts or discourses or codes, we begin to think again of initiating the young into what has to be understood as a *conversation,* written or spoken, perhaps begun, as Michael Oakeshott has written "in the primeval forests and extended and made more articulate in the course of centuries. . . . Education, properly speaking is an initiation into the skill and partnership of this conversation in which we learn to recognize the voices, to distinguish the proper occasions of utterance, and in which we acquire the intellectual and moral habits appropriate to conversation. And it is this conversation which, in the end, gives place and character to every human activity and utterance" (1962, pp. 198–9).

This has been widely quoted in discussions of Philosophy of Education in recent years. But if it is to count in the present context, we need to hold in mind that the great *conversation,* like culture itself, becomes subject to transformations by means of critique and reflexivity. Of particular interest to today's educational philosopher is the matter of plurality and pluralization. We can no longer speak in abstract terms about "Mankind" or "the child" or even "the partnership of this conversation." We are being asked to think of persons in their plurality, in their distinctiveness, no one a duplicate of any other. At once, we are learning to acknowledge the worth and power of different cultures and civilizations, out of which identities are being negotiated. We are varying and complicating our notion of the historical past and the multiple heritages that study the past. At once, we are striving towards untried conceptions of our society—always composed of newcomers, but now made up of newcomers who cannot be submerged in some conforming whole. To learn to "recognize the voices" now is to pay heed where educators seldom paid heed before: to living beings of all classes, from almost countless countries on the globe. We are being asked to recognize the sound of exile, of expulsion, of abandonment; we are being asked, as never before, to attend to the voices of all sorts of women, men, and children too, to empower them to make meanings in the disparate, sometimes savagely unequal lives they live. Maurice Merleau-Ponty wrote that we are "condemned to meaning" and that "true philosophy consists in relearning how to look at the world . . ." (1967, p. xx). If that world, that "reality", is understood to be variously interpreted experience, "learning to look" (certainly for educators) may mean learning how to reflect with others upon intersubjectivity itself and upon the possibilities of strangers coming together to relearn and to transform. The philosopher's obligation may involve enabling all sorts of persons to think about the ways they direct their attention, the vantage points they take, the naming, the caring, the concern.

In these days, it may not be sufficient to work at constructing the world as meaningful, to achieve the various often contending texts, to *see.* Philosophers may recognize the place of deconstruction at the same time, deconstruction as an intellectual move to complement what we have learned in the past about concept clarification, about what John Passmore called "critico-creative thinking" (1972, p. 36) and about what R.S. Peters described as "qualities of mind" that might be called "human excellences". To deconstruct, according to Jacques Derrida, is to "practice an *overturning* of the classical opposition and a general displacement of the system" (1982, p. 329). He means the disclosure of certain oppositions that are built into our language and that shape our thinking: white/black; male/female; cognitive/affective; literal/figurative—all binary oppositions, with the superior member of each pair set ahead of the other. Derrida describes the system as one of hierarchical logocentrism. Logocentrism suggests that a center, an essence, a fixed principle lies at the heart of what we write too much of the time. The notion of the hierarchical has to do with the subordination of terms and the constitution of the subordinate terms as other, to be grasped as what the first excludes.

Reaching back into the Scriptures, we can see the origins of such hierarchies in Eve being born from Adam's rib; we can find it in the opposition Toni Morrison dramatizes when she speaks of the white man constructing the black man as other, defined in terms of what the white excludes. Derrida wants to overcome the privileging of the *logos* and the systematized, the abstract and the universal. He wants to make questionable concepts like *presence* and *center* and to allow for a decentering, a move towards fluidity and process. There are complexitities, of course; but Derrida is offering us a novel way of looking at ourselves and our texts in ways equivalent to "relearning how to look at the world."

What counts as Philosophy of Education in the face of all this? Can we construct and deconstruct, and still preserve? We may find ways of shaping the kind of "common world" Hannah Arendt had in mind when she wrote:

> Education is the point at which we decide whether we love the world enough to assume responsibility for it and by the same token save it from that ruin which, except for renewal, except for the coming of the new and the young, would be inevitable. . . . She went on: And education, too, is where we decide whether we love our children enough not to expel them from our world and leave them to their own devices, nor to strike from their hands their chance of undertaking something new, something unforeseen by us, but to prepare them in advance for the task of renewing a common world (1961, p. 196).

The questions throb. What can philosophers do to make "renewal" in such terms meaningful? What can be done to permit the values of freedom of expression, of opinion to continue having a liberating effect in a multi-faceted "common world"? How can we permit a democratic philosophy to retain some permanent value in spite of our discoveries of the "unforeseen"?

Some of the high points in democratic philosophy may have been reached in discourse generated by the Civil Rights movements, feminist movements, and movements for the gay and lesbian persons among us, for the disabled, the excluded. Vaclav Havel in *Letters to Olga* wrote:

> Are there any visible signs that an "existential revolution" is happening in the world today? I can't help feeling that if you are open to hope, you can find timid signals in many things: in movements of youth in revolt

such as have broken out periodically since the 1950s, in genuine peace
movements, in varied activities in defense of human rights, in liberation
movements (as long as they don't degenerate into mere efforts to
replace one kind of terror with another) . . . in ecological initiatives, in
all the constantly recurring attempts to create authentic and meaningful
communities that rebel against a world in crisis, not merely to escape
from it, but to devote their full efforts—with the clear-sighted deliberation and humility that always goes with genuine faith—to assume
responsibility for the state of the world (1988, p. 372).

There have been as many disappointments as triumphs since this was written a decade or more ago in a prison cell; but what Havel said remains
relevant, in part because he avoided a totalizing vision, because he moved
beyond text to particulars, because he spoke of community and deliberation
and responsibility.

There are implications here for an approach to morality that may find a
place in the teaching of Philosophy of Education today. Our problem, in
many places, is still one of reconciling experiences of connectedness, embed-
dedness, caring, and obligation with the desire some of us nurture for
regulatory norms of some sort—again, for an incarnation of principles that
presumably define our democracy. We have not yet found a place for the
feminist ethic founded in "caring" in the spheres of power and public policy
(Noddings 1984); and, surely, one of the concerns that must count is the
concern for transforming public spaces to allow articulate and principled
action on the part of human beings who know what it signifies to be "I" to
another's "Thou" (Buber 1970), to refuse reification and submergence in an
"It-world" (p. 96).

Buber was troubled by the spectre of such submergence. He asked
whether the greatness of statesmen and businessmen did not depend on their
way of seeing human beings. The point was to see human beings as "centers
of services and aspirations that have to be calculated and employed according to their specific capacities" (p. 96). The point was for human beings to
confront each other in meaningful relationships. Striving for this, striving to
prepare the grounds for it in classrooms (through dialogue, through the reading of journals, through collaboration in learning), educators cannot but be
aware of how much is deflected by the languages still in use, most poignantly
in the schools. There is constant talk about the ways in which schools meet
the demands of technology, prepare for the workplaces, and offer training in
skills. There is a reiteration of the centrality of "outcomes," curriculum tools,
competencies. We speak of the young as "human resources," not as persons
with the potential for thinking for themselves and the potential to choose.
Our Enlightenment-rooted orientations to human dignity, to human rights,
to the rule of reason slip too easily into process-product approaches, not to
speak of preoccupations with outputs and efficiency.

Joseph Conrad's *Heart of Darkness* (for all its now apparent colonial tone) speaks to these matters even today. Marlow, who has just returned from a long immersion in the African wilderness, is meeting with his company's officials on a yawl anchored in the Thames. He is reminding the lawyer, the accountant, and the director of companies how the early Romans must have felt when they first landed in the wilderness that would one day be England. They faced, he says, as he has faced, "the incomprehensible." Then he bursts out: "Mind, none of us would feel exactly like this. What saves us is efficiency—the devotion to efficiency" (1952, p. 221). He is thinking of the indifferent cruelty of the ivory traders along the river in the Congo, the natives roped together, the ruthless raping of their land. Efficiency, he knows, becomes a screen. It becomes what Milan Kundera called a folding screen "set up to curtain death" (1984, p. 253); to exclude "everything from its purviews which is essentially unacceptable in human existence" (p. 248). Philosophy has traditionally worked to break through the screens, even as it has pursued its "love of wisdom," and its struggles against mystifications and bewilderments. The difference today is in the loss of old legitimations, of anchor points; but the struggle and the search go on. Conrad spoke of the necessity of values as "barriers against nothingness." Many existentialists, conscious of living towards their own deaths, have written about choosing themselves as indispensable or, as in the case of Sartre on at least one occasion, choosing themselves *as if* for all human beings. Values may be groundless; but an act of rebellion, a taking of initiative, a repairing of a lack can create values. We are characterized, wrote Sartre, by our going beyond a situation, by our orienting ourselves to something still to come which we are trying to bring into being. "This is what we call the *project*" (1963, pp. 91–92). Starting with the project (doing philosophy, teaching young people), we develop a *praxis* that opens into what has not yet been. "A flight and a leap ahead, at once a refusal and a realization, the project retains and unveils the surpassed reality which is refused by the very movement which surpassed it. Thus, knowing is a moment of *praxis,* even its most fundamental one" (p. 92). It can be said that if teaching is our project, and if teaching responds to a need or a lack (absence of literacy, susceptibility to indoctrination, inarticulacy), the *praxis* created by the teacher builds a kind of wall against meaninglessness; it brings value into the world.

The search for value, like the search for meaning, may be negated by those who are, in Hannah Arendt's language, "thoughtless." She had in mind an "absence of thinking" as in the case of Adolf Eichmann, and the use of cliche-ridden language: "Cliches, stock phrases, adherence to conventional, standardized codes of expression and conduct have the socially recognized function of protecting us against reality, that is, against the claim on our thinking attention that all events and facts make by virtue of their existence" (1978, p. 4). It is not only language that raises the folding screen, as most of us know. In Christa Wolf's *Accident: A Day's News,* a German woman narrator contemplates "the desire of most people for a comfortable life, their tendency to believe the speakers on raised platforms and the men in white coats" (1989, p. 17). Surely, this mode of unthinking acquiescence is of direct concern to the educational philosopher. The narrator's feelings of desperation are in part occasioned by two important material facts: the fallout from the Chernobyl accident is spreading over the German countryside she inhabits, and her brother is having delicate brain surgery which (although she cannot know it in advance) he does survive. Reading this, we are reminded of the significance of context, even—and perhaps especially—in the "doing" of educational philosophy these days. At the end of the novel, the narrator also summons *Heart of Darkness:*

> How he managed to free himself from concepts such as "device," "effect"—the hardest thing of all. But enough for today. That writer, he knew the meaning of sorrow. He set right out into the blind spot of that culture to which he also belonged, and not in thought alone. Fearlessly into the heart of darkness. . . . So does this person speak to me. So shy, I could hardly expect to find such words as "hate" and "love" in his works. "Greed" I found often. Greed, greed, greed . . . (p. 108).

In the course of the story, the narrator has been doing domestic tasks; she has been talking to her daughter on the phone, reporting about the pollution, asking about her grandson playing "me Punch" in the kitchen. She has been waiting in dread for news from the hospital. There are tears, bad dreams, memories; and finally, "how difficult it would be, brother, to take leave of this earth." Perhaps it is the circumstances of a woman's life that keep her so grounded, that help her refuse words like "device" and "effect". But is it necessarily a feminine tendency to link the prevalent thoughtlessness and denial with the actuality of "men in white coats"? And that last affirmation of "this earth," which she knows is terribly polluted by the nuclear leak, perhaps spoiled, but which calls out for rescue, cleansing, and a kind of provocative care. Is that necessarily a woman's affirmation as she feels the china cup in her hand, the soft earth under her feet? Or is it the kind of interest and concern that can be taught?

The hunt for ivory described by Conrad, the "Grand March" Kundera brings to life as he makes us feel the pressure of ideology and marching tunes, the accident at Chernobyl that gives rise to Wolf's intermeshing themes: all point to actual, material consequences of patriarchal and colonial thinking. They are entangled not only with patterns of speech, but with actualities that attentive readers are enabled to *see.* Paradoxically, perhaps, they grasp them by bringing into existence an unreal, imagined world, the *as if* world of the novel. Making the enactments and perspectives of a novel objects of their experience, they not only become increasingly aware of the traces of other texts. Sartre wrote that the literary object "though realized *through* language, is never given *in* language," and that the reader must always invent (under the guidance of the author) the revelation the writer has undertaken by means of language and project beyond the words "a synthetic form" (1949, pp. 41–44). What we project is an event within our consciousness provoked by imagination. We summon up a Marlow, a German woman writer, a Violet on her way to Harlem in the 1920s; we lend them, as it were, our lives. Granted, they are not empirically *real;* they are not to be found on the river, in the streets, on the fields; but they are intended by acts of imagining, perceiving, judging consciousness. At the very least, urged beyond language, we experience the space between what we have projected and the actuality, the materiality of a world that cannot be represented, but which can be lived.

Frequently, as Sartre reminded us, novels like those mentioned appeal to our freedom by presenting the world insofar as it demands human freedom. "And if I am given this world with its injustices, it is not so that I might contemplate them coldly, but that I might animate them with my indignation, that I might disclose them and create them with their nature as injustices, that is, as abuses to be suppressed" (pp. 62–63). Richard Rorty and others have spoken of the absence of an underlying authority we can turn to when we want to support judgments of what is offensive or what needs repair. The only way to think about the world in any case, writes Rorty, is by means of language:

> One can use language to criticize and enlarge itself, as one can exercise one's body to develop, strengthen and enlarge it, but one cannot see language-as-a-whole in relation to something else to which it applied, or for which it is a means to an end. The arts and sciences, and philosophy as their self-reflection and integration, constitute such a process of enlargement and strengthening. But philosophy, the attempt to say "how language relates to the world" but saying what *makes* certain statements true, or certain actions or attitudes goor or raional, is, in this view, impossible (1982, p. xix).

We can take this seriously and, at once, hold in mind the likelihood that Cixous's Amnesty Lecture had actual consequences in the form of increased donations, letters to prisoners, protests to government representatives. Whether such words as hers (or ours, as philosophers of education) appeal to people's indignation or, as in Albert Camus's *The Plague* (1948) to some shared determination to refuse complicity, or to a set of beliefs shared by members of the community, we would like to believe that they do more than simply extend the conversation Oakeshott described. This is not meant to imply that the articulations described were endowed with a kind of universal referentiality. They did not come as if "from nowhere" (Putnam 1981, pp. 49–50). They were uttered by situated beings whose words were like a *call* to those who paid heed, a call to action of a sort, to take initiatives, to heal, to repair. And, in doing so, to create values—surely a central concern in philosophy.

To search for some single source of legitimacy or to turn to a single standard or norm would be to cancel out heterogeneity and difference, both so prominent in our own day. To think monologically, in fact, would be to overlook the plurality of logics that exist, the local discourses, the particular *little* stories not always accounted for in contemporary philosophy. What of consensus, however? What of the kind of communicative action Jurgen Habermas hoped would lead to significant agreements or to the recognition of a "universal interest everyone can acknowledge"? (1987, p. 235). For Lyotard and Hans-Georg Gadamer, and perhaps for modern educational philosophers, there might be a turn towards practical judgment, or what is called *phronesis* (Lyotard 1985), taking into account a variety of narratives and entangled language games. For some (Gadamer 1981, p. 80), phronesis is linked to a dialogue among persons who have regard for one another, who share the same local community. Cixous turns to poetry with somewhat the same relationship in mind: "by sharing unhappiness, by being strangers together, people and poet reconstitute an internal homeland" (1993, p. 207). Cixous then asks questions that might lead us to the heartland of what might count as Philosophy of Education today. She speaks of how a prison summons up the thought of freedom in its full splendor, the thought of freedom, "the duty to be free." And, after a moment, "We who are free, are we helping to expand the realm of freedom on this earth, are we responsible? Do we need a camp, a prison, a war, to free us from our indifference to ourselves and from our fear of others? So we do not forget our good fortune?" (p. 219).

Whatever counts as Philosophy of Education today must begin in queer questions, those not susceptible to logical or empirical resolutions. Whatever shape they take, they must be defined with the contexts of multiple transactions, those in which diverse human beings are intimately involved. Even if they extend to the far reaches of metaphysics or are limited to the clarification of terms, they are posed within the frames of overlapping institutions—public shools, local and state bureaucracies, communities, universities—the carriers of heritage. Most often, they are articulated in the local spaces where educational dialogue is most likely to occur. Some may focus on critical consciousness; some on personal choosing and commitment; some on social or political resistance; a few, overarching frameworks erected to combat relativism and the anarchy so many see "loosed upon the world" (Yeats 1959, p. 186). Some of us may come to realize that the situations in which we do philosophy are hermeneutical situations, situations in large measure familiar because we have been struggling to make sense of them over the years.

Whoever we are, we have engaged the traditions made available to us against the background of our lived lives and the prejudgments we have made over time. The horizons of our lived experiences have been, to one degree or another, open. A horizon, writes Gadamer, signifies a range of vision "including everything that can be seen from a particular vantage point" (1975, p. 315). As more and more perspectives open for us, as we see into wider and wider worlds, our lived vantage points remain crucial if we, like so many others in this moment of time, reject the possibility of a universal vision or an objective ground. Once we accept the notion of vantage point, we become aware that no one has a total vision from any place in the world. We see aspects, profiles; whole visions—landmarks, historical studies, short stories—they always lay ahead to be achieved. One of the great powers of imagination is that it opens the possibility of such achievement; it opens vistas on what might be, what is not yet. Imagination moves us out of confinement, through the windows of the actual, so that we can summon up alternative realities. We can break with the frozen, the reified, as we can with the purely formal and abstract. The poet Wallace Stevens, who pondered so deeply the relations between imagination and reality, said in dealing with his "rationalists":

> Rationalists, wearing square hats,
> Think, in square rooms,
> Looking at the floor,
> Looking at the ceiling.
> They confine themselves
> To right-angled triangles.
> If they tried rhomboids,
> Cones, waving lines, ellipses—
> As, for example, the ellipse of the half moon—
> Rationalists would wear sombreros (1954, p. 75).

The ellipse of the half-moon is an expansion, not a substitution. Even to suggest a glimpse of the half-moon is to bring an open window into view, a possibility of looking beyond what here is fixed and ordinary. When the image of the rationalists wearing sombreros appears, it suggests as well that rationalists—no more than any other selves—are not to be understood as fixed, predefined, or mere essences. They can wear square hats and sombreros; they can become as well as be.

We end in some manner where we began—with talk of language, power, and identity. We end with the unanswered questions about diversity and relativism, with aching questions about who inhabits and who dominates a fading public sphere. There is the need to enable all kinds of persons to break with confinement and to challenge hollow prescriptions and formulae; at once there is the need to make a community in which a plurality of persons can participate and through participations choose their projects and themselves. We are told on all sides that we cannot decide whether our lives add up to anything or not, no matter how unified our narratives. Life, according to Rorty, ought to be viewed as "a web of relations to be rewoven, a web which time lengthens every day" (1989, pp. 42–43). There is always more to be woven; the quilt, the carpet, are forever incomplete.

The idea of webs takes on increasing importance as we ponder the bringing into being of new orders, new modes of communication at a time of shifting identities, reaching towards an inclusiveness never seen before. We want, as we think about what counts as Philosophy of Education, to affirm identity and difference and to do so, when we can, by means of dialogue. In the midst of so much discussion of pluralization and the relation of diverse others to the changing self, Hannah Arendt's words about weaving webs of relationship may take on a new meaning. She was writing about action and speech, and about human beings' "agent-revealing" capacities and about the world of things out of which so many of our interests rise.

> These interests constitute, in the word's most literal significance, something which *inter-est,* which lies between people and therefore can relate and bind them together. Most action and speech are concerned with this in-between, which varies with each group of people, so that most words and deeds are about some wordly objective reality in addition to being disclosure of the acting and speaking agent. . . .
>
> Since this disclosure of the subject is an integral part of all, even the most "objective" intercourse, the physical, worldly in-between along with its interests is overlaid and, as it were, overgrown with an altogether different in-between which consists of deeds and words and owes its origin exclusively to men's acting and speaking directly *to* one another. This second subjective in-between is not tangible, since there are no tangible objects into which it could solidify; the process of acting and speaking can leave behind no such results as end-products. But for all its intangibility, this in-between is no less real than the world of things we visibly have in common. We call this reality the "web" of human relationships. (1958, pp. 182–3)

Yes, Arendt was thoughtless enough to focus on *men* as a generic term; she paid little heed to the patriarchal domination even of the "in-between"; she saw little possibility of the encounters in the private world affecting and perhaps transforming what happened outside where people could appear before each other "as the best they knew how to be." Nevertheless, she did see persons in their plurality, with all their distinctive perspectives, engaging in new beginnings, being in process, refusing essentialism. Involved in action as they were, they found their action, their beginnings falling into already existing webs.

The disclosure of each person and the setting of each new beginning start, for Arendt, a new process which emerges as the unique life story of the newcomer and affects the life stories of all those with whom she comes in contact. The stories are the outcomes of action; but no one can be the author of any eventual outcome. Again, we are in touch with a process and with an ongoing interchange, a dialogue, often an imaginative dialogue that sustains the telling and allows for no solidification. Out of the process, in which increasing numbers may be involved, the common world emerges. It is always susceptible to renewal and continually being brought into being. Constituted as it must be from many vantage points, from many fused horizons, it may turn out to be a multi-faceted world and a strangely inclusive one. Diverse meanings will emerge, highlighting dimensions of the webs that interconnect and sometimes delicately catch the light.

Entanglement cannot be overcome; nor can the effects of power on perspective, choice, and even dialogue. Michel Foucault's concept of power/knowledge is still here to be confronted by educational philosophers, along with the idea that certain knowledges are "disqualified," while others have been thought to be elite. Opposed as Foucault was to scientism and positivism, and to the confusions in the social and the natural sciences, he was unwilling to set aside the claims of formal knowledge because of the corruptions of institutionalization. The research project that interested him did not posit an empirical-positivist dualism. What it did was "to entertain the claims to attention of local, discontinuous, illegitimate knowledges against the claims of a unitary body of theory which would filter, hierarchicize, and order them in the name of some true knowledge and some arbitrary idea of what constitutes a science and its objects" (1980, p. 83). He wanted to reactivate local, minor, popular, and perhaps subjugated knowledges in opposition to the hierarchies in which so much of knowledge had been thrust. Foucault wanted to detach the power of truth "from the forms of hegemony, social, economic and cultural, within which it operates at the present time" (p. 113).

It is not a question of overwhelming "erudition" with the formerly disqualified. Nor is it a matter of identifying the cognitive with the hierarchical or the hegemonic. Yes, it is a matter of constructing and deconstructing once again. It is a matter of attaining the kind of thoughtfulness so important to Hannah Arendt, who was so horrified by thoughtlessness and heedlessness that she called upon her readers passionately "to think what we are doing" (1958, p. 5). That, in many respects, is what Foucault has done: thinking in terms of problems, in terms of questions. According to Foucault:

> Thought is not what inhabits a certain conduct and gives it its meaning; rather, it is what allows one to step back from this way of acting or reacting, to present it to oneself as an object of thought and question it as to its meaning, its conditions, its goals. Thought is freedom in relation to what one does, the motion by which one detaches oneself from it, establishes it as an object, and reflects on it as a problem (Rabinow 1984, p. 388).

Thought, the pursuit of meanings, freedom, and concern: there is no final summing up the themes of what counts as Philosophy of Education. Passion should infuse all these: the passion of sensed possibility and, yes, the passion of poetry and the several arts. Thinking of ourselves as subjects reaching out to others and attending to the shapes and sounds of things, we may resist the anaesthetic in our lives and the drawing back to anchorage. We have to know about our lives, clarify our situations if we are to understand the world from our shared standpoints, our standpoints as philosophers of education ready to commit ourselves to small transformations as we heed the stories, the multiplex stories, as cautiously we work to transform.

BIBLIOGRAPHY

Archambault, R. (1965), ed. *Philosophical Analysis and Education.* (New York: The Humanities Press).

Arendt, H. (1961). *Between Past and Future.* (London: Faber and Faber).

Arendt, H. (1978). *On Thinking.* (New York: Harcourt, Brace Jovanovich).

Arendt, H. (1958). *The Human Condition.* (Chicago: The Chicago University Press).

Bakhtin, M. (1981). *The Dialogic Imagination.* (Austin: The University of Texas Press).

Barthes, R. (1967). *Writing Degree Zero.* (Boston: Beacon Press).

Belenky, M.F., Clinchy, B.M., Goldberger, N.R., Tarule, J.M. (1986). *Women's Ways of Knowing.* (New York: Basic Books).

Bishop, E. (1983). *The Complete Poems.* (New York: Farrar Straus and Giroux).

Bordo, S. (1990). "Feminism, Postmodernism, and Gender-Scepticism," in L.J. Nicholson, ed., *Feminism/Postmodernism,* pp. 133–156 (New York: Routledge).

Buber, M. (1970). *I and Thou.* (New York: Charles Scribner's Sons).

Butler, J. (1992). "Contingent Foundations: Feminism and the Question of 'Postmodernism'," in J. Butler and J.W. Scott, eds. *Feminists Theorize the Political* (New York: Routledge), pp. 3–21.

Camus, A. (1948). *The Plague.* (New York: Alfred A. Knopf).

Cixous, H. (1993). "We Who Are Free, Are We Free?" *Critical Inquiry,* Winter 1993, 19(2): 201–19.

Conrad, J. (1952). "Heart of Darkness," in *Three Great Tales.* (New York: Modern Library).

Derrida, J. (1982). *Margins of Philosophy.* (Chicago: University of Chicago Press).

Dewey, J. (1931). *Art as Experience.* (New York: Minton, Balch & Co.).

Dewey, J. (1916). *Democracy and Education.* (New York: The Macmillan Co.).

Dewey, J. (1958). *Experience and Nature.* (New York: Dover Publications).

Dewey, J. (1954). *The Public and its Problems.* (Athens, OH: The Swallow Press).

Foucault, M. (1980). *Power/Knowledge.* (New York: Pantheon Books).

Freire, P. (1970). *Pedagogy of the Oppressed.* (New York: Herder and Herder).

Gadamer, H.-G. (1975). "Hermeneutics and Social Science," in *Cultural Hermeneutics* 2: 306–315.

Gadamer, H.-G. (1981). *Reason in the Age of Science.* (Cambridge, Mass.: MIT Press).

Gates, H.L. (1988). *The Signifying Monkey.* (New York: Oxford University Press).

Geertz, C. (1983). *Local Knowledge.* (New York: Basic Books).

Gilligan, C. (1981). *In a Different Voice.* (Cambridge: Harvard University Press).

Green, T. F. (1971). *The Activities of Teaching.* (New York: McGraw-Hill).

Habermas, J. (1971). *Knowledge and Human Interests.* (Boston: Beacon Press).

Habermas, J. (1987). *The Philosophical Discourse of Modernity.* (Cambridge: MIT Press).

Harding, S. (1986). *The Science Question in Feminism.* (Ithaca: Cornell University Press).

Hartsock, N. (1987). "Rethinking Modernism: Minority vs. Majority Theories," *Cultural Critique* (7), pp. 187–206.

Havel, V. (1988). *Letters to Olga.* (New York: Dodd Mead).

Hawthorne, N. (1969). "Earth's Holocaust," *The Portable Hawthorne,* ed. M. Cowley (New York: Viking Press).

Hirst, P. (1965). "Liberal Education and the Nature of Knowledge," in R.D. Archambault, ed. *Philosophical Analysis and Education* (London: Routledge and Kegan Paul).

Horkheimer, M. and Adorno, T.W. (1972). *Dialectic of Enlightenment.* (New York: Seabury Press).

Irigaray, L. (1985). *Speculum of the Other Woman.* (Ithaca: Cornell University Press).

Keller, E.F. (1985). *Reflections on Gender and Science.* (New Haven: Yale University Press).

Kundera, M. (1984). *The Unbearable Lightness of Being.* (New York: Harper and Row).

Lacan, J. (1977). *Ecrits.* (London: Penguin Books).

Lyotard, J-F. and Thebaud, J.L. (1985). *Just Gaming.* (Minneapolis: University of Minnesota Press).

Lyotard, J-F. (1984). *The Postmodern Condition.* (Minneapolis: University of Minnesota).

MacIntyre, A. (1981). *After Virtue.* (Notre Dame: University of Notre Dame).

Merleau-Ponty, M. (1964). *The Primacy of Perception.* (Evanston: Northwestern University Press).

Merleau-Ponty, M. (1967). *Phenomenology of Perception.* (New York: The Humanities Press).

Morrison, T. (1992). *Playing in the Dark: Whiteness and the Literary Imagination.* (Cambridge: Harvard University Press).

Nietzsche, F. (1967). *On the Genealogy of Morals.* (New York: Vintage Books).

Noddings, N. (1984). *Caring: A Feminine Perspective on Ethics and Moral Education.* (Berkeley and Los Angeles: University of California Press).

Oakeshott, M. (1962). *Rationalism and Politics And Other Essays.* (London: Methuen).

Passmore, J. (1972). "On Teaching to be Critical," in *Education and the Development of Reason,* ed. R.F. Dearden, P.H. Hirst, and R.S. Peters. (London: Routledge & Kegan Paul).

Peters, R.S. and Hirst, P. (1970). *The Logic of Education.* (London: Routledge and Kegan Paul).

Peters, R.S. (1967). *Ethics and Education.* (Glencoe, Ill.: Scott, Foresman).

Phillips, D.C. (1981). "Post-Kuhnian Reflections on Educational Research," in J.S. Soltis, ed., *Philosophy and Education* (Chicago: University of Chicago Press).

Putnam, H. (1981). *Reason, Truth, and History.* (New York: Cambridge University Press).

Rabinow, P., Ed. (1984). *The Foucault Reader.* (New York: Pantheon Books).

Rorty, R. (1989). *Contingency, Irony, and Solidarity.* (New York: Cambridge University Press).

Rorty, R. (1982). *Consequences of Pragmatism: Essays 1972–1980.* (Minneapolis: University of Minnesota Press).

Rorty, R. (1979). *Philosophy and the Mirror of Nature.* (Princeton: Princeton University Press).

Said, E. (1978). *Orientalism.* (New York: Pantheon Books).

Said, E. (1992). *Culture and Imperialism.* (New York: Alfred A. Knopf).

Sartre, J-P (1956). *Being and Nothingness* (New York: The Philosophical Library).

Sartre, J-P (1949). *Literature and Existentialism.* (New York: The Citadel Press).

Sartre, J-P (1963). *Search for a Method.* (New York: Alfred A. Knopf).

Scheffler, I. (1943). *Reason and Teaching.* (Indianapolis: Bobbs Merrill).

Schutz, A. (1967). "On Multiple Realities," *Collected Papers* I, *The Problem of Social Reality.* (The Hague: Martinus Nijhoff).

Spivak, G.C. (1990). *The Post-Colonial Critic.* (New York: Routledge).

Stevens, W. (1954). "Six Significant Landscapes," *The Collected Poems of Wallace Stevens.* (New York: Alfred A. Knopf).

Toulmin, S. (1990). *Cosmopolis.* (New York: The Free Press).

Wittgenstein, L. (1968). *Philosophical Investigations.* (New York: Oxford University Press).

Wolf, C. (1989). *Accident: A Day's News.* (New York: Farrar, Straus, and Giroux).

Woolf, V. (1962). *To the Lighthouse.* (London: Everyman's Library).

2

The Discourse of
Philosophy of Education

Walter Feinberg

Maxine Greene situates Philosophy of Education within the discourse about
rights, self, rationality and power and provides an analysis that emphasizes
deconstruction and renewal. In developing this narrative she raises the most
important issues that contemporary philosophers and philosophers of educators must come to address—how traditional (Western) conceptions of rights
can be mobilized to generate renewal without reinforcing hierarchy and
domination. To put the problem slightly differently: How can the liberating
features of the language of human rights be maintained while avoiding using
the concept of rights—developed by white, Western, bourgeois males—to
lord it over others who have not yet reached the stage of development where
they can appreciate the wisdom of the Enlightenment tradition? Although
Greene echoes Cixous's ambivalence regarding this conception of rights and
the "inalienable" self that it attaches to, she also shares, I think, correctly,
Cixous's reluctance to abandon the concept completely.

Given this dilemma, Greene believes the principle role of philosophers of
education is to find a way to "expose the inadequacies (and the racism, and
the sexism) in so much of the discourse without disposing of the texts themselves." The texts are patriarchal expressions of communications "tightly
constrained by rules of logic, linearity, and (on occasion) a range of technical
controls," limiting the free flow, imaginative, and spontaneous conversation

24

that characterizes healthy and productive human relationships. Rights talk interrupts the discourse and is patriarchical to the extent that, in doing so, the father in *To the Lighthouse* becomes the interpreter of reality and the final arbiter of truth. It becomes colonial when it "has not only imposed a 'right' way . . . ; it has in many cases deformed, belittled . . . what has been considered 'undeveloped,' implicitly regressive."

In addition to the philosopher's task of exposing the inadequacies of language without disposing of the text, Greene proposes an additional task for philosophers. True philosophy, she tells us quoting Merleau-Ponty "'consists in relearning how to look at the world.' . . . 'Learning how to look' (certainly for educators) may mean learning how to reflect with others upon intersubjectivity itself . . . The philosopher's obligation may involve enabling all sorts of persons to think about the ways they direct their attention, the vantage points they take, the naming, the caring, the concern."

Deconstruction serves as an important tool for engaging in this reflection by revealing the hierarchical binary relations that provide the framework for much of the discourse on Philosophy of Education. In disclosing how much of our thinking is governed by hierarchical binaries such as white/black, male/female, cognitive/affective we have taken an important step in, as Derrida puts it, "*overturning* of the classical opposition and a general displacement of the system." In this way, Derrida, according to Greene, believes that we can "overcome the privileging of the logos and the systematized, the abstract and the universal."

The obligation to relearn how to look at our world—in Merleau-Ponty's terms—is carried on as an intergenerational, as well as an individual project; when it takes on generational proportions, it suggests the role that Philosophy of Education may play in this enterprise. Greene accepts Hanna Arendt's idea that education is the commitment we make when we both provide the material, spiritual, and intellectual support that enables our children to "undertake something new" and at the same time "prepare them in advance for the task of renewing a common world." For Greene, this means that Philosophy of Education serves, among other things, as a reminder of the traditions within which our lives are woven while at the same time reminding us that the vantage point which that tradition provides is, like all vantage points, partial and incomplete. In this recognition, Philosophy of Education provides the release for imagination and for opening "vistas on what might be, what is not yet." Hence, Philosophy of Education is involved in self-development and self-formulation which requires attending to the silences in our own tradition and our own history and therefore breaking through that aspect of the Enlightenment tradition that has served to subordinate women, people of color, and non-Western peoples.

These insights are not just academic or abstract, but have a profound impact on schools and other educational institutions. They are responsible for many of the demands to establish schools that serve a single ethnic or racial group or a single gender. Both the The Corporate School and the New Concept School, private schools serving African-American students in the Chicago area, have received high praise not only for the academic achievement of their students but for instilling a strong sense of racial pride rooted in African and African-American ideals. Researchers have praised all-girls schools for the self assurance, assertiveness, and sense of competence that they nurture. Other institutions have also been influenced by the rejection of the Western-centered philosophy that has dominated our thinking for more than a century. Museums must reexamine entire displays developed when the savage/civilized binary was taken for granted as the appropriate framework in which to show the *progress* of *man*.[1] The imperative that Greene describes is already taking place. Part of the problem for philosophers of education is whether a field more accustomed to academic argument and conceptual analysis has a role to play in the important changes that are encompassed by Greene's observations. I will argue that there is an important role for Philosophy of Education to play, but in making this argument I will need to complement Professor Greene's conception of the field itself by bringing another discourse into focus.

Greene's placement of Philosophy of Education within an intergenerational context is valid: an important task of educational scholarship is to examine the factors involved in intergenerational reproduction and disruption.[2] Philosophy of Education serves as a reflective analysis and evaluation of the intergenerational reproduction of knowledge, skills, and sensibilities.[3] Contemporary philosophical discourse about education should be located within the context of the discourse about rights, self, rationality and power. However, I want to suggest that the discourse Greene describes need not constitute Philosophy of Education, at least as presently conceived. It could simply reflect a philosophical discourse about education (this is but one feature of the discourse of Philosophy of Education). Another side is a discourse about institutions that are intended to educate. The term school can be used to indicate such institutions, but in doing so it is important to remember that formal schooling is but one representation of such institutions. *Schooling* is used here to indicate institutions that take on intentional or expected educating functions, and discourse about such institutions grounds the field of Philosophy of Education as much as the discourse about rights, power, and self.[4]

Without the institutions and practices that are explicitly intended to educate, the profession of Philosophy of Education as we know it today would not exist. This is not to say that there are not educational problems that can be dealt with philosophically without necessarily referencing institutional practices. Questions about the nature of knowledge, the character of teaching, the nature of moral education and virtue need not be addressed in relationship to any ongoing institutional practice. However, when they are addressed in this way they can be situated within a standard philosophical discourse such as epistemology, philosophy of mind, and social philosophy.

This discourse takes on the characteristics of Philosophy of Education when it is informed by or centered on institutional practice.

Hence Philosophy of Education is institutional philosophy. It is a reflection on the aims of actual organizations and the practices of established institutions that are involved in some official or semi-official way in educating people. It is for this reason that courses in Philosophy of Education are not usually found in philosophy departments and it reflects the fact that the organ of Philosophy of Education—the Philosophy of Education Society—arose out of the efforts of a group of educators.[5] To remind us that Philosophy of Education has something to do with schooling—a reminder that Greene, whose work in schools is legendary, does not need—is not to say that each and every issue philosophers of education address must bare immediately on the work of teachers. Issues of educational policy as well as evaluation and goals may be quite indirectly related to classroom practice but are certainly important concerns for people in the field of Philosophy of Education. Nor is it to say that schools must be accepted as the best or most appropriate sites of learning. Arguments for de-schooling are important and provocative—although not especially convincing—and they certainly have a place in philosophical debates about the kinds of institutions that educate. Arguments about de-schooling are philosophical when they seek careful reflection on existing practices and the framework of institutional discourse, and they count as Philosophy of Education because they are truly about schools. It is not to say that Philosophy of Education is not often well served by people whose graduate degree is in philosophy rather than Philosophy of Education. It is simply to observe that a philosophical discourse about education that is informed by the practices of schools and other educational institutions is a discourse in Philosophy of Education. In this sense of the term, Philosophy of Education is somewhat more like scholastic philosophy than it is metaphysics; and it has a practical goal—the improvement of the institutions through which the activity of educating is advanced. Unlike much of scholasticism, however, Philosophy of Education does not begin the discourse by ruling out reformation or revolution.

This is not meant as an essentialist definition of Philosophy of Education, but a description of the actual practices that are presently identified as Philosophy of Education and it identifies a role that is recognizable both by those within the field and those outside of it. To the extent that it serves as a definition, it does so through recognizing that definitions perform certain functions in relation to ongoing practice and that they are not completely separable from the institutions which sustain the practices. There is a real sense in which Philosophy of Education is what philosophers of education do when they see themselves doing Philosophy of Education. However, this operational definition should not be taken too far, for if philosophers of education did not relate their discourse to an ongoing institution there would be very little to distinguish their discourse from other forms of philosophy that are concerned with rights, power, self, or that attempt to understand knowledge and the possibility of its transmission. In this sense, Dewey was probably wrong when he equated all philosophy to Philosophy of Education. True, Philosophy of Education asks most of the interesting questions of philosophy, but it answers them in relation to on-going institutional practice.

To describe Philosophy of Education in this way is to acknowledge the importance of the history and practices of the Philosophy of Education Society and to embrace the concern that R. Bruce Raup expressed in its founding to improve "teaching in the Philosophy of Education in schools for the education of teachers and in other educational institutions."[6] Whether or not Raup overemphasized the importance of teachers colleges for Philosophy of Education—and I think he did—the more important point is the need to situate the field at the intersection of two discourses—one philosophical and the other institutional. Teachers colleges and schools of education make the latter discourse more likely and more easy to sustain. It is not, however, the only possibility.

The conception of Philosophy of Education that I have offered, partial as it is, delineates the activities of philosophers of education from the work of philosophers, even those with explicitly educational concerns. The difference is not only in the nature of the work itself but in the discourse within which the works are situated. That the work of a philosopher of education is situated within a professional discourse about the existing practices of schools or other ongoing educating institutions is reflected in the standards used to evaluate work in the field. The philosophical community is rightly concerned with the rigor and originality of the argument, a concern which philosophers of education should also share. However, the community of philosophers of education must also be concerned to reflect an informed and up-to-date awareness of the actual work and issues of the schools or of policies and research that pertain to contemporary educational practices. This does not mean that people who are identified as philosophers will not on occasion write articles or books that are informed about school practice. Nor does it mean that philosophers of education may not sometimes be poorly informed about the activities of schools. The point has to do with the expectations of the field rather than with just how well someone inside or outside of the field may meet those expectations. Or, to put the matter slightly differently: A philosopher who makes mistakes about school practice may still meet the standards of good philosophy. However, a philosopher of education who is consistently uninformed about educational practices and research is failing to meet the standards of the field.

The different discourses in which philosophy and Philosophy of Education are situated have an influence on the way in which the concerns of education are explored. Nevertheless the two have a good deal in common. For example, both philosophers and philosophers of education are likely to address such fundamental questions as what counts as education, how education can be distinguished from indoctrination, training and the like—questions that were popular among the last generation of both analytic philosophers and philosophers of education and which remain important questions. This common ground is reflected in many of the common texts and issue that are shared by both fields. Plato's discourse on justice in *The Republic,* Rousseau's discussion of freedom in *Emile,* Dewey's reframing of democracy in *Democracy and Education* and R.S. Peters's exploration of the aims of education are likely to be treated in classes taught by both philosophers and philosophers of education. Moreover recently, the influence of feminism, Marxism and postmodernism is being felt within both the philosophical community and the field of Philosophy of Education and has added to each a new concern about whose interests are served by different conceptions of knowledge and different assigned aims.

Philosophy of Education departs from a philosophical interest in education in the high level of interdependence between the work of empirical educational researchers and the work of philosophers of education. Philosophers of education must both mine the findings of empirical traditions to understand the constraints and possibilities of human development and, as practitioners of institutional philosophy, they must critically analyze the extent to which methodological frameworks may reinforce institutional practices that arbitrarily restrict educational discourse. It is at this point that the rights discourse and the institutional discourse intersect.

Institutional philosophies such as Philosophy of Education or Philosophy of Medicine have a complicated relationship to the practical knowledge that is carried on within the institution itself. In the Philosophy of Medicine, the philosopher does not need to be able to perform the technical work of the nurse or the physician or to share the same knowledge base. She does, however, need a working understanding of the organization and structure of healthcare, the availability and benefits of certain kinds of treatment, and a general conception of health and disease. If, for example she was concerned with a just distribution of healthcare, she would need to know the relative benefits, say, of introducing a new water treatment plant in Third World countries as opposed to the development of a new open heart surgical unit. Each has its costs and its benefits, but in many countries the former is likely to service the needs of the vast majority of a population, while the latter benefits only the few who are wealthy enough to survive to the age where heart disease becomes a serious problem. Both the philosopher of medicine and the philosopher of education need, in Greene's phrase, to be able to imagine other arrangements. This imagination, however, is but one stage in a larger process. They must have the philosophical tools to evaluate present practices against alternative possibilities. In these evaluations, conceptions of justice, fairness, autonomy, and independence must begin to inform the existing institutional standards.

Within institutions the meaning of concepts is established through their historical use. The feminist critique of rights that Greene draws upon is powerful precisely because the institutional history of this term is mixed, serving both liberationist, and non-liberationist goals. When institutional meanings are confronted by feminist and other critical scholarship, the historically encrusted meanings are reconstituted as objects of discourse and criticism to be held up against more honorific understandings. As institutional philosophy, Philosophy of Education confronts the practices and present meanings of existing institutions. Moreover, as Greene notes, deconstruction provides an instrument for revealing frameworks of domination and subordination and overturning—to use Derrida's phrase—"the classical oppositions."

Although deconstruction may encompass critical method and philosophy, it is at best a moment in the Philosophy of Education. In Philosophy of Education, the exposure of institutional meanings provides a promissory note that the possibility of reconstruction will be considered and that serious attempts will be made to reconstitute meanings in new and non-dominating ways. To enter this phase of institutional philosophy, it is important to expose the limits of deconstruction by asking what purpose we might wish to, as Greene advocates, "practice an *overturning* of the classical opposition and a general displacement of the system." What is the reason to bring to consciousness such oppositions as "white/black; male/female; cognitive/affective; literal/figurative" if not because we operate under some notion that certain voices and certain purposes have been wrongly silenced. Yet deconstruction itself is silent when it comes to the question of reconstruction.[7] This is a silence that Philosophy of Education cannot share.

Maxine Greene poses the dilemma of reconstruction eloquently:

> This differs considerably from a conception of objectively existing frameworks in which we can somehow ground a normative order of consequence for young people in our schools. Yet it remains difficult to set aside our commitments to theoretically-grasped principles like freedom, justice, and equality. Similarly, for all our familiarity with the problematic of the "Enlightenment Project" (Horkheimer and Adorno 1972), we are still drawn to idealistic renderings of reason linked to progress and to humanism. They continue to draw us towards them, either as regulatory norms or unrealized possibilities. In a moment of shattered frameworks and alternations between scepticism and hopelessness, they seem to glow in the dark as reminders of what might be, and of what is still to be achieved.

Reconstruction requires that the floating scepticism that energizes the deconstructive project yield some reminders—as Greene puts it of "what is still to be achieved". Such reminders can be found by examining feminists' and deconstructionists' insights and by exploring the larger project which supports these insights. Greene's scepticism of scepticism provides a way to reveal the nature of this project.

When Derrida speaks of overturning the classic oppositions which have much "to do with the way we think and speak" and I would add, feel and act, he is not just proposing a random rejection without any direction in mind. Because the overturnings are of systems of dominance and subordination he clearly seeks a world where, if these hierarchies are not eliminated altogether, they are at least not taken for granted and allowed to exert a decisive but subliminal influence on our structures of discourse. Similarly, when feminists reject the ideas of dead white men, they are not rejecting their ideas just because they are old or because they came from white males. They are rejecting them because they sense that there was woven into their expression a system of privilege which has been perpetuated through and along side of the ideas. They do not accept the view that the ideas can be separated from their expression. Instead, they hold that the way a person lives is connected to the ideals he expressed. For example, the fact that Jefferson continued to hold onto his slaves during his lifetime, tells a good deal about the conception of rights that he had in mind when he authored the founding documents. Without identifying this system of privilege as the object of deconstruction's scepticism, it is simply impossible to understand why we should overturn this opposition rather than that one; or, why we should worry about overturning any opposition whatsoever. And without similarly identifying this system of privilege as the object of feminists' concern, we are simply relegated to a behavioral paradigm where the difference between being silenced and being quiet is erased. Yet if these are indeed the core projects of these two movements, there is every reason, as Greene affirms "not to set aside our commitments to . . . principles like justice, freedom and equality." The object is in fact to see them for the role they can play in liberating dominated groups while also understanding how they have been sometimes used otherwise. This may very well mean not an out-of-hand rejection of the writings of white males, but a renewed exploration in order to understand both the possibilities they helped to articulate—often as oppressed subjects themselves—and the avenues they blocked as they expressed themselves through the images, norms, and conceptual distinction of their own period and gender. The project also requires the resurrection of ideas of woman, native peoples, people of color, and blue collar workers whose words were less likely to be provided a public forum.

For philosophers of education concerned about classroom activities and relations, it is very important to be clear about the direction one is taking and the principles that are being supported.[8] As a pacifist, a person may indeed agree that gay people should not be discriminated against in the military—because they believe that discrimination anywhere is wrong. This need not, however, be taken as supporting the military. Similarly, take a teacher who is concerned about the tendency for the boys to dominate the classroom conversation. For this reason the teacher tries to call on girls before boys, to encourage reluctant girls to raise their hand and to teach boys to be patient while a girl is speaking. Consider the different reasons a philosopher of education might give for viewing this *bias* in favor of the girls in a positive light. One reason might have to do with the cash value assertiveness plays in our society. The adage "children should be seen and not heard" just is not good advice for raising children—whether girls or boys—in late twentieth century America. Yet to advance assertiveness for this reason is not to overturn a classical opposition, but to affirm an existing and widespread social value—the value of assertiveness. A philosopher of education who is not wild about assertiveness may, like the pacifist, support the activity for other reasons, say, women have an equal right to good jobs and income and in this society they need to be assertive to secure them. Another likely reason is that children learn more when they engage in active discussion in class, but as a general principle this seems incomplete. Children learn more when they are active participants in a *good* discussion. And a good discussion involves people seeking clarity and truth while they are also concerned about the quality of the relationships that enables the search for clarity and truth to continue in a reasonably unthreatening atmosphere.

There are at least two compelling reasons for the concern about silencing. The first is that people who want to speak have a right to do so and if others systematically monopolize the conversation, this right is being denied. This reason has very little to say about the quality of what is said, but it has a lot to say about the way in which traditional rights doctrines can be used to advance progressive agendas. Systematic silencing in school can be a special and most serious violation of such a right because of the long-term consequences it entails as girls learn eventually to silence themselves.

This reason for objecting to the systematic silencing of girls is an example of how our sensitivity to rights actually guides critical scholarship. Granted, it calls for a more extended discussion of rights and the way different groups are advantaged and disadvantaged in learning to exercise them. Yet the discussion cannot begin without some awareness of what it means to have a right and when it is appropriate to equate the inability to exercise a right with its violation. A second reason for concern about the girls' silence is that they likely have something important to say and that the silence denies everyone the benefit of their insights.

Although there are at least two reasons for concern about the silence, they mandate considerably different institutional responses. There is a vast institutional difference between the right a person has to speak and the concern that a person be heard. The first is often therapeutic activity—an activity that is undertaken because of a personal deficiency and as a step on the way to something else. The second is a way to promote clarity and truth-seeking by assuring that as many different perspectives can be considered in a deliberation.

Philosophers of education have a stake in the way this distinction is developed because they are engaged in a practice that is centered on the improvement of educational institutions. And, while removing silences—whether for reasons of rights or for reasons of truth—is likely to improve the lives of children, education is advanced when the former also serves the latter.

An important feature about institutions and practices as far as Philosophy of Education is concerned is that they constrain discourse in certain ways that transcend simple logical possibilities. Discourse here entails intervention in ongoing activities. To become conscious of an institutional practice as a practice (rather than an unchangeable act of nature) is to force a decision about whether to endorse the practice through allowing things to be, or to intervene in a way that will change the practice. In the arena of Philosophy of Education arguments are framed within the context of existing practices and possibilities. Historical and social factors must be accounted for and taken into account. Here, ongoing practices exist in a way that constrains action and provides the framework for normative discourse. Philosophy of Education reflects on existing practices as they relate to schools or other educative institutions. Such reflection is most importantly about the aims of those institutions as they are embedded in practices.

NOTES

1. Appreciation to Willard Boyd, President of the Field Museum for this insight.

2. Walter Feinberg, *Understanding Education: Toward a Reconstruction of Educational Inquiry,* Cambridge: Cambridge University Press, 1983 pp. 147–74.

3. Ibid.

4. Because schools and other educative institutions exist within a network of supporting institutions and practices, the scope of Philosophy of Education is wide ranging, encompassing critiques of popular culture, media, and economic practices as they impinge upon the education of the young.

5. For a most useful history of this organization see James M. Giarelli and J. J. Chambliss, "The Foundations of Professionalism: Fifty Years of the Philosophy of Education Society in Retrospect" *Educational Theory*, Summer, 1991 41(3): 265–74.

6. As quoted in Giarelli and Chambliss., p. 268.

7. In referring to deconstruction I am not speaking of its use strictly as a literary method in, say the work of Barbara Johnston. I am addressing its limitation when used as a devise for social criticism. The extreme of this, of course, would be in the work of Paul DeMan.

8. It is important to see the opposition between principled and relational thinking that has recently been made to characterize the difference between male and female thinking, not as a logical opposition, but as built into genderized practices that could be otherwise.

3

Counting Down to the Millennium

D.C. Phillips

The closing of a century (and even more significantly for some, the ending of a millenium) will soon be upon us. Such occasions have always served as stimuli for humans to reflect upon where they have been and where they are going. With her usual powerful and suggestive prose, Maxine Greene has sketched the intellectual context in which our reappraisal must take place of what Philosophy of Education is about, as we move into the new age.

Her account is truly "millenial"; she shows that over the past few decades great, even shattering, changes have occurred in both the realm of ideas and the socio-political setting in which our intellectual labor takes place. Thus, voices that previously were suppressed, or that faced great difficulty in becoming audible in public, are finally being heard—and the messages that these voices are conveying present fundamental challenges to the received order of ideas, concepts, assumptions, and practices. Our task has now become, Greene tells us in a vivid way, to decide how to maintain the best of the centuries-old Enlightenment tradition and how to meld this (perhaps small) residue with the insights that are being offered by the newly vocal feminist and minority scholars (including—to add to the complexities—those from non-Western cultures). With Hélène Cixous she finds herself "in tension with regard to a desire for the old standards and an acknowledgement of post-modern scepticism and questioning." Thus Greene assigns those of us in Philosophy of Education a daunting task—one made no easier by the dual facts that our profession is declining in numbers, and that even in more settled times it never had much influence on those who occupy positions of power in society (no matter whose voice was representing our field).

I accept the general picture that Maxine Greene has painted of the tumultuous intellectual and social times in which we live; but I interpret this picture differently. Rather than seeing the situation in terms of an undermining of the old Enlightenment tradition and a multi-directional quest for the new, I see it as having the potential for an exciting and liberating extension of the Enlightenment vision—a vision that has taken us centuries to fully appreciate and which may take us even longer to realize in practice both in education and socio-political life. (Whether we can afford to wait much longer is another matter—and one upon which I presume Greene and I agree: the sooner the liberating changes take place, the better.) Furthermore—and here I am in further disagreement with Greene—I see postmodernism as pointing the road to disaster, rather than illuminating the path to salvation. The unresolved (and unresolvable?) tensions in this general position are clearly represented in Greene's essay. To attain the social and educational goals that she and I share, she needs to embrace old-fashioned Enlightenment (and even "patriarchal") concepts and values (Siegel 1994, argues a parallel point).

My manner of proceeding will not resonate with most of those who share Greene's predilection for postmodernism. As Christopher Norris puts it, these days those who resist postmodernism are "mostly treated . . . in tones ranging from reproof (mild or firm) to pitying fondness."

> Quite simply, any talk of truth, reason, valid argument, critique or other such "Enlightenment" notions is enough to mark one out as hopelessly *derriere-guarde,* or as a last-ditch defender of some obsolete creed . . . whose deplorable effects are witnessed everywhere around us, and whose imminent demise must surely be welcomed by all right-thinking persons. (Norris 1993, p. 285)

Forced to make a choice between these negative reactions, I would settle for the reader's "pitying fondness." But Norris's words serve as a nice introduction to my first point.

The Argument from the Persistence of Social Pathology

Human ideals and precepts—whether social, political, moral, or religious—often fail when put into practice. Christianity, the religion of the "Prince of Peace," led to non-peaceful abominations such as the Inquisition, persecution, horrendous sectarian wars, and in some contexts it gave support to slavery and apartheid. The ideas of Marx were taken as the basis for the communist system that recently was overthrown by long-suffering citizens in the former USSR. But were Christianity and Marxism refuted by—or even responsible for—the horrors committed in their names? Was the educational and philosophical thought of John Dewey refuted by the clear excesses of the last years of the progressive movement in education in the decade of the 1950s? For that matter, is the ideal of protection of the natural environment in some way invalidated or tarnished by the fact that some industrialists (and not only in the post-Enlightenment West) continue deliberately to despoil it?

One line of thought would be that, yes, Christianity, Marxism, the philosophy of John Dewey, and ideals like environmental protection stand condemned on the evidence of these consequences. On the other hand, a strong case can be made that the fault does not lie necessarily with the ideas, but with their execution. Fallible and often shortsighted or avaricious humans, working in less than perfect social and organizational settings, botched the translation of the ideal into practice—or thwarted it altogether. Was Marx really responsible for the excesses of Stalin and the Communist State; or Jesus for the acts of sadistic inquisitors? The alternative account is a familiar one to those who work in the field of Philosophy of Science: A theory or hypothesis is tested by deducing from it some consequence that can be checked by experimental or observational means; but in order to carry out such a test, scientists must make use of *auxiliary assumptions* (other theories and data, calculations, laboratory work with equipment and chemicals and so on, must all play a role in conducting a test). If the result of a test is negative—that is, if the predicted result is not obtained—the conclusion cannot be drawn that the theory is at fault, for the trouble might well lie with one of the auxiliaries. (There are inumerable examples of all this in the history of science; for a further discussion, see Phillips 1987.)

There is a lesson to be learned here that, I would claim, is relevant for appraising the mode of argument used by Greene and others who are in the radical contemporary feminist and postmodernist camps. For the position they hold is this: The Enlightenment tradition—the tradition that has given us the impressive corpus of modern science (including medicine) and mathematics, modern technology (with its contributions to modern health, transportation, communication, and agriculture), and ideals of justice and freedom for the individual (those ideals, for example, that are embodied in the U.S. Bill of Rights)—is defective because wars have not disappeared, because inequality and injustice are still present in modern societies, and because women and members of ethnic minorities and the gay community have not yet achieved full equality and often suffer egregious discrimination. It should be apparent, however, that this is not a valid line of argument.

Like all traditions in human intellectual history, the Enlightenment tradition is not without flaws. The problems that Greene and others point to (and they are genuine and serious problems) can equally or more plausibly be explained as being due to the defective ways these ideals have been put into practice—and, no less importantly, as being due to the defective humans who have put them into practice (or who have pretended to put them into practice). Without really considering and excluding other possibilities, Greene seems to believe that "the repressive aspects of Western philosophy derive primarily from phallocentrism and colonialism"—ignoring the evidence that non-Western, non-colonial societies have been just as repressive, as are (and were) the tribal communities of Africa and the pre-colonial Americas.

Perhaps the problem lies deeper in human nature than Greene is willing to admit, and cannot be conveniently passed-off onto those ideals that have been promulgated in the West since the time of the Enlightenment. (The choice of diagnosis here, of course, has major implications for what remedy we educators will adopt.) Greene offers a revealing succession of examples to make her case: The Chernobyl disaster, the death sentence passed on Salman Rushdie by the religious leaders in Iran, the suppression of Native American cultures, Hiroshima, the Holocaust, and Stalin's Gulag are all offered as evidence that modern technical rationality (one child of the Enlightenment) is at fault. The facts that are troublesome for this case are overlooked: Tribal societies all over the globe have constantly committed atrocities upon each other; Rushdie was condemned by a group which has rejected Western ideals—but is protected by a society that espouses them; Stalin and Hitler were psychopathic monsters—not unlike some spawned in non-Western societies—and they were opposed by many heroic people of Enlightenment disposition; in the ancient pre-Enlightenment world entire populations of conquered cities were sometimes unmercifully slaughtered; enlightened figures like William Wilberforce protested vigorously against the enslavement or unjust treatment of native populations; Bertrand Russell—a rationalistic Enlightenment-style philosopher if ever there was one—was willing to be jailed (on more than one occasion) for his pacifist and anti-nuclear weapons views; and quintessential Enlightenment thinkers like John Locke argued eloquently for religious toleration.

Following on from the differing diagnoses of the contemporary intellectual and social scenes that we offer, Greene and I also differ in the implications we see for education, and for Philosophy of Education. But before turning to this important matter, there are other (postmodernist) fish to fry.

The Postmodernist Attack on the Enlightenment Tradition

Earlier in my discussion a critique was offered of one line of reasoning that seems to be followed by Greene and many other postmodernists: the persistence of injustice and other social pathologies does not, by itself, offer a challenge to the validity of the social ideals or the intellectual tools developed within the Enlightenment tradition (see Norris 1993, p. 286, for a similar point). Some commentators have offered an interpretation of postmodernism that may throw light on why social pathology is seen the way it is within this framework: it has been pointed out that postmodernism is, in part, "the product of [social] desperation," and that it reflects "disillusioned optimism"—"the strain of seeing one's hopes and dreams come to nought may lead some to recoil in frustration" (Rosenau 1992, p. 11; she provides references to other works offering similar diagnoses of postmodernism).

I do not believe that it is fruitful to pursue too far the psychological motivations that might lie behind the adoption of intellectual positions (interesting as this may be). In our role as philosophers we should focus instead upon the reasons or warrants that are offered in support of these intellectual positions or frameworks. (To use Richard Rorty's terminology, this is our unique contribution, as a profession, to the "conversation of Mankind" (Rorty 1979)). Now, postmodernists do offer a line of argument—one that is reflected in Greene's essay—to the effect that the philosophical, and especially the epistemological, program of the Enlightenment, from Descartes down to the present, has been headed in quite the wrong direction. As one critic of postmodernism, Ernest Gellner, described it:

> There is also an alternative and also rather interesting path, leading from the alleged overcoming of the theory of knowledge, of "epistemology," an overcoming which is acclaimed as the great achievement of twentieth century philosophy. It is associated with names such as Wittgenstein, Heidegger, Rorty, and others. In so far as epistemology is an enquiry into difficulties facing the mind in its pursuit of knowledge of external reality, one might have expected that a movement so acutely imbued with a sense of these difficulties, indeed one which turns them into a kind of self-titillating house speciality, would treat epistemology as a welcome ally. But this is not always so. (Gellner 1992, p. 37.)

Elsewhere in the same book Gellner adds the names of Rabinow and Foucault to the list of those who helped to develop the "interesting" anti-epistemological "path" that he was criticizing; it is relevant to note that all these authors are mentioned approvingly in Greene's essay. (The only serious omission from Gellner's list is Jean-Francois Lyotard.)

As philosophers we need to examine the warrant that is offered for this far-reaching anti-epistemological position. If epistemology is dead, there is an incredible amount of *post-mortem* activity—the vast majority of professional philosophers, whose speciality it is (as Gellner pointed out) to examine sceptical arguments about the epistemic endeavor, do not consider that postmodernists and others have made anything like a serious case, and they continue in their epistemological labors with unabated enthusiasm. An interesting case in-point is provided by the recent encyclopedic *A Companion to Epistemology* (Dancy and Sosa 1992), where Lyotard does not even appear in the index, where Rorty's anti-epistemological work is assigned only a couple of very brief discussions, where postmodernism is mentioned (in passing) on only one occasion, and where the topic "The Death of Epistemology" is discussed in less than three and a half pages (in a volume of well over five hundred pages). Now, Greene and others might respond that this shows how stubborn and how blinkered in intellect most Enlightenment-tradition philosophers are; but this response would be one which "psychologizes" the opponents, and it is one which sidesteps the necessary intellectual task of examining the *grounds* or *warrants* that traditional philosophers have for their rejection of postmodernist doubts about epistemology. (Michael Williams, in the Dancy and Sosa volume, describes several problems that the "death of epistemology" group have to grapple with; and although he acknowledges that it "remains to be seen" whether the concerns about epistemology "will prove to have been exaggerated", he reports that the "rumors [about the death of epistemology] have died down" after their widespread circulation in the 1970s. (See Williams 1992, p. 88.)

This is not a watertight case against postmodernism (clearly I have not attempted to offer such a case), but rather the more modest point that postmodernism is *highly controversial,* philosophically speaking, and that its chief assertions have been criticized—a point one could never discern from the writings of contemporary educational theorists who draw upon this tradition as if it had the status of Holy Writ (and here, unfortunately, I must include Greene's essay). The moral is that we must be cautious in advocating sweeping conclusions or implications for Philosophy of Education on the basis of premises that are at worst extremely dubious and at best subject to major controversy.

Can Postmodernism Point the Way to Reform?

There is another serious problem that arises within the context of the program being pursued by Greene in her essay, one that probably has led to the tension she feels about the Enlightenment tradition. (For, it will be remembered, although she finds it intellectually bankrupt, as well as colonialist and paternalistic—as does Cixous—Greene cannot abandon it completely.)

The place to start to make the problem clear is with Lyotard's postmodernist "incredulity toward [justificatory] metanarratives" (Lyotard 1984, p. xxiv). Lyotard judged as dubious the accounts—the grand legitimizing metanarratives—that have been developed over the last couple of hundred years to justify or warrant the epistemological claims of modern science (that is, the accounts that have been given to justify its status as *knowledge*). I will not develop the obvious point that, in order to make his case, Lyotard found it necessary to present a grand metanarrative of his own which presumably, to be consistent, ought to be viewed with incredulity. (Even within the Enlightenment tradition itself there has been no attempt to paper over the problems. There has been ample recognition of the epistemic difficulties, although these have not always been the ones that engaged Lyotard's attention. These problems usually have not been regarded as insurmountable. Newton-Smith provides a detailed and extended example involving what some regard as the less-than-successful attempts to show that belief in the current theories of science is rational (Newton-Smith 1981).)

Now, the problem for Greene, Cixous, and others is that the same "Lyotardian" scepticism can be (and has been) turned against legitimizing discourse in the socio-political and moral realms as well. The whole apparatus of human rights, duties, obligations, religious toleration, human dignity, the value of democracy, and so on, which was intended to have application across the human race (despite the obvious flaws in putting this apparatus into practice, as touched upon earlier), was a product of the "totalizing" paternalistic and colonialist Enlightenment tradition. So presumably all this needs to be abandoned, or subjected to incredulous inspection.

But what happens if this traditional apparatus is jettisoned? Can we seriously contemplate stripping people of rights, or of obligations, and so on? It is clear that Greene sensibly recoils from this prospect. Yet, as a postmodernist, she has to be extremely wary of the universal pretensions of our moral codes; and she stresses the need to honor individuals who develop their own meanings and values in the socio-cultural settings in which they find themselves, she wants us to respect other "language games" or Wittgensteinian "forms of life," and she wants us to "acknowledge the worth and power of different cultures and civilizations, out of which identities are being negotiated." In short, she has to retreat to a form of relativism (although, strangely, her claims of course are meant to apply to *all* of her readers—such is the dilemma faced by relativists who try to give advice!). It should be noted that this relativism is no accident; for, as Ernest Gellner points out, "the postmodernist movement, which is an ephemeral cultural fashion, is of interest as a living and contemporary specimen of relativism" (Gellner 1992, p. 24).

This relativistic position leads to some clear problems, which is why Greene and Cixous are ambivalent. Do we want to honor a cultural group's right to practice female circumcision, for example (to cite a case that I believe has deeply divided feminist postmodernists), or do we want to remain mute about the Salman Rushdie case, or about tribal hatreds that currently are tearing apart central Africa in so bloody a manner? The obvious route, here, is to make use of our traditional beliefs about human rights and so on, whether or not they are inheritances from the Enlightenment. And the problems do not just arise when we look at examples drawn from overseas cultures, for the same dilemma arises when we turn to policy within our own society—we either have a basis for advocating educational and social policies and interventions across the diverse groups which make up our society, or we are relativists who avoid "totalizing" frameworks, especially when they (supposedly) have colonialist and paternalist origins (whatever that might mean).

The Role of Philosophy of Education

It is time to turn to the implications of this discussion—and of Greene's—for our roles as educators and philosophers of education.

I do not wish to exaggerate the differences between Maxine Greene and myself on these matters, for, if we go to a sufficient level of abstraction, it is clear that we both hold that philosophers of education face the task of rethinking and reexamining the repertoire of traditional beliefs (including philosophical ones) in the light of the intellectual and socio-political climate in which we now find ourselves. It is worth stressing in this context that it is not only postmodernists who hold that we ought to be incredulous. Philosophers are a sceptical and somewhat argumentative breed whose stock in trade has always been the critical examination of contemporary views—as the history of mainstream Western philosophy from the life (and death) of Socrates down to Bertrand Russell and many of our own contemporaries bears witness. (I do not regard the rich and complex Enlightenment tradition as perfect, as foreclosing further inquiry and debate. It is simply that I do not see that it needs to be abandoned or that inquiry needs to start over; it is a vibrant tradition that is far from being univocal, and overall I see it as being more on track than off.)

I do not want to paint a false picture, to gloss over the major differences that exist at a less general level between Greene's position and my own. For she seems to think that the pressing problems of our times, insofar as they impinge on philosophers of education, are at base intellectual in nature—they are problems that stem, in her view, from the general bankruptcy of Enlightenment ideas (including technical rationality). While acknowledging that we have serious philosophical work to do, when it comes to the general contribution that philosophers of education can make to society and to the alleviation of the problems that beset it, my account diverges markedly from hers. A major task in the socio-political context is an *educational* rather than a philosophical one: the task of teaching our philosophical material more effectively, so that the epistemic and socio-political ideals we have developed and defended have more purchase in the lives of our students. It does not profit us to have developed a strong notion of human rights, for example, if individuals (including policymakers) in our own society and around the world can abandon this whenever the mood takes them. Nor is it helpful for our educational system to produce people who espouse allegiance to critical rationality but who can be swayed by the first argument that comes along that preys on raw emotions or appeals to crass self-interest. Philosophers must discover how to make our ideals *living ideals,* ones which individuals will be faithful to in their everyday activities. Being Enlightenment figures in our daily lives is no easy matter, but at least there are some fine heroes and heroines from the history of our tradition for us, and our students, to emulate.

BIBLIOGRAPHY

Dancy, Jonathan, and Sosa, Ernest, eds. *A Companion to Epistemology*. Oxford: Blackwell, 1992.

Gellner, Ernest. *Postmodernism, Reason and Religion*. London: Routledge, 1992.

Lyotard, Jean-Francois. *The Postmodern Condition: A Report on Knowledge*. Manchester: Manchester University Press, 1984.

Newton-Smith, W.H. *The Rationality of Science*. Boston: Routledge, 1981.

Norris, Christopher. *The Truth about Postmodernism*. Oxford: Blackwell, 1993.

Phillips, D.C. *Philosophy, Science, and Social Inquiry*. Oxford: Pergamon Press, 1987.

Rorty, Richard. *Philosophy and the Mirror of Nature*. Princeton, NJ: Princeton University Press, 1979.

Rosenau, Pauline. *Post-Modernism and the Social Sciences*. Princeton, NJ: Princeton University Press, 1992.

Siegel, Harvey. "Radical Pedagogy Requires 'Conservative' Epistemology," paper presented at the Annual Conference of the Philosophy of Education Society of Great Britain, Oxford, April 1994.

Williams, Michael. "Death of Epistemology". In Dancy, J., and Sosa, E., eds., *A Companion to Epistemology*. Oxford: Blackwell, 1992, pp. 88–91.

PART TWO

VARIATIONS
FROM/ON
THE "CANON"

4

Education for Domestic Tranquillity

Jane Roland Martin

R.S. Peters worried about aims talk in relation to education on the grounds that it was incoherent.[1] I worry for different reasons. Whereas in the United States, at least, it is taken for granted that instructional methods will have to vary according to time and place and that curriculum is also subject to change, it is frequently assumed that the aims of education are—or at least should be—always and everywhere the same. It is also a given that these are individual aims: that they have to do with the development of individuals. In proposing here that domestic tranquillity become an overarching aim of education,[2] I make no claims of universality. While I feel sure that domestic tranquillity is an appropriate educational aim for societies besides my own, I do not pretend to speak for any but end-of-the-century United States. Moreover, although I do not for a moment deny that, to insure domestic tranquillity, individuals will have to learn to think and act in some ways rather than others, I am treating this as a holistic aim: one that has to do with the state of society rather than the development of individuals. In so doing I purposely leave open the question of whether it is reducible to a set of individual aims.

Historians seem to agree that the inclusion of domestic tranquillity on the list of ends that the framers of the United States Constitution hoped to insure was in large part a response to the fear of insurrection occasioned by Shays' Rebellion.[3] Frustrated by high taxes, high interest rates, declining farm prices, farm foreclosures, and the imprisonment of those who could not pay their debts, Massachusetts farmers, in the summer of 1786, began protesting the actions of their legislature. By fall and winter, these protests had become armed confrontations, although with almost no bloodshed. By February 1787 Daniel Shays and his men were routed but the fear of further rebellion—if not in Massachusetts then in Virginia or New Hampshire—haunted the men who were soon to frame the new constitution. The adoption of the concept of a strong national government is in part due to Shays and the debt-ridden farmers of Massachusetts. The inclusion in the Preamble to the Constitution of the "domestic tranquillity clause" is no doubt to be accounted for in this way, too. As constitutional scholars remind us, however, the language of the framers outlives the immediate concerns of 1787.[4] Thus, in the 1990s we need to ask what significance the domestic tranquillity clause had when the Constitution was written and what it might have now.

Even for the founding fathers this clause must have had meaning beyond just that of preventing rebellion, for the term "domestic" conveys a double message. Had they spoken of *civic* tranquillity, it might justifiably be concluded that their interest was simply in insuring governmental stability. Indicating on the one hand that internal as well as foreign disturbances can constitute threats to that stability, use of the term domestic casts the new nation in a special light. If England had once been home to the colonists, now the United States of America was their home.

Surprisingly enough, despite the fact that during the last two decades or so the concept of the domestic sphere has been investigated at some length, the relativity of the domestic has scarcely been noted. By *relativity* I mean that what one takes to be a domestic sphere or realm varies according to one's point of view. Thus, whereas the drafters of the Constitution, implicitly adopting an international perspective, viewed the United States itself as the domestic—for them, what scholars today call the public or civic realm *was* the domestic realm—recent scholarship locates the domestic within a culture or country.

It is one thing to notice the relativity of the domestic, and quite another to show that the founding fathers' vision of the civic as a realm of the domestic has theoretical and practical significance for education. Moreover, to say that from one standpoint the domestic and the public or civic are contrasting notions whereas from another the public or civic *is* the domestic, is to say very little if the domestic is not given content. I can only begin to fill in the notion of an expanded domestic *realm* and to argue for the importance of taking seriously the founding fathers' concern with domestic tranquillity. I hope it will become clear as I proceed, however, that if we in the United States increase *our* own vision of the domestic to match that of the framers, we must also enlarge *their* understanding of tranquillity to meet the realities of life at the end of the twentieth century.

Domesticating Society

Despite its variability, for us today the term domestic in its primary sense pertains to the family or home or household. In enlarging the concept of the domestic, I am therefore asking about the kind of home we want our nation to be and the kind of family we want its inhabitants to be. There is another sense of domestic, however, one that commentators overlook. Think for a moment about domestic animals. In the West's cultural consciousness they are not simply nice gentle beings who happen to have been invited to live in our homes or farmyards. They are tamed creatures, beasts, whose fierceness has been trained or bred out of them.

In the classic story of domestication, which is not about animals but about women, Shakespeare makes it clear that to domesticate is to make gentle *and* obedient. Shakespeare may not have used the term domestic in *The Taming of the Shrew,* but Petruchio's taming of Kate has all the marks of a domestication. Invoking the images of roaring lions, an angry boar, and neighing steeds when in Act I he determines to marry Kate, in the last scene of the play, Petruchio assures his friends, and his servant who had likened Kate to a wildcat, that he would wager twenty crowns on the obedience of his hawk or hound, but he would venture twenty times as much on his wife's.

What does Kate's taming bode, Petruchio is asked: "Peace it bodes, and love and quiet life, And awful rule and right supremacy; And, to be short, what not, that's sweet and happy?"[5] In other words, it bodes domestic tranquillity. Whether Petruchio's supremacy in his private home will contribute to Kate's happiness we can never know. One thing is clear: her submission to his commands is not an aspect of their domestic tranquillity that one would want to see replicated in society at large. Conflicting with the most basic principle of democracy as well as with the ideal of sex equality, Kate's docile obedience to her husband's authority mimics the very political relationship the founding fathers were determined to avoid. Shays' Rebellion may have moved them to strengthen the Union but it did not undermine their faith in the very self-government Kate renounces in marriage. Indeed, upon hearing about Daniel Shays, Thomas Jefferson even allowed that "a little rebellion now and then is a good thing, and as necessary in the political world as storms in the physical."[6]

Fortunately, both history and contemporary experience reveal that the domestic tranquillity Petruchio foresaw for himself and Kate need not turn on "awful rule and right supremacy." Indeed, just as the British learned that awful rule and right supremacy contain the seeds of domestic intranquillity, studies of family violence showing that the incidence of physical abuse in the private home is much higher where the husband presumes to be the head of the household than where both spouses view themselves as equal, teach us an analogous lesson.[7]

The ends of peace, love, and happiness both in the private and the public home surely require the gentling of characters like Kate—although not through Petruchio's training methods. Even in her relations with her father and sister she behaved abominably. But in humans, if not in roaring lions and angry boars, making gentle does not have to entail—and from both an ethical and a political standpoint ought not to entail—making obedient. Thus, in determining the implications of an expanded conception of the domestic, let us bracket Kate's subservience and Petruchio's corresponding mastery of her without losing sight of her new found gentleness. In keeping this in focus we must, of course, be ever mindful that in history, as in Shakespeare's play, a woman's gentleness has been part and parcel of her subservient status; indeed, has been a factor contributing to her domination. Thus, although the two aspects of domestication as taming—making gentle and making obedient—are analytically independent, in practice it may not be so easy to detach the one from the other. Nevertheless, if we value the peace, love, and happiness that Shakespeare attached to the private domestic realm, and if we believe that these goods should characterize the entire social realm as well, we had better try to accomplish just this.

I need scarcely say that the domestic tranquillity Petruchio anticipated in his life with Kate does not characterize U.S. society in the late twentieth century. In our private homes wife beating is rife: one does not know whose statistics to believe but one volume I have read reports that two million women are beaten by their husbands each year while in 1987 a *Boston Globe* article quoted an expert in the field as saying that 600,000 women in the United States are severely assaulted four or more times a year by their husbands.[8] The incidence of child abuse is also staggering: this same volume reports that two million children are victims of abuse annually.[9] In addition, man-girl incest is estimated to involve at least one percent of all girls.[10]

The spaces of our public home are plagued by violence too: our schools play host to vandalism and assaults on teachers and students, our sports arenas to brutality and rioting, the streets of our cities to mugging, murder, gang terrorism, rape. The violence permeating our public home is not only physical. In *Redesigning the American Dream,* Dolores Hayden detailed the way billboards, bus placards, store windows, public art turn urban space into a "landscape filled with images of men as sexual aggressors and women as submissive sexual objects."[11] Her chilling account of this landscape as experienced by two women traveling to work in Los Angeles in June 1981 holds all too true, I fear, for urban dwellers in just about every American city today.

It must be emphasized that our public home has not always been an unsafe place in which to live. Violence in the sense of the physical or psychological violation of persons has not always been the norm.[12] Indeed, in 1786—the very moment when our founding fathers judged domestic tranquillity to be in jeopardy—a Boston newspaper was moved to write:

> In America mobs are noisy and stop courts—in Great Britain they are
> riotous and pull down houses. In England or Ireland a man is liable in
> the most peaceful times to be robbed at noon. In America any man is
> safe at midnight in the largest cities and surrounded with a Hampshire
> convention or a Worcester mob.[13]

How paradoxical! For us, the domestic tranquillity the founding fathers
sought to preserve is relatively unproblematic. I do not mean to suggest that
either the fear or the possibility of insurrection is entirely a thing of the past.
Nonetheless, it seems safe to say that although the *civic* form of domestic
intranquillity that worried our founding fathers is by no means extinct,
another kind of domestic intranquillity—an *anti-social* form that seems to
have been relatively unproblematic for them—is by far the greater danger
today. Tearing the social fabric as surely as rebellion unties civic bonds,
domestic violence writ large violates the very rights of life, liberty, and the
pursuit of happiness that the Constitution is intended to protect.

Social reality demands that we expand the founding fathers' understanding of domestic tranquillity and that we reclaim the civic or public realm as a
domestic domain. It requires that all of us take on the task of erasing domestic violence and intranquillity in our society and inscribing domestic
tranquillity in its place.

Four Arguments against Domesticity

As it happens, in nineteenth century United States an image of the private
home as a realm of tranquillity to which one returned at the end of the day
from an untranquil outside world gained currency.[14] Needless to say, this
model had limited application. It did not capture the experience of those
women who, having left home to work in factories or as "domestics," had no
home to return to at day's end. Nor did it do justice to the experience of those
whose full-time job it was to create and maintain the home. Having no place
to retreat *from,* this home could not be *women's* haven. As for the experience
of those women, including slaves, who both ran a home and worked outside
it, the model at best fit imperfectly. To be sure, some women—notably slaves
and in a later period black domestic workers, but undoubtedly others as
well—suffered so cruelly in the world outside home that despite the work to
be done their own home must have seemed a place of rest.[15] Yet by representing home as a sanctuary in an evil world, the model effectively hid from view
the domestic violence that made it for many women, whether rich or poor,
white or black, an unsafe place to be.

The vision of home as haven was at best, then, an illusion masking the
realities of women's existence. Yet it is a mistake on this account to dismiss
out of hand the sense of connection and intimacy, the safety and security, the

peace and love, that our public home lacks today. The question for us should be: How can we write these things large without repeating the patriarchal structure on which that nineteenth century ideal was predicated?

First, several common objections to the domestication of society must be addressed. One is that because the private home is a major site of violence in the United States today, to project its qualities onto the whole realm is the height of folly. If we want to reduce the violence of the civic sphere, had we not better look anywhere but there for our model of the nation itself? I agree that the enormous gap between the realities of private homes today and Petruchio's dream of peace, love, and quiet life should give us pause. We need not fear, however, that if we conceptualize the civic as a realm of the domestic it will become polluted by these realities. Indeed, since the larger society is already a sphere of violence, we should be asking if its violent nature does not adversely affect the tranquillity of the private home. Analysts tend to place the blame for wife and child abuse on the home itself: on the relationships and configurations of both the present abusive home and the childhood home of the victim and the victimizer.[16] But behavior in the private home is affected by the larger societal context. Would private violence flourish in a domesticated society? Would the private home be such a dangerous haven were it situated in a safe and loving world? Rather than assume that the failings of the private home invalidate the project of domesticating society, we should perhaps expect the private home to reap the benefits of a domesticated civic or public realm.

A related objection is that because home as haven is a myth masking the exploitation and domination of women, to project the qualities it attributes to the private home onto our public home is to guarantee women's subordination in society at large. The conclusion that the cost of this form of domestic tranquillity is women's oppression simply does not follow from the premise, however. In the first place, we now know—if we did not always—that both sexes are capable of doing the physical and intellectual labor required to make a home a safe, warm, secure place. If one assumes that only females have a capacity for intimacy and love, then for its emotional labor domestic tranquillity will inevitably have to rely exclusively on women. But to grant this premise about intimacy and love is to embrace an unwarranted biological determinism. True, psychologists are discovering that females in our culture tend to be more nurturant and to have developed stronger bonds of intimacy than males. But this asymmetry is best regarded not as a consequence of biology but as a problem to be overcome by education.

A third objection to conceptualizing the nation as a domestic realm is that literature, science, philosophy, the fine arts, if not civilization itself, is put at risk. It is instructive to consider at least William James's version of this argument for, in the early part of this century, he gave voice to fears that many still have today. According to James, the higher forms of literature and fine art bring home to us "human nature strained to its uttermost and on the rack."[17] And here, in turn, is his judgment on that small domesticated society of Chautauqua, circa 1890—"This order is too tame, this culture too second-rate."[18] Given these premises one must conclude that, in his view, a society has to place human nature on the rack if it is to produce great works.

The most that can be said for James's definition of first-rate literature is that it is far too limited. Ironically, his "happy week at the famous Assembly Grounds on the borders of Chautauqua Lake" is the very stuff on which Jane Austen's inspiration thrived.[19] No doubt George Eliot could also have found sufficient drama in that middle class society. Nor are Austen and Eliot the only major writers whose work belies James's argument. Henry James would be considered a mediocre writer on his brother's criterion as would John Keats, Anton Chekhov, and Emily Dickinson. Moreover, it should not be thought that if domestic tranquillity prevails there will be no pain, conflict, or misfortune. People will still get sick, things will still happen to them that are outside their control—they will still die. Luck, accident, contingency; conflicts of desire, loyalty, obligation will continue to be inescapable and unsettling features of life.[20] One need not worry too much, then, that in projecting the values of safety and security, peace and love onto the whole social sphere we will be ridding human existence of all danger and risk. Nor need we fear that the gentling of society will usher in an era free from tension and conflict.

Actually, James's dismay at Chautauqua derived only in part from his fear that high culture would be flattened. The more pressing problem in his view was that in this tranquil community there was no call for the virtues that he identified with manliness. In complaining about the absence of precipitousness, by which he meant "strength and strenuousness, intensity and danger,"[21] and in calling Chautauqua "too tame,"[22] James was in fact expressing his admiration for "the sterner stuff of manly virtues" and his disapproval of any order that did not actively encourage their expression.

James's argument from lost masculinity would very likely be made by many in the U.S. today. Yet the conclusion that society should not be domesticated only gains support if his admiration for a Ramboesque version of masculinity is justified. As a factor contributing heavily to the domestic intranquillity that now characterizes our public sphere, it is anything but. Indeed this conception of masculinity, representing as it does a barrier to the domestication of society, is best viewed as an obstacle to be overcome, not a reason for rejecting the project. We should not underestimate how hard it will be for U.S. culture to renounce this particular construct of gender. Because masculinity is a cultural construct, and because both masculinity and femininity have highly variable cultural meanings that can change over time, and the very opposition between masculinity and femininity is itself a cultural product, the argument from lost masculinity is best viewed as a reminder of the seriousness of the task at hand, and not of the undesirability of that task.

Domesticating Education

Even if the U.S. judicial system were inclined to give due weight to the domestic tranquillity clause of the Constitution, it would be remiss to view one of the most important issues of our age as primarily a matter of law. A conception of the nation as home, of public space as a place of safety and security, of the relationship among citizens as one of harmony and shared goals rather than antagonistic claims: all this constitutes a reorientation of thought, feeling, and action. For this new perspective, and for the knowledge and skill that must accompany it, we must look not just to legislation but to education.

Unfortunately, education is premised on the very split between the domestic and the civic that an enlarged vision of the domestic challenges. This culture, if not every culture, takes the function of education to be that of transforming those who have to that point lived their lives in the domestic realm into members of the public or civic realm. Assuming that membership in the one realm is natural, we see no reason to prepare people to carry out the tasks and activities associated with it. Perceiving membership in the other realm as something to be achieved and therefore as problematic, we make the business of education preparation for carrying out the tasks and activities associated with it. Our culture's very conception of education, not only rests, then, on the distinction between the civic and the domestic; it views domestic life as that which we must learn to go beyond.

As a matter of fact, almost all of us continue to live in homes and be members of families[23] even as we take our place in society at large. Yet although to go beyond is not necessarily to leave behind, we nevertheless think of becoming educated not simply as a process of acquiring new ways of thinking, feeling, and acting. For us it is also a matter of casting off the attitudes and values, the patterns of thought and action associated with the domestic. Considering these latter to be impediments to the successful performance of society's productive processes, we demand that education move us away from the domestic realm and all it represents even as it equips us for life in the public realm.

In a real sense, then, *all* formal education in our culture is civic education. With the exception of those home economics courses—sometimes now called family studies—that many children in school never even take, education today is not concerned with life in the domestic realm. Liberal education, vocational education, the general education provided by our elementary and secondary schools: these are all forms of civic education, not in the narrow sense of citizenship instruction or training in patriotism, but preparation for life in the public world of work, politics, and high culture.

If all education is civic and our perspective is shifted so as to perceive the civic as the domestic, then all education becomes domestic. This does *not* mean that all teachers become home economics teachers. Just as there is a broad and a narrow sense of civic education, so too there is in the case of domestic education. When all education is seen as civic, civic education in the limited sense of citizenship or patriotic education or education about one's country's form of government becomes one among many elements of civic education broadly understood. Similarly, when the civic is seen as the domestic, domestic education in the limited sense of home economics becomes one among many elements of domestic education writ large.

When our perception of the civic changes, so must our vision of education. As an expanded domestic realm promises to supplant an ethic of violence and violation with one of safety and security, peace and love, our new vision will reorient educational theory and practice. One who makes the insuring of domestic tranquillity a central aim of education claims for young people a very special quality and kind of moral instruction, and for society a very special kind and quality of moral life. This new vision does not simply infuse formal programs in moral education with goals and objectives derived from our interest in insuring domestic tranquillity. It requires that *all* aspects of educational endeavor be made consistent with and reflective of this end.

What does this bode for the nation's schools, colleges, and universities? At the very least it bodes a commitment to the safety—the bodily and psychological integrity—of students and to education in the 3Cs of care, concern, and connection. It bodes, therefore, a shift away from teaching methods and classroom practices that, shunning these virtues, inhibit collaboration and cooperation, as well as a rejection of the privileged status now bestowed on education for spectatorship.[24] Equally important, it bodes a greater subject matter inclusiveness that, along with an increased respect for difference and diversity, transmits an appreciation of domesticity itself.

As it now conducts our young from the domestic into the civic or public realm, school teaches them to devalue that place called home and the things associated with it. Its lessons, constituting a hidden curriculum in anti-domesticity, are conveyed as much by the silences of the curriculum as by the explicit derogation of the domestic.[25] If we are to insure domestic tranquillity, school's complicity in transmitting a hidden curriculum in anti-domesticity must be acknowledged. Because U.S. society has assigned responsibility for carrying out the tasks and activities of the private home on the basis of gender, the well-documented silences about—and the negative portrayals of—women are implicated too. Because its prejudices have placed African-Americans closer to nature than to culture, the silences about and negative portrayals of black men as well as about women of all races are also implicated. The connections between education's implicit denigration of women and African-Americans, on the one hand, and the domestic on the other are seldom if ever acknowledged. Nevertheless, the strands of these three hidden curricula are interwoven.

It is essential to raise to consciousness school's hidden curricula about race and gender if the harm done by the present hidden curriculum in anti-domesticity is to be redressed.[26] All of us have absorbed the lessons of this latter curriculum so well, however, that its eradication will not be accomplished easily. Nor will it be easy to persuade educators in the various fields of knowledge to give legitimacy to domestic study, for they themselves devalue the domestic. To insure domestic tranquillity in our private homes and in the larger society we must teach our students and ourselves to value domesticity so that domesticity will become everyone's business.[27]

Conclusion

For good reason, the founders made the new nation the site of the domestic. Some two hundred years later we must reclaim their insight into the relativity of the domestic without accepting the domestic boundaries they took for granted. Today, if not in Daniel Shays' lifetime, a domestic/public split separating our *home*land from other lands is as fraught with danger as was the fragmentation of states inherent in the Articles of Confederation that the founding fathers rejected. In an age in which not merely the nation, indeed not merely the human species, but *all* life is at risk, the earth itself must be seen for what it is—our home. "We have inherited a large house," Martin Luther King once said, "a great 'world house' in which we . . . must learn somehow to live with each other in peace."[28] The domestic tranquillity we seek in our private homes and need desperately to extend to our national home must be projected onto the whole world and ultimately onto the whole planet and these projections must then be turned back onto all facets of education.

NOTES

1. See, e.g., R.S. Peters, "Aims of Education—A Conceptual Inquiry" in R.S. Peters ed., *The Philosophy of Education* (London: Oxford University Press, 1973), pp. 11–34.

2. The thesis of this essay is developed more fully in Jane Roland Martin, *The Schoolhome* (Cambridge: Harvard University Press, 1992). A good deal of the material it contains was first presented in a series of unpublished papers and in Jane Roland Martin, "To Insure Domestic Tranquillity: Liberal Education and the Moral Life," *Working Papers Series* #8, Project on Interdependence, Radcliffe College, Cambridge, MA.

3. See, e.g., Marian L. Starkey, *A Little Rebellion* (New York: Knopf, 1955); Howard Zinn, *A People's History of the United States* (New York: Harper and Row, 1980); Allen Weinstein, "Massachusetts Uprising Affected the U.S. Constitution," *Boston Globe,* February 2, 1989.

4. Paul Freund, "What They Said, What They Read," *New York Times Book Review,* March 15, 1987, pp. 3, 20–21.

5. William Shakespeare, *The Taming of the Shrew,* in Hardin Craig ed., *The Complete Works of Shakespeare* (Chicago: Scott, Foresman and Company, 1951), p. 181.

6. Starkey, *Rebellion,* p. 4.

7. Pamela Reynolds, "Violence at Home," *Boston Globe,* March 29, 1987, pp. A15, A17.

8. John Langone, *Violence* (Boston: Little Brown, 1984), p. 124; Reynolds, "Violence at Home."

9. Langone, *Violence,* p. 134.

10. Wini Breines and Linda Gordon, "The New Scholarship on Family Violence," *Signs,* 8 (Spring, 1983): 521.

11. Dolores Hayden, *Redesigning the American Dream* (New York: W.W. Norton, 1984, p. 221).

12. Newton Garver, "What Violence Is," in Jeffrie G. Murphy, ed., *An Introduction to Moral and Social Philosophy* (Belmont, Calif.: Wadsworth Publishing Co., 1973), pp. 332–38.

13. Starkey, *Rebellion,* p. 63.

14. Hayden, *American Dream,* p. 68ff.

15. Jacqueline Jones, *Labor of Love, Labor of Sorrow* (New York: Basic Books, 1985); but cf. Toni Morrison's portrayal of Pauline Breedlove in *The Bluest Eye* (New York: Pocket Books, 1970).

16. See, e.g. Reynolds, "Violence at Home."

17. William James, "What Makes a Life Significant" in *Talks to Teachers* (New York: W.W. Norton, 1958), p. 174.

18. Ibid. p. 173.

19. Ibid. p. 172.

20. For a discussion of the place of these in morality see Martha C. Nussbaum, *The Fragility of Goodness* (Cambridge: Cambridge University Press, 1986).

21. William James, "The Moral Equivalent of War," in Richard Wasserstrom ed., *War and Morality* (Belmont, Calif: Wadsworth Publishing Co., 1970), p. 174. For a fuller discussion of this point see Jane Roland Martin, "Martial Virtues or Capital Vices? William James' Moral Equivalent of War Revisited," *Journal of Thought,* 22 (Fall, 1987): 32–44.

22. Ibid. p. 173.

23. Although not necessarily traditional nuclear ones.

24. For a fuller discussion of this point see Chapter 3 of Martin, *The Schoolhome.*

25. For a fuller discussion of this point see Chapter 5 of Martin, *The Schoolhome.*

26. For more about what do to with a harmful hidden curriculum see Jane Roland Martin, "What Should We Do with a Hidden Curriculum When We Find One?," *Curriculum Inquiry,* 6 (1976): 135–151.

27. For a fuller discussion of this point see Chapter 5 of Martin, *The Schoolhome.*

28. Quoted in Diana L. Eck, "Responses to Pluralism: Worldviews in an Interdependent World," *Working Papers Series #4,* p. 20, Project on Interdependence, Radcliffe College, Cambridge, MA.

5

Pragmatism: The Aims of Education and the Meaning of Life

Alven Neiman

Once upon a time philosophers lived and thrived within a world thought to be composed of essences or natures. Their beliefs about these entities led them quite naturally to make claims about the good for human life—the ultimate meaning of life and the aims of education. Today it is no longer fashionable for philosophers of education to believe in essences: contingency, flux, and Heraclitus, rather than Parmenides, Plato, and Aristotle, are in vogue. One of the most important causes of this change is the work of philosophical pragmatists such as Dewey and James. This essay will begin to lay the ground work for thinking again, from a pragmatic point of view, about the status, after essences, of questions about ultimate meaning and purpose. The ramifications of this beginning will be considered for questions about the aim of education.

This essay will first return to a philosophical garden of Eden where talk of growth as the aim of education was tied in simple and relatively unproblematic ways to talk of natures. Next I shall examine what I shall refer to as a philosophical fall from grace. After pragmatism had the courage to take the theory of evolution seriously, the link between growth, meaning and educational aims could never be so simple as it was in the garden. There are some questions about the very use of a term like growth, given the fall from essence and meaning.

This fall, taken to its extreme, leads to a kind of nihilism or (if I may be so bold) "continental irrationalism" in educational theory. Dewey's contextual use of terms like "good," "growth" and "meaning" is meant to provide a middle ground between these nihilists and the ever present keepers of the essentialistic tradition; but how useful is such contextualism in this regard? My intent is to begin to imagine ways in which this project of the middle road might be brought to fruition.

There is a space to be found between Dewey's own quasi-positivism and his better, richer inclinations. In this space, the well-known neo-pragmatist Richard Rorty will play a role as quasi-villain, representing, at least, Dewey's worst self. Steven C. Rockefeller's *John Dewey: Religious Faith and Democratic Humanism* and several concurrent articles demonstrate how Dewey, at least in his better moments, avoided the modern tendency to reduce the traditional religious search for ultimate meaning to either nonsense, childish fantasy, or irrationality.[1] His picture of Dewey lets us find room to optimistically wonder about the capacities of philosophical pragmatism to satisfy the most deeply felt and perennial human concerns and to remind us that Dewey's teacher William James still has much to teach us, after Darwin, about life, and its meaning.

Today, years after the heyday of positivism, it is fashionable to discount the concern for an ultimate or final meaning or purpose of life. It seems naive to many to think we need to take seriously the concerns of supposedly arcane, provincial thinkers such as Augustine, St. Theresa, Pascal, and Kierkegaard when educational aims are thought of. Part of the reason for this is that, pragmatists especially, are so obviously grounded in the anti-essentialistic, Darwinistic thinking of our patron saints, especially Dewey, and that after essences no such talk makes sense. Rockefeller's work on Dewey is exciting, because it allows pragmatists to remain true to the genius of our saints, while opening us up to the concerns of saints other than our own. It allows us to imagine ways in which we can perhaps both reject essentialism and properly acknowledge the sorts of longings that no merely contingent event or being can satisfy. It allows us to consider, without embarrassment, how education might properly both cultivate and help to satisfy a longing that no merely human thing, in fact no thing at all, can touch.

The Garden and the Fall

Let us return, then, at least briefly to a time when philosophers lived within a world of stability, a world in which the eternal was as open to view as change and flux are now. In such a world all living things, such as Aristotle's proverbial acorn, lived and grew in accord with their telos. While not all acorns became oak trees, all were, at least, *meant* to. And given such an inherent purpose or natural striving, the acorn's progress or lack thereof might properly be judged. Certain ways of treating, or "educating" the acorn as more or less proper, could be understood in so far as they either helped or hindered the natural progression or *growth*.

So much for acorns. What of human beings? What of *their* education? Just as acorns might be used as paper weights or projectile weapons, humans, can be trained or twisted in any number of ways that are false to their nature. But nature, it was thought, bestows a meaning or purpose upon humans as well as acorns. While they can become efficient at auto mechanics or bridge or corporate finance, they can also be educated as *real* human beings. They can, through proper education, become what nature has *in mind* for them. The true education, true liberal education is, on this scheme, that which allows things to grow most naturally, to become what they are by nature meant to be, to achieve their ultimate purpose.

This talk of natures and meaning reaches its most developed form in the West in Thomism and its philosophical relatives.[2] Here a root metaphor of the Aristotelian, that of the artifact, is most clearly utilized and strenuously developed. Acorns or people can be thought of easily as *meant* to do something, when they are thought of as purposely created; thus things are *endowed* with meaning through the motivation of their creator. *The* meaning of human life, understood within the medieval context is to come to know and love God. Medieval patterns of learning and education follow on the basis of the now familiar pattern.[3] Important in this regard is the idea of *all* meaning, whether of words, or events, or things, communities of persons, human life as a whole, or simply of Being, *as endowments*. I shall return to this idea later.[4]

So much for the philosophical garden. What of the fall? The story of the developments in science, culture, and society, in which the world was evacuated of *transcendentally endowed* meaning, is well known. The tale is told sometimes as a triumphant overcoming of stupidity and intransigence; sometimes as a tragedy. In any event, the net result is seen to be a world in which meaning can no longer be found in nature or meta-nature, as a whole, but must be found or created within the realm of our interaction with the world around us.

In Dewey's description of this process, there are both acute problems and intriguing possibilities, but always hope and good cheer.[5] The major idea for Dewey in this regard is that, *fixed* and/or *eternal* ends or ideals ought to be done away with. These include, of course, any teloi said to exist beyond the realm of time and chance, either in a realm of essence existing now or in a world existing somehow at the end of, or beyond history. Dewey, alongside these descriptions, typically tried to argue that the postulation of such worlds functioned to disguise imposition of power by one group over another; in doing so they prevented the development of true social intelligence.

Aspects of this vision will be discussed in more detail later. First, what, in general, are the implications of this process for the matter at hand? The writer, John Rodman, in the provocative essay "The Dolphin Papers" provides a lively answer:

> The only real revolutionary stance is that "nature" is the greatest con-
> vention of all. Perhaps there are no natures, no essences—only
> categories and paradigms that human beings mentally and politically
> impose on the flux of experience in order to produce illusions of cer-
> tainty, definiteness, distinction, hierarchy. Apparently, human beings
> do not like a Heraclitan world; they want fixed points of reference in
> order not to fall "into" vertigo, nausea. Perhaps the idea of nature or
> essence is man's ultimate grasp for eternity. The full impact of the theo-
> ry of evolution (the mutability of species—including man) is thus still
> to come.[6]

Where once were found in the garden, beings with eyes, fins, thumbs, with
minds that transparently evidenced design and a designer, now there are
only the workings of natural selection, mechanism, contingency, and brute
manipulation. What meaning the world and human life is to have must, it
seems, be provided by us, by human purpose insofar as it can provide some
form to this chaos. The idea that some meanings might be more or less
objectively present becomes an anachronism.

Rodman's formulation directs us to one way in which continental "postmodern" thought currents have recently come to interact with pragmatism.
There, in reaction to the loss of essence, to "the death of God," is found a kind
of Sartrean nausea, anxiety and despair in the face of a world of flux. In such
a Darwinian world, it is claimed any talk of human nature or ultimate meaning and its connection to liberal education can and should be deconstructed
(i.e. shown to be based either on the Thrasymachian, Nietzchean will to
power, or on childish desire for security in a brave new world). Typically,
however, in such writings there is an implied value orientation (e.g. Sartre's
Marxism, Nietzschean metaphysics, or many current versions of "politically
correct" democratic faith) that in fact cannot be justified upon its own
premises. What remains most problematic in these "postmodern" accounts is
why their own theses on human liberation and flourishing aren't simply more
illusion, more lies, more escape from reality or imposition of dogma.[7]

One response to this kind of post-Darwinian, pragmatic philosophy is a
kind of reactionary romanticism, in which the garden of essence is said to
exist even now, to exist beyond the misty fog of secular confusion, muddle-
headedness, and vainglory. Nothing much will be said here about such
currents. Pragmatism rules out such a philosophy. Now, the claims of
Deweyan pragmatism provide some sort of third way, or middle road
between nihilism and essentialism.

Growth and Meaning

In Deweyan pragmatism, a sophisticated attempt is found to make sense of
meaning after the fall. Dewey's allegiance to naturalism leads him to under-

stand human life and thought as, first of all, the activity of a biological organism concerned with a satisfactory adjustment to the environment. For Dewey this picture stands in sharp contrast to the view, before the fall, of human activity as most characteristically understood as the doings of a disembodied mind, a ghost in the machine. Knowledge is understood as advancing awareness of the antecedents and consequences of experiences, useful for *coping,* for problem solving. The *meaning* thereby grasped of objects and events contrasts sharply with a more traditional understanding of knowledge as *copying,* or adequate representation, of a reality that is said to exist prior to human activity.

Recent attempts of pragmatists such as Richard Rorty to embellish this account of meaning suggest its relative incompleteness. Rorty's account of growth and meaning is a forcible reminder of the problems involved in retaining talk of growth and meaning after the fall. An interest in continental writers such as Sartre and Nietzsche leads him to conceive of the human search for meaning in terms of a process of self-creation. On the Aristotelian model *true,* objective growth involves the conforming of a thing to a *preestablished telos.* But for Rorty at least, it can consist only of developing ones *own* meanings and identity in response to the particular problems, situations, desires faced in life. Instead of meaning or purpose endowed by nature or design one finds what has been referred to by T.V. Morris as the "do it yourself" approach that is also found in Sartre's existentialism.[8]

As Rorty, in a piece entitled "Education Without Dogma" notes, it is hard to understand what, in this context, distinguishes proper from improper growth, healthy development from mutation, malignancy, or even chaos. His gloss here, on the problem is provocative:

> This notion of species of animals gradually taking control of its own evolution by changing its environmental conditions leads Dewey to say, in good Darwinian language, that "growth itself is the moral end" and that to "protect, sustain and direct growth is the chief *ideal* of education." Dewey's conservative critics denounced him for fuzziness, for not giving us a criterion of growth. But Dewey rightly saw that any such criterion would cut the future down to the size of the present. Asking for such a criterion is like asking a dinosaur to specify what would make for a good mammal or asking a fourth-century Athenian to propose forms of life for the citizens of a twentieth-century industrial democracy.[9]

The implication, at least from Rorty's perspective, is that the pragmatist's growth must be taken as solely a contextual matter. Growth and the good are in each case relative to one's particular context. Here Rorty, it must be noted, can refer to contextualism in Dewey's *own* writing. Good in any given situation is (to use Dewey's own contextualist gloss) ". . . the meaning that is experienced to belong to an activity when conflict and entanglement of various incompatible impulses and habits terminate in an orderly release in action."[10]

The human animal, on this account, brings certain values or desires to a particular context. This humanly given meaning is, as evolving aim or end in view, a result of previous interactions between self and environment. And previous interaction also, to the extent intelligence has been involved, resulted in a sense of the meaning of things understood as cause and effect connection, or "knowledge meaning." The history of human life is a history composed of desire and knowledge, both evolving in the face of new problems, impediments, conflicts.[11]

So opposed to *The Meaning of Life* or *The Aim of Education* the *meanings* and *aims* are found in evolving context. In his credal essay, "What I Believe" Dewey writes that there is no reason to decide (as my essentialists and nihilists think we must) between *ultimate meaning* or *absolute meaninglessness*. "There are many meanings and many purposes in the situations with which we are confronted, one . . . for each situation. Each offers its own challenge to thought and endeavor, and presents its own potential values."[12] Pragmatic growth, as it is developed in Rorty seems to function, within any given context, as merely a kind of place holder. It serves to mark in each case an achieved equilibrium, at any given moment, between evolving desire/meaning and a continually evolving environment.

How well does this account, after the fall, respond to the dialectic of nihilism and essentialism? It can be argued that pragmatism, as understood so far, can *to some extent* respond to the premise common to both of these viewpoints; once again this is the claim that the absence of *essence* or *telos* implies the crudest sort of relativism. Measurement of growth, of the good in each situation, can be objective in a way that measurement of the worth of ice cream cannot. Either perceived conflict, and entanglement of habits of an organism are overcome or not. Moreover, we can imagine traditions of thought characterized in terms of an evolving problematic and knowledge moving in directions that might be characterized as more or less rational in terms of the ability to solve problems that are at least partially constitutive of what that tradition is.[13]

But what can be said to the essentialist who holds out for *ultimate* meaning, for *meaning* beyond meanings, for the possibility of *growth,* beyond growths? The history of pragmatism reveals several different strategies of response. First one finds, especially in Rorty, but also perhaps in Dewey, a response in terms of sense and nonsense. A second response comes in terms of relative health/maturity. A third can be understood in terms of an overarching theory or sense of rationality. I want to conclude this section by briefly elaborating what these strategies are about.

Various forms of positivism, linguistic and otherwise, have agreed that in some way or another the classic philosophical questions are in some way illegitimate or ill-formed. It is as if the quests of philosophers like Plato were misguided in the same way as attempts to discover the color of the number 3. Thus Kant famously in his *Critique of Pure Reason* compared the study of metaphysics to the attempt to milk male goats.

In a rather famous case of this kind, the philosopher J. L. Austin argued that the question "What is real?" (or "What is *really* real?"), upon which traditional ontology has been founded, is based on a mistake. "Real," Austin claimed, is "a Trouser word." It makes sense only when *worn* upon one linguistic context or another. Duck hunters can speak well of *real* ducks, in contrast to decoys; cake bakers can speak of *real* frosting, as opposed to the kinds that come out of cans, etc. Obviously the contextual analyses of meaning in Dewey and Rorty discussed earlier can be understood, in *this* context as reductions of supposed ultimacy. It reminds us of one typically pragmatic response to questions about "the view from nowhere" or from "God's eye view."[14]

Another strategy is to talk of good and bad questions in terms of maturity and immaturity. Freud and Marx both suggest in their writings that the desire for God, for meaning/purpose endowed by a transcendent being, for an endowment of meaning external to human desire, belief and action, exhibits a kind of childishness that should at best be humored and in the long run extirpated. This line of discussion is exhibited sometimes in Dewey and often in Rorty. Rorty, in his essays often uses the psychological ploy of asking his readers to choose meaning over *Meaning* in order to demonstrate the maturity and courage needed to leave the search for essence and antecedent reality behind to enter a brave new world of contingency.[15]

A third strategy, recently made use of in Rorty's work, is perhaps most clearly reminiscent of Dewey's most typically acknowledged approach to meaning and meanings. In his famous paper "The Influence of Darwin on Philosophy" Dewey argues that sometimes the most important result of an intellectual revolution is not merely the answering of some important question or question(s), but, rather, the replacement of one set of questions with another.[16] Thus in the passage from "What I Believe," quoted earlier, Dewey may be taken as simply recommending, in light of our current problems and projects, that we give up, on pragmatic grounds, one type of traditional quest. Once we get beyond the quest for *the purpose* and *the meaning* of life we can get down to the task of making the democratic way of life a reality. One can, I believe, find in Rorty's work many similar kinds of arguments against taking traditional philosophical problems seriously, in favor of *action,* the writing of plays and novels, direct political work, engagement in a post-philosophical culture.[17]

The motivation up until now for making reference to Rorty's use of Dewey, is, in the end, to argue that there are resources in Dewey, but perhaps not in Rorty, for acknowledging and satisfying legitimate yet ultimate elements of the quest for meaning. Neopragmatism, not only in the work of Rorty, but also in others, has failed to stress Dewey's religious quest for meaning. In Rockefeller's portrayal of Dewey, pragmatism and democratic faith can only prevail, and only deserve to prevail, if these religious elements in Dewey's philosophy are taken seriously. Pragmatism, in other words, must transcend Rorty's attempts to discredit the concern for ultimate meaning in that philosophy.

Dewey and Ultimate Meaning

One of the most stunning features of Rockefeller's work is the way in which it demonstrates Dewey's constant preoccupation with the sorts of questions referred to earlier, those having to do with ultimate meaning. In fact, Rockefeller suggests that we can find in Dewey's overall project ". . . a depth and fullness of meaning that is not commonly appreciated."[18] He finds there ". . . a distinctively democratic way of liberation and community . . . (that) involve(s) an ideal possibility for the future development of the social, economic, moral and religious life of the species worthy of humanity's shared faith and devotion."[19] He believes that Dewey's philosophy, his *religious faith* in democracy, is special and unique insofar as it provides a reconstruction of perennial religious ideals that saves what is good in them in the face of the challenges of secular enlightenment thinking. The promise of his work is that it lets us imagine that Dewey's philosophy and democracy might actually take not only science and enlightenment seriously, but also the longings that essentialists have tried to cherish and nourish. His work serves to admonish would-be pragmatic positivists that they cannot count on Dewey's authority to bolster their intuitions about meaning. Thus chastized, pragmatism may then go beyond the quasi-positivism of both the nihilists and Rorty's neo-pragmatism to respond to essentialism's most basic concern.

On Rockefeller's account, Dewey's description of the religious disposition has both an activist and contemplative element.[20] Rockefeller demonstrates how it was that Dewey, after leaving Hegelianism behind for a more naturalistic Darwinistic world view, first stressed the former. It, for Dewey, involves a kind of unification within the self, and between the self and a community composed of those committed to making an ideal possibility, a democratic way of life, into a reality. This activist element of Dewey's democratic faith most clearly parts with his earlier Idealist viewpoint, a viewpoint in which the unity of the actual and ideal was taken as antecedently realized rather than sought for.

According to Rockefeller this element is also stressed in Dewey's relatively late work *A Common Faith*. There Dewey speaks of God as the imagined reality of the ideals of democracy, as well as all personal and natural elements that contribute to such a reality. This idea of God, Dewey believed, might be of value as ". . . a poetic device for unifying interests, generating emotions, and inspiring action."[21] Such a notion, believed in and acted on might, Dewey hoped, provide the proponents of democracy with a sense of natural piety, a solidarity of love and trust among those acting in the present for their predecessors, and their hoped for successors.

To imagine why so many find Dewey's God lacking, consider, once again, his pragmatist successor Richard Rorty. Criticisms of Rorty's choice of "solidarity" over "objectivity" look a lot like the sort of criticisms that were, according to Rockefeller, raised against *A Common Faith*.[22] Many of Rorty's critics have faulted him for failing to acknowledge the possibility of truth beyond any merely human ideas or ideals, of any meaning beyond meanings found in human knowledge or desire. Is, for example, our trust in, our commitment to, the democratic faith justifiable outside of what we, we who reside within the boundaries of *our* tradition, simply and contingently believe? Is there no ground for our faith beyond our ultimate commitment to Rorty's final vocabulary? Rorty dismisses questions of this sort, suggesting that, for example, they are as vacuous as the worries as to whether "God is on our side."[23] But why do such worries or the desire to directly answer them need to be vacuous?

As Rockefeller notes, the paradox of our social and political life today has to do with the West's growing apathy in the face of democratic renewal elsewhere.[24] While Eastern European nations seek examples of wisdom and courage from us, the West flounders in malaise. And perhaps there is good reason for this state of paralysis. In the face of the evils of the world wars, the Holocaust, the proliferation of nuclear weapons, and the growing ecological crises, there is perhaps good reason to wonder about our faith in democratic liberalism. Perhaps the West should wonder whether it has the resources to counter, for example, the nihilism discussed earlier. There is nothing in the activist religious faith so far discussed to counter such worries beyond hope in desperate need of justification. How can our continued allegiance, with all our heart and soul, be motivated?

If essences or natures to foster a continued faith cannot be appealed to, what can be done? According to Rockefeller, Dewey's account has the resources to at least begin to deal with such worries. To this general end Dewey, according to Rockefeller develops a further, contemplative element of the democratic faith. This element can be specified more fully by briefly returning to Dewey's idea of growth.

In several of the best recent articles on the subject, Daniel Pekarsky speaks of an element in Dewey's idea of growth beyond what I have referred to as increased knowledge, as well as the development of new aims in new contexts.[25] Pekarsky calls the element "appreciation." Examples of increased appreciation may or may not involve added knowledge of antecedents or consequences. It signals, for Pekarsky, an element of meaning in growth that, unlike knowledge meaning is concerned not with mere biological adaptation, with instrumental prediction, or control with problem solving, but, rather, with the kind of unifying perception characteristic of aesthetic or even religious experience. In Rockefeller's account, Dewey's life was primarily a search not simply for better ways of surviving within nature but, rather for a special kind of appreciation. Dewey refers to this kind of appreciation towards the end of *Human Nature and Conduct:*

> Infinite relationships of man and his fellows already exist. The ideal
> means . . . a sense of these encompassing continuities with their infinite

reach. This meaning even now attaches to present activities because they are set in a whole to which they belong and which belongs to them. Even in the midst of conflict, struggle and defeat a consciousness is possible of the enduring and comprehensive whole.[26]

Moreover, Rockefeller suggests quite persuasively that Dewey had himself achieved such a sense of his place within the whole, and a sense of peace constitutive of most mysticism.[27] He achieved, in other words, some sense of support in meaning beyond anything merely human, or merely natural. The problem for Rockefeller, and for us, is this: Can Dewey explain what he here sought and obtained, within the bounds of his naturalistic, anti-essentialistic philosophy? Can he justify his own need, and explain its legitimate fulfillment?

The quest for ultimate meaning is a quest that takes us beyond the ongoing battle of Deweyan democrats against chaos and evil. For Rockefeller, it leads, in Dewey's own life, to a deeper truth of harmony, wholeness, peace. It is the unity beyond duality that lies behind Dewey's entire project; it is, as Dewey himself put it, what provides him in his struggles ". . . a peace beyond understanding." Dewey saw in his intimations of such peace a sense of what democratic life might in the end provide us. The question is not whether Dewey really did achieve the sorts of experiences described above. Rather, given Dewey's own acknowledgment of a human need for such experiences, we must ask, as Rockefeller insists, how the search and attainment of it is possible within the bounds of a naturalistic, anti-essentialistic philosophy? Again, can Dewey justify his own need and explain its legitimate fulfillment within his own modes of conceiving the real? As Rockefeller puts the problem:

> Does Dewey's naturalistic view of the world make intelligible how ultimate meaning is possible? . . . Does his account of the religious form of experience have implications for an understanding of reality that are not fully articulated in his metaphysics and idea of the divine? Does Dewey's own religious experience point to a depth dimension of reality that is not adequately expressed in his philosophical language?[28]

And finally, if it does, how can democratic education help point the way to others?

The Limits of Pragmatism

In a number of essays, William James argues that ultimately the only solution to the problem of pessimism is religious faith, a faith in an order beyond human beings and nature "in which the riddles of the natural order can be explained," and "in which the true significance of our present mundane life consists." James in these essays usefully demonstrates the limits of scientific,

enlightenment ways of knowing and being; even the best of scientific knowing leaves out, and must leave out, an understanding of human beings as
knowers, lovers, scientific theorizers. In these remarks James is signaling his
belief that mere meanings and purpose, unrelated to what I've referred to as
ultimate meaning or purpose, will never satisfy the human psyche.[29]

But James goes beyond these criticisms of what I've referred to as positivistic pragmatism. He also criticizes those I've called essentialists, for attempting
to dogmatically capture the higher order of meaning in the categories of
some conceptual framework or other. Men need faith, James says, but
". . . (they) can live and die by the help of a sort of faith that goes without a
single dogma or definition." What is needed is not intuitive access to the
realm of *truth,* but an awareness that our truths, our meanings, our purposes
are not the only or final ground.[30]

Rockefeller's discussion of Dewey provides important evidence in favor of
these Jamesean conclusions. Dewey, according to Rockefeller, often falls into
the errors of scientism. But in the end, his Dewey at least begins to recognize,
as James more consistently does, that naturalism is not enough. Rockefeller's
portrait of a man who, more strenuously and honestly than any other natu-
ralist, tried to comprehend the *entire* range of human experience, provides
important testimony that even the most strenuous of naturalisms leaves us,
in its explicit pronouncements, with the most important issues in the life of
human beings untouched.

Perhaps the weakest yet most suggestive part of Rockefeller's book is his
attempt to make room for meaning and mystery within the world of Dewey's
Experience and Nature. His attempt to link Dewey's world system to the work
of mystical theologians such as Meister Eckhart and philosophers such as
W. T. Stace is certainly interesting and instructive.[31] But his project, and
Dewey's fails because of its latent dogmatism; because of its fall into metaphysics. Neither Dewey's pragmatism nor nihilism seem able to wholly give
up the attempt to capture the *absolute* truth about things in philosophical,
metaphysical language. Thus, both fail to properly respect what really matters. I want to suggest that after the fall, it is not simply essentialism, but
metaphysics, ontology, that must go.

Nihilists and positivists, even sophisticated quasi-positivists such as
Foucault and Rorty, claim to bypass metaphysics. But in their tirades against
essentialists they constantly evoke the metaphysics of nominalism and contingency, freedom and power. Even Dewey's own sophisticated philosophical
project, so far ahead of James's in so many ways, goes astray when it tries to
capture the essence of things, the God's eye truth, even though that truth
appears to be a Heraclitean one. Dewey's pragmatism fails, in the end,
because it (to use Rorty's language) rejects all "metanarratives" as ahistorical
and dogmatic, yet in *Experience and Nature* tries to codify its conclusions as
metanarrative. And, as Rockefeller's project implies, the attempt to reconcile
that metanarrative with ultimate meaning is full of difficulty.

Perhaps a suggestion, such as Rockefeller's, that those who cherish Dewey's pragmatism at its best, ought to pay homage to Eckhart, Dionysus the Aeropagete, Buber, and the Mahayana Buddhist thinkers, will even (or especially) at the end of the elaborate discussion, seem confusing and or annoying. The point, here, can be clarified by reference to both a philosopher Dewey admired, William James, and another philosopher who revered James, Ludwig Wittgenstein. Within the pragmatic universe our best guide to a responsible extension of a purely naturalistic philosophy is the *subversive* naturalism of James and Wittgenstein. I want to try and briefly restate and extend Rockefeller's suggestions by referring to the thought of these men, thought that is surely better known and more easily adaptable to Dewey's pragmatism than that of the thinkers Rockefeller himself refers to.

Like Dewey and Rorty, James sometimes steps into metaphysics. But no pragmatist better explains the paradoxes involved in trying to describe the inexpressible than does James. Take for instance his remark in the preface of "The Will to Believe" that describes his radical empiricism:

> For (the radical empiricist) the crudity of experiences remains an eternal element thereof. There is *no possible point of view* from which the world can appear an absolutely single fact. (my italics)[32]

No possible point of view. That the *philosophical* way things are, is not hard, or even impossible to know, but simply is *not*. Even this is misleading. Wittgenstein, at least as described by Ray Monk, hints at a similar reality. According to Monk, Wittgenstein, both in his earlier and later writing, rejected philosophical theory and metaphysics. But he did this not to banish mystery and wonder but instead to clear the way for it. Pragmatism in education and elsewhere does best when it not only subscribes to the improvements Dewey and Rorty make in pragmatic philosophy, but also when it continues to honor the concern for ultimate meaning in the manner suggested so insistently in James and Wittgenstein.[33]

How can these ideas be applied to education? One suggestion is that in teaching the democratic faith and its implications not only those who countenance Dewey's activist faith but also those who have aspired to and preached his contemplative vision need to be studied, taught, and revered. To some extent, writers like Emerson, James, Whitman, and Dewey can be used to inspire students to do both. But this use is possible only if pragmatists resist the now popular tendency to *deconstruct*, that is reduce the urge for the contemplative vision to Nietzschean power or irrationality. Such deconstructions too often follow essentialism into dogma. In the discovery of power as a force behind knowledge, too often ignored is the quest for meaning. If the main thrust of this essay is right, then educators are justified in presenting the quest of "holy fools" as heroic, even while they insist on tolerance of the many different ways of describing the results of such a quest.

An examination of the lives and work involved in such heroism leads to a concern with such indirect forms of language as irony, analogy, and metaphor. Educators need to take much more seriously the possible uses of such language in intimating a reality that in the end cannot adequately be conceptualized. Obviously the study of poetry as a vehicle for such an understanding can be valuable in helping students imagine such a reality and the questioning it may provoke.

Also useful in this regard are the works of such thinkers as Plato and Aquinas, Buber and Kierkegaard, as well as James himself. Too often and too easily it is assumed that the canonical writers of philosophy were consistently intent on obtaining accurate representations of a world beyond the natural world. If writers such as David Burrell are to be taken seriously, it might be better to see these philosophers as engaged in attempts at making our languages more flexible instruments for *knowing* the unknowable. For example, Burrell tries to show that Aquinas' doctrine of analogy can be taken as a logical as well as a metaphysical doctrine.[34] Similarly the irony of Socrates, as well as that of James, works as a way of exercising restraint in our claims to know the world, as well as a means to new possibilities for hope and solace, peace within the arena of struggle. In the past I have credited Rorty in this regard, but I fear I was too generous. Rorty's irony, infected as it is through contact with continental irrationalism too often ends up sounding like nihilism. What is needed is a less dogmatic irony, perhaps an irony in philosophy and education inspired by James in which the concern for the really important, ultimate things are left unsaid but constantly pointed towards with respect and humility.[35]

Finally, René Arcilla has recently argued that pragmatic educators have good reason for taking seriously a type of education in metaphysics that culminates in the Heddeggerian question: "Why is there something rather than nothing?"[36] Arcilla's suggestion for enacting an education into "the miracle and mystery of existence" suggests the ultimate concern not only of Heiddegger but also of Monk's Wittgenstein, Rockefeller's Dewey, as well as of William James. I see no reason why this sort of education in wonder cannot be early reconciled with Dewey's activist faith. Arcilla's suggestions, as well as my own, are meant to allow within liberal education a concern for the spiritual quest that transcends all sectarian, credal positions that aim to codify James's religious faith or its denial.

After essences it is not easy to take seriously the essentialist's concern for ultimate meaning. One sure way to fail is to replace, as Rorty does, the essentialist's simplistic view of language as mirror with an equally misguided idea of language (literally) as a tool. Another is to respond to the Fall by codifying Nietzsche's ontology of power and cruelty as a new dogma of human nature. A third is to reduce all desire for cosmic meaning and assurance to childish obsession and fantasy. Naturalism is, as Wittgenstein and James of all the recent philosophers most fully understood, all right, as long as it is seen not simply as the whole truth but rather, as that part of the truth that can, at any given time, most easily be affirmed.

After the Fall any confidence in delimiting a human *telos* is misguided, but it would be a mistake to infer from this that the seekers of ultimate truth referred to in this essay have nothing to teach. As Ray Monk notes, Wittgenstein was fond of categorizing modernity as a dark time, much darker, in fact, than the Dark Ages. Dewey's stirring faith in intelligence is surely a useful corrective to Wittgenstein's rather blind hatred of science and enlightenment. But the corrective is truly useful and not incendiary if we see Dewey's *entire* faith as it is, as a whole piece, including not only knowledge and meaning but positing all sorts of *appreciation* as crucial. The point for education is that even beyond *mere* intelligence, *appreciation* is the most important thing of all.

Perhaps, in the end, there is no garden. Perhaps the garden never was, and never will be. And yet there is nothing more important than the garden. For if there is no garden, then the fallen world as described by most of its quasi-positivist proponents is equally imaginary. It is myth, it is metaphysics. Perhaps what is needed most in this dark time is a means of shedding that ancestral blindness that keeps our eyes focused on, rather than beyond, the garden and the Fall. For it is only beyond (and, of course, not literally beyond) that what is true resides. In this essay, I have signaled my desire that educators might begin the work, so long overdue, of opening eyes of appreciation for this realm and its proponents.[37]

NOTES

1. Steven C. Rockefeller's *John Dewey: Religious Faith and Democratic Humanism* (New York: Columbia University Press, 1992). See also Rockefeller's "John Dewey, Spiritual Democracy and The Human Future," *Cross Currents* (Fall 1989) 39 (3):300–21, and "John Dewey: The Evolution of a Faith," in Maurice Wohlgelernter, ed., *History, Religion and Spiritual Democracy: Essays in Honor of Joseph C. Blau.* (New York: Columbia University Press, 1989) pp. 5–34.

2. For good examples of this thinking in contemporary philosophy see Jacques Maritain, *Education at the Crossroads* (New Haven: Yale University Press, 1943) and Mortimer S. Adler, *Reforming Education: The Opening of the American Mind* (New York: Collier Books, 1990).

3. For a good account see Jean Leclerq, *The Love of Learning and the Desire for God* (New York: New American Library, 1962).

4. For the metaphor of meaning as endowment I am indebted to my colleague T.V. Morris, in his *Making Sense of It All: Pascal and The Meaning of Life* (Grand Rapids, Michigan: Wm. B. Erdmans Publ. Co., 1992), especially Chapter 4, "The Meaning of Life."

5. Examples abound in Dewey's work. See, for example, his *The Quest of Certainty*

(Carbondale: Southern Illinois University Press, 1988) and also *Reconstruction in Philosophy* (Boston: Beacon Press, 1957).

6. Rodman, "The Dolphin Papers," *North American Review* 2 (1974): 13–26, p. 16.

7. For an account of these "postmodern currents" and their tendency towards inconsistency see my "Education, Power and the Authority of Knowledge," *Teachers College Record,* 88 (1986): 64–81. I especially have in mind here Foucault at least as he is understood in James Miller's superb *The Passion of Michel Foucault* (New York: Simon & Schuster, 1993). Foucault, at least as portrayed by Miller, never quite escapes the kind of self contradiction discussed here. To take one example: How can a philosophy that is so intent upon relativizing all claims to knowledge of nature so uncritically accept the view of human nature proposed in Nietzsche's work? I'll say more about this in my last section.

8. Morris, p. 57ff. The Sartre I have in mind here is that of his famous *Existentialism and the Human Emotions* (New York: Citadel Press, 1985).

9. Rorty, "Education without Dogma," *Dissent,* Spring 1989, pp. 198–204.

10. John Dewey, *Human Nature and Conduct* (Carbondale & Edwardsville: Southern Illinois Press, 1988) p. 146.

11. I here gloss, in an extremely compressed way, discussions on aims and inquiry found in any number of Dewey's texts including *Human Nature and Conduct.* Rorty's use of these ideas as well as of Dewey and James' adaptation of Darwinism is presupposed here.

12. John Dewey, "What I Believe," reprinted in Gail Kennedy, ed. *Pragmatism and American Culture* (Boston: D.C. Heath and Company, 1950) pp. 23–31, pp. 26–27.

13. My sense is that pragmatism can make use, to some extent of Alasdair MacIntyre's account of rationality within traditions as developed in his "Epistemological Crises, Dramatic Narratives and the Philosophy of Science," *The Monist* (1977):453–472. What pragmatism *can't* easily make use of, I believe, is MacIntyre's later gloss of the account in terms of truth as correspondence or adequacy in his *Whose Justice? Whose Rationality?* (Notre Dame: University of Notre Dame Press, 1988) Chapter 18ff.

14. For Austin's discussion see his *Sense and Sensibility* (New York: Oxford University Press, 1961). For similar strategies used against what Thomas Nagel calls "The View from Nowhere," see Rorty's "Solidarity or Objectivity?" in his *Objectivity, Relativism and Truth: Philosophical Papers* Volume 1 (Cambridge University Press, 1991) pp. 21–34.

15. See Rorty's "Solidarity or Objectivity?" but also his *Contingency, Irony, Solidarity* (Cambridge University Press, 1989). Dewey sometimes uses the same kind of talk. For an example again see his "What I Believe."

16. This piece appears in a collection of essays also entitled *The Influence of Darwin on Philosophy* (Bloomington: Indiana University Press, 1965) pp. 1–19. See also Rorty's "Just One More Species Doing Its Best," *London Review of Books* 25 July 1991, pp. 3–7.

17. Here one finds a striking example, and modification, of Rorty's use of Dewey in his advocacy of novels and, more generally, works of art in the place of philosophy in a new liberal Utopia. Again see *Contingency, Irony, Solidarity*.

18. Rockefeller, "John Dewey, Spiritual Democracy and the Human Future," *Cross Currents* (Fall 1989), 39 (3): 301.

19. Again p. 301.

20. The following remarks most specifically follow Rockefeller's discussions in Chapter 10–12 of his book, footnotes in 1 above. Earlier chapters of the book can be seen as laying a groundwork for these.

21. Rockefeller, p. 323.

22. For discussions of criticism of Dewey's *A Common Faith* see Rockefeller Chapters 10–11. Typical criticism of Rorty's infamous "relativism" can be found in Richard Bernstein, "Rorty's Liberal Utopia" *Social Research* (Spring 1990) 57(1): 30–72.

23. For an especially good example of Rorty's penchant for such quasi-positivist dismissals, see his "Hermeneutics, General Studies and Teaching," *Synerges* 2 (1986): 1–15.

24. For Rockefeller's attempt to place his project in this context see the prologue to *John Dewey,* pp. 1–26, as well as his *Cross Currents* essay, footnoted above.

25. See, for example, Pekarsky's "Dewey's Conception of Growth Reconsidered," *Educational Theory* (Summer 1990) 40(3): 283–94.

26. Dewey, *Human Nature and Conduct,* p. 226.

27. See Rockefeller's discussion of Dewey's claim to a peace that surpasses understanding, pp. 492ff.

28. Rockefeller, pp. 532.

29. See James, "Is Life Worth Living," in his *The Will to Believe and other Essays in Popular Philosophy* (New York: Dover Publications, 1956) pp. 51. For a contemporary critique of science from a perspective similar to that of James see Walker Percy's essay "The Fateful Rift: The San Andreas Fault in The Modern Mind," reprinted in his *Signposts in a Strange Land,* ed. by Patrick Samway (New York: Farrar, Straus and Giroux, 1992) pp. 271–79. The connection between Percy's concerns here and James are striking, and worth further examination.

30. James, "Is Life Worth Living," p. 56.

31. Rockefeller, pp. 536ff.

32. James, *The Will to Believe,* p. ix.

33. Monk's interpretation appears in his magnificent biography *Ludwig Wittgenstein: The Duty of Genius* (New York: Penguin Books, 1990). See also M. O'C Drury's contribution to Rush Rhees, ed. *Recollection of Wittgenstein.* (Oxford: Oxford University Press, 1984). To get a sense of how I began to construe James as irony, one might compare the passage from the preface of *The Will to Believe* with Samuel Hynes' reading of irony as "a view of life which recognized that experience is open to multiple interpretations, of which no one is simply right, and that the coexistence of incongruity is part of the structure of existence." (This is

quoted from Hynes' *The Pattern of Handy's Poetry* by D.C. Muecke, *Irony and the Ironic* (London: Metheuan and Co., 1982), p. 31.

34. See, for example, Burrell's *Exercises in Religious Understanding* (Notre Dame: University of Notre Dame Press, 1972) for good treatments, in this vein, of Anselm, Aquinas, Augustine, Kierkegaard, and Jung. Also see his recent and superb treatment *Knowing the Unknowable God: Ibn-Sina, Maimonides, Aquinas* (Notre Dame: University of Notre Dame Press, 1986).

35. See my "Ironic Schooling: Socrates, Pragmatism, and the Higher Learning," *Educational Theory* (41) 1991: 371–383.

36. See Arcilla's "Metaphysics in Education after Hutchins & Dewey," *Teachers College Record* (93) 1991: 281–89.

37. The reference, of course, is to James's "On a Certain Blindness in Human Beings" printed in his *Talks to Teachers on Psychology, and to Students on Life's Ideals* (New York: Dover Publications, 1962). Note James's reiteration of his radical empiricist rejection of "the God's eye view" in the preface. "According to that philosophy the truth is too great for any one actual mind even though that mind be dubbed "The Absolute" to know the whole of it. The facts and worths of life need many cognizers to take them in. There is no point of view absolutely public and universal. Private and uncommunicable perceptions always remain left over." This passage, along with the earlier reference to the preface of *The Will to Believe,* signals for me the central core of a Jamesian irony of special value in our quest to speak well of the unspeakable.

6

Permit Them to Flourish[1]

Philip W. Bennett

Essences

Alven Neiman's worry that talking about the aims of practices like educating necessarily commits one to a philosophically suspect essentialism is a worry I don't share. People do talk about aims, goals, purposes, and functions, and when they talk, people understand one another, or certainly so it seems. They understand one another: agree and disagree, "the game is played";[2] that when they so talk they are necessarily engaged in unaware metaphysics seems unlikely to me.

Aim or Aims?

I'm not worried about essences. I'm not worried about speaking of the aim or the overarching aim of education, as Jane Roland Martin does, but I am mindful of Wittgenstein's reminder that we tend towards a craving for generality.[3] I think it safer to speak here of *aims,* that may include *both* "domestic tranquillity" and "an appreciation" for the unsayable (following Martin and Neiman). There are many different kinds of activities that get called education, and it is likely that under certain circumstances one or another aim or purpose might be more fitting than some other for those circumstances. Teaching a child to swim and teaching that child to operate a computer both

73

involve education, but the activities in question might have no one thing in common; so too with the aim sought.

Schooling

Both Martin and Neiman easily equate education with schooling. Pink Floyd agree. In their rock opera *The Wall,* schoolchildren chant:

> We don't need no education
> We don't need no thought control
> No dark sarcasm in the classroom
> Teacher, leave us kids alone![4]

But equating the two, while easy and natural, is worth resisting or at least noting. Schoolchildren have been well educated (if not educated well) long before they make it to kindergarten. And the very reforms that Martin endorses when and where implemented come in reaction to prior training. The violence she abhors doesn't arise out of a vacuum.

Schooling is one thing; educating another. I think it fine to propose new aims for schooling; or more specifically, new aims for the public school systems as they exist in the United States at this time. But let's not forget all that goes on outside the classroom, in front of the television, on the street, in the kitchen, at the mall, on the corner.

And if we are looking to propose new aims or purposes for public schooling in the U.S. it is worth asking what purpose schooling currently serves. In her introduction to *The Golden Notebook* Doris Lessing offers one answer, one similar to Pink Floyd's:

> Ideally, what should be said to every child, repeatedly, throughout his or her school life is something like this:
> "You are in the process of being indoctrinated. We have not yet evolved a system of education that is not a system of indoctrination. We are sorry, but it is the best we can do. What you are being taught here is an amalgam of current prejudice and the choices of this particular culture. The slightest look at history will show how impermanent these must be. You are being taught by people who have been able to accommodate themselves to a regime of thought laid down by their predecessors. It is a self-perpetuating system. Those of you who are more robust and individual than others, will be encouraged to leave and find ways of educating yourself—educating your own judgment. Those that stay must remember, always and all the time, that they are being molded and patterned to fit into the narrow and particular needs of this particular society."[5]

Thought control, indoctrination: not a pretty picture. Do these exaggerations merely express the pain of growing up under the British system, or do they illuminate a part of the picture, or do they both illuminate and express? It does seem that one of the purposes that school currently plays is to make students fit into the system, to make them good consumers and producers, to make them good citizens, to make them into good (here meaning *fitting*) "bricks in the wall."[6]

School also serves the purpose of getting young people out of the home, so that parents/care-givers can be in the market place. It also serves the purpose of keeping young people out of the market place for a time, so they are less likely to compete directly with their parents or their peers' parents for McJobs.

I am here referring of course to the "hidden curriculum"; an important part of it is a kind of domestication, with a heavy emphasis on obedience and conformity.

Begin at the Beginning

A child is born. Not in a vacuum but into societies that are currently set up in very irrational ways. Very oppressive ways. Very hurtful ways. What we see at the beginning or soon thereafter is a little one struggling to know, to learn, to figure out the world, but doing so in a context where s/he is currently being hurt, and not given adequate support to learn from those hurts.

Children naturally want to learn about their environment and themselves. That curiosity about the world, that thirst for understanding, that wanting to know, is an inherent quality in humans and certain other animals. It is easy to speculate about its evolutionary origins—after all, humans come with so little in the way of instinct—but it is hard to deny that the thirst is there.

And when it looks like the thirst isn't there, this isn't because some of us have it and some of us don't; it is because this thirst can be altered, interrupted, even blocked.

Some of this interruption is due to accident. Some of it is due to particular family patterns. But most of it is due to systematic, society-approved and reinforced misinformation and abuse: oppression. And it begins at birth.

What is the first question? Not: Is it healthy? Two hands, two feet? No, it's: Is it a boy or a girl? The mistreatment begins then.

Gender. Class. So-called "race," or skin color. Ethnicity. Size. Age. Later, issues around sexuality and the choice of partners and looking normal, that is, not being crazy, or not too crazy.

We Get Hurt, We Heal

When a child is hurt, be it physical, emotional, psychological, the child will easily and naturally respond to that hurt in a healing way. This is not something that we learn to do; it, like the curiosity and growth that accompany it, are part of our inherent nature. This natural healing response is quite miraculous and powerful.

Cuts close up, skin regrows. These healing processes are accompanied on the "outside" by responses that often are associated with emotions: sobbing, laughing, shaking, sweating, storming, but also yawning, stretching, scratching, and talking.

But at a very early age this natural healing process gets interrupted. Big boys don't cry. Proper young ladies don't make a fuss. What are you crazy, or something? Stop that fidgeting or I'll give you something to fidget about.

What It Might Look Like

It could look like this. A young one gets hurt. She finds the safety and comfort of an attentive adult. She cries, shakes, or does whatever she needs to do to deal with the hurt. She learns from the experience; processes the information, and goes about her business, a bit wiser. Learning; learning from our mistakes as well as our successes, is part of what it is all about.

What It Does Look Like (Mostly)

But instead it is much more like this. A young one gets hurt. And there is no one to go to; they are all too busy or too sunk in their own despair, or simply absent. Or when present, unable to be attentive. Or, out of embarrassment, interrupt the tears with some foolishness about hushing up there, it's not so bad. Or directly humiliate the young one for his tears, or her fears. And instead of learning from the hurt, the young one's intelligence is obstructed.

Suppose the particular hurt took the form of being told how stupid you are. (If we were stupid this wouldn't hurt; it is only because we are not that it does.) Instead of processing this hurtful experience and learning the lesson here—that sometimes people say hurtful things about you that really have nothing at all to do with you personally—in the absence of the healing experience what is left is a confusing response that perhaps I *am* stupid, or at least I'm stupid about this—if it's a little girl, plug in math—what is left is a stunting of the natural growth process, a block to inherent brilliance, a crimp in intelligence that may develop into a rigidity of thought or feeling.

This is especially so when the hurtful misinformation gets repeated, and repeated, and repeated. This is part of what any oppression has at its core: misinformation and hurtful mistreatment based on it that goes unprocessed, because the very *healing process itself* is targeted by oppression, partly through gender—big boys don't cry, young ladies don't raise their voices—and mostly through what some refer to as mental health systems oppression, that is visions of normality that dictate not showing strong feelings.

But a Sketch

This is all very incomplete, but I need to lay this out before attempting any comments about the aims of education, since the young ones who show up at our schools are people about whom this is true, or so I believe. It is also true about those who are there to teach these young ones. They too have been hurt; most of their wounds are due to the very oppressions they should address in educating.

Violence: Individual and Structural

Martin's conception of domestic tranquillity is at least partially reactive: it is in response to the violence that she sees as the norm in U.S. society at this time. Borrowing from Newton Garver's oft reproduced article, she defines violence as the "physical and psychological violation of persons."[7] In the realm of the physical, she reminds us of spousal and child abuse, including sexual abuse. In our public spaces, "our schools play host to vandalism and assaults on teachers and students, our sports arenas to brutality and rioting, the streets of our cities to mugging, murder, gang terrorism, rape." As for psychological violation, she mentions the use of public spaces—billboards and the like—to propagate images of women as victims and men as aggressors.

Martin is not to be faulted for the incompleteness of these lists, but what gets left out entirely does say something about her understanding of violence and thereby her vision of the tranquillity that is to replace it. There is no reference to the institutional or structural violence of poverty, or the violence that accompanies the oppressions that serve to hold the owner/worker class structure in place. (They divide us from one another—men versus women, White versus Black, to keep our focus off of our true source of misery.)

Martin's failure to recognize structural or institutional violence leads to a nostalgia for the good old days of the eighteenth century. Violence "has not always been the norm." She quotes with approval a Boston newspaper from 1786 contrasting the U.S. with England or Ireland—where a man is liable to be robbed at noon, while in America "any man is safe at midnight in the largest cities." In the eighteenth century our founding fathers were much more concerned with the "*civic* form of domestic intranquillity" (rebellion) than with the "*antisocial* form" that we face today.

It is puzzling that some significant form of antisocial violence was lacking in the eighteenth century. The treatment of Blacks, the treatment of women, the treatment of the majority living in poverty gets ignored in favor of focussing on street crime and the safety of a man walking at midnight. This particular blind spot threatens to undermine the potential scope of Martin's revisioning, and diminishes the potentially revolutionary implications of an analysis of domestic tranquillity.

Responding to Violence

Giving proper attention to domestic tranquillity is not "primarily a matter of law," says Martin. We must look "not just to legislation but to education." This too is disturbing, but that may be because I've lived most of my adult life with politicians playing the crime card and demanding "lawn odor."

But what is more disturbing is the notion that education, following on our proper revisioning of the realm of the domestic and civic, requires that we "supplant an ethic of violence and violation with one of safety and security, peace and love." It is the reference to an "ethic of violence and violation" that stops me cold. What can this possibly mean? The medicine for young people is a "very special quality and kind of moral instruction." The malady? Training in an ethic of violence? This training brought about by the media? Rambo movies, ice hockey, trash television?

Again Martin is not to be faulted for not providing an analysis of the causes of violence. But in the absence of a better hint than her reference to an "ethic of violence and violation," her prescriptions become less powerful due to the threat of vagueness.

Some of Where It Comes From

I return to my sketch. The violence we face today has its root cause in the interlocking systems of oppression, and attempting to replace violence with a vision of peace and tranquillity can only be accomplished by ending those oppressions; but especially the economic exploitation that fuels them. Anything short of this will always remain reactive and rearguard. And ending oppression is something that education writ large can take as one of its proper aims. So too for education as schooling, though we will need to go far beyond multiculturalism or the Three C's.

When people are hurt, the natural, human response is to heal through emotional release. When this avenue is denied, as it is in presently-constituted societies, humans substitute coping for emotional release. We cope by adopting roles, and these roles basically fall into two classes: the mistreator or oppressor role and the victim role. Behind any given oppression, are people being hurt and then acting on or out of that hurt in accordance with one or the other of these roles.

Consider racism. What is racism but the societally-enforced and socially sanctioned misinformation and mistreatment of people of color by Whites. Whites are forced into the oppressor role; people of color into the victim role. But beneath the oppressor role that Whites adopt is undischarged pain and fear. Children are not born racists. It is beaten into them. Though some may find it paradoxical to note, Whites too are hurt by racism. They are not hurt in anything like the same way or to the same degree as people of color, but they are hurt. W.E.B. Du Bois saw this:

> Unfortunate? Unfortunate. But where is the misfortune? Mine? Am I, in my blackness, the sole sufferer? I suffer. And yet, somehow, above the suffering, above the shackled anger that beats the bars, above the hurt that crazes there surges in me a vast pity—pity for a people imprisoned and enthralled, hampered and made miserable for such a cause, for such a phantasy![8]

The same can be said about sexism, classism, and *all* the other oppressions: beneath the oppressor roles that get played out lie unhealed pain and fear. So too with street violence and *all* the sources of domestic intranquillity.

Education for Healing

I see violence as the acting out or "dramatizing" of unhealed painful emotions.[9] Usually it comes in the course of acting on the role of oppressor inside one oppression or another; inside sexism, when it is violence against women; inside racism, when it is violence against people of color. Oppression gets internalized, and much of the violence of the streets, which is in our cities predominately Black on Black, can be traced to internalized racism.

Do I know this to be true? No, but I think it is a pretty good guess, and it is one that fits the facts. It gives us more to go on than vague references to an "ethic of violence." And it has definite implications for the aims of education, and for taking seriously, as I do, Martin's particular aim of domestic tranquillity.

A necessary means towards achieving the end of domestic tranquillity is creating environments that promote healing. This means combating the widely accepted mythology about emotions, a mythology that is crumbling all around us. (When Edward Muskie teared up, it was a scandal; George Bush's frequent public tearing up, was looked upon [almost] with compassion.) It means providing young ones with the opportunity to get their feelings out so that they are not left inside rigid roles of victim or oppressor. It means consciously and directly addressing the oppressions that formalize the hurt they experience, addressing them on all levels, not just *cognitively*.

Domestic Tranquillity

When poverty is seen as violence, domestic tranquillity has radical economic implications. When the earth is seen as our home and domestic tranquillity is extended, as Martin does at the end of her paper, to global dimensions, the connections between corporate capitalism and ecological devastation cannot be ignored. Again, Martin's aim has radical economic implications.

Five Cs, not Seven

To the three Cs of care, concern and connection, I would add, following Martin, collaboration and cooperation, but I would want to explicitly address competition and consumerism, and show how both undermine the other five.

One of the implications of taking seriously collaboration and cooperation, and scorning competition, will be eliminating the grading system and all the consequences attendant upon it. The implications of our hidden (and not so hidden) curriculum concerning competition are huge and an important part of any conversation about education and its aims. I wish space permitted me to say more here about them.[10]

Appreciation for the Unsayable

I want to conclude with a remark about Neiman's goal of appreciation. It is clear from his references that he is thinking of students in colleges and universities, or upper-level secondary students: young ones will not go far with Buber and Kierkegaard. But I think his goal can be and should be seen as a reasonable one for all of us, in and outside of school. It is probably best nurtured in the young through dance, art, poetry and all the other activities that often are the staple of kindergarten and disappear increasingly through the grades. But why? The embarrassment one would encounter now in encouraging a high school class to take time for a circle dance, would not be there under less oppressive conditions, and certainly would not be there if it had been part of the curriculum all along.

But questions about ultimate meaning are often difficult to give attention to in the midst of confusion and suffering. These questions and the means to encourage their flourishing will be much easier to address once we dismantle our present oppressive societies—or rebuild them as they crumble from their own internal contradictions.

NOTES

1. The reference is to a poem by Harvey Jackins, that begins: "O Parents, Teachers, and all such Instructors, permit them learn." Much of the theory about oppression, violence and emotional healing in this paper is due to the work of Harvey Jackins and his colleagues and friends in the Re-evaluation Counseling communities, of which I am a part. See Jackins, *The Human Side of Human Beings: The Theory or Re-evaluation Counseling* (Seattle: Rational Island Publishers, 1978).

2. The reference is to Ludwig Wittgenstein, *The Philosophical Investigations* (Oxford: Blackwell, 1953). See sections 654 and 655 and elsewhere.

3. Ludwig Wittgenstein, *[Preliminary Studies for the Philosophical Investigations, Generally Known As] The Blue and Brown Books* (Oxford: Blackwell, 1958), pp. 17–18. LW notes that the "craving for generality" can be understood in a number of ways, one being the "contemptuous attitude towards the particular case."

4. Roger Waters/Pink Floyd, "Another Brick in the Wall, Part II," *The Wall*, Columbia Records, NY, 1979.

5. From Doris Lessing's Introduction to *The Golden Notebook* (New York: McGraw-Hill, 1962), pp. xxiii–xxiv.

6. Pink Floyd, Ibid.

7. Newton Garver, "What Violence Is," in Jeffrie G. Murphy, ed., *An Introduction to Moral and Social Philosophy* (Belmont, CA: Wadsworth, 1973), p. 332.

8. W. E. B. Du Bois, *Darkwater* (New York: Harcourt, Brace and Howe, 1920), pp. 33–34.

9. See, for example, Alice Miller, *For Your Own Good: Hidden Cruelty in Child-Rearing and the Roots of Violence* (New York: Farrar, Straus, Giroux, 1983) and her case study of Hitler.

10. See Perry Saidman, *Competition: An Inhuman Activity,* pamphlet available from Seattle: Rational Island Publishers, 1994.

RATIONALITY
AND REASON

7

Reasonable Doubt:
Toward a Postmodern Defense
of Reason as an Educational Aim[1]

Nicholas C. Burbules

> It is . . . reasonable to be reasonably wary of the rational.
> —Michel Serres[2]

"Be reasonable," we are sometimes told, and in many contexts this is felt as a rebuke or, even worse, a command to silence one's thoughts and feelings. When reason is held to be a strict adjudicator of legitimate and illegitimate expression, the effect is often to suppress beliefs and values that do not measure up to its standards. This conception of rationality has fallen under withering attack by current postmodern writers, especially those speaking from poststructuralist and feminist perspectives.[3] In this essay, I want to consider whether these criticisms mean that "reason" must be abandoned entirely as an ideal, or whether, instead, the ideal should be retained but reconstructed along less formal, transcendental, and universal premises. Defending the latter view, I suggest what this ideal might mean in educational settings.

Some Postmodern Criticisms of Rationality

The dominant philosophical tradition in the West, certainly since Descartes, has been to regard a particular type of rationality as the fundamental method for investigation into truth. Ernest Gellner defines it as "an individualistic attempt to set up rationally the limits and nature of the genuinely knowable world."[4] The story of this Cartesian conception of reason, "intellectually perfectionist . . . and humanly unrelenting," and how it emerged as the presumed basis for credible thought, has been a major subject of investigation in recent years: "Whatever sorts of problem one faced, there was a supposedly unique procedure for arriving at a correct solution."[5] This procedure was based upon logical deduction, strict rules of evidence, and an avoidance of the distorting tendencies of affect; a method of investigation in which the force of correct answers was thought to be rationally, intrinsically, compelling (that is, "true"). For Descartes, it was possible to doubt *everything,* but not reason itself.[6]

Yet, as Gellner, Alasdair MacIntyre, Richard Rorty, Stephen Toulmin, and others have argued, even within the Western tradition there have been very different conceptions of reason, an understanding of which can inform a broader and less monolithic conception of what "good reasoning" entails.[7] Specifically, some of these authors—Rorty is probably the best-known example—have pointed out that an overemphasis on the epistemic functions of reason, and within that a privileging of a particular scientistic approach to inquiry, has skewed the discussion away from moral and political dimensions that are actually at the heart of decisions about what to believe and how to act. The great myth of this narrow view of rationality, Rorty explains, is that without a strict criterion of truth, we will be left to rely only on "taste, passion, and will."[8] A sharp demarcation between the rational and the irrational (or nonrational), and the implication that without the protection of the former there is no alternative but the latter, is one of the trademarks of this particular tradition.

More recently, philosophers of quite different schools of thought have preferred to think in terms of different *kinds* of reasoning. Reasoning can be conceived in different and in broader terms than simply in terms of rationality.[9] Yet the literature in Philosophy of Education has been slow to pursue this line of inquiry: the chief philosophical writers in education who focus on reason or critical thinking (Robert Ennis, John McPeck, Richard Paul, Israel Scheffler, and Harvey Siegel) all, to varying degrees, begin with the premise that reasoning equates with rationality.[10] They consider any attempt to discuss alternative rationalities as tantamount to creeping relativism, and maintain that it is especially important for educators, above all, to defend the value of rationality.

For better or for worse, the trend of thought in much of contemporary philosophy seems to be running against this view. Indeed, rather than a modest opening up for consideration of alternative forms of reasoning, many critics now simply want to throw out the concepts of reason or rationality as the remnants of a misguided Enlightenment tradition that, whatever its original liberal intent, has become stultifying, monolithic, and insensitive to cultural diversity. Drawing from a variety of sources, but especially in "post-modern" circles of discussion, many philosophers simply take it for granted that reason is no longer an important topic, except as a target of criticism. In response to these criticisms, any defense of reason is regarded as inherently suspect; a sentiment that is being asserted with increasing force and certitude. Richard Bernstein, by no means an unsympathetic observer of postmodernism, expresses puzzlement and alarm over this trend:

> Why is there a rage against Reason? What precisely is being attacked, criticized, and damned? Why is it when "Reason" and "Rationality" are mentioned, they evoke images of domination, oppression, repression, patriarchy, sterility, violence, totality, totalitarianism, and even terror? These questions are especially poignant and perplexing when we realize that not long ago the call to "Reason" elicited associations with autonomy, freedom, justice, equality, happiness, and peace.[11]

In my view, it is crucial for concerned scholars to acknowledge this "rage against reason" as a real intellectual and political movement, one with thoughtful and articulate defenders.[12] Many of their criticisms and challenges seem to me convincing. Yet the question remains whether it is possible to abandon any talk of "rationality" altogether without replacing that category with something similar or, as Harvey Siegel among others has suggested, whether the very effort to *argue* against rationality commits one implicitly (and self-contradictorily) to some of the very standards being purportedly rejected.[13]

In this essay, the substance of these criticisms can be replied to with a reconceptualization of rationality: the alternative term "reasonableness."[14] This different way of thinking about rationality provides the guidance and structure needed for coherent thought in epistemic, practical, and moral matters without proclaiming the existence of transcendental and universal standards that are problematic from a postmodern point of view. This position can be considered in the postmodern spirit—a revision and going-beyond of modernist conceptions and presuppositions—rather than an *antimodern* rejection of the entire enterprise of seeking any objective and generalizable basis for resolving competing claims about truth, value, or proper course of action.[15] The antimodern position makes an error that is the mirror image of that made by certain defenders of rationalism: assuming that if reason means anything, it means rationality in the Cartesian sense, and that any other forms reason might take stand or fall along with those Cartesian premises.

The postmodern view is rooted in *doubt* rather than *denial*. It asks, skeptically, what follows socially and politically from advocating a formal, universal standard of rationality to which people must be expected to conform; it asks who is silenced, who is intimidated, who is excluded when this and this only defines the standard of credible discourse; it holds in suspense an allegiance to any particular mode of thought, when the entire historical and cultural record urges us in the direction of pluralism and tolerance for diversity in these matters. In this sense, doubting the Cartesian method of rationality (something Descartes himself was unable to do) can be carried out in the name of a more inclusive and flexible understanding of reason; yet one that need not deny or reject the specific achievements of that method, within certain areas of human thought and practice. Our doubt can be a reasonable doubt.

Rationality and Reasonableness

Where does the postmodern critique of rationality leave us? What is left if the idea of rationality is abandoned as a neutral arbiter of the rules of clear thinking; a dispassioned means for reaching indubitable conclusions; a universal guide to human thought and conduct; and a timeless story line, playing itself out across the history of human evolution as we pursue the capacity for pure and untainted ratiocination? What if, instead, reason is regarded as a human invention and achievement, one that is hardly arbitrary, since it has arisen in similar forms under many different circumstances and constraints, but one that is neither necessary nor universal? What if reason is regarded as a practice growing out of communicative interactions in which the full play of human thought, feeling, and motivation operate? What if the only basis for generalizing the merits of reason is a concrete, specific, educative process in which others are engaged in this way of thinking: if successful *this shows* that it is generalizable, and if it fails it shows that it is not? Finally, what if the benefits of reason are grounded in nothing more or less than that which answers certain kinds of questions, solves certain kinds of problems, adjudicates certain kinds of disagreements; not because it is the essential or necessary guide to all human thought and action?

What is left is a good deal of the architecture of what we actually *do* when reasoning (logical deduction is a useful way to think through certain arguments, for example), but with a much more modest set of claims about its range of utility or its generalizability to persons and groups who might have evolved different ways of answering questions, solving problems, and adjudicating disagreements. In its place are some very general human traits that more broadly guide reflective thought and action. In short, a conception of reason—reasonableness—can be maintained in the face of postmodern criticisms without falling entirely into relativism.[16] Discriminations can be made between more or less "reasonable" and "unreasonable" thoughts or actions—and of the contexts that promote them—that do not rest on the sharp, and rather harsh, dichotomy of "rational" and "irrational" that has characterized many previous discourses about reason.[17]

I want to suggest instead that "reasonableness" refers to the dispositions and capacities of a certain kind of person, a person who is related in specific

contexts to other persons—not to the following of formal rules and procedures of thought. Although a reasonable person is one who will tend to have,
and offer, reasons to support his or her choices of belief and action, these are
the manifestation of something more basic about this sort of person. A characterization solely in terms of "reason-giving" or "reason-following" confuses
the symptom with the source of reasonable dispositions. A common trend,
for example, in much current writing on critical thinking is to suggest the
limitations of "logicality" as an approximation of what a critical thinker is
and does; rather, we need to supplement the skills of logical reasoning with
dispositions to apply them in contexts of practice.[18] In some cases, unfortunately, the characterization of these dispositions is rather thin: the difference
between the logical rule "always test a syllogism for valid structure" and the
"disposition to test syllogisms for valid structure" is hardly worth talking
about. Similarly, the "rational passions" discussed by Israel Scheffler and others, such as a passion for rigor and clarity, are sometimes little more than the
rephrasing of formal criteria in an emotive language.[19]

For this reason, along with others, I prefer the term "virtues" to "dispositions." Virtues are flexible aspects of character, related to our sense of self and
integrity, but also fostered and encouraged by the communities and relations
with others that provide the context in which we decide and act. We express
virtues out of the choices we make, because of the types of people we are, in
relation to the actions and choices of those around us. The term "disposition"
does little to suggest this richness and complexity.[20] "Disposition" tends to
refer to individual tendencies, often ascribed from an external perspective
through observation and behaviorist inference. A virtue, on the other hand,
is not a mere expression of habit, but an expression of judgment and choice;
virtues will be enacted in different ways in different contexts, and in relation
to different persons. Hence they cannot be analyzed solely as individual pos-
sessions: persons acquire, maintain, and express the virtues that they do
partly because of the relations they have to others, and how those others act
in response to them.[21]

A better understanding of reasonableness as a human characteristic and
achievement requires a deeper account of how virtues affect conduct: they
are not simply the activating sentiments that motivate us to apply the formal
rules we have learned, but the aspects of character that bring us to care about
learning or paying attention to such standards in the first place. They are part
of who we are. A person who is reasonable wants to make sense, wants to be
fair to alternative points of view, wants to be careful and prudent in the
adoption of important positions in life, is willing to admit when he or she
has made a mistake, and so on. These qualities are not exhibited simply by
following certain formal rules of reasoning. They are enormously more complex than that, since they are manifested in a broad range of situations that
are not governed by formal rules. Because they are more basic and extensive
than any set of rules, these virtues might even be manifested in specific situa-

tions by ignoring some of these rules (as when someone violates the norm of strict precision and accuracy in trying to express a simple idea to a child). In this view, it is because persons are reasonable, or want to be, that they should concern themselves with "logicality" as a useful heuristic for ordered thought—not vice versa. We can assess the reasonableness, or not, of many beliefs and actions only by understanding them in the context of a larger process of deliberation, reflection, discussion, and change, it is in *how* and *when* persons change their minds that their reasonableness, or not, manifests itself.[22] Simple and dichotomous characterizations of "rationality" do not help us in making these sorts of judgments.

This perspective on reasonableness is in many ways premodern, and part of the story that Gellner and others recite is the submersion of this character-driven view of reason in the modernist era of Cartesian hegemony. Rationality, Gellner points out, is itself a concept with a history. It has not been consistent and monolithic, even within the Western tradition.[23] Toulmin reminds us, for example, that:

> For sixteenth-century humanists, the central demand was that all of our thought and conduct be *reasonable*. On the one hand, this meant developing modesty about one's capacities and self-awareness in one's self-presentation. . . . On the other hand, it required toleration of social, cultural, and intellectual diversity. It was unreasonable to condemn out of hand people with institutions, customs, or ideals different from ours. . . . Instead, we should recognize that our own practices may look no less strange to others, and withhold judgment until we can ask how far those others realized their positions by honest, discriminating, and critical reflection on their experience.[24]

Similarly, Rorty says that reason

> names a set of moral virtues: tolerance, respect for the opinions of those around one, willingness to listen, reliance upon persuasion rather than force. These are the virtues which members of a civilized society must possess if the society is to endure.[25]

Finally, Charles Taylor notes:

> Rationality involves more than avoiding inconsistency. What more is involved comes out in the different judgments we make when we compare incommensurable cultures and activities. These judgments take us beyond merely formal criteria of rationality, and point us toward the human activities of articulation which give the value of rationality its sense.[26]

Notice what a different conception of reason this approach leads us to: one sensitive to cultural difference and diversity; modest about its claims to universality; situated in human relations and moral reflection; grounded more in practical, social activities of speaking, listening, and reflecting than in dispassioned logical deduction or a scientistic search for "facts." Evidence and analysis are pertinent to careful reasoning, of course; but these methods must take their place in a larger context of choices about weighing multiple sources of information, appreciating the merits of other perspectives, and in that light judging carefully the potential *limits* of one's methods and theory. Their epistemic value cannot be divorced from their effects on our moral and political lives.

This discussion leads to a second and related dimension of reasonableness: the capacity to enter into communicative relations in which persons together inquire, disagree, adjudicate, explain, or argue their views in the pursuit of a reasonable outcome (that is, an outcome that the participants, after careful deliberation, are satisfied with). The virtues of reasonableness Rorty mentions are manifested in the ways that persons speak with and listen to one another. Reason is an enacted, imperfect, social process, not the application of mechanical rules of inquiry. Validity depends not only on the formulation of an idealized case, but on its being heard, questioned, and responded to by others. Rorty terms this change a shift from "argument" to "conversation."[27] Jürgen Habermas speaks, similarly, about the shift from "formal" to "procedural" rationality; because formal reason has stressed "what is universal, supra-temporal, and necessary over what is particular, variable, and accidental," it has given an "idealistic casting" to the concept of reason.[28] Instead, Habermas's recent works constitute a sustained and detailed argument that claims about truth or moral rightness can be supported only through *actual* conversational engagements among persons with different points of view. If such communicative relations cannot be entered into and sustained, reason is not possible. Reason, in the words of Seyla Benhabib, comes to be seen as "the contingent achievement of linguistically socialized, finite, and embodied creatures."[29] This communicative aspect is chiefly what makes the pursuit and attainment of reasoned positions a practical and contextual endeavor. The adequacy of the processes of reasoning and conversation is judged by the practical efficacy and social acceptability of the conclusions they derive; and the reliability of these conclusions is judged by the thoroughness and care of the processes by which they were reached.

It is important to see the *critical* dimensions of this view of reasonableness as well. Among other things, it shows the individualistic bias underlying the Cartesian view of reasoning. Reasonable views should be seen as the product of social interactions, whether directly or indirectly. No one can be expected to be reasonable in entirely unreasonable circumstances; and a corollary of this insight is that the characterization of "unreasonableness" is often more a critique of social circumstances rather than a criticism of persons. Contexts in which people are discouraged from careful deliberation and reflection; where dubious beliefs, values, tastes, and manners are enforced through strong social or institutional coercion; where hasty or overly simplistic choices are pressed upon persons; where there are few opportunities for intersubjective discussion and consideration of alternatives, are all *unreasonable* contexts, by which I mean that they are both the consequence of poorly-considered and oppressive social choices, and that they are likely to result in unreasonable thoughts and actions by persons within them. These circumstances are rampant in our society. This way of thinking about reason implies a strong social critique, an analysis of power and ideology as distortions to human thought and action, not only as an arid analysis of "sloppy thinking" or invalid syllogisms (although these formal errors of reasoning are sometimes the symptoms of those larger distortions). One dimension of this social critique should include the way in which the hegemony of a particular, narrow, instrumental conception of rationality has—whatever its benefits within a more limited context—often *hindered* and *limited* the formation of those social relations and practices that are required to develop a balanced and intersubjectively meaningful appreciation of the world.

The Cartesian conception of rationality is both epistemic and teleological; it is held to be the only avenue toward reliable knowledge, and held to be certain of success in yielding correct, final answers, if its methods are properly followed. This faith can be regarded today only with scepticism. The work of Thomas Kuhn and other historians and philosophers of science has deeply undermined the belief that even scientists proceed in a purely rational way.[30] A heavy irony is that both rationalist philosophers and certain postmodern ones share the argument that once this particular conception of reason is given up, there is nothing left but an "anything goes" relativism. Both are, in my view, mistaken.[31] Instead, we need to begin with the premise that the process of reasoned inquiry is manifested in the thoughts, conversations, and choices that the actual persons involved pursue toward some conclusion—and if they are reasonable people, this conclusion is as reliable as any can be. Of course, that conclusion might be mistaken, but it can be recognized as such and rectified only through a further extension of the same process. The epistemic dimension of reasonableness is thereby inverted, the question is no longer: What procedures of inquiry or argument are most likely to yield the truth? but rather, When people have sought to understand the truth of their situation, what are the general patterns of investigation that they have settled upon over time?

Among these patterns of investigation, the rules of logic or scientific inquiry play an important part, but a limited one, because they are effective as such only in social contexts of communication, practice, and judgment. The difficult question, then, concerns the nature of these contexts, and what it means to conduct ourselves reasonably within them. As a way to begin that investigation, I will propose four interdependent qualities that seem central to reasonableness: objectivity, fallibilism, pragmatism, and judiciousness. They can be translated from the formal, decontextualized language of "rationality" to a discourse more concerned with personal character, practical contexts, and communicative relations.[32] My purpose is to show that these virtues of reasonableness are both richer and more effective when they are understood in this way. They are better able to withstand certain postmodern criticisms, and they can better help to guide and inform our educational projects.

Four Virtues of Reasonableness

Striving for objectivity. What, in fact, is necessary in order for a person to adopt an objective standpoint? One element is an attitude of tolerance, the capacity to regard alternative positions without a "rush to judgment." An objective person is one who can withhold his or her own opinions in an engagement with other points of view. This capacity is fostered, not primarily by the exercise of certain intellectual skills, but by the exercise of a demeanor and capacity for restraint. There are many other aspects of tolerance as well: being able to recognize what one's owns biases might be, acknowledging the limits of one's capacity to appreciate fully the viewpoints of others, and caring enough about others to exert the effort necessary to hear and comprehend what they are saying. Lacking such tolerance, a person cannot enact that component of reasonableness called "objectivity". The acquisition and exercise of these characteristics is clearly not a purely cognitive/rational endeavor. On the contrary, objectivity in this sense has nothing to do with a lack of commitment, caring, or feeling.

Objectivity is supported, not by the position of holding no view, but by the position of having regarded enough other views thoughtfully and sympathetically to realize that each has something to be said for it, so that one is distanced somewhat from the attitude that there is or can be one "best" way of all. This sort of pluralism is fostered, of course, partly by having been exposed to a sufficient range of differences, but also by engaging them in some process of give-and-take that has enabled one to consider seriously the merits of each. This, it seems to me, is a chief talent of persons whom we consider to be "objective"—and it is, I think, a fundamentally different analysis of that virtue than those normally found in the literature. There was a time when authors on rationality found it unremarkable and unproblematic to offer such comments as: "thinkers who think rationally think alike."[33] It is difficult to imagine many philosophically-informed people embracing this position now. Indeed, today many more or less coherent ways of constructing an identity and form of life that, however strange and "irrational" they might appear from the outside, seem to be meaningful and coherent for the people who occupy them. Reasonableness, if it is to be a sustainable virtue, must acknowledge the fact of difference, perhaps irreconcilable difference, as a condition of the social world, and take its direction not from an ethnocentric presumption of superiority,[34] or the erasure of difference in the name of presumed consensus around a unified truth, but in a thoughtful and sensitive engagement across differences, even as it leaves some of those differences in place.[35] As Benhabib puts it: "It is crucial that we view our conceptions of the good life as matters about which intersubjective debate is possible, even if intersubjective consensus . . . remains unattainable in these areas."[36]

What this line of argument suggests is that in the pursuit of objectivity, values such as tolerance and pluralism are *methodological* as well as *moral* edicts. Our thinking will be richer, more balanced, and more fair when we are able to hear and consider a variety of alternatives. Being able to do so requires not only some intellectual capacities, but also aspects of character, personal relations, and social contexts that encourage and support the development of this virtue. We all know persons who have great intellect but who cannot detach their critical capacities sufficiently to hear and consider alternative points of view. To that degree, they lack what I am calling "objectivity." Similarly, persons who can listen to anything and not react critically to it seem to lack a kind of discernment. At both extremes, these people fail to be reasonable.

Objectivity, therefore, is not a result of uncaring neutrality or of ostensibly holding no position. Nor does a tolerance and appreciation for many alternative points of view imply a relativistic embrace of simply *any* view. It involves an awareness of and reflection upon positions one does hold, and what their consequences are for other people. Feminists writing about epistemology have written revealingly on this topic, and have made the crucial point that relativism is no friend to the feminist project, that some supportable sense of objectivity is crucial in the endeavor to have others recognize the insights of feminist study and critique as "real" and "valid." But feminists also want to rethink what objectivity means:

> [O]ne's social situation enables and sets limits on what one can know; some social situations—critically unexamined dominant ones—are more limiting than others in this respect, and what makes these situations more limiting is their inability to generate the most critical questions about received belief. . . . [Feminism] argues against the idea that all social situations provide equally useful resources for learning about the world and against the idea that they all set equally strong limits on knowledge.[37]

The view that Sandra Harding and others call "standpoint epistemology" argues that all knowing begins with a subject position (any thinker or inquirer is first of all a person, with certain characteristics, in a particular situation) and the potential effects of that position (privilege, for example) on the possibilities and limits of his or her "objectivity" in investigating a particular subject. But in order to do this fully, one must accept the reality of that situation and the heightened objectivity that can result from taking it into account. As Lorraine Code puts it: "Knowledge is always *relative to* (i.e., a

perspective *on,* a standpoint *in*) specifiable circumstances. Hence it is constrained by a realist, empiricist commitment according to which getting these
circumstances right is vital to reflective action."[38]

In this sense, the distinction between objectivity and subjectivity has been
misdrawn. First, it is overly dichotomous: elements of subjectivity, and an
acknowledgment of such, are *part of* attaining objectivity. Our limited and
imperfect, but sincere, attempts to understand our own biases or blind spots,
and to question how our social status, position, or identity place us in particular and sometimes problematic relations to others with whom we seek
understanding, is the best protection of objectivity that we can have. We cannot forget, ignore, or set aside those aspects of our identity; we can only act
as self-reflectively as possible within them. This leads to a quite different
understanding of objectivity. Second, if one believes that a conversational
engagement with others is crucial to the intersubjective negotiation of
knowledge and value claims, then one can prejudge neither the superiority
of one position nor the nihilistic incomparability of all positions. As Donna
Haraway argues:

> The alternative to relativism is not totalitarianism and single vision. . . .
> The alternative to relativism is practical, locatable, critical knowledges
> sustaining the possibility of webs of connections called solidarity in pol-
> itics and shared conversations in epistemology.[39]

Hence, the acquisition and expression of this virtue cannot be an individual achievement. Developing tolerance, for example, depends upon the
kinds of communicative and other social interactions one has had with others throughout the course of one's life. Viewing these capacities in the context
of real human interactions also helps make clear when tolerance might *not* be
a reasonable response: when one has reached the limits of one's capacities to
remain detached, or when certain points of view are so repugnant that it is
unrealistic and unreasonable to be expected to judge them.

The rationalist conception of objectivity has dominated discussions of
what it means to be reasonable, to the point where many critics conclude
that the idea of "objectivity" should be abandoned. This would be a mistake
for at least two reasons: because there are cases in which a capacity for objectivity in the sense of being able to hear competing points of view and to
consider their merits is crucial to making fair and reliable decisions; and
because effective social critique (whether feminist or not) rests upon the
claim that a particular point of view is more objective in that it is more
self-conscious, reflective, and considerate of different points of view. Being
able to make and substantiate such a claim is crucial to the development of
any theory and practice that scrutinizes and criticizes the status quo and asks
people to consider their lives from a better vantage point. In this sense of
objectivity, then, some views are more reasonable than others.

Accepting fallibilism. One of the great insights of modern philosophy is Karl Popper's reminder not to be afraid of making mistakes, because it is only through the discovery of error, through some process of falsification, that we are driven to change.[40] Indeed, Popper's recommendation seems to extend far beyond the confines of scientific hypothesis testing—where it is typically applied—to a broader vision and attitude toward life. In a variety of contexts, both personal and professional, intellectual and emotional, we all have experienced failure, error, frustration, and disappointment. If we can live with these, as we must, it is usually with the understanding that they have formed us, taught us something, strengthened our capacity to endure change. In this broader sense, the acceptance of fallibilism is also a component of a reasonable character.

What is involved in this virtue? First, it requires certain commitments, or certain risks, that run the possibility of error. Purposely hiding behind obscurantism, withholding commitment, or playing it safe by only conforming to the conventional and obvious, are all ways of avoiding mistakes—and hence, ultimately, of avoiding learning and change. Second, it requires a capacity to recognize that one is wrong, which is fundamentally linked with the capacity to *admit* (to one's self, and to others) that one was wrong. This includes our capacity to hear and respond thoughtfully to the criticisms of others. Third, it involves a capacity for reflection, as we ponder not only that we have *made* a mistake, but also why it happened and how we can change to avoid repeating it in the future. Once again, there are individuals who have all the intellectual skills one could admire, but who find it difficult to acknowledge error. This is a defect from the standpoint of a reasonable character. However, it would be a mistake to regard this entirely as a shortcoming of the individual, and not as a breakdown in a broader developmental context that implicitly and often explicitly rewards unreasonable conduct. Sometimes it is dangerous to admit error, and sometimes the damage done to personal relations or self-esteem make admission of one's mistakes a punishable offense. In the university context, for example, the rise of an "adversary method" as the primary model of academic engagement frequently rewards those who are most vigorous in defending their own point of view and attacking those of others.[41]

Notice, please, that I am not suggesting that the give-and-take of criticism within communities of inquiry is illegitimate; on the contrary, it is a crucial process in a culture that recognizes fallibilism as the pivot point of change. But when this process takes place in a system of "high stakes" rewards and punishments; when certain aggressive aspects of personality and verbal style are falsely taken to be proxies for a healthy critical process; when the pressures and power relations of such contexts are such that certain prospective participants are intimidated from entering the conversation, then the *forms* of debate and critical interaction are mistaken for the *substance* of carefully and sympathetically comparing the merits of a range of points of view and subjecting them to some process of thoughtful scrutiny and revision.[42] It should be no surprise in these contexts that people have developed a razor-sharp capacity to dissect the ideas of others, but a stultified capacity to alter or abandon their own presuppositions.

Reasonableness, on this view, expresses a capacity for change, a change prompted by one's own recognition and acknowledgment of error, but also supported by a social environment in which this process is regarded with favor, not disdain. "Falsifiability" is normally taken in the literature to be a description of the characteristics of a theory or research program; but it includes more than this, since theories are held by persons, and because research programs comprise individuals with various personal, institutional, and (often) financial interests in maintaining and perpetuating their positions. Hence "falsifiability," and conceptual change as a result, are achievable not only because of the features of a particular intellectual framework, but because of the capacities for facing up to, and responding to, error on the part of those who hold it, and the contexts and social relations that encourage or discourage such responses.

Fallibilism, too, implies a particular view of learning: that we gain new understandings not only by the accumulation of novel information, but by the active reconstruction of our frameworks of understanding. This sort of change requires that we encounter and interact with radically different points of view from our own; which means, of course, that we must exist in contexts that support and encourage difference—but which also means that we must have the capacity and willingness to engage others in a communicative interchange that makes the meaningful juxtaposition of different views possible. An inherent part of this process is the surprise, puzzlement, or even outrage we might feel at first in encountering a novel point of view or unexpected piece of evidence. Accepting fallibilism has a strong affective component. Without the "shock of the new," we often lack the motivation to rethink our assumptions. Yet there is little value in romanticizing the sentiments accompanying the intellectual process of trial, error, and change. These can be difficult and disturbing experiences, whether in academic, intellectual settings (such as seeing one's ideas questioned and criticized by a colleague) or in personal ones (such as realizing and coming to grips with one's own prejudiced attitudes toward a particular person or group).[43]

Maintaining a pragmatic attitude. In using the term, I am not trying to invoke a specific school of thought: the "pragmatism" of Dewey, James, or Peirce. Rather, I am referring to a deeper underlying attitude which characterizes that general world view: a belief in the importance of practical problems in driving the process of intellectual, moral, and political development. Such an outlook is sensitive to the particulars of given contexts and the variety of human needs and purposes. Most important, pragmatism reflects a tolerance for uncertainty, imperfection, and incompleteness as the existential conditions of human thought and action. Yet it also recognizes the need for persistence in confronting such difficulties with intelligence, care, and flexibility.

The central lesson of fallibilism in philosophy, from Socrates to Popper, is that we proceed, not towards truth, but away from error. It is much easier to know when we are wrong than when we are right; and the philosophical consequence of this insight is a distrust of teleological conceptions of rationality. Certain approaches to inquiry are relied upon, including the conversational ones discussed earlier, not because they will yield a convergence around truth or agreement, but because experience has shown them to be reliable ways of avoiding certain egregious kinds of mistakes. There is no guarantee built into them to produce what we seek; we merely expect that whatever they yield is more likely to be dependable than what we might garner from other approaches. Such a commitment to a process of inquiry or negotiation, without certainty of its results, is what defines the pragmatic attitude, and is also a primary feature of reasonableness.

A reasonable person is frequently in situations where insufficient information is available, where problems appear intractable, where outcomes are unpredictable. Here, most of all, their capacities are tested. In such difficulties, what makes the responses of a person reasonable and reliable is whether they can approach the present problems with an open mind, a willingness and capacity to adapt, and persistence in the face of initial failure or confusion. In this case (as in the others I have discussed) this virtue operates at a much deeper and more pervasive level than any particular set of skills or strategies—although certainly having some appropriate skills, having experience with similar situations, and having some track record of success in coping with them are also relevant to whether a person will respond constructively to a new challenge. Also supportive of such capacities are social contexts (including educational contexts) in which an emphasis on success is not exaggerated; in which failure or frustration are accepted as inevitable conditions of growth; and in which offering cooperative assistance and constructive suggestions—or asking for them—are socially and personally acceptable options. Once again, this provides a quite different characterization of the person who is reasonable, and of the type of context that fosters and supports reasonable conduct.

Judiciousness. One of the reasons that a virtues account of reasonableness is prior to, and not just a supplement for, an emphasis on "logicality" is that a reasonable person requires the ability to judge, to distinguish situations in which a rational calculation in the narrow sense might be called for, and when it is not. We need to build into the concept of reasonableness an awareness of its own limitations: a reasonable person is one who knows when *not* to try to figure certain things out in a particular rational way, and who regards the skills of rationality and the assessment of reasons as simply heuristics in the much more complex process of trying to decide what to believe and what to do—heuristics that can help guide choices, but not govern them. It is not reasonable to try to apply the analysis of logic, or the strict rules of evidence, or the critique of informal fallacies, to each and every situation; people react with amusement, puzzlement, or actual antipathy to those who do.

Part of judgment is a capacity for prudence and moderation, even in the exercise of reason itself. We are not always reasonable. We occasionally fail to act upon our own best inclinations. We frequently fall short of our aspirations. Acknowledging and accepting this in ourselves and in those around us, and asking others to accept it in us, are related to the acceptance of fallibilism and the willingness to embrace imperfection and incompleteness that is part of the pragmatic spirit: the recognition of the patterns of gray-on-gray that typically characterize human choice and action. There is often more than one reasonable thing to believe, to say, or to do; and it is part of the fallacy of Cartesian conceptions of rationality that they seek a determinative calculus that will converge on the one "best" or "right" answer.

Here, as in the other virtues of reasonableness the key quality is being able to hold competing considerations in balance, accepting tensions and uncertainty as the conditions of serious reflection. Such broad capacities as paying attention to "relevant" information, respecting complexity, keeping an open mind to alternative points of view, and appreciating the limitations of one's tools of inquiry, as well as their utility, are not rule-governed or formal capacities—yet without exercising such traits, we cannot be reasonable.[44]

The attainment of reasonableness is a matter of degree: sometimes we are more reasonable than at other times; around some people we are more reasonable. Our aspiration is not to cross some sharp boundary from the "irrational" to the "rational," but to improve, through a process of learning and development, our capacities to be reasonable, and those of others with whom we interact. This awareness should *increase* our sense of interdependence and kinship with others, and provide a healthy counterbalance to the smug confidence that we can answer every question, solve every problem, or resolve every dilemma on our own.

Finally, those whom we respect as reasonable are judicious about when and how they follow the dictates of argument in the strict sense of the term, and they are receptive to the influence of other kinds of persuasion as well. In the actual practice of human communication, strict and conclusive argument is very rare; alongside that is an enormous range of interlocutory styles, including questions, allusions, unsubstantiated suggestions, metaphors, and other tropes, as well as an even broader range of expressions, gestures, touches, tonal utterances ("hmmm?"), and other kinds of communication. The capacity of all these sorts of utterances to move us is *extra-rational* only in a very narrow sense of that term. To be reasonable in social contexts of interaction entails remaining open to the influences of other avenues of mutual exploration, negotiation, and the pursuit of understanding. A respect for the force of reason is crucial, as is the attempt to be clear, coherent, and accurate in what one says. But it is not everything.

Reasonableness as an Educational Aim

In my discussion of reasonableness and the virtues that partly constitute it, I have emphasized the interdependence of personally developing certain capacities with finding contexts in which other people possess and exhibit these virtues in their actions and interactions with one another, and with us. Concretely, we attain the degree of reasonableness that we do because of the reasonableness of those around us; the process of exploring and adjudicating different positions catches up its participants in an edifying dynamic. In other words, the educational question of fostering and encouraging the virtues of reasonableness is intrinsic to the question of their nature and worth; we might say we pursue and value certain kinds of interactions because they yield reasonable outcomes, but it is just as true to say that we respect and trust those outcomes because of the interactions that gave rise to them.

A fair question is: Who is the *we* being talked of here? Is reasonableness simply another version of rationality; an artifact of modern, Western, patriarchal culture? Do these virtues simply represent a middle class conception of polite conduct, elevated peremptorily to the status of a set of universal standards? As I have tried to characterize it, reasonableness is not culturally imperialistic or biased toward masculine conceptions of rationality: these sorts of standards are maintained, in one guise or another, by all sorts of people, in many different cultures and in various historical contexts. The virtues of reasonableness are features of reflective thought and practice that are continually invoked by disparate persons and groups with otherwise quite different systems of belief, value, and action; and this fact suggests that they are far from arbitrary.

These virtues are not "universals," their adoption is not mandatory for those who might not share them. But I believe that their benefits can be made apparent to others through a process of communicative interchange that is itself consistent with the values it advocates (that is, it would not depend upon coercion or other indirect means of manipulation). In one sense, these virtues are *generalizable,* in the sense that others might be persuasively brought to recognize them. This claim is performative, in the sense that its credibility depends on being able to fulfill it in practice. This is a very different claim than one of *universality*, which asserts that these qualities are incumbent upon persons whether they personally recognize and value them or not. Generalizability is a pragmatic achievement; it yields only what Benhabib and Michael Kelly call a "weak universalism."[45] This perspective focuses more on the necessary conditions for certain kinds of intersubjective explorations to occur, and less on a belief in consensus as the likely or "best" result of such engagements. Any resulting agreements that do occur are substantiated in a concrete, particular sense, not a transcendental one: "The emphasis now is less on *rational* agreement, and more on sustaining those normative practices and moral relationships within which reasoned agreement *as a way of life* can flourish and continue."[46]

This conception of reason is not subject to some of the same criticisms that postmodern theorists have leveled against the traditional conception of rationality. Conceiving of reasonableness as a set of virtues does not commit us to a belief in a master narrative or a pure meta-discourse; on the contrary, characterizing reason as a concrete, imperfect, human attainment responds sympathetically to the criticism that rationality has been abstracted from the field of human interrelationships and politics. The virtues of objectivity, fallibilism, pragmatism, and judiciousness each can be explored in ways that do justice to the diversity of human thoughts, values, and forms of life, without falling into a relativism that is unable to recommend or criticize any manner of thinking. While being flexible enough to accommodate a broad range of human processes of communication, investigation, or negotiation, these four virtues also provide a basis for excluding others that can be shown to be counterproductive to intelligent, committed, and caring thought and action. In a postmodern framework, these are the sorts of criteria that are needed: not determinative in the sense of presuming to pick out the one best manner of approaching a problem, but not leveling of all possible alternatives either. It is the hallmark of a reasonable person to be able to consider a range of worthy possibilities, and to acknowledge the potential benefits inherent in each, without becoming incapable of choosing or judging between them—even while acknowledging at the same time that others might legitimately choose from among that range differently.

I hope that readers who reject a particular, narrow conception of Cartesian rationality can recognize something quite different in the account I am proposing here. On the other hand, I hope that readers who consider rationality to be the grounding of their world view can come to see a broader and more inclusive sense of the term. This will require both kinds of readers to set aside certain presuppositions about what "rationality" has come to mean, and what is good or bad about it. While purposely borrowing terminologies such as objectivity, I have tried to give these concepts a very different meaning from their ordinary use.

Finally, this conception of reasoning has an essential *educational* element, not only because of the general problem of how to foster and encourage these characteristics in others, but because the conception requires an educational process at the level of its very definition and justification. In each of the four virtues I have discussed, the process by which we exercise and cultivate these virtues involves us in a set of communicative interactions (and more specifically, educative interactions) with others. These virtues ought to be conceived as *social,* as well as *individual,* attainments. They are neither acquired nor exercised in isolation.

Reasonableness represents an educational aim because it is bound to and illuminates fundamental aspects of how the process of learning itself occurs:

through encountering new, challenging, and often conflicting ideas; through making mistakes and trying to learn from them; through persisting through levels of difficulty and discouragement to something new and worthwhile; and through learning to judge in practice both the applicability and the limits of the general principles and skills one acquires. Each of these, in turn, depends upon a range of communicative and other relations the learner forms with other people. Through these relations we learn to be reasonable.

NOTES

1. This essay has benefited from the comments and suggestions of Kal Alston, Rupert Berk, Chip Bruce, Robert Ennis, Wendy Kohli, Melissa Orlie, Ralph Page, Suzanne Rice, Harvey Siegel, Kenneth Strike, and the participants in the Philosophy of Education Discussion Group at the University of Illinois. Previous versions of this argument were presented formally before the California Association for Philosophy of Education and the Philosophy of Education Society, where colleagues also helped me to develop my thoughts on this subject. See Nicholas C. Burbules, "Rethinking rationality: On learning to be reasonable," in *Philosophy of Education 1993,* Audrey Thompson, ed. (Urbana, IL: Philosophy of Education Society, forthcoming).

2. Michel Serres, "Literature and the exact sciences," *SubStance* (1989) 18(2): 4.

3. These criticisms are discussed in detail in a longer version of the present essay, "Reasonableness as an educational aim: Postmodernism and normativity in the philosophy of education," which is currently in review for publication.

4. Ernest Gellner, *Reason and Culture: The Historic Role of Rationality and Rationalism* (Cambridge, Mass.: Blackwell, 1992), p. 15.

5. Stephen Toulmin, *Cosmopolis: The Hidden Agenda of Modernity* (Chicago: University of Chicago Press, 1990), pp. 199–200.

6. Rene Descartes, *Meditations* in Ralph Eaton, ed., *Descartes Selections* (New York: Charles Scribner, 1927), pp. 88–165.

7. See Gellner, *Reason and Culture,* especially pp. 1–29; Alasdair MacIntyre, *Whose Justice? Which Rationality?* (Notre Dame, IN: University of Notre Dame Press, 1988); Richard Rorty, *Philosophy and the Mirror of Nature* (Princeton, N.J.: Princeton University Press, 1979); Toulmin, *Cosmopolis: The Hidden Agenda of Modernity.*

8. Richard Rorty, *Consequences of Pragmatism* (Minneapolis: University of Minnesota Press, 1982), pp. 164, 171–72.

9. See, for example, Richard Foley, "Some different conceptions of rationality," in Ernan McMullin, ed., *Construction and Constraint: The Shaping of Scientific Rationality* (Notre Dame, IN: University of Notre Dame Press, 1988), pp. 123–152; Ian Hacking, "Language, truth, and reason," in Martin Hollis and Steven Lukes, eds., *Rationality and Relativism* (Cambridge, Mass.: MIT Press, 1982), pp. 48–66; David Schmidtz, "Rationality within reason," *Journal of*

Philosophy, (1992) 89(9): 445–86; Douglas Walton, "What is reasoning? What is an argument?" *Journal of Philosophy*, (1990) 87(8): 399–419.

10. For a lucid overview of this tradition, including an analysis and critique of some of the views I am defending in this essay, see Harvey Siegel, "Reason and rationality" in J. J. Chambliss, ed., *Philosophy of Education: An Encyclopedia* (New York: Garland, forthcoming). For a specific debate over the views of reason discussed here, see Nicholas C. Burbules, "The virtues of reasonableness," and Harvey Siegel, "The rationality of reasonableness," in Margret Buchmann and Robert Floden, eds, *Philosophy of Education 1991* (Normal, Ill.: Philosophy of Education Society, 1992), pp. 215–24 and 225–33.

11. Richard J. Bernstein, *The New Constellation: The Ethical-Political Horizons of Modernity/Postmodernity* (Cambridge, Mass.: MIT Press, 1993), pp. 32–33.

12. An interesting and provocative attempt to engage these issues "from the outside" can be seen in Clive Beck's presidential address to the Philosophy of Education Society, "Postmodernism: Pedagogy and the philosophy of education," in Audrey Thompson, ed. *Philosophy of Education 1993* (Urbana, IL: Philosophy of Education Society, forthcoming).

13. Harvey Siegel, *Relativism Refuted* (Boston: Reidel, 1987).

14. Preliminary versions of this argument can be found in Nicholas C. Burbules, "The virtues of reasonableness," *Philosophy of Education 1991*, Margret Buchmann and Robert Floden, eds. (Normal, IL: Philosophy of Education Society, 1992), 215–24; Nicholas C. Burbules, "Rationality and reasonableness: A discussion of Harvey Siegel's *Relativism Refuted and Educating Reason*," *Educational Theory*, (1991) 41(2): 235–52.

15. For a longer discussion of the postmodern/antimodern distinction, see Nicholas C. Burbules and Suzanne Rice, "Dialogue across differences: Continuing the conversation," *Harvard Educational Review*, (1991) 61: 393–416.

16. Nicholas C. Burbules, "The virtues of reasonableness," and "Rationality and reasonableness." See also Emily Robertson, "Reason and education," in Buchmann and Floden, eds., *Philosophy of Education 1991*, pp. 168–180.

17. For similar arguments, see Max Black, "Reasonableness," in R.F. Dearden, P.H. Hirst, and R.S. Peters, eds., *Education and the Development of Reason* (Boston: RKP, 1972), pp. 199–200 and 205–6; and R.S. Peters, "Reason and passion," in *Education and the Development of Reason*, pp. 214–16.

18. See Robert H. Ennis, "A taxonomy of critical thinking dispositions and abilities," in Joan Boykoff Baron and Robert J. Sternberg, eds., *Teaching Thinking Skills: Theory and Practice* (New York: W.H. Freeman and Co., 1987): 9–26; Richard W. Paul, *Critical Thinking: What Every Person Needs to Survive in a Rapidly Changing World* (Rohnert Park, CA: Center for Critical Thinking and Moral Critique, 1990); and Harvey Siegel, *Educating Reason: Rationality, Critical Thinking, and Education* (New York: Routledge, 1988).

19. Israel Scheffler, "In praise of the cognitive emotions," in *In Praise of the Cognitive Emotions* (New York: Routledge, 1991), pp. 3–17.

20. See, on the other hand, Gilbert Ryle, "A rational animal," in R.F. Dearden, P.H. Hirst, and R.S. Peters, *Education and the Development of Reason*, pp. 176–193.

21. See Suzanne Rice and Nicholas C. Burbules, "Communicative virtues and educational relations," in H.A. Alexander, ed., *Philosophy of Education 1992* (Urbana, IL: Philosophy of Education Society, 1993), pp. 34–44 and Nicholas C. Burbules and Suzanne Rice, "Can we be heard?" *Harvard Educational Review.* This reappropriation and revision of Aristotle's conception of virtue has been strongly influential in feminist moral theory. See especially the work of Martha Nussbaum, *The Fragility of Goodness* (New York: Cambridge University Press, 1986) and *Love's Knowledge* (New York: Oxford University Press, 1990).

22. For an excellent discussion of this point, see Hugh G. Petrie, *The Dilemma of Enquiry and Learning,* (Chicago: University of Chicago Press, 1981), pp. 122–23, 186; and Stephen Toulmin, *Human Understanding* (Princeton, NJ: Princeton University Press, 1972), p. 84.

23. Gellner, *Reason and Culture,* p. 9.

24. Toulmin, *Cosmopolis,* p. 199.

25. Richard Rorty, "Science and solidarity," in John Nelson, Allan Megill, and Donald McCloskey, eds., *The Rhetoric of the Human Sciences* (Madison: University of Wisconsin Press, 1987), p. 40.

26. Charles Taylor, "Rationality," in Hollis and Lukes, eds., p. 105.

27. Richard Rorty, *Philosophy and the Mirror of Nature,* pp. 170–171, 317–318; see also Richard Rorty, *Consequences of Pragmatism,* p. 165.

28. Jurgen Habermas, *Postmetaphysical Thinking: Philosophical Essays* (Cambridge, Mass.: MIT Press, 1992), pp. 38, 39, 117.

29. Seyla Benhabib, *Situating the Self: Gender, Community, and Postmodernism in Contemporary Ethics* (New York: Routledge, 1992), p. 8.

30. T.S. Kuhn, *The Structure of Scientific Revolutions* (Chicago: University of Chicago Press, 1970); for an excellent set of case studies of just how imperfect the process of science is, see Michael Lynch and Steve Woolgar, eds., *Representation in Scientific Practice* (Cambridge, Mass.: MIT Press, 1990).

31. For similar arguments, see Richard J. Bernstein, *Beyond Objectivism and Relativism* (Philadelphia: University of Pennsylvania Press, 1983); Joseph Margolis, *Pragmatism Without Foundations: Reconciling Realism and Relativism* (Oxford: Basil Blackwell, 1986); and Paul Tibbetts, "Representation and the realist-constructivist controversy," in Michael Lynch and Steve Woolgar, eds., *Representation in Scientific Practice,* pp. 69–84.

32. These properly should be regarded as clusters of virtues, not discrete characteristics; nor are these necessarily the only virtues of reasonableness. I do not make any special claims to comprehensiveness here. For two related, though different accounts, see John Dewey's discussion of "traits of individual method" in *Democracy and Education* (New York: Macmillan, 1916), pp. 203–10; and Anthony Quinton's four virtues of belief, in "On the ethics of belief," in Graham Haydon, ed., *Education and Values: The Richard Peters Lectures* (London: The Institute of Education, 1987), pp. 37–55.

33. D. Pole, "The concept of reason," in R.F. Dearden, P.H. Hirst, and R.S. Peters, *Education and the Development of Reason* (Boston: RKP, 1972), p. 154.

34. See Richard Rorty, *Contingency, Irony, and Solidarity*.

35. Burbules and Rice, "Dialogue across differences."

36. Seyla Benhabib, "In the shadow of Aristotle and Hegel: Communicative ethics and current controversies in political philosophy," in Michael Kelly, ed., *Hermeneutics and Critical Theory in Ethics and Politics* (Cambridge, Mass.: MIT Press, 1990), p. 16. See also Burbules and Rice, "Dialogue across differences."

37. Sandra Harding, Rethinking standpoint epistemology: 'What is strong objectivity'?" in Linda Alcoff and Elizabeth Potter, eds., *Feminist Epistemologies* (New York: Routledge, 1993), pp. 54–5, 61; see also Lorraine Code, "Taking subjectivity into account," in *Feminist Epistemologies*, p. 41; Helen Longino, "Subjects, power, and knowledge: Description and prescription in feminist philosophies of science," in *Feminist Epistemologies*, pp. 101–20, and Helen Longino, *Science as Social Knowledge* (Princeton, NJ: Princeton University Press, 1990).

38. Code, "Taking subjectivity into account," p. 40.

39. Donna Haraway, "Situated knowledges: The science question in feminism and the privilege of partial perspective," in *Simians, Cyborgs, and Women: The Reinvention of Nature* (New York: Routledge, 1991), p. 191.

40. Karl R. Popper, The *Logic of Scientific Discovery,* (New York: Basic Books, 1959).

41. Janice Moulton, "A paradigm of philosophy: The adversary method," in Sandra Harding and Merrill B. Hintikka, eds., *Discovering Reality: Feminist Perspectives on Epistemology, Metaphysics, Methodology, and Philosophy of Science* (Dordrecht, Holland: Reidel, 1984), pp. 149–164.

42. See my discussion of how debate can take dialogical and nondialogical forms in Chapter Six of *Dialogue in Teaching: Theory and Practice* (New York: Teachers College Press, 1993).

43. See also Nicholas C. Burbules, "The tragic sense of education," *Teachers College Record,* (1990) 91(4): 468–79.

44. For a very different view of judgment, in the context of teaching, see Hugh G. Petrie, "Knowledge, practice, and judgment," *Educational Foundations,* (1992) 6(1): 35–48.

45. Seyla Benhabib, *Critique, Norm, and Utopia: A Study of the Foundations of Critical Theory* (New York: Columbia University Press, 1986), p. 265; Benhabib, "In the shadow of Aristotle and Hegel," in *Situating the Self,* pp. 35–37; Michael Kelly, "MacIntyre, Habermas, and philosophical ethics," in Michael Kelly, ed., *Hermeneutics and Critical Theory in Ethics and Politics,* p. 83. Habermas seems to be making some steps in this direction; see *Postmetaphysical Thinking,* pp. 136, 139.

46. Benhabib, *Situating the Self,* p. 38.

8

Educating for Emancipatory Rationality

Wendy Kohli

The Enlightenment conception of reason essentially denoted the capacity to know reflectively and bring to realization a way of life consistent with what should be. It was, then, critical, practical, and comprehensive—critical in the sense that it provided criteria for evaluating the given, practical in that it served as a guide to enlightened practice, and comprehensive to the extent that it offered the basis for understanding and determining the ends of human life.[1]

In the most general sense of progressive thought, the Enlightenment has always aimed at liberating men [sic] from fear and establishing their sovereignty. Yet the fully enlightened earth radiates disaster triumphant.[2]

Investments and Beliefs:
Critical Grounding for a Rehabilitated Reason

Elsewhere, I have explored what is at stake in postmodern discourse for philosophers of education, thinkers who historically have grounded their work in the normative and the universal.[3] Here I continue that exploration in relation to reason and rationality, acknowledging at the start my tempered affinity with modernist thought and practices, including my investment in the liberatory potential of reason. As a feminist with my intellectual and political roots in Marxism and the Critical Theory of the Frankfurt School, I have had a contradictory relationship to rationality: at once criticizing reason in the name of reason, and at the same time privileging the role of reason in emancipating human beings from all forms of domination.[4] My commitment to Critical Theory resides in its powerful critique of modern society (particularly the rationalization of the life-world), the domination of nature, and the reduction of action to instrumental means. With regard to the latter, I am particularly interested in the diminution of the possibility for real democracy where individual agents in community take action to determine their futures.

I valued particularly the early work of Max Horkheimer and Theodor Adorno, with their negative critique of modernity that continued the Marxist agenda of analyzing "modern societies in the light of a normatively grounded idea of an emancipated society."[5] Their analysis of the "eclipse of reason," showed how Enlightenment reason lost its liberatory potential when it allied itself with industrial capitalism, becoming primarily instrumental, and ultimately, oppressive. At the same time, they were not satisfied with only criticizing capitalism. Their comprehensive framework let them uncover the negative moment in Marxism, the tendency toward technical rationalization. The Frankfurt School social theorists exposed a Marxism that fell short of its utopian promises when it supported state capitalism—a highly bureaucratized, hierarchical, totalitarian system. Moving the criticism beyond political economy to that of instrumental reason opened the way for Critical Theorists to take a look at the entirety of technical civilization, including the relations of domination between humans and nature, and to some extent those between men and women.[6] The focus of their project, as David Ingram points out, was the paradox posed by the role of reason: "How could rational enlightenment cease to be a force for emancipation and become an instrument of total domination?"[7]

Habermas "stood on the shoulders" of Horkhemier and Adorno, going beyond their "negative critique" by developing a theory of communicative action that allowed him to make categorical distinctions between instrumental and communicative rationality.[8] For Habermas, communicative rationality "expresses a conception of rationality which a speaker must acknowledge, who understands the internal relationship between the raising of intersubjective validity claims and the commitment to give and be receptive to arguments."[9] One important ethical consequence of this understanding of rationality is that "only those norms and normative institutional arrangements are valid . . . which individuals can or would freely consent to as a result of engaging in certain argumentative practices."[10] Implicit in Habermas's theory of communicative processes are the modernist (and some would say, problematic) assumptions that those involved in such communication are committed to "truth, rightness and truthfulness (or authenticity)—whenever they try to reach a mutual understanding . . . and that rational persons are inherently oriented toward something like an unconstrained democratic community."[11]

Attending to Feminist Critiques of Reason and Rationality[12]

It is risky for a feminist to rehabilitate the Enlightenment belief in reason as a means to freedom in this postmodern epoch. There are compelling warnings to avoid such a stance. Various feminists, through their trenchant critiques of rationality within ethics and epistemology have exposed, among other things, the identification of reason with maleness and un-reason with femaleness. Geneveive Lloyd reminds us of the powerful Cartesian legacy we have inherited: "The search for the 'clear and distinct,' [involves] the separating out of the emotional, the sensuous, the imaginative."[13] This separating, this shedding of the sensual and the corporeal, required a particular kind of training. Men had to *learn* to be rational; they had to be trained out of soft emotions and their sensuousness.[14] And women were "excluded from this training in reason."[15] Without this necessary training for rationality women were "*left* emotional, impulsive, fancy ridden"—less rational than men.[16]

Accompanying this distorted inheritance is a gendered division of labor with regard to reason and the emotions: women "are to provide comfort, relief, entertainment and solace for the austerity that being a Man of Reason demands."[17] Women are taught, with some exceptions, that "reason rather than emotion [is] regarded as the indispensable faculty for acquiring knowledge."[18] Emotions were seen not only as unimportant to knowing and acting, but they were viewed as "nonrational and often irrational urges that regularly swept the body rather as a storm sweeps over the land."[19]

How are we to respond to this gendered dichotomy between reason and emotion? Valerie Walkerdine, Marie Fleming, Elizabeth Minnich, and other feminists have argued that it isn't just a matter of "add women and stir" to the traditional conception of "rational man." We must move beyond the construction of the rational self as a "profoundly masculine one," and reason as a "capacity invested within the body and . . . mind of the man, from which the female was, by definition, excluded."[20] This will require, among other things, eradicating the reason/emotion split and the myth of the "man of reason as an ethical ideal" that has been cultivated since Descartes.[21]

Alison Jaggar has taken on the difficult task of transforming the relationship between reason and emotion and suggests that "emotions may be helpful and even necessary rather than inimical to the construction of knowledge."[22] She argues that "human emotions are neither instinctive nor biologically determined. Instead, they are socially constructed on several levels."[23] Drawing on contemporary sociological and anthropological research, she suggests that human emotions are "simultaneously made possible and limited by the conceptual and linguistic resources of society."[24] She also maintains that emotions "are wrongly seen as necessarily passive or involuntary responses to the world. Rather, they are ways in which we engage actively and even construct the world."[25]

One implication of this perspective is that people can be taught different ways to understand and experience emotions. Emotions are not inherently *natural,* biological. Just as identities are socially constructed, so too are the meanings that are attached to feelings and emotions. Emotions depend on our perceptions of our situations "as well as on the ways that we have learned or decided to respond to them."[26] They also depend upon how we are constituted by race, class, gender, and sexuality. As Jaggar and other feminists note, throughout western history "reason has been associated with members of dominant political, social, and cultural groups and emotion with members of subordinate groups."[27] In order to have a reconstructed notion of reason (and by implication, of emotion), we must transform the hegemonic relations that reinforce this distorted relationship and "construct a model that demonstrates the mutually constitutive rather than oppositional relation between reason and emotion."[28]

Another dimension of the feminist critique is the problematic universalizing of enlightenment reason and the sovereignty of the unified, human/ rational self. Instead of taking for granted as humanly inclusive the "concepts, theories, objective methodologies, and transcendental truths" that are part of the received tradition, feminists such as Sandra Harding and Christine DiStefano are urging an examination of the way these products of enlightenment are marked by gender, class, race, and culture.[29] Not to examine these markers is to perpetuate a "fiction" based on "distortions, perversions, exploitations and subjugations."[30] Lois McNay continues this critique; these "supposedly objective, impartial standards such as universal reason . . . are in fact historically situated and contingent terms, often extrapolations of masculine characteristics and values that serve to legitimize and reproduce a dominantly masculine culture."[31]

Feminists have also made particular charges against Critical Theory, even with its supposed "emancipatory" reason. Seyla Benhabib, citing the research of Carol Gilligan, focuses on the communicative ethics of Habermas. She criticizes his theory on the grounds that "like other formalistic, universalist moral theories, [he] only accommodates the moral perspective of the 'generalized other'."[32] Benhabib also notes that Habermas' work, like most modern moral and political theory, tends "to subordinate the standpoint of the concrete other, which it consigns to the private sphere of the family, to the standpoint of the generalized other, which is legally institutionalized in the public sphere."[33]

Benhabib extends her criticism by challenging Habermas's strong reliance on consensus and instead offers it "more as a regulative *ideal.*"[34] She insists that it is more important to focus on the validity of the procedures or process than on the reaching of agreements. For her, the procedures must be "radically open and fair to all."[35] It is her insistence on radical openness that insures more inclusive public discourse than Habermas. She is committed to welcoming "the voices of those whose 'interests' may not be formulable in the accepted language of public discourse."[36] Benhabib wants them in the conversation for moral ends; she believes that their "very presence in public life may force the boundaries between private needs and public claims, individual misfortunes and collectively representable grievances."[37]

Drawing on Hannah Arendt's concept of "enlarged thinking," Benhabib retains a universalizing ethics while taking the stance of the concrete other. This enables us to see "every moral person as a unique individual, with a certain life history, disposition and endowment, as well as needs and limitations."[38] Benhabib's goal, similar to mine, is to retain a kind of "postEnlightenment" universalism while at the same time acknowledging the historical situatedness of identity and politics. Part of her effort is to name gender as one of the contingencies of modern communication and ethics, something Habermas neglects to do.

It is this neglect of gender by Habermas that leaves most feminists cautious about relying on a theory of communicative reason as the basis for a more democratic, rational society. Even Benhabib's commitment to the inclusion of women in dialogue is suspect for, as Marie Fleming asks, "how [is this inclusion] possible within a system of valuing in which women are structurally and necessarily devalued? The participants in communicative reason may be equal, but they are also masculine."[39] This is the case, Fleming insists, even with Benhabib's energetic "effort to make room for the 'other' sex" in communicative discourse.[40] At the same time, Fleming reluctantly grants that there just may be some saving grace in communicative reason. She resists rejecting it out of hand given that it "privileges the dialogical and promises to accommodate the historical," two key criteria for a feminist reconceptualization of reason.[41]

These feminist analyses extend and transform other philosophical criticisms that have targeted the all-too-familiar dualisms separating reason from emotion, mind from body, knowledge from experience, means from ends, theory from practice, public from private. Abstract, static, instrumental, regulative reason, with its accompanying bifurcations, has undergone the (varying) scrutiny of phenomenologists, pragmatists, Marxists, Critical Theorists and poststructuralists, as well as philosophers informed by Eastern religions.

Situating my own thinking in a Critical-feminist context, I share many of these concerns and am aware of the limiting, even exclusionary features of the dominant Western view of reason, even *critical* reason. But I also agree with those feminists who have argued that at particular historical junctures, reason has served as a liberating force for women and other subordinated groups.[42] Hence, I want to "reconstruct" reason's liberatory potential, taking into account these important criticisms. I believe, along with Chris Weedon that, "we cannot afford to abandon reason entirely to the interests of patriarchy. Reason, like experience, requires both deconstruction and reconstruction in the interests of feminism,"[43] and in the interests of Philosophy of Education. By rescuing reason from its instrumental purposes, and from the seventeenth century legacy of the disembedded/disembodied (male) ego, we may be more able to articulate what it means to educate rational persons-in-community with the capacity to create a more rational society. From a Habermasian point of view, this "more rational society" would be one that did not allow "scientific and technological values to occlude or otherwise prevent moral and aesthetic values from having a structure-building effect for society as a whole; nor would it be fully rational if the economy and state absorbed the communicative lifeworld."[44]

Creating such a rational society requires an expanded, integrated, even transformed notion of reason that takes into account the oppressive social conditions that keep particular groups of people marginalized, labeled, and disempowered. It also requires new practices to empower people to move out of and beyond their subjugated positions. These practices, including but not limited to "public, unrestricted discussion, free from domination,"[45] are embedded in a radical notion of democracy that is committed to the liberation of all people.

Reason, Difference and Oppression

Any notion of dialogical or communicative reason must take into account the differences between and among people. Without attending to the particular, situated experiences of different groups of people, different subjectivities, different identity positions, concepts such as freedom, democracy, and equality ring hollow.

When I speak of "difference" I do not mean simply the variety or diversity of human experience. I mean the *persistent social* differences that result from systemic practices that create unequal and difficult conditions for people to flourish. These differences are the social effects of *oppression:* "the systematic, institutionalized mistreatment of one group of people by another."[46] In contemporary United States, oppression takes such forms as racism, sexism, classism, ageism, adultism, homophobia, anti-Semitism, and ableism.

By incorporating a theory of oppression into a reconstructed understanding of communicative rationality, we may be better able to explain why it is that people don't all "come to the table as equals"; why some people, even some groups of people have the "dispositions" necessary to engage in "rational discourse" and others do not; why some have been "defined out" of the entire process. We need to move away from looking at differences in one's capacity to think and act "rationally" as simply individual deficiencies. Instead, they must be seen as the social effects of oppression.[47]

The flipside to the externally imposed, institutionalized forms of oppression is *internalized* oppression. Gloria Yamato states it powerfully when she says members of the targeted group are emotionally, physically, and

> spiritually battered to the point that they begin to actually believe that their oppression is deserved, is there lot in life, is natural and right, and that it doesn't even exist. The oppression begins to feel comfortable enough that when "ol'Massa lay down de whip, we got's to pick up and whack ourselves and each other."[48]

Several early Frankfurt School theorists, like Herbert Marcuse, who tried to integrate Marx with Freud understood this concept without naming it as such. Their analysis convinced them that traditional Marxism "was inadequate in comprehending the subjective dimension of social life."[49] Marcuse articulated this important realization when he asked rhetorically:

> Are revolutions perhaps not only defeated, reversed and undone from outside; is there not perhaps in the individuals themselves already a dynamic at work which *internally* negates a possible liberation and gratification, and allows them to submit not only externally to the forces of denial?[50]

This insight is similar to those expressed decades ago by Franz Fanon and Paulo Freire and by contemporary feminist theorists such as bell hooks, Audre Lorde, and Toni Morrison, who have written movingly about the "subjective dimension of the reproduction of domination."[51]

Members of certain targeted groups, such as women, working class people, people of color, or gay and lesbian people, "internalize" the misinformation that circulates in the "external" society. When we take in the systematic lies and distortions about ourselves that are filtered through institutions such as schools and the media, we begin to believe them. We also begin to develop certain "patterns of feeling and modes of behavior" that reflect negative self-images, negative identities.[52] These patterns of feeling often take the form of powerlessness, anger, fear, or hopelessness. They also may be seen by others, particularly those who have more power or status, as deficiencies.

Those of us committed to expanding liberty and social justice, to furthering a substantive participatory democracy, to having a more comprehensive understanding of a truly "rational" society, need to understand the pervasive and persistent existence of internalized oppression and how it shapes virtually every social situation, every dialogue, every communicative interaction. It is inadequate to equate one's capacities for rational discourse in terms of individual "dispositions." Those capacities must be unpacked with a theory of internalized oppression to see that dispositions can have a silencing effect on some and a privileging effect on others. "Race, gender, class and sexual identity" is not just a slogan or political litany, although it may sound like that to some. We *are* raced, gendered, sexed, classed and this has important implications for the way we think and act, for how others interact with us.

Reason, Emotion and Communication

To a great extent, given the way the discourse of reason has been inscribed in Western cultural practices, most people who have suffered under oppressive conditions often seem "un-reasonable" in public conversation; they do not fit the profile or have the attributes needed in the dominant (white, middle class, masculine) discourse.

Furthermore, these marginalized groups may end up exhibiting attitudes, beliefs and behaviors that become reified as identities; the *effects* of oppressive conditioning are conflated with the *essence* of who they are. For example, women become in the eyes of many, care-taking, emotional, intuitive, passive, irrational, beings. The historical conditions responsible for these characteristics are often overlooked, leaving us with essentialized understandings of *what it means to be a woman*. Some feminist analyses of "women's voice" and "women's ways of knowing" promote this essentialism.[53] Those resisting this ahistorical view of women's identity, such as Elizabeth Minnich, observe that

> what we find by studying the "woman's voice" *now* may not only not be *the* woman's voice, but may specifically not be the or a, voice that we would hear had women not been oppressed so systematically for so long.[54]

Benhabib, and to a certain extent Habermas, want to accommodate difference in their communicative scenarios. In fact, Benhabib is explicitly committed to those who have been marginalized by their "different" language, habits and affect. Yet, those who are "different," those who have been excluded, those who have experienced years of oppressive conditioning, may have many *feelings* attached to their difference. Their emotions may be at odds with the way the dominant culture expects them to respond. They may even express what Jaggar calls "outlaw" emotions, those emotions experienced by "subordinated individuals who pay a disproportionately high price for maintaining the status quo."[55]

So, it is not just about *including* more voices or perspectives in the conversation. These newly included voices may be amplified by anger, even rage. They may be diminished by fear, embarrassment, or inadequacy. And they may be filled with grief and grievance. Neither Benhabib nor Habermas acknowledges the complexity of the affective dimensions of communicative reason. What happens to these feelings when they enter the conversation? How are they incorporated? If expressed, can the communication remain "reasonable?"

Most "rational" people would agree that a conversation in which deep anger or rage is expressed, particularly if directed at some of the participants, would not meet the criteria of a mutually-respectful dialogue. Yet, to be truly committed to enlarging the conversation, to creating a more inclusive public discourse, it will no longer do to render these feelings invisible or to see them simply as moral deficiencies. Any theory of communicative reason that is reaching for more radical democratic participation must incorporate a strategy for dealing with the emotions that are intricately related to historically marginalized, disenfranchised groups. One possible strategy is to encourage people to take turns listening to one another as they vent feelings associated with the forms of oppression they suffer due to their particular location in society. Once the feelings are expressed, listened to, and reflected upon, clearer thinking may result, leading to better communication.

It is possible for men and women, for those in dominant positions and those in subjugated positions, to live more "rationally" in the world. But this will require more than developing the skills of rational argument and critical thinking, or attaining a degree of linguistic proficiency, or even developing communicative virtues.[56] It will entail the development of new structures and processes that attend to the emotional effects of internalized oppression.

An expanded notion of the practice of communicative reason that builds in such opportunities to express, in mutually agreed upon sessions, these feelings associated with one's socially constructed identities and one's experience on the margins, must be developed.[57] If this is done, we will be in a better position to create truly democratic communities that can support rational communication and interaction of equals. Through this reinvigorated "communicative reason," the inherent connections between thought and feeling, mind and body, reason and emotion, public and private will have been acknowledged. And we will be able to think and act more clearly (rationally) as a result.

Educating for Reason and Rational Action: A CODA

Enlightenment thinkers from Hobbes and Descartes to Rousseau, Locke and Kant believed that reason is a natural disposition of the human mind, which when governed by proper education can discover certain truths. It was furthermore assumed that the clarity and distinctness of these truths or the vivacity of their impact upon our senses would be sufficient to ensure intersubjective agreement among like-thinking rational minds.[58]

Historically, rational thought was supposed to lead to enlightened action, to the development of rational citizens who would perfect the world. There was a direct link between reason and freedom, reason and democracy, reason and action. Reason was to bring light into the darkness, to disabuse people of superstition and tradition, to liberate them from certain forms of bondage.

The transformation of the Enlightenment ideal of reason to the modern, instrumental form that has engulfed us in the twentieth century has led to a paralysis; many of us are skeptical of the possibility to effect systematic change. For too long, those who have criticized particular social/political/economic arrangements such as monopoly capitalism, have failed to provide the theoretical insight for why oppressed people at times appear to collude in their own oppression.

Social theorists, even dialectical Marxists, have subscribed to a notion of ideology that assumes "social subjects create culture and consciousness in a straightforward, rational, linear way proceeding to revolutionary action."[59] Even those with the most emancipatory theories have failed to see the important role emotions play in social change. Those social theorists who continue to separate reason from emotion, and who do not understand the emotional/psychological dimensions of oppression, end up with an inadequate theory of change. Even those who understood the powerful effects of hegemony, such as Antonio Gramsci, and who paid attention to the "structures of feeling" that are deeply embedded in us, such as Raymond Williams, did not make the connection that we *need to express emotions* in order to think and act more clearly and powerfully.

I am interested in educating people to see their oppression more clearly, to encourage them to discharge the feelings that are keeping them fearful, powerless, or enraged, and then assisting them to act decisively on their clear thoughts and analysis of the situation before them.

This educative process is similar to and extends Freire's notion of a "pedagogy of the oppressed," and resembles feminist pedagogy as well. Both of these liberatory pedagogies offer a way for people to reclaim their rationality and their power. A missing piece for both of these approaches may be what Sherover-Marcuse calls the "practice of subjectivity."[60] This practice would "begin the healing of wounds sustained in an oppressive society."[61]

Modern educational theory and practice is riddled with Cartesian rationalism, with a narrow, static, instrumental view that separates the wheat from the chaff, the "rational" from the "irrational." So often, those in the latter category "just happen" to be women, people of color and other politically and socially marginalized groups. It is also a view of rationality that excludes other ways of thinking, other ways of being rational. Education is infused with an exclusive notion of rationality that limits and delimits our possibilities for creativity, democracy and freedom. It leads to immense conformity, for if we cross the border, we are often labeled "irrational." The fear of being called a witch, or "crazy," or in philosophical circles "wrongheaded," keeps most of us in line, most of the time.

My vision is that we dismantle the societal conditions that deny women, people of color, poor people, Jewish people, gay and lesbian people, disabled people, men—all of us—our full humanity. I think that through a reconstructed view of rational action we can begin to do just that.

NOTES

1. Frank Hearn, *Reason and Freedom in Sociological Thought* (Boston: Allen and Unwin, 1985), p. 15.

2. Max Horkheimer and Theodor W. Adorno, *Dialectic of Enlightenment* (New York: Herder and Herder, 1972), p. 3.

3. Wendy Kohli, "Postmodernism and the 'New' Pedagogies: What's At Stake in the Discourse?," *Education and Society*, Volume 9 Number 1 (1991), 39–46.

4. See Stephen Leonard, *Critical Theory in Political Practice* (New Jersey: Princeton University Press, 1990), p. 9.

5. Albrecht Wellmer, "Reason and Utopia and the *Dialectic of Enlightenment*," in Richard Bernstein, ed., *Habermas and Modernity* (Massachusetts: MIT Press, 1985), p. 50.

6. See the essay "Juliette or Enlightenment and Morality" in *Dialectic of Enlightenment*, pp. 81–119.

7. David Ingram, *Critical Theory and Philosophy* (New York: Paragon House, 1990), p. 59.

8. Wellmer, in Bernstein (1985), p. 51.

9. Wellmer, in Bernstein (1985), p. 52.

10. Seyla Benhabib, *Situating the Self: Gender, Community and Postmodernism in Contemporary Ethics* (New York: Routledge, 1992), p. 24.

11. Ingram, *Critical Theory and Philosophy* (1990), pp. 185–86.

12. There is no *one* feminist position on rationality, or on *anything* for that matter. There is a range of diverse and even contradictory philosophical and political positions under the rubric of feminist theory/philosophy. I am merely sketching out some of the common objections to the traditional Enlightenment notion of reason.

13. Genevieve Lloyd, "The Man of Reason," in Garry and Pearsall, ed., *Women, Knowledge and Reality: Explorations in Feminist Philosophy* (Boston: Unwin Hyman, 1989), p. 116.

14. Lloyd, in Garry and Pearsall, p. 117.

15. Lloyd, in Garry and Pearsall, p. 116.

16. Lloyd, in Garry and Pearsall, pp. 116–17.

17. Lloyd, in Garry and Pearsall, p. 117.

18. Alison Jaggar, in Garry and Pearsall, p. 129.

19. Jaggar, in Garry and Pearsall, p. 130.

20. Valerie Walkerdine, *Schoolgirl Fictions* (London: Verso, 1990), p. 67.

21. Lloyd, in Garry and Pearsall, p. 118.

22. Jaggar, in Garry and Pearsall, p. 131.

23. Jaggar, in Garry and Pearsall, p. 134.

24. Jaggar, in Garry and Pearsall, p. 135.

25. Jaggar, in Garry and Pearsall, p. 137.

26. Jaggar, in Garry and Pearsall, p. 138.

27. Jaggar, in Garry and Pearsall, p. 141.

28. Jaggar, in Garry and Pearsall, p. 141.

29. Christine DiStefano, "Dilemmas of Difference," in Linda Nicholson, ed., *Feminism/Postmodernism* (New York: Routledge, 1990), p. 73.

30. Sandra Harding as quoted in Garry and Pearsall, p. 75.

31. Lois McNay, *Foucault and Feminism: Power, Gender and the Self* (Boston: Northeastern University Press, 1992), p. 91.

32. Ingram, *Critical Theory and Philosophy,* p. 207.

33. Ingram, *Critical Theory and Philosophy,* p. 208.

34. Benhabib, *Situating the Self,* p. 9.

35. Benhabib, *Situating the Self,* p. 9.

36. Benhabib, *Situating the Self,* p. 9.

37. Benhabib, *Situating the Self,* p. 9.

38. Benhabib, *Situating the Self,* p. 10.

39. Marie Fleming, "Women's Place in Communicative Reason," in Elizabeth Harvey and Kathleen Okruhlik, eds., *Women and Reason* (Michigan: University of Michigan Press, 1992), p. 256.

40. Fleming in Harvey and Okruhlik, p. 253.

41. Fleming, in Harvey and Okruhlik, p. 248.

42. Elizabeth Harvey and Kathleen Okruhlik, "Introduction," in Harvey and Okruhlik, p. 2.

43. Chris Weedon, *Feminist Practice and Poststructuralist Theory* (Oxford: Basil Blackwell Ltd., 1987), p. 10.

44. Ingram, *Critical Theory and Philosophy* (1990), p. 186.

45. Jurgen Habermas, *Toward a Rational Society: Student Protest, Science and Politics* (Boston: Beacon Press, 1970), p. 118.

46. Gloria Yamato, "Something About the Subject Makes It Hard to Name," in Gloria Anzaldua, *Making Face, Making Soul: Creative and Critical Perspectives by Feminists of Color* (San Francisco: Aunt Lute Books, 1990), p. 20.

47. See for example Valerie Walkerdine's poststructuralist account of reason and gender in *Schoolgirl Fictions,* pp. 67–73.

48. Yamato in Anzaldua, p. 20.

49. Erica Sherover-Marcuse, *Emancipation and Consciousness: Dogmatic and Dialectical Perspectives in the Early Marx* (Oxford: Basil Blackwell, 1986), p. 134.

50. Herbert Marcuse as quoted in Sherover-Marcuse, p. 134.

51. Sherover-Marcuse, p. 135.

52. Sherover-Marcuse, p. 135.

53. See for example the work of Mary Bilenky, et al., *Women's Ways of Knowing* (New York: Basic Books, 1986).

54. Elizabeth Minnich, *Transforming Knowledge* (Philadelphia: Temple University Press, 1990), p. 115.

55. Alison Jaggar, in Garry and Pearsall, p. 144.

56. See the companion piece to mine by Nick Burbules in this volume.

57. Not to be misunderstood, I am not calling for "free for alls" where anyone has license to dump on other people. I am speaking about structured exchanges with agreed upon guidelines.

58. Benhabib, *Situating the Self,* p. 4.

59. See my essay, "Raymond Williams, Affective Ideology, and Counter-Hegemonic Practices," in Dennis Dworkin and Leslie Roman, *Views Beyond the Border Country: Raymond Williams and Cultural Politics* (New York: Routledge, 1992), pp. 115–16.

60. Sherover-Marcuse, *Emancipation and Consciousness,* p. 135.

61. Sherover-Marcuse, *Emancipation and Consciousness,* p. 135.

9

Reconceiving Reason

Emily Robertson

Defending Rationality as an Educational Ideal

Despite the current "rage against reason,"[1] neither Burbules nor Kohli proposes abandoning the development of rationality as an educational ideal. Instead each seeks to "reconstruct" or rehabilitate" that ideal as depicted in the traditions of Western philosophical thought. They criticize a particular conception of reason, not rationality itself. Along with postmodernist critics of reason, they reject "the fantasies of the Positivist, who would replace the vast complexity of human reason with a kind of intellectual Walden II."[2] But neither are they content to simply "unmask the imaginary purity of reason."[3] Rejecting both the myth of pure reason and the reduction of all rational discussion to relations of power, they attempt to develop a more adequate understanding of reason as embodied in human relationships.

For Burbules, the problem with the dominant Western philosophical account of rationality lies in its focus on an overly narrow conception of reason that assumes objective and universal standards sufficient to resolve disputes about truth, value, or action. Against this account, Burbules affirms a conception of rationality compatible with fallibilism and pluralism, one which rejects the "formal, decontextualized language" of "Cartesian rationality" for "a discourse more concerned with personal character, practical contexts, and communicative relations." He emphasizes that knowing how to think well is not sufficient for being rational; traits of character are required as well, indeed, are more primary components of rationality, or reasonableness. Burbules argues for developing the virtues of reasonableness—striving for objectivity, accepting fallibilism, maintaining a pragmatic attitude, and judiciousness—against what he sees as the tendency of traditional Philosophy of Education to emphasize acquiring specific techniques of rational thought and critical thinking skills. Given that rational patterns of thought cannot always (perhaps even, often) be made explicit in sets of rules, these virtues, Burbules believes, are an essential part of rationality, and not simply dispositions to apply the rules of reason. They are "very general human traits that . . . broadly guide reflective thought and action," are "part of who we are," and explain why we care about abiding by standards for rational judgment in the first place. The merits Burbules finds in rationality as reasonableness include: its acknowledgment of alternative forms of reasoning (which makes it less open to postmodernist charges that reason is a source of oppression or domination); its insistence that epistemic value is not independent of moral and political value; its grounding of rationality in social relations (with the implication that irrationality may be the result of social circumstances rather than individual error); and its recognition of the role of "commitment, caring, and feeling" in rationality. For these reasons, Burbules believes that reasonableness is a more fruitful guide for our educational aims than is the conception of reason he rejects.

For Kohli, neither the "skills of rational argument and critical thinking" nor the development of "communicative virtues" of reasonableness are enough to help us "live more rationally." The rationality Kohli seeks is strongly tied to participatory democracy and the consensual development of social norms and normative institutional arrangements through dialogue. Her concern is for full and free participation of all members of society in this dialogue. She is concerned that we understand how "internalized oppression" may diminish oppressed persons' capacities for rational dialogue conducted according to conventional standards. She argues that capacities for rational discourse cannot be understood simply in terms of individual dispositions: "We must unpack those capacities with a theory of internalized oppression. When we do, we will see that dispositions can have a silencing effect on some and a privileging effect on others." Those who have suffered from oppression may seem "'unreasonable' in public conversation; they do not fit the profile or have the attributes needed in the dominant (white, middle class, masculine) discourse." Furthermore, even if these voices are included in the conversation, they "may be amplified by anger, even rage, . . . diminished by fear, embarrassment or inadequacy, and . . . filled with grief and grievance." How can these feelings be expressed and acknowledged in a reasonable conversation, Kohli wonders? She holds that the prospects for enlisting a communicative reason in the interest of a more radically democratic politics will require developing strategies for dealing with the emotions of marginalized groups. She proposes holding meetings in which such emotions can be "expressed, listened to and reflected upon" so that "clearer thinking may result, leading to better communication."

I agree with Burbules' and Kohli's shared goals of reconstructing reason and defending the development of (a reconstructed) rationality as an educational aim. Each focuses on neglected aspects of rationality, the virtues of reasonableness and the role of emotion in rational discourse, a focus which expands our understanding of rationality without denying the contributions of previous work on this topic in Philosophy of Education. For example, developing the virtues of reasonableness is not a sufficient educational goal for one interested in fostering rationality: training in particular traditions of rational thought is required as well (I imagine Burbules would agree). Being willing to entertain alternative points of view, open to admitting error, sensitive to human needs and purposes, and cognizant of the limits of reason will not in themselves allow one to decide between two scientific hypotheses, make wise judgments in moral matters, or construct a sound philosophical argument. Thus Burbules's proposals do not so much replace the tradition's emphasis on modes of reasoning as supplement it. And Kohli's efforts to rehabilitate emancipatory rationality reinstate a traditional connection between reason and freedom, although she, like Burbules, would reserve the right to substantially modify that tradition. In the following, I have chosen to concentrate on two aspects of their work: Burbules's attention to the social construction of rationality and Kohli's account of the relationship between emotion and reason.

The Immanence and Transcendence of Reason

Putnam has argued that "reason is . . . both immanent (not to be found outside of concrete language games and institutions) and transcendent (a regulative idea that we use to criticize the conduct of *all* activities and institutions)."[4] A similar distinction is made by Habermas in his theory of communicative rationality, the theory Kohli attempts to reconstruct and make the basis for her defense of reason as a means to freedom. Habermas says that, in the making of validity claims for propositions and norms,

> the validity laid claim to is distinguished from the social currency of a de facto established practice and yet serves it as the foundation of an existing consensus. The validity claimed for propositions and norms transcends spaces and times, *"blots out" space and time;* but the claim is always raised *here and now,* in specific contexts, and is either accepted or rejected with factual consequences for action.[5]

For one who agrees with this view, as I do, an acceptable account of rationality must properly acknowledge *both* the immanence and the transcendence of reason. Achieving this goal means resisting the tendency within the philosophical tradition to emphasize one at the expense of the other. Habermas has observed that

> ever since Plato and Democritus, the history of philosophy has been dominated by two opposed impulses: One relentlessly elaborates the transcendent power of abstractive reason and the emancipatory unconditionality of the intelligible, whereas the other strives to unmask the imaginary purity of reason in a materialist fashion.[6]

Burbules's reconceptualization of rationality causes concern in that, in trying to give proper due to the sense in which reason is a "human invention . . . growing out of communicative interactions," Burbules has depreciated the necessary transcendence of reason. He says that, on his view, "the epistemic dimension of reasonableness . . . is inverted": the question is no longer, "What procedures of inquiry or argument are most likely to yield the truth?" but rather, "When people have sought to understand the truth of their situation, what are the general patterns of investigation that they have settled upon over time?" It is true that the only procedures and standards for pursuing truth are embodied in traditions of rational inquiry which have evolved over time in the context of actual investigations. Nevertheless, that those standards themselves can be rationally criticized shows that the conception of rationality is not to be wholly identified with any existing standards.

What is the relationship between the transcendent and the immanent aspects of reason? Transcendent reason expresses a truth about what is ordinarily meant when we assert that one proposition provides a reason for believing another. Immanent reason expresses the facts of our actual epistemic situation, that is, it provides the correct description of our practices of appraisal and evaluation. In asserting that R is a good reason for believing P, we don't mean to be relativizing the truth of our claim to our own conceptual framework, nor is any such relativization implicit in what is said. However, evaluation, appraisal, reason-giving is in fact always done from the perspective of some framework or other. As McCarthy has said, "We can make historically situated and fallible claims to universal validity."[7]

Those who deny the immanence of reason take the linguistic point embodied in the transcendence of reason as establishing the existence of criteria of rationality independent of time and place that can be employed in the evaluation of all existing traditions of rationality. They engage in what Putnam describes as "characteristic philosophical fantasies" (in which he includes the positivists' search for the ideal language, an inductive logic, and the empiricist criterion of significance).[8] Those who deny the transcendence of reason attempt to "naturalize" reason by identifying it with humanly constructed and evolving traditions of rationality; they in effect deny the distinction between epistemology and sociology. For example, in showing that the currently existing traditions embody sexist or racist assumptions, some critics take themselves to have undermined reason itself. Yet, what appear to be challenges to reason per se on closer inspection often are attacks on some particular conception of reason as embodied in a given intellectual tradition; they frequently are attempts to "unmask the imaginary purity of reason in a materialist fashion." Understood as critiques of existing traditions, as (in Kohli's terms) "criticizing reason in the name of reason," they can be enormously helpful. But if they reject truth for rhetoric and reason for power, they deny any role to the regulative idea of reason as transcendent.

Reason is immanent within the myriad substantive traditions of inquiry that arise as human beings in specific historical and cultural locations attempt to understand their world and decide how to live in it. Philosophical theories of rationality are sometimes attempts to criticize, or rationally reconstruct, particular traditions of reason, as in the Philosophy of Science, for example. On the other hand, some theories are attempts to analyze reason as transcendent, to understand the function of this "regulative idea."

As part of a general characterization of reason as a regulative idea, I agree with de Sousa that rationality is "a teleological concept," a view Burbules "distrusts."[9] On the teleological conception, rational belief aims at truth, rational action at success, rational desire at the good, and so on, however these end states are defined.[10] Burbules prefers to think of us as proceeding "not towards truth, but away from error." But the regulative idea of rationality as aiming at truth reminds us of the point of the enterprise. Embedded in the concept of rational judgment is the assumption that some ways of forming beliefs or deciding how to act or what ends to seek are more likely to meet with success than are others. The modes of judgment and the reasons they provide are not properly thought of as *merely* instrumental means to their ends, however, but must recommend the belief or action in question: rationality is a normative concept.[11] Nevertheless, if a well-designed experiment was thought no more reliable a method for assessing the truth of a scientific hypothesis than flipping a coin, it would not form part of a tradition of scientific rationality.

Thus, on the teleological analysis, to abandon the regulative idea of rationality would require either rejection of the goals of rationality (truth, strategic success of action, a good life, etc.) or extreme scepticism about the claims of any forms of judgment (any traditions of reason) to be better ways of reaching these goals. Perhaps some critics have taken one of these routes. More common are criticisms of particular philosophical accounts of reason as transcendent, or of particular traditions of how to achieve rationality in belief, desire or action, currently, especially of accounts stemming from positivism.

This brief sketch of the standpoint of rationality requires further elaboration. Nothing follows from the bare teleological analysis of rationality about the character or success of any substantive tradition of rational thought. The lesson of the immanence of reason is that accounts of reason as transcendent do not generate criteria of rational assessment. Furthermore, the teleological analysis should be understood as compatible with the following observations concerning the actual institutions and practices of reason (reason as immanent): (1) Rationality of thought or action is neither necessary nor sufficient for success. Irrational beliefs can be true and rational ones false. Irrational actions can achieve the agent's goals and rational ones fail. Rational forms of thinking do not need to be algorithms such that, when followed rightly, they must yield the correct results. All that is required for the concept of rationality to have purchase is that some forms of thinking typically are better than others in achieving the desired results. (2) Forms of rational judgment are not necessarily formalizable in explicit rules. Rationality may require tacit knowledge which can be taught and learned without being made explicit. (3) Rational judgment does not always yield one best answer—one true description of the world, one best way to live. Alternative beliefs and courses of action may be rational in the same circumstances. Rationality does not require us to "give up our pluralism."[12] (4) As it is commonly put these days, the practices of rational thinking are "human constructions." However, it doesn't follow that there are no constraints on our constructions. If mind does not mirror the world, neither does it make it up. Our traditions of rationality may reflect our interests and choices, but some traditions prove better than others in accomplishing our purposes. (5) It must be acknowledged, however, that our "purposes" are not entirely independent of our traditions of rationality, and, hence, are not totally external measures of success. Methods, standards, and goals of rationality evolve together. None of them is sufficiently independent to provide foundations for the others. Yet, from science to ethics, it does not follow that "anything goes;" relativism is not a necessary consequence of the failure of foundationalism.[13]

What is the significance of the distinction between reason as immanent and reason as transcendent for understanding the development of rationality as an education aim? I have suggested that the regulative idea of rationality, interpreted according to the teleological analysis, reminds us of the point of the enterprise. Commitment to the ends of rationality in its various domains is a constitutive part of the ideal. To teach the current traditions of rational thought, and even the communicative virtues, without conveying the point of it all, without fostering a passion for the pursuit of truth or for leading a morally good life or being an effective agent, is to teach the forms of rationality without the purpose.

Reason and Emotion

A friend once said to me in the midst of a conversation, "You're the most *reasonable* person I know." It was not a compliment. Although I didn't initially understand his perspective, I've come to realize that what he wanted from me in that moment was not my rational assessment of his situation, but my emotional support. He wanted me to acknowledge that the world was unfair, that he had been wronged, and that I supported him. Determining a rational response could wait. This anecdote suggests the kind of relationship between emotion and reason I believe Kohli has in mind. I think she is right to be concerned about the affective dimensions of rationality. However, I worry that her account of venting or discharging feelings in order to proceed with clearer thinking may be read as reinforcing an unwarranted dichotomy between reason and emotion, a dichotomy both Kohli and Burbules want to overcome. In place of this view I would suggest a more cognitive role for the emotions, one in which emotions are seen as a potential source of knowledge and hence as part of the rational process. Emotions have a role in determining rational action. Like Jaggar, I think "emotions may be helpful and even necessary, rather than inimical, to the construction of knowledge."[14] Emotions are complex and difficult to understand, however, both philosophically and scientifically. The following is a sketch of some of the possibilities.

The relationship between emotions and rationality can be viewed in at least two ways. First, emotions can themselves be judged as rational or irrational. For example, fear can be an appropriate or inappropriate reaction to one's circumstances. When education of the emotions is taken as an educational goal, it is sometimes this element of appraisal which is emphasized. More complex, and more controversial, is the issue of the cognitive role of emotion, if any, in rationality as a whole, its place in the formation of beliefs and of judgments about how to act. Traditionally, though not uniformly so, emotion has been regarded as a distorting influence which needs to be suppressed or overcome in the search for truth. But recent work in both philosophy and neurology suggest a positive role.

Neurologists Hanna and Antonio Damasio have reported that some persons who have sustained injuries (through strokes, tumors, or accidents) to a specialized region of the frontal cortex experience difficulty with personal and social decision-making and with the processing of emotion.[15] In the cases they have studied, the patients' lives took a dramatic turn for the worse after their injuries. Once responsible members of their communities, they no longer could be trusted to honor their commitments, had difficulty holding jobs, and lost respect for social conventions. However, tests showed no intellectual or neuropsychological impairment. The subjects "ability to tackle the logic of an abstract problem, to perform calculations, and to call up appropriate knowledge and attend to it remains intact."[16]

The Damasios devised an experiment in which five patients, along with a control group, were shown slides which included violent scenes and pictures of nudity along with neutral scenes. Physiological responses of the subjects such as pulse and blood pressure were monitored. These responses are controlled by the autonomic nervous system and are not normally subject to conscious control; they are hypothesized to be associated with some emotional states. Unlike the control group, the five patients showed no physiological reactions to the nude or violent pictures when viewing the slides passively.[17]

The Damasios hypothesize that the damaged region of the subjects' brains is connected to other brain regions that store emotional memories, and that people with damage to this region lose covert awareness of emotional reactions and this impairs their ability to make social and moral decisions. They believe that "emotion and its underlying neural machinery participate in decision-making within the social domain."[18]

This is speculative material, but it does suggest that emotional awareness may play an important role in practical judgment. Exactly what role is not clear. Should emotions be regarded, like perception, as a source of knowledge? Or do they make a different contribution? The Damasios suggest that the feelings evoked in particular circumstances may be associated with memories of past experiences involving either pleasure or pain. Thus emotions function as a warning or anticipation of future consequences and hence guide the decision-making process.[19] A more complex view of emotional perception is suggested by Sherman:

> Often we see not dispassionately, but because of and through the emotions. So, for example, a sense of indignation makes us sensitive to those who suffer unwarranted insult or injury, just as a sense of pity and compassion opens our eyes to the pains of sudden and cruel misfortune. We thus come to have relevant points of view for discrimination as a result of having certain emotional dispositions. We notice through feeling what might otherwise go unheeded by a cool and detached intellect. To see dispassionately without engaging the emotions is often to be at peril of missing what is relevant.[20]

This account is compatible with de Sousa's view that emotions direct the subject's attention to particular aspects of the environment, thus stimulating thought in certain directions. In his view, they do not themselves provide reasons for action, but "like scientific paradigms" are "a source of reasons."[21] This might be one way of explaining the behavior of the persons described by the Damasios. Lacking covert awareness of their emotional states, they do not attend to features of the situation that would attract the attention of normal subjects.

How helpful the emotions are in making rational decisions will depend, of course, on their appropriateness to the agent's situation. The emotions an individual experiences and the contexts that evoke them are at least partially determined by the cultural context whatever the "neural machinery" involved. Feeling shame, for example, requires a set of intersubjective meanings and social practices without which experiencing this emotion would be inconceivable. Fear and the physical responses associated with it may be more deeply rooted in our evolutionary past, but its meaning, the objects that evoke it, and appropriate manifestations of it are all culturally relative. As Jaggar says, "we absorb the standards and values of our society in the very process of learning the language of emotion, and those standards and values are built into the foundations of our emotional constitution."[22] Thus an inappropriate emotional response might be either the result of an individual's misreading of her or his situation or the result of social biases which have shaped habitual emotional reactions. The Damasios' research suggests that emotions play an important role in practical judgment. But whether they help us be more effective agents or make sound moral judgments depends on more than an unimpaired brain. It requires as well critical reflection on our characteristic responses and efforts to reeducate ourselves when our emotions are inconsistent with our best judgments. And, of course, we should also be alive to the possibility that recalcitrant emotions might be showing us the failure of our theories to be in touch with human possibility. Emotions likely are neither immutable biologically-based responses, nor infinitely plastic social constructions.

I have argued that rationality requires not only the acknowledgment of emotions but also their positive contribution in practical judgment, as well as critical analysis of emotions as socially-conditioned, habitual responses. This suggests a complex set of aims for the education of the emotions. First, adults shape the emotional responses of children in developing "the perceptions constitutive of emotions," in Sherman's phrase. In elaborating a form of education in the spirit of Aristotle, Sherman suggests that "part of what the parent tries to do is to bring the child to see the particular circumstances that here and now make certain emotions appropriate." For example, the parent tries to get the child to see "that what the child took to be a deliberate assault and cause for anger was really only an accident."[23] Second, we sometimes may have reason to reassess our habitual emotional perceptions of situations. What was once conventionally regarded as "harmless flirting," for example, is now understood to be "sexual harassment" and the sense of what emotions are appropriate in that context changes. Here, too, emotions have a role to play in critical evaluation and are not merely called upon to passively adjust to new intellectual evaluations. Jaggar argues that what she calls "outlaw emotions," emotions that are conventionally unacceptable, can form the basis for social criticism when these emotions are experienced by subordinated individuals and made the basis for a critical subculture, as when welfare payments generate resentment rather than gratitude.[24] Sherman suggests that the naive emotional responses of children can be instructive to adults who have repressed or over-intellectualized their responses.[25] Finally, while sometimes emotions yield straight away to new information, our learned, deeply habitual emotional responses frequently lag behind our altered judgments. We find ourselves experiencing racist and sexist emotions in conflict with our beliefs. How to change ourselves in such circumstances is an educational project we all face.

Conclusion

One positive upshot of the discussions of reason in this book is a richer, more complex conception of rationality as an educational aim. One of my teachers once asked the class whether we would choose to be always rational if we knew our wishes would be granted by some omnipotent power. Only a few said yes. I suspect those who declined the offer imagined they were being asked if they wanted to be like Mr. Spock, the Star Trek character famous for his rational control and absence of emotion. Perhaps one difficulty in portraying a rational life as appealing is part of a general problem known to novelists of making good characters attractive: somehow irrationality and evil seem more interesting. But I think it also points to a failure of our theories. Burbules worries that the virtues he depicts might be taken as merely "a middle-class conception of polite conduct." And Kohli points out that not everyone can see themselves as participants in a friendly dialogue. As Bernstein says, "sometimes what is required to communicate—to establish a reciprocal 'we'—is rupture and break—a *refusal* to accept the common ground of the 'other.'"[26] An educational aim has to be made compelling for students. It has to represent an appealing form of life they can see themselves enacting. Until we can offer a conception of rationality that has room for passionate commitment as well as open-mindedness, emotion in addition to intellect, rupture as well as consensus, and social justice as both a condition and outcome of rational dialogue, we may not have many takers.

NOTES

1. Richard Bernstein, "The Rage Against Reason," in Ernan McMullin, ed., *Construction and Constraint: The Shaping of Scientific Rationality* (Notre Dame: University of Notre Dame Press, 1988), pp. 189–221.

2. Hilary Putnam, *The Many Faces of Realism* (LaSalle, IL: OpenCourt, 1987), p. 8.

3. Jurgen Habermas, *The Philosophical Discourse of Modernity* (Cambridge, MA: MIT Press, 1987), p. 324.

4. Hilary Putnam, "Why Reason Can't be Naturalized," *Synthese* 52(1982), 8.

5. Habermas, pp. 322–3. See also Jurgen Habermas, *Postmetaphysical Thinking* (Cambridge, MA: MIT Press, 1992), p. 139.

6. Habermas, *The Philosophical Discourse of Modernity*, p. 324.

7. Thomas McCarthy, "Scientific Rationality and the 'Strong Program' in the Sociology of Knowledge," in McMullin, *Construction and Constraint,* p. 82.

8. Putnam, "Why Reason Can't be Naturalized," p. 8.

9. Ronald de Sousa, *The Rationality of Emotion* (Cambridge, MA: MIT Press, 1987), p. 163.

10. There are weaker and stronger senses of rationality, depending upon the perspective from which the evaluation is conducted. For example, in the minimal sense, an agent's actions are rational if they can be explained by her or his beliefs and desires. Any genuine action is rational in this sense. But the same action may have been based on unwarranted beliefs or inappropriate desires, such that in a larger evaluative context the action was not rational. I take it that when rationality is thought of as an educational ideal, something more than minimum rationality is the goal. See Richard Foley, "Some different Conceptions of Rationality," in McMullin, *Construction and Constraint,* pp. 123–52.

11. See Roderick Firth, "Epistemic Merit, Intrinsic and Instrumental," in *Proceedings and Addresses of the American Philosophical Society* 55(1981), 5–23. See also J. David Velleman, *Practical Reflection* (Princeton: Princeton University Press, 1989), especially Chapter 7.

12. Putnam, *The Many Faces of Realism,* p. 77.

13. I have defended this view in Emily Robertson, "Reason and Education," in Margaret Buchmann and Robert E. Floden, eds., *Philosophy of Education 1991* (Normal, IL: Philosophy of Education Society, 1992), pp. 168–80.

14. Allison M. Jaggar, "Love and Knowledge: Emotion in Feminist Epistemology," in Elizabeth D. Harvey and Kathleen Okruhlik, eds., *Women and Reason* (Ann Arbor: University of Michigan Press, 1992), p. 117.

15. Hanna Damasio, Thomas Grabowski, Randall Frank, Albert M. Galaburda, Antonio R. Damasio, "The Return of Phineas Gage: Clues About the Brain from the Skull of a Famous Patient," *Science* 264 (1994), 1102–1105. See also Sandra Blakeslee, "Old Accident Points to Brain's Moral Center," *The New York Times,* May 24, 1994, pp. C1 and C14 and Sandra Blakeslee, "The Brain May 'See' What Eyes Cannot," *The New York Times,* Jan. 15, 1991, pp. C1 and C8.

16. Damasio et. al., p. 1104.

17. Blakeslee (1991), p. C8.

18. Damasio et. al., p. 1104.

19. Blakeslee (1991), p. C8.

20. Nancy Sherman, *The Fabric of Character: Aristotle's Theory of Virtue* (Oxford: Clarendon Press, 1989), p. 45.

21. de Sousa, p. 198.

22. Jaggar, p. 130.

23. Sherman, p. 171.

24. Jaggar, p. 131.

25. Sherman, p. 173.

26. Bernstein, "The Rage Against Reason," in McMullin, *Construction and Constraint,* p. 216.

10

Postmodernism, Ethics, and Moral Education

Clive Beck

A View of Ethics Influenced by Postmodernism

What follows is a view of ethics "influenced" by postmodernism. But that is not a very accurate historical description, since it turns out that I have been something of a postmodernist most of my life, and certainly since before I first heard of the philosophical movement(s) which go by that name. Reading literature on postmodernism, however, has helped me clarify and extend some of my "natural" tendencies in that direction.

Postmodernism does not provide many explicit statements on ethics. However, it does offer some, especially through the writings of Richard Rorty, to whom I will give special attention. My emphasis on Rorty creates a difficulty, since some people question the extent to which he is a true postmodernist. (Not having the space to deal adequately with this issue, I must simply say that in this paper I will follow the fairly general practice of regarding Rorty as a postmodernist (as he himself does); and also that his views on ethics are broadly compatible with those of other key postmodernists.)

Anti-foundationalism

People commonly see morality as part of the bedrock of life, a foundation that is unchanging and universal. According to postmodernists, however, there is no such foundation, in morals or any other sphere. Rather, values are a cultural construction, changing over time and varying from culture to culture. There is no external moral reality which ethical inquiry seeks to uncover. Rather, humans create morality, in accordance with their varied interests, traditions, and circumstances. Moral values are not "objective," written in the heavens somewhere. They arise within human life.

In this vein, Richard Rorty stresses the *accidental* nature of morality, its contingency. We just happen to value the things we do: "what counts as being a decent human being is relative to historical circumstance."[1] Rorty rejects the "traditional Kantian backup" to morality as "an ahistorical distinction between the demands of morality and those of prudence."[2] This outlook may also be described as *pragmatic:* morality is accepted as it is found, emerging historically within our culture. We do not impose external "shoulds" and "oughts."

In line with his rejection of external, fixed foundations, Rorty sees morality as grounded in ordinary human emotions and motivation: he proposes an *internalist* view of ethics. He argues that traditional Christianity made the mistake of trying to detach morality from emotions, especially those of solidarity and fellow-feeling: "From a Christian standpoint (the) tendency to feel closer to those with whom imaginative identification is easier is deplorable, a temptation to be avoided."[3]

Now, to a considerable extent I accept the anti-foundationalist, pragmatic, internalist approach to ethics sketched above. And I will not repeat here the many compelling demonstrations postmodernists have given in support of it. However, I believe the approach must be qualified, modified, and supplemented in several ways.

To begin with, the approach places too much emphasis on the *cultural* determination of moral values, to the neglect of other factors. Societies cannot just decide to value *anything,* in a kind of cultural wish fulfillment. There are certain "hard facts"—about human nature, the natural environment, political structures, economic processes, even cultural development itself—to inquire about, while also consulting the latest cultural opinion.

Second, the postmodernist approach places too much emphasis on the fact that reality is "historical," "in play," "on the way," "in process," constantly changing. For there is also considerable *continuity* in reality, and specifically in values. Dewey spoke of *enduring* interests and values, and Charles Taylor talks of tentative frameworks. While these are not absolutely fixed or eternal in the manner envisaged by traditional metaphysicians and moral theorists, they are nevertheless very important.

Third, postmodernists place *too* much emphasis on the concrete and the local to the neglect of the general. It is true that a broad notion such as that "humans seek happiness," understood stereotypically, can desensitize us to the variety of concrete goals which cultures and groups pursue. However, when properly understood and used, such generalizations serve a vital function.

The notion that humans want to be happy, or that they want to survive, or be healthy, or have friends, or find meaning in life, can give general direction to individual and group life. And without such generalizations it would be difficult to think our way through many problems. (Postmodernists seem to experience a similar need. While condemning the making of generalizations they often themselves appeal to general values such as equality, freedom, diversity, playfulness, innovation, suspicion, dialogue, community).

Finally, while postmodernists are rightly critical of the frequent use of theory to impose beliefs and values on local communities and sub-groups, they unfortunately tend to reject theory altogether, seeing it as *inherently* distorting and tyrannical. Although reality does not have an external, fixed foundation it does have many internal continuities which are important (though shifting) reference points in achieving well being. It is possible and necessary, then, to develop *theory* which links particular values and actions to enduring values and frameworks.

Pluralism

Postmodernists pride themselves in encouraging a hundred flowers to bloom, in accepting and indeed celebrating diversity. This outlook is linked to the belief, already noted, that there is no ultimate foundation to life, that knowledge—including moral knowledge—is conditioned by changing human interests and traditions. Different communities and interest groups construct values to suit their particular needs and culture.

Rorty's acceptance of difference is seen, for example, in his endorsement of Freud's non-judgmental approach to morality. Says Rorty: "Freud shows us how something that seems pointless or ridiculous or vile to society can become the crucial element in the individual's sense of who she is. . . ."[4] He helps us see how "the private poem of the pervert, the sadist, or the lunatic" may be "as richly textured and 'redolent of moral memories' as our own life."[5]

This championing of diversity, however, while a major contribution of postmodernism, has often been at the expense of an awareness of commonality. To some extent, the postmodernists' emphasis on diversity is an absolute value, unreflectively adopted. Why *should* we assume that only differences exist and not commonalities (if only partially and temporarily)? And why *should* we celebrate difference more than commonality? Commonalities offer at least as many advantages as differences; and at any rate both, insofar as they exist, must largely be accepted in good pragmatic spirit.

Further, it seems absurd to approach new people or new cultures with a completely open mind on value matters, wondering, for example, whether they would mind being killed, or having their health ruined, or being made to suffer, or being separated from their family and friends. Rather, we should assume that they do share these basic values and concentrate on finding out, through dialogue, the form in which they value them. In the unlikely event that they do not value these things *at all,* that will become apparent as the dialogue proceeds.

Anti-authoritarianism

According to postmodernists, knowledge—including moral knowledge—reflects the interests and values of those who produce it. Michel Foucault, for example, sees concepts and rules with respect to sexuality as embodying and furthering the interests of power elites.[6] Postmodernism, then, exposes paternalism as the overrated arrangement that it is: "paters" (and "maters") again and again put their own interests above those of the people in their "care." In order to counter this natural bias, moral inquiry must be conducted in a democratic, non-authoritarian manner so that the interests of the various parties are taken into account as much as possible. Moral values should not be fashioned by one group (parents, teachers, academics, or clergy) and simply transmitted to another group (offspring, students, or ordinary members of the public). Everyone must get into the act of creating morality.

Lyotard's emphasis on smaller rather than larger communal groups, his attack on "grand narratives," and his proposal to do away with professors may all be seen as reducing the role of authority in knowledge and value production, thus increasing self-determination.[7] Similarly, according to Thomas McCarthy, Derrida's notion of the "play of differance" in language "points us in the direction of democracy."[8] Rorty, too, suggests a radically non-authoritarian approach by downplaying the role of intellectuals. For Rorty, intellectuals are "just a special case" among inquirers, with a distinctive language and methodology.[9] In fact, knowledge production is everyone's business, and people of all walks of life produce knowledge (including moral knowledge) with equal competence.

Insofar as people try to *help* each other in moral matters, a key non-authoritarian procedure is that of dialogue. Dialogue is important for several reasons: to understand better other people's situation and needs, to give them better advice; to learn from them as they give us feedback about *our* values; and it provides a means whereby compromises may be arrived at which are consented to and understood by all parties. Among postmodernists, Rorty is the one who has most emphasized dialogue or "conversation." He says, for example, that "our culture, or purpose, or intuitions cannot be supported except conversationally";[10] and that "*conversation* (is) the ultimate context within which knowledge is to be understood."[11]

While a non-authoritarian approach to ethics is crucial, however, postmodernists have sometimes questioned the need for power structures of *any* kind. And as a number of writers have pointed out, a complete flight from power runs the danger of leaving the small and the weak even more vulnerable than before. Thomas McCarthy, for example, says that while it is important "to interrogate and revise received notions of liberty, equality, justice, rights, and the like," as Derrida does, so that their use in the service of domination is exposed, nevertheless "to disassemble without reassembling them may rob excluded, marginalized, and oppressed groups of an important recourse." He goes on:

> It is sheer romanticism to suppose that uprooting and destabilizing universalist structures will by itself lead to letting the other be in respect and freedom rather than to intolerant and aggressive particularism, a war of all in which the fittest survive and the most powerful dominate.[12]

Ethics must support a type of democracy which is not just a free-for-all but in which there is a systematic pursuit of goals, using whatever structures—theoretical, political, economic—are necessary to that end. Of course, such talk of systematic action, means-end strategies, and so on will be interpreted by many as lapsing back into modernism, into "mechanistic," "rationalistic" thinking. But I see no alternative. In my view, if we do not systematically and powerfully pursue ends, employing various means as necessary, we can hardly be described as having values or morality at all.

Solidarity

Rorty and other postmodernists, either explicitly or by implication in their scholarly practice, place a great deal of emphasis on solidarity with and concern for others. Again and again they reject oppressive power, manipulation, exploitation, violence, the inflicting of harm by some humans on others. And, more positively, they attempt to promote community, respect, and mutual help. With this emphasis, of course, I am in full accord.

However, I believe that Rorty provides too "thin" an account of moral motivation (and others offer virtually no account at all), thus leaving us not much better off *in practice* than under the Kantian conception. To show a significant degree of interest in the well being of others, we must see in detail how it is connected to our own well being and that of our inner group. Once again we see the need for a complex set of interrelated ideas—"theory," no less—if morality is to work.

There is an explanation for Rorty's meager account of moral motivation. Because of his interest in private "irony" and a poetic rather than a theoretical approach to life, he is concerned enough to separate private from public morality. He believes that linking the two constrains personal inventiveness and originality. While in the public domain we should be altruistic, in private we should maximize originality. But *why* make an absolute out of personal innovation in this way? With such an approach one has no option but to arbitrarily *assert* public responsibility as a value, and run the risk of having one's assertion rejected.

Some Implications for Moral Education

There are a great many implications of the foregoing for moral education. I only have space to outline a few of the most obvious ones. It should be noted that in what follows I will often use the term "moral education" in a fairly broad sense to include what is sometimes called "values education." This is in keeping with the broad view of morality presented in this paper.

A Comprehensive Approach

My research on moral education has led me to the view that moral learning should be integrated with learning in general. Separate units, projects, or even courses in ethics do have a place, but it is often difficult to gain acceptance for them; and anyway, the great bulk of moral learning takes place through other subjects, through the "hidden curriculum," and through the organization and atmosphere of the classroom and school.

Such a perspective ties in with the postmodernist linking of facts and values. Morality is not a separate domain, with its own foundations. Rather, morality must be developed in the context of the study of culture, politics, economics, history, literature, art, science, and technology. We must know relevant "facts" in order to have sound "values." And without sound values in general we cannot know what is *morally* good and right.

One implication of this is that schooling must become much more effective in terms of teaching about the world and life. Children cannot be taught how to behave just by passing on a handful of moral principles and rules. School studies must cover a wide range of fields in considerable depth. This is a tall order; but I feel it is feasible so long as we have a sense of direction, which attention to values can give us. At present a lot of time is wasted in schools with busy-work—whether of a traditional or progressive kind—or in mastering largely irrelevant material. Without an adequate overall plan for schooling, sufficient integration between different subjects and activities and between the different levels of schooling cannot be achieved: kindergarten, primary, junior, intermediate, senior. Further, without a clear sense of the value of what is being studied, students lack the motivation to learn effectively.

Whatever subject or topic is being studied, values must be considered an integral aspect. In this way the value-relativity of the "facts" will be highlighted; students (and teachers) will constantly grow in their understanding of values in general and in their own personal value outlook; and students (and teachers) will have greater incentive to study the phenomena in question.

This will only work, however, if an open approach to values is taken. The moment students sense that the study of a subject is being used to "push" a particular value position which they cannot accept, they will lose interest.

Identifying and Accepting Differences

To deal with values throughout the curriculum and in the life of the school, we should encourage a pluralistic approach. Legitimate differences in ways of life should be identified around the world, in the local community, and in the school itself. It should be recognized that differences often simply reflect differences in circumstances; or the choice of different but equally good ends in life or different but equally good means to the same end. Actual cases of difference in the school should be approached in this spirit: children who are often late for school because of lack of support at home; children who are very serious about their school work and not so keen on sports; children who are exceptionally interested in music or art; and so on. (In this way, the tyranny of the peer group can be undermined.) In classroom studies, a great deal of time should be spent looking at examples—from history, literature, current affairs, students' and teachers' own lives—of moral difference: differences in family patterns, treatment of children, treatment of parents, sexual behavior, sexual orientation, attitudes toward birth control and abortion. Part of the point of this study is to see the legitimate reasons people have for their differences; but another part is to learn often to accept moral differences even when the purpose of them cannot be seen.

The study of differences should not be just in terms of cultural and social sub-groups: ethnic, religious, gender, or class. *Individual* differences should be studied among people of the same sub-group or category. (We should not assume, for example, that a woman from India will be interested in exchanging curry recipes, or that a man from Spain will enjoy bull fighting and not mind hot weather.) Social and cultural studies in schools have often been an exercise in stereotyping. The focus rather should be on learning to make *qualified* generalizations: Many Spaniards enjoy bull fighting (but many do not); Many French people like red wine with their lunch (but some prefer Coke).

Finding Foundations for Life and Morality

Moral education involves pointing out commonalities and continuities as well as differences and changes. People need "foundations"—if only of a provisional kind—to give direction and meaning to life. We need to study "metaphysics" with our students (metaphysics across the curriculum!). We need to see patterns in what we and others want in life and how to achieve it in order to know what is moral and how to live "the good life." We need to identify "basic" values in life—health, happiness, friendship, community, discovery, fulfillment—the things which ultimately make life seem good and worthwhile. Consideration of such values can help students form their value outlook, and also enable them to see greater similarity from culture to culture than is often acknowledged.

Much of our time in schools should be spent identifying commonalities in people: in students, teachers, family, and community. In casual conversation and school assemblies, in formal studies and discussions, attention should be drawn to similarities in goals, desires, joys, fears, problems. So much effort is expended in schools preaching against prejudice of various kinds. But the main cause of prejudice is an exaggerated belief in the difference between people of various sub-groups and categories.

Even at a global level we can find things in common, which may form an important part of our "foundation" in life. Schools in the West are already involved to some extent in promoting globalism through school-wide celebrations and classroom studies of world geography and children of other lands. A more adequate treatment of global issues should be developed, one which avoids stereotyping and superficial generalization but nevertheless notes commonalities among human beings.

A Non-authoritarian Approach

The anti-authoritarianism of postmodernism has many implications for moral learning in schools. When moral judgments are made (about the goals of the school, interpersonal behavior, academic requirements, dress codes, methods of discipline) the opinions of students should be taken more seriously than at present. And in the formal study and discussion of values, a dialogue approach should be used much of the time. Teachers should recognize that they, like their students, have extensive and fundamental learning needs in the area of values; and that they can learn a great deal from students—even at the elementary level—given their wealth of life experience. For teachers to learn from students, there must be a radical shift of subject matter to "life issues" (what Nel Noddings has called "centers of care")[13] so that students are interested and have something to contribute. Teachers should largely serve as chair, facilitator, or coach rather than moral "expert." They should say what they think, as noted before, but ensure that students feel free to do the same. Teachers are of course designated and paid to create learning programs. But they should involve students as much as possible in the design of the programs, and should see them as *for themselves as much as for their students;* indeed, if teachers are not constantly learning, they hinder the learning of their students. Teachers and students should be seen as learning morals together.

A non-authoritarian approach does not mean an unstructured, contentless pedagogy. Teachers should have at the ready ideas for meaningful individual and small group projects, along with a fund of "content" such as stimulating quotations from literature on values, excellent stories, and videos that bear on moral issues, learning materials that highlight key moral questions, and encourage discussion, and relevant excerpts from newspapers and magazines. But the use to which this material is put should be a constant subject of open discussion and decision making.

A non-authoritarian pedagogy paves the way for an emphasis on relationships in the school—between teachers and students, students and students, teachers and teachers—as largely "ordinary" ones from which moral learning is possible. The school structure and ethos should be such that school members are able to form close friendships, engage in genuine conversations about life, and express everyday emotions. Teachers should feel that they are getting to know children and adolescents, and students that they are getting to know adults.

Building a Basis for Altruism

As Rorty has pointed out, solidarity or other-regarding morality must be based in ordinary human emotions and motivations if it is to be possible at all. In the educational setting, this implies seeing the task of moral education not as one of moralizing and preaching in order to shame children into altruism *against* their inclinations, but rather of helping to extend their sympathies and loyalties. This can be done partly through formal study and discussion but perhaps even more by developing warm, genuine relationships in the school and classroom which lead naturally to greater mutual understanding and inclusiveness.

Altruism requires going beyond the types of motivation postmodernists have mentioned. Teachers must promote a systematic study of the links between individual, group, and societal well being. Such a detailed understanding of the reasons for altruism, which can begin even in kindergarten, will help students not only to know when they should help other people but also to have the necessary motivation to do so. Theoretical moral understanding of this kind has not been advocated by postmodernists, or for that matter by either traditional or progressive educators; but it is an essential basis for moral judgment and action. Once again, there is a need to modify and go beyond postmodernism while taking advantage of its insights.

NOTES

1. Richard Rorty, *Contingency, Irony, and Solidarity* (Cambridge: Cambridge University Press, 1989), 189.

2. Richard Rorty, "Postmodernist Bourgeois Liberalism," in Robert Hollinger ed., *Hermeneutics and Praxis* (Notre Dame, IN: University of Notre Dame Press, 1985), 214–5.

3. Rorty, *Contingency, Irony, and Solidarity,* 191.

4. Ibid., 37.

5. Ibid., 38.

6. See for example Michel Foucault, *The History of Sexuality* (New York: Random House/Vintage, 1990, orig. 1976), esp. 11–13.

7. Jean-Francois Lyotard, *The Postmodern Condition,* Geoff Bennington and Brian Massumi, trans. (Minneapolis: University of Minnesota Press, 1984), *passim.*

8. Thomas McCarthy, "The Politics of the Ineffable: Derrida's Deconstructionism," in Michael Kelly ed., *Hermeneutics and Critical Theory in Ethics and Politics* (Cambridge, Mass.: MIT Press, 1990), 161.

9. Rorty, *Contingency, Irony, and Solidarity,* 37.

10. Rorty, "Pragmatism, Relativism, and Irrationalism," as quoted in Bernstein, *Beyond Objectivism and Relativism,* 201.

11. Richard Rorty, *Philosophy and the Mirror of Nature* (Princeton, NJ: Princeton University Press, 1979), 389.

12. McCarthy, "The Politics of the Ineffable," 157–8.

13. Nel Noddings, *The Challenge to Care in Schools: An Alternative Approach to Education* (New York: Teachers College Press, 1992), e.g., xiii, 70–1, 173–7.

11

Care and Moral Education

Nel Noddings

Increased interest in moral education in the past few years has led to vigorous debate among moral educators. In addition to the ongoing dialogue between cognitive-developmentalism and character education,[1] the ethic of care has been introduced as a perspective on moral education.[2] Because the ethic of care has roots in both feminism and pragmatic naturalism, and because moral education is at its very heart, it holds interest for educators as well as philosophers.

An Ethic of Care and Its Source

Like deontological ethics—ethics of duty and right—the ethic of care speaks of obligation. A sense that *I must* do something arises when others address us. This "I must" is induced in direct encounter, in preparation for response. Sometime we, as carers, attend and respond because we want to; we love the ones who address us, or we have sufficient positive regard for them, or the request is so consonant with ordinary life that no inner conflict occurs. In a similar fashion, the recipients of such care may respond in a way that shows us that our caring has been received. When this happens, we say that the relation, episode, or encounter is one of natural caring. The "I must" expresses a desire or inclination—not a recognition of duty.

At other times, the initial "I must" is met by internal resistance. Simultaneously, we recognize the other's need and we resist; for some

137

reason—the other's unpleasantness, our own fatigue, the magnitude of the need—we do not want to respond as carers. In such instances, we have to draw on ethical caring; we have to ask ourselves how we would behave if this other were pleasant or were a loved one, if we were not tired, if the need were not so great. In doing this, we draw upon an ethical ideal—a set of memories of caring and being cared for that we regard as manifestations of our best selves and relations. We summon what we need to maintain the original "I must."

Now why should we do this? Why, that is, do we recognize an obligation to care? If we were Kantians, we would trace our obligation to reason, to a commitment that logic will not allow us to escape. But in the ethic of care we accept our obligation because we value the relatedness of natural caring. Ethical caring is always aimed at establishing, restoring, or enhancing the kind of relation in which we respond freely because we want to do so.

An ethic of care does not eschew logic and reasoning. When we care, we must employ reasoning to decide what to do and how best to do it. We strive for competence because we want to do our best for those we care for. But reason is not what motivates us. It is feeling with and for the other that motivates us in natural caring. In ethical caring, this feeling is subdued, and so it must be augmented by a feeling for our own ethical selves.

Kant subordinated feeling to reason. He insisted that only acts done out of duty to carefully reasoned principle are morally worthy. Love, feeling, and inclination are all supposed by Kant to be untrustworthy. An ethic of care inverts these priorities. The preferred state is natural caring; ethical caring is invoked to restore it. This inversion of priority is one great difference between Kantian ethics and the ethic of care.

Another difference is anchored in feminist perspectives. An ethic of care is thoroughly relational. It is the *relation* to which we point when we use the adjective "caring." A relation may fail to be one of caring because the carer fails to be attentive or, having attended, rejects the "I must" and refuses to respond. Or, it may fail because the cared-for is unable or unwilling to respond; he or she does not receive the efforts of the carer, and therefore caring is not completed. Or, finally, both carer and cared-for may try to respond appropriately but some condition prevents completion; perhaps there has been too little time for an adequate relation to develop and the carer aims rather wildly at what he or she thinks the cared-for needs. A relational interpretation of caring pushes us to look not only at moral agents but at both the recipients of their acts and the conditions under which the parties interact.

Of course, the adjective "caring" is often used to refer to people who habitually care. There are people who attend and respond to others regularly and who have such a well-developed capacity to care that they can establish caring relations in even the most difficult situations. But, at bottom, the ethic of care should not be thought of as an ethic of virtue. Certainly, people who care in given situations exercise virtues, but if they begin to concentrate on their own character or virtue, the cared-for may feel put off. The cared-for is no longer the focus of attention. Rather, a virtue—being patient, or generous, or cheerful—becomes the focus, and the relation of caring itself becomes at risk.

From this very brief exposition of an ethic of care, we can see that moral education is at its very heart. We learn first how to be cared for, how to respond to loving efforts at care in a way that supports those efforts. An infant learns to smile at its caregiver, and this response so delights the caregiver that he or she seeks greater competence in producing smiles. Caregiver and cared-for enter a mutually satisfying relation. Later, the child learns to care for others—to comfort a crying baby, pet a kitten, pat a sad or tired mother with a murmured, "Poor mommy!"

The source of adult caring is thus two-fold. Because we (lucky ones) have been immersed in relations of care since birth, we often naturally respond as carers to others. When we need to draw on ethical caring, we turn to an ethical ideal constituted from memories of caring and being cared for. Thus the ethic of care may be regarded as a form of pragmatic naturalism. It does not posit a source of moral life beyond actual human interaction. It does not depend on gods, nor eternal verities, nor an essential human nature, nor postulated underlying structures of human consciousness. Even its relational ontology points to something observable in this world—the fact that *I* am defined in relation, that none of us could be an *individual,* or a *person,* or an entity recognizably human if we were not in relation.

It is obvious, then, that if we value relations of care, we must care for our children and teach them how to receive care and to give care. Further, our obligation does not end with the moral education of children. Contrary to Kant, who insisted that each person's moral perfection is his or her own project, we remain at least partly responsible for the moral development of each person we encounter. How I treat you may bring out the best or worst in you. How you behave may provide a model for me to grow and become better than I am. Whether I can become and remain a caring person—one who enters regularly into caring relations—depends in large part on how you respond to me. Further, ethical caring requires reflection and self-understanding. We need to understand our own capacities and how we are likely to react in various situations. We need to understand our own evil and selfish tendencies as well as our good and generous ones. Hence moral education is an essential part of an ethic of care, and much of moral education is devoted to the understanding of self and others.

The Components of Moral Education

Modeling, the first component of moral education in the care perspective, is important in almost every form of moral education. In the character education tradition, for example, it is central because exemplars constitute the very foundation of moral philosophy.[3] In the care perspective, we have to show in our modeling what it means to care.

There is a danger in putting too much emphasis on the modeling component of caring. When we focus on ourselves as models, we are distracted from the cared-for; the same peculiar distraction occurs, as we have seen, when we concentrate on our own exercise of virtue. Usually, we present the best possible model when we care unselfconsciously, as a way of being in the world. When we do reflect, our attention should be on the relation between us and the cared-for: Is our response adequate? Could we put what we have said better? Has our act helped or hindered? We do not often reflect on our observers and what our behavior conveys to them. And this is as it should be.

But sometimes we must focus on ourselves as models of caring. When we show a small girl how to handle a pet, for example, our attention may be only peripherally on the pet. Our focal attention is on the little girl and whether she is learning from our demonstration. Similarly, as teachers, we often properly divert our attention from a particular student to the whole class of watchers. What does our behavior with this particular student convey to the class about what it means to care? As I said earlier, the shift of focus has its dangers and carried too far, it actually moves us away from caring.

In quiet moments, in the absence of those we must care for, reflection is essential. Not only should we reflect on our competence as carers, but we can now also consider our role as models. If I am, as a teacher, consistently very strict with my students "for their own good," what am I conveying? One teacher may emerge from such reflection satisfied that caring rightly forces cared-fors to do what is best for them. Another may emerge appalled that her efforts at care may suggest to students that caring is properly manifested in coercion. If the two get together to talk, both may be persuaded to modify their behavior, and this observation leads logically to the second component of moral education in this model.

Dialogue is the most fundamental component of the care model. True dialogue is open-ended, as Paulo Freire wrote.[4] The participants do not know at the outset what the conclusions will be. Both speak; both listen. Dialogue is not just conversation. There must be a topic, but the topic may shift, and either party in a dialogue may divert attention from the original topic to one more crucial, or less sensitive, or more fundamental.

The emphasis on dialogue points up the basic phenomonology of caring. A carer must attend to or be engrossed in the cared-for, and the cared-for must receive the carer's efforts at caring. This reception, too, is a form of attention. People in true dialogue within a caring relation do not turn their attention wholly to intellectual objects, although, of course, they may do this for brief intervals. Rather, they attend non-selectively to one another. Simone Weil described the connection this way:

> The love of our neighbor in all its fullness simply means being able to say to him: "What are you going through?" It is a recognition that the sufferer exists, not only as a unit in a collection, or a specimen from the social category labeled "unfortunate," but as a man, exactly like us. . . . This way of looking is first of all attentive. The soul empties itself of all its own contents in order to receive into itself the being it is looking at, just as he is, in all his truth.
>
> Only he who is capable of attention can do this.[5]

The other in a dialogue need not be suffering, but carers are always aware of the possibility of suffering. If the topic-at-hand causes pain, a caring participant may change the subject. Dialogue is sprinkled with episodes of interpersonal reasoning as well as the logical reasoning characteristic of intellectual debate.[6] A participant may pause to remind the other of her strengths, to reminisce, to explore, to express concern, to have a good laugh, or otherwise to connect with the other as cared-for. Dialogue, thus, always involves attention to the other participant, not just to the topic under discussion.

Dialogue is central to moral education because it always implies the question: What are you going through? It permits disclosure in a safe setting, and thus makes it possible for a carer to respond appropriately. Dialogue provides information about the participants, supports the relationship, induces further thought and reflection, and contributes to the communicative competence of its participants. As modes of dialogue are internalized, moral agents learn to talk to themselves as they talk to others. Such dialogue is an invitation to ever-deepening self-understanding. What do I really want? What was I trying to do when I acted as I did? What (good or evil) am I capable of? Am I too hard on myself? Am I honest with myself? One important aim of dialogue with others or with self is understanding the "other" with whom one is in dialogue.

Dialogue as described here rejects the "war model" of dialogue. It is not debate, and its purpose is not to win an argument. It may, of course, include intervals of debate, and both participants may enjoy such intervals. But throughout a dialogue, participants are aware of each other; they take turns as carer and cared-for, and no matter how great their ideological differences may be, they reach across the ideological gap to connect with each other.

One organization that has put aside the "war model" of dialogue is a group of women on opposite sides of the abortion issue; they call themselves Common Ground. (Actually, several organizations using this name have sprung up around the country, but the one to which I refer here is in the San Francisco Bay Area.) The purpose of Common Ground is not for each side to argue its own convictions and effect a glorious victory over ignorant or evil opponents. Rather, the explicit primary goal is to "reject the war model of the abortion argument and fully recognize that human beings, not cardboard cut-outs, make up the 'other side'."[7] The women of Common Ground describe themselves as "frustrated and heartsick at what the abortion contro-versy has done to traditionally female values such as communication, compassion, and empathy." But can an issue like abortion be resolved through communication, compassion, and empathy? That question misses the whole point of the approach being discussed here. The point of coming together in true dialogue is *not* to persuade opponents that our own position is better justified logically and ethically than theirs. The issue may never be resolved. The point is to create or restore relations in which natural caring will guide future discussion and protect participants from inflicting and suf-fering pain. Many of the women of Common Ground continue their advocacy roles in pro-life or pro-choice organizations because advocacy/adversary roles are the only ones widely accepted in American politics. But their advocacy functions are deepened and softened by the goal of Common Ground—to maintain caring relations across differences. Strategies that participants might once have considered against faceless adversaries are now firmly rejected.

Common Ground may well achieve desirable practical outcomes beyond a cessation of violence and name-calling. Already, women of opposing views on abortion have agreed on other goals: providing aid to existing children who are needy, helping poor mothers, defending women who are deserted or abused. Energies have been diverted from condemning and fighting to accomplishing positive, cooperative goals and, more important, to the estab-lishment of relations that will allow ideological opponents to live constructively with their differences.

Talk, conversation, and debate are used in every form of moral education, but often the focus is on justifying moral decisions. Cognitive programs of moral education concentrate on helping students to develop moral reason-ing. In sorting through dilemmas, students learn to justify the positions they take and to judge the strength of other people's arguments. It is certainly worthwhile to exercise and strengthen students' powers of reason, but advo-cates of the care perspective worry that students may forget the purpose of moral reasoning—to establish and maintain caring relations at both individ-ual and societal levels. Of course, advocates of a cognitive approach to moral education may deny that caring relations are central to moral reasoning. They may argue, instead, that the purpose of moral reasoning is to figure out what is right. This involves an evaluation of principles and selection of the one that should guide moral action. If this were done regularly by everyone, they might argue, we would achieve a just society and reduce individual suf-fering considerably. But care advocates worry about principles chosen and decisions made in abstract isolation, and we worry, too, about the assump-tion that what is right can be determined logically, without hearing what others are actually going through.

The theoretical differences between care and justice perspectives are too many and too deep to explore here. However, one point is especially relevant to the present discussion. There is some evidence that students exposed to cognitive approaches often come to believe that almost any decision can be justified, that the strength of their arguments is what really counts.[8] Cognitivist educators are not happy with this result, but to change it, they have to lead students toward concepts that help to anchor their thinking. They usually depend on a procedural mechanism to determine right or wrong. Care theorists more often line up with consequentialists here. In trying to figure out what is right, we have to find out what is good for the people involved. But this does not make us utilitarians, either. We do not posit one stable, abstract, universal good and try to produce that for the greatest number. Rather, we must work to determine what is good for this person or these people and how our proposed action will affect all of those in the network of care. Dialogue is the means through which we learn what the other wants and needs, and it is also the means by which we monitor the effects of our acts. We ask, "What are you going through?" before we act, as we act, and after we act. It is our way of being in relation.

A third component of moral education in the care perspective is practice. One must work at developing the capacity for interpersonal attention. Simone Weil thought that this capacity could be developed through the "right use of school studies"—especially subjects like geometry.[9] But all of us know people who are wonderfully attentive in an intellectual field and almost totally insensitive to people and their needs. To develop the capacity to care, one must engage in caregiving activities.

In almost all cultures, women seem to develop the capacity to care more often and more deeply than men. Most care theorists do not believe that this happens because of something innate or essential in women. Care theorists believe that it happens because girls are expected to care for people, and boys are too often relieved of this expectation. This is an open question, of course, but the hope of moral educators is that both sexes can learn to care. Indeed, most care theorists oppose any position that confines caring to women because it would tend to encourage the exploitation of women and undermine our efforts at moral education. Caring is not just for women, nor is it a way of being reserved only for private life.

What sort of practice should children have? It seems reasonable to suggest that, just as girls should have mathematical and scientific experience, boys should have caregiving experience. Boys, like girls, should attend to the needs of guests, care for smaller children, perform housekeeping chores, and the like. The supposition, from a care perspective, is that the closer we are to the intimate physical needs of life, the more likely we are to understand its fragility and to feel the pangs of the inner "I must"—that stirring of the heart that moves us to respond to one another.

Similarly, in schools, students should be encouraged to work together, to help one another—not just to improve academic performance. Teachers have a special responsibility to convey the moral importance of cooperation to their students. Small-group methods that involve inter-group competition should be monitored closely. Competition can be fun, and insisting that it has no place whatever in cooperative arrangements leads us into unnecessary confrontation. But, if competition induces insensitive interactions, teachers should draw this to the attention of their students and suggest alternative strategies. Such discussions can lead to interesting and fruitful analyses of competition at other levels of society.

Many high schools—more independent than public—have begun to require community service as a means of giving their students practice in caring. But a community service requirement cannot guarantee that students will care, any more than the requirement to "take algebra" can ensure that students will learn algebra in any meaningful way. Community service must be taken seriously as an opportunity to practice caring. Students must be placed in sites congenial to their interests and capacities. The people from whom they are to learn must model caring effectively, and this means that they must be capable of shifting their attention gently and sensitively from those they are caretaking, to those they are teaching. Students should also participate in a regular seminar at which they can engage in dialogue about their practice.

The last component of moral education from the care perspective is confirmation.[10] To confirm others is to bring out the best in them. When someone commits an uncaring act (judged, of course, from our own perspective), we respond—if we are engaging in confirmation—by attributing the best possible motive consonant with reality. By starting this way, we draw the cared-for's attention to his or her better self. We confirm the other by showing that we believe the act in question is not a full reflection of the one who committed it.

Confirmation is very different from the pattern found in many forms of religious education: accusation, confession, forgiveness, and penance. Accusation tends to drive carer and cared-for apart; it may thereby weaken the relation. Confession and forgiveness suggest a relation of authority and subordinate and may prevent transgressors from taking full responsibility for their acts. Further, confession and forgiveness can be ritualized. When this happens, there is no genuine dialogue. What happens does not depend on the relation between carer and cared-for, and the interaction is not aimed at strengthening the relation. Hence it has little effect on the construction of an ethical ideal in either carer or cared-for, since this ideal is composed reflectively from memories of caring and being cared for.

Confirmation is not a ritual act that can be performed for any person by any other person. It requires a relation. Carers have to understand their cared-fors well enough to know what it is they are trying to accomplish. Attributing the best possible motive consonant with reality requires a knowledge of that reality, and cannot be pulled out of thin air. When carers identify a motive and use it in confirmation, the cared-for should recognize it as his or her own. "That is what I was trying to do!" It is wonderfully reassuring to realize that another sees the better self that often struggles for recognition beneath our lesser acts and poorer selves.

Philosophical Issues

The model of moral education discussed here is based on an ethic of care. That ethic has an element of universality. It begins with the recognition that all people everywhere want to be cared for. Universality evaporates when we try to describe exactly what it means to care, for manifestations of caring relations differ across times, cultures, and even individuals. In roughly similar settings and situations, one person may recognize a cool form of respect as caring, whereas another may feel uncared for without a warm hug.

Because of its beginning in natural attributes and events, caring may properly be identified with pragmatic naturalism. John Dewey started his ethical thought with the observation that human beings are social animals and desire to communicate. The ethic of care begins with the universal desire to be cared for—to be in positive relation with at least some other beings. We note that human beings do in fact place a high value on such relations, and so our most fundamental "ought" arises as instrumental: If we value such relations, then we ought to act so as to create, maintain, and enhance them.

As Dewey filled out his moral theory, he moved rapidly to problem solving—surely one aim of communication. As we fill out an ethic of care, we concentrate on the needs and responses required to maintain caring relations. The difference need not be construed as a gender difference, but it may indeed be the case that the care orientation arises more naturally and fully from the kind of experience traditionally associated with women. Dewey himself once remarked that when women started to do philosophy, they would almost surely "do it differently." This observation in no way implies that a gender difference must forever divide philosophical thinking. Mutual influence, critical reciprocity, may produce models that incorporate elements of both perspectives. However, it may be years before female philosophies are themselves fully developed. Will we finish up at the same place by a different route? Or will even the endpoint be different? These are intriguing questions for contemporary moral philosophy.

Whereas there is an element of universality in the ethic of care, we cannot claim universality for the model of moral education. Probably all moral educators incorporate modeling and practice in their educational programs, but many would reject confirmation, and some would reject the focus on dialogue, emphasizing instead commandment and obedience. Proponents of caring do not regard the lack of universality as a weakness. On the contrary, many of us feel that insistence on universal models is a form of cultural arrogance. Here we differ strongly with Kohlbergians on at least two matters: First, we see no reason to believe that people everywhere must reason or manifest their caring in identical ways; second, although we put great emphasis on intelligent action, we reject a narrow focus on reason itself. It is not just the level and power of reasoning that mark moral agents as well developed but the actual effects of their behavior on the relations of which they are part. Moreover, it is not so much the development of individual moral agents that interests us but the maintenance and growth of moral relations, and this is a very different focus.[11]

Care advocates differ also with certain aspects of character education. Although we share with Aristotelians and others who call themselves "communitarians" the conviction that modern moral philosophy has put far too much emphasis on individual moral agents wrestling in lonely isolation with logically decidable moral problems, we also fear the Aristotelian emphasis on social role or function. This emphasis can lead to hierarchies of virtue and demands for unwavering loyalty to church or state. Different virtues are expected of leaders and followers, men and women, bosses and workers. Further, educational models tend to suppose that communities can arrive at consensus on certain values and/or virtues.

Early in this century, the Character Development League sought to inculcate in all students a long list of virtues including obedience, industry, purity, self-reliance, courage, justice, and patriotism.[12] Probably both Kohlbergians and care advocates would agree that school children should have many opportunities to discuss such virtues and that they should read and hear inspiring stories illustrating the exercise of virtue. But to rely on community consensus is to lean on a wall made of flimsy material and colorful paint. If we all agree that honesty is somehow important, we probably disagree on exactly how it is manifested and how far it should be carried. Whereas Kant would have us never tell a lie and Charles Wesley spoke approvingly of the ancient father's statement "I would not tell a wilful lie to save the souls of the whole world,"[13] most of us would lie readily to save a life, a soul, or even the feelings of someone, if doing so would cause no further harm. Indeed, we might feel morally obligated to do so.

From a care perspective, we might begin with *apparent* consensus but with the frankly acknowledged purpose of uncovering and developing an appreciation for our legitimate differences. The need to do this—to respond to the universal desire for care (for respect, or love, or help, or understanding) underscores the centrality of dialogue. We must talk to one another. Sometimes we are successful at persuading them, sometimes they persuade us, and sometimes we must simply agree to go on caring across great ideological differences. Unless we probe beneath the surface of apparent consensus, we risk silencing divergent and creative voices. We risk also, allowing a core of powerful authorities to establish a fixed set of approved virtues and values.

A central question today in debate over the introduction of values education is exactly the one alluded to above: Whose values? One group would press for its own; another would press for consensus. Care theorists would answer, "Everyone's!" But, with cognitivists, care theorists would subject all values to careful, critical scrutiny and, with character educators, we would insist that the effects of our choices on our communities and the effects of our communities on our choices be treated with appreciation. We would insist that our community—nation, town, classroom, family—stands for something, and we would attempt to socialize our children to the stated standards.[14] But we would do this with a respectful uncertainty, encouraging the question *why*, and recognizing our responsibility to present opposing alternatives as honestly as we can. Despite sometimes irresolvable differences, students should not forget the central aim of moral life—to encounter, attend, and respond to the need for care.

This reminder is well directed at moral educators as well. Although we differ on a host of issues in moral philosophy and psychology, as educators, we have a common aim—to contribute to the continuing moral education of both students and teachers. With that as our aim, we, too, should reject the war model and adopt a mode of constructive and genuine dialogue.

NOTES

1. See Larry P. Nucci, ed., *Moral Development and Character Education* (Berkeley: McCutchan, 1989).

2. See Nel Noddings, *Caring: A Feminine Perspective on Ethics and Moral Education* (Berkeley and Los Angeles: University of California Press, 1984); also *Women and Evil* (Berkeley and Los Angeles: University of California Press, 1989); and *The Challenge to Care in Schools* (New York: Teachers College Press, 1992).

3. For the foundation of this approach, see Aristotle, *Nicomachean Ethics,* trans. Terence Irwin (Indianapolis: Hackett, 1985).

4. Paulo Freire, *Pedagogy of the Oppressed,* trans. Myra Bergman Ramos (New York: Herder and Herder, 1970).

5. Simone Weil, "Reflections on the Right Use of School Studies with a View to the Love of God," in *Simone Weil Reader,* ed. George A. Panichas (Mt. Kisco, N. Y.: Moyer Bell Limited, 1977), p. 51.

6. See Nel Noddings, "Stories in Dialogue: Caring and Interpersonal Reasoning," in *Stories Lives Tell: Narrative and Dialogue in Education,* ed. Carol Witherell and Nel Noddings (New York: Teachers College Press, 1991), pp. 157–70.

7. Stephanie Salton, "Pro-life + pro-choice = Common Ground," *San Francisco Chronicle,* August 30, 1992, A15.

8. Instructors at the University of Montana, which now requires all undergraduates to take two courses in ethics, have noted this unfortunate result of the dilemma approach.

9. Weil, "Right Use of School Studies."

10. Confirmation is described in Martin Buber, *I and Thou,* trans. Walter Kaufmann (New York: Charles Scribner's Sons, 1970).

11. The relational perspective is described in psychological terms in Carol Gilligan, *In a Different Voice* (Cambridge: Harvard University Press, 1982); see also Mary F. Belenky, Blythe M. Clinchy, Nancy R. Goldberger, and Jill M. Tarule, *Women's Ways of Knowing* (New York: Basic Books, 1986).

12. See James Terry White, *Character Lessons in American Biography for Public Schools and Home Instruction* (New York: The Character Development League, 1909).

13. Quoted in Sissela Bok, *Lying: Moral Choice in Public and Private Life* (New York: Vintage Books, 1979). p. 34.

14. Even Lawrence Kohlberg acknowledged the need to socialize children. See Kohlberg, "Moral Education Reappraised," *The Humanist* 38 (Nov.–Dec., 1978): 13–15. In this article Kohlberg accepts the need to "indoctrinate." I do not think we need to indoctrinate. We socialize but always encourage students to ask *why*.

12

Extending the Boundaries
of Moral Education

David E. Purpel

I am very pleased that this volume has included consideration of moral education as one of its themes and surely the papers by Professors Noddings and Beck testify to the critical importance of the topic as well as to the seriousness that many educators attach to it. These two articles strike me not only as intellectually helpful and insightful but even more importantly, they represent sensitivity, concern, and commitment in regard to profoundly important issues. Both articles seem to situate their discourse within two spheres—one being the broad realm of academic theory (basically philosophical and psychological) and the other being the more applied if more narrow world of schools. Both neatly interweave theoretical complexities and questions with the challenges of curricular and instructional practice and in so doing they provide insight into both. I believe both analyses could be easily extended to involve wider social, political, cultural, spiritual, and personal issues and indeed, I believe would benefit from it. It is this belief that provides the focus of this essay.

Social and Cultural Context

The idea that a great deal of energy should be put into examining and fostering the impulse to care is extremely appealing, sensible, and moving to me (I am pleased to have the chance to participate in such efforts). In doing so, my first and most powerful impulse is not so much to consider questions regarding the mechanisms of caring (important as that might be) but rather to note the *enormous amount of caring needed,* or put another way, to register and witness the incredible degree of human pain and suffering in our midst. As educators and citizens, I believe that the reality of immense and unacceptable human suffering ought to be the primary point of departure for our work and that the degree to which we reduce that suffering be the true measure of the value of our work. What I want to discuss first in this essay, therefore, is the matter of *unnecessary* human suffering, particularly that which is the consequence of socially constructed realities, policies, and practices; in other words, to examine the social and cultural sources of the pain that cries out for the caring. A primary concern is to examine the source and nature of the suffering and in that process face the possibility of our complicity in it and the necessity of reflecting on our responsibility for its alleviation. As educators and citizens we are then required to see ourselves not only as potential healers but also as perpetrators, accomplices, and victims of suffering. (Let me say as strongly as I can that this is not in any way meant to diminish the importance of caring for the needy in situations where we do not know the origins of the suffering or when that issue does not seem particularly relevant.) It is clear to me that the injunction to care for our neighbor includes the responsibility to deal with the symptoms and effects as well as the source of the pain. My position, however, is that an inclusive orientation toward suffering (as it intersects with caring) involves considerations of etiology as well as symptomology. If a child comes to us weeping, we can exercise caring by comforting the child *or* by intervening in the source of the child's pain—my ideal is that we do both.

There is no infallible way to distinguish between necessary and unnecessary suffering. This difficulty should not stop us from relying on that formulation for providing us with important insights. The distinction provides us with a very useful heuristic: pursuing the question as to whether the pain could have been prevented or not is a useful and evocative process. Beyond that, it is not very difficult to figure out that poverty, homelessness, and social privilege are not inevitable but that death and loss are. We do not need to have penetrating analytic skills to know that our culture has created class and caste distinctions, but that nature necessitates that we experience pain when we lose those we love. Pain that is the consequence of attempts at establishing intimacy and the deep disappointment that results from failures to attain particular aspirations may seem inherent in the very nature of experience, but it is also clear that at least part of the source of this pain is rooted in certain cultural values and expectations. We need to comfort children who feel rejected because of their particular appearance or consciousness, as well as children who feel inadequacy because of poor school performance. There are, however, other issues that are vital and present: Is this pain inevitable? Is *all* we can do about such situations is provide sympathy and help in overcoming their deficiencies? How did we get to the point where these phenomena got defined as deficiencies and are we to accept them as such in perpetuity? Is not all suffering that is rooted in a sense of inadequacy culturally determined and hence unnecessary? Are we willing to say instead that although some of this suffering may not be inevitable and is certainly unfortunate, but nonetheless, a necessary consequence of other beneficent values (maintaining standards, competition, achievement)?

However, I want to move as quickly as possible from abstract notions of social context to the particulars of the United States of the 1990s, for it is vital that when we talk of caring and of ethical commitments that we avoid the sins of blindness and denial of what surrounds us. My belief is that there is an obscene and ghastly degree of unnecessary human suffering not only on a global scale but within our own communities and neighborhoods, that this is mostly a function of policies and practices made by those in power (who are among other things usually well educated). My guess is that those who have made far-reaching decisions in foreign policy, investment strategy, city planning, banking policy, with such devastating and tragic effects have very good analytic and interpretive skills and are likely to be as sensitive interpersonally as most people in other groups. Moreover, the source of much of this misery is the moral cancer of privilege, hierarchy, and ruthless competition which not only permeates institutional education but is legitimated and rationalized there. To put it bluntly, formal education has major responsibility for much of the rampant unnecessary human suffering not only because its graduates have the power, and not only because it embodies the very callousness, hierarchy, and inequity that contribute to the general suffering, but also because of its power to validate and justify a meritocratic ethic. It is an ethic which structures winners and losers, in which those who win do so at the expense of others, and an ethic of advantage, privilege, and hierarchy that has produced unemployment, underemployment, poverty, hunger as well as luxury, comfort, wealth, and ease. Tragically, formal education has become a vital part of the process by which these privileges are distributed or, to put it in moral terms, by which human dignity is rationed. Thus, we have a social and economic system that, although it has generally and broadly created enormous wealth and contributed profoundly to our well being, it (we) has (have) failed to provide justice for all. We have a culture at war with itself as it affirms both equality and freedom both dignity for all and privilege for some, implicitly supporting greed while struggling publicly to embrace *agape*.

The implications of this ongoing, persistent, very real, very horrible pain, inequity, and injustice has consequences for developing a caring consciousness and encouraging students to engage in ethical discourse. First it must be remembered that moral issues are social in character and are heavily involved with the particularities of history, beliefs, structures, and controversies of the community. When people act they act in a particular setting and when they are asked to act or think morally they need to do so in a particular context. When we strive to help people develop a moral consciousness, we need to address the moral dimensions of those aspects of U.S. society and culture in the 1990s that shape our lives. I have no doubt that philosophical and psychological insights are absolutely necessary and extremely useful dimensions of promoting a moral consciousness, but to exclude or marginalize the social, historical, cultural, political, and economic contexts is at best to render the process of moral education as benign if not irrelevant and at worst, to contribute to social irresponsibility.

The classroom setting is an important site for witnessing and acting on moral issues. It is certainly vital that we attend to those individuals with whom we interact, however distantly or intimately and that we do so with care and compassion. Such settings require careful study and analysis and merit our concern but they do not exhaust the realm of those who require care and consideration. What of those in pain who we do not see or encounter and what of those suffering unnecessarily whose identity is not known to us? Does not our imagination allow us to make such people real and their pain palpable? Does not our moral responsibility extend beyond those with whom we can have personal experiences to groups and individuals who though absent are linked to us? Again, I affirm the importance of encouraging us to be caring, sensitive, and compassionate when we are together, but this must not be at the cost of denying the intense pain that is anonymous, elsewhere, and endemic or at the expense of accepting responsibility for its amelioration.

It is of course important to not only offer comfort to those who are immediate but also to confront one's role in the source of that pain. As difficult as that process is in intimate settings and small groups, it pales in comparison with the complex task of sorting out our responsibilities for the existence of wide ranging and pervasive suffering and its alleviation. *What cannot and must not be denied if we are to present ourselves as moral beings is the harsh and persistent reality of immense ongoing unnecessary human suffering and our profound responsibility to confront our role in its origins and persistence.* We must go further and reflect on why this urgent concern is so absent from educational practice and so painfully neglected in educational theory. I believe that part of the explanation for this absence and neglect is to be found in the tangled and contradictory notions of psychological denial, political complicity, intellectual rationalization, moral anguish, and personal confusion. This knot of human paradoxes and dilemmas calls for a consciousness of compassion and humility for ourselves and each other, especially when we seek not only to describe and act on our moral responsibilities but to endeavor to instruct others in this process.

What must be confronted is the moral consciousness of a society and culture that countenances unnecessary suffering and more particularly, how the educational system participates in the development, preservation, and legiti-mation of that consciousness. This consciousness is one which seems to put enormous stress on personal achievement, individual success, and material well being and a society which accepts continuous and unbridled competi-tion as the proper way to determine who is to have how much success and dignity. This consciousness has moved into phase of what has been called "hyper-individuality" and into an era of increasingly harsh conflict, division, and hostility such that it has prompted some to remind us that in such an ethic we may well be eroding our impulse to be caring.

In our concern for moral education, we need to be concerned with the necessity to care for those in pain and to become better informed about the source of the pain. The source is often within the school and classroom set-ting and that means that not only are personal sensitivities and interpersonal relationships involved but so are school policies, community mores, and issues of even larger social and cultural contexts. Such situations require us to respond with the healing that comes from the warmth of human relation-ships and spontaneous, freely given compassion. In addition, we also need to examine the sources of that pain which require analysis, knowledge, and interpretation. It is not only unnecessary but undesirable to separate out rea-son from feeling for even when we deal with the need to care at the interpersonal and classroom levels we are faced with the task of responding to both the etiology and the symptoms of suffering. However, to limit the agenda of moral education to intellectual understanding of general and hypothetical moral issues and/or to responding personally to immediate pain is to invite denial and despair regarding the social and cultural structures that precipitate so much of human suffering. It is certainly a loving and caring thing when we comfort a child who weeps over failing a test and it strikes me as morally right to provide further support to reduce the likelihood of more failures and to ameliorate the anguished responses to such disappointments. *That is simply not enough in an education that aspires to being morally grounded.*

Much of the pain is rooted in a constellation of social, economic, cultural, and political conditions that has structured the necessity and inevitability of such pain. Among the anguishing aspects of responding to this pain is the moral and intellectual necessity of determining that which is socially and cul-turally constructed, endorsed, and affirmed even in the face of the suffering. With this responsibility comes the issue of our complicity and attitude towards such policies. Do we as educators support and condone such poli-cies and do we as citizens participate knowingly and willingly in a system in which we are likely to benefit at the expense of others and cause pain and suffering? It is schools after all that insist on grading people and on continu-ally testing them on their achievement in a culture that is obsessed with the pernicious doctrine that a person is as "good" as his or her work. It is as if we were at one moment to bash someone over the head (we often do this as teachers in the name of maintaining standards) and then in the next moment demand that we care about the pain (but not the bash). Are we to say: People shouldn't cry when they are bashed or that they should wear helmets in school? or perhaps even that a little bashing is *good* for you? Furthermore, what does it say about the moral consciousness of educators if their response is that they are merely acting on the social and cultural imperatives and that the pain that educators inflict attendant to school life is not to be taken personally? Educators are cultural leaders, cultural creators, social activists who work in schools, universities, academies, and are moral agents required to take responsibility for their participation in this process. To selectively truncate and narrow that realm of responsibility is intellectually problematic and politically troublesome, particularly when our future as a people, community, and even as a planet is at risk.

The most horrendous moral outrages of our time are embodied in the incredible amount of unnecessary human suffering. To limit our response to these outrages to analysis and compassion is to increase the risk of becoming numb to the cries of human suffering and decrease the impulse and will to transform ourselves into a much more loving and just community. We must not only weep, bind up the wounds, comfort the troubled; we must do more than strive to gain philosophical insight into the moral significance of human events. We must also trouble the comfortable; express our outrage at oppressors, bear witness and delve into ways that specific social and cultural institutions and attitudes can be reconstructed to meet our highest aspirations and deepest commitments. There is hunger, misery, and despair, in the land: We must constantly ask why this is *not* the central and burning issue that occupies the center of every discussion of educational policy and practice. A morally valid education surely includes processes in which we are called upon to deeply reflect on our moral discourse and to analyze our history and social institutions especially those that nourish our impulse to be compassionate and connected. It needs also to deal with matters of moral agency, which requires affirmation and commitment as informed by an understanding of that which promotes injustice and inequity, and by a faith that defiantly rejects the inevitability of unnecessary human suffering.

Spiritual Context

I do not believe that our scholarly oath and inclination to be sceptical and critical ought to keep us from recognizing and accepting the reality that there is incredible human suffering in our midst and that a great deal of it is of human making. Surely, there is a great deal of uncertainty and controversy regarding their causes, origins, and solutions, but let us not obscure the reality of this suffering behind the screens of professional scepticism and obsessive academic precision. When it comes to understanding the origins of good and evil, I confess to both wide-eyed fascination and profound humility and am reduced (exalted?) to seeing these questions as mystery, for it is clear to me that important and vital as social and cultural contexts are, there is more here than meets the eye. Clive Beck and Nel Noddings have in their essays raised a number of intriguing and helpful, albeit vexing questions about these elusive and intangible issues. I want to note some of them, more as items on a continuing agenda for meditation than as problems to be resolved through analysis.

There are a number of passages in the two essays relating to this agenda that struck me as powerfully evocative. Speaking to both the impulse to care and to resist caring, Nel Noddings says: "In doing this, we draw upon an ethical ideal—a set of memories of caring and being cared for that we regard as manifestations of our best selves and relations. We summon what we need to maintain the original 'I must'." I accept this view as not only profoundly true but one that is also deeply mysterious—where does the "I must" come from? When we "draw and summon," what is it we are calling upon and what is the origin of the impulse to draw and summon? What about the idea of a best self? Is it already formed waiting to be awakened or is it totally constructed by will and contingency? Are there also less good selves within us including a worst self? What is the source of the impulse to make the distinction between good and bad? Noddings offers a hint of one possible source of such impulses when she says: "The supposition, from a care perspective, is that the closer we are to the intimate physical needs of life, the more likely we are to understand its fragility and to feel the pangs of the inner 'I must'—*that stirring of the heart that moves us to respond to one another* (my italics)." "Spiritual"? Wow!

Professor Beck raises similar questions: "People need 'foundations'—if only of a provisional kind—to give direction and meaning to life. We need to study 'metaphysics' with our students (metaphysics across the curriculum!). We need to see patterns in what we see and others want in life and how to achieve it in order to know what is moral and how to live the 'good life'. . . ."

Metaphysics is a necessary part of the quest for goodness and at the same time these ideas raise several questions. How are the "loose ends" to be connected to the fabric of critical analysis and rational thinking? How loose are these ends and to what are they connected? Is metaphysics only to be studied rather than affirmed? And of course, to raise the explosive issue of giving direction and meaning to life is to bring forth a flood of the most profound and baffling questions of human existence regarding our origins, nature, and destiny, questions that are as vital in their relevance and importance as their discussion is absent in the schools and in the literature on moral education.

It is clear that moral dilemmas, problems, and issues are manifested in any number of spheres—interpersonally, in school settings, in the community, society, nation, planet. It is also clear that serious thought, reflection, and study is required in addressing these issues and equally clear that we should be nourishing the inner emotive and intuitive processes that are also significantly involved in such attempts. If the mind and the body are to be nourished and trusted then so also do we need to attend to matters of the spirit with all the elusiveness and problematics that this concept brings with it.

Personal Context

Not only does moral education involve social, psychological, and metaphysical inquiry but it also requires personal self-reflection and individual soul searching. Each of us engages in some form or another in the troubling and daunting task of searching for and acting on meaning and I believe that those of us who are educators ought to integrate this quest into our professional responsibilities. My view is that educators need to share that struggle and infuse personal reflection into the intellectual and ideological dimensions of their work not only as legitimate self-reflection but as a necessary part of genuine dialogue. We all come out of some tradition, some life-view, some basic posture towards our existence which are, of course modified and altered by experience and reflection but still in some way inform who we are and what we do. Perhaps more to the point, we need to share our current struggles and address the basic questions of meaning as they influence our ongoing work and in so doing we join self-reflection, research, learning, and teaching. I would like to present a very brief sample of what I have in mind not only for purposes of illustration but to take the opportunity to be involved in the process I have suggested.

I am a first-generation American, the son of Russian-Jewish immigrants who fled from pogroms in which two of my grandparents were murdered. I was raised as and clearly identify myself as Jewish but my education in Jewish traditions was meager if not distorted and my identification was primarily cultural and ethnic. In more recent years, I find myself drawn to Jewish religious traditions and have begun fairly serious reading and study and am increasingly interested in integrating that study into my teaching and writing. It has become increasingly clear that in a general way this background has in one way or another informed my work but it is only recently that I have made a conscious effort to clarify and extend these influences.

I have accepted as the grounding for my approach to educating for moral consciousness a set of ideas that emerges from what is called the Prophetic tradition (which has its origins in the Biblical prophets who engaged in non-stop moral critique of current social policies). It represents a paradigm which combines the spiritual and the social by insisting on holding the community to its sacred covenants and one which combines severe criticism with profound hope. Abraham Joshua Heschel's stunning book *The Prophets* not only made this paradigm accessible to me but his enormous intellectual power, profound spirituality, and energizing eloquence have provided me with a solid and continuing source of insight and direction. Perhaps two short quotes can provide a taste of that power:

The prophet seldom tells a story, but casts events. He rarely sings, but castigates. He does more than translate reality into a poetic key; he is a preacher whose purpose is not self-expression or the "purgation of emotion" but communication. His images must not shine, they must burn. The prophet is intent on intensifying responsibility, is impatient of excuse, contemptuous of pretense and self-pity. His tone, rarely sweet or caressing, is frequently consoling and disburdening: his words are often slashing, even horrid—designed to shock rather than edify. . . . The prophet is concerned with wrenching one's conscience from the state of suspended animation.

Above all, the prophets remind us of the moral state of a people: Few are guilty, but all are responsible. If we admit that the individual is in some measure conditioned or affected by the spirit of society, an individual's crime discloses society's corruption. (Heschel 1962, pp. 7, 14, 16)

Heschel has provided me with a number of deeply satisfying formulations some of which I accept as compelling and convincing even though I have yet to assimilate them into my work. There are still others that confound and baffle me, but my respect for Heschel's passionate arguments does not allow me to dismiss them. As an example of the former I offer his very convincing notions on the importance of awe and mystery to the educative process, ideas that I accept as "true" even as I recognize that they have yet to have any real impact on my personal or professional life. Heschel says in *Who is Man?*:

The world presents itself in two ways to me. The world as a thing I own, the world as a mystery I face. What I own is a trifle, what I face is sublime. I am careful not to waste what I own; I must learn not to miss what I face. . . . All we have is a sense of awe and radical amazement in the face of a mystery that staggers our ability to sense it. . . . Knowledge is fostered by curiosity; wisdom is fostered by awe. *Awe precedes faith; it is the root of faith.* We must be guided by awe to be worthy of faith. (My italics) (Heschel 1965, p. 89)

I know that if I were to fully embrace these ideas it would change my life but here I find myself resisting that which persuades me. An important example of a belief that Heschel holds as central but that I have great difficulty in accepting involves the crucial matter of our relationship to the transcendent. In the conclusion of *Who is Man?*, he says:

Of one thing, however, I am sure. There is a challenge that I can never evade, in moments of failure as in moments of achievement. Man [sic] is inescapably, essentially challenged on all levels of existence. It is in his being challenged that he [sic] discovers himself as a human being. Do I exist as a human being? My answer is: *I am commanded—therefore I am.* There is a built-in *sense of indebtedness in the consciousness of man,* an awareness of *owing gratitude,* of being *called upon* at certain moments to

> reciprocate, to answer, to live in a way which is compatible with the grandeur and mystery of living. (My italics) (Heschel 1965, p.111)

I along with countless others continue to struggle with the meaning, significance, and implication of such ideas, knowing that in spite of my scepticism and confusion, they cannot be dismissed. I find it possible to resist as Heschel provides, but unable to ignore his questions since they are so deeply connected to issues of moral consciousness. And so the struggle continues.

This very short excursion into my thoughts on moral education is not intended primarily to be autobiographical as much as it is an attempt to embody an approach to the area of moral education that strives to widen and deepen its dimensions. I believe the field would be further enriched by work that delves into the multiplicity of perspectives that give it light and direction—the social, cultural, political, psychological, metaphysical, spiritual; the classroom, the family, the personal, the existential and the essential; the personal struggles and the enduring traditions. It should be no surprise that the effort to develop moral consciousness and responsibility should require such a comprehensive approach nor should we be daunted by the perplexity, ambiguity, and complexity of the task. In fact, we need to take pains to be clear on just how serious and profound the issues are lest we contribute to the dangers of reductionism, oversimplification, and sentimentality. What we must always remember is that when to seek to educate morally, we are undertaking *the* most important *and* challenging of tasks and in so doing we are required to be both bold and humble; critical and affirmative; open and committed. The commitment and contributions of Professors Beck and Noddings offer powerful reasons to be optimistic about the future of such efforts in a time when they are so desperately needed.

BIBLIOGRAPHY

Heschel, Abraham Joshua, *The Prophets* (New York: Harper and Row, 1962).

Heschel, Abraham Joshua, *Who is Man?* (Palo Alto: Stanford University Press, 1965).

KNOWLEDGE AND CERTAINTY IN UNCERTAIN TIMES

13

For the Stranger in My Home: Self-Knowledge, Cultural Recognition, and Philosophy of Education

René Vincente Arcilla

As a philosopher of education, a lot of my work consists of teaching philosophical texts to prospective or actual teachers. Among other things, I try to encourage these students to recognize their better, more ideal selves, hopefully their teaching selves, in the ideas of these authors, and so to appreciate how the call to stand for something—for the good of teaching, for example—is continuous with the call to learn how to read the idealism of others. Indeed, some may recognize in this way of being a Philosophy of Education teacher the ideas of, among others, Michael Oakeshott and Stanley Cavell. They focus learning on the quest for self-understanding. Learning from them, I try to suggest that the best, most honest teaching comes out of such an understood self (as distinct from a mastered professional role).[1]

Of course this effort is bound to meet its challenges. One which I have encountered repeatedly is that some students refuse to recognize themselves in another's ideas because they fear that those ideas are rooted in a culture antagonistic to themselves and their ideals. Among students resistant to my attempts to teach European philosophy are those who belong to cultures that Europe has oppressively colonized. Since I come from such a culture myself, this challenge to philosophical learning has given me particular pause. Should I or anyone encourage students to recognize their ideal selves in the terms of an historically hostile culture? What are the dangers in doing so? Is there anything nevertheless promising in such teaching? If so, how can this promise be protected?

These questions of mine have received focus and stimulation from a recent essay of the philosopher Charles Taylor, "The Politics of Recognition."[2] Taylor argues that when modern philosophers realized that self-understanding depends on "dialogical recognition," they in effect allied the traditionally philosophical quest for self-understanding with a new multiculturalist "politics of recognition" stemming from the modernist commitment to democracy. This strikes me as a useful way to understand our moral scruples about hegemonic assimilation and our growing interest in cultural diversity. What worries me, though, is that philosophical and political elements of that interest appear to be in uneasy tension, a tension that could threaten the philosophical learning I want to encourage. To offer one response to this tension and to the above set of questions, I would like to sketch a variant of Taylor's argument, one that links his multiculturalist politics to a quest for self-defamiliarization. The educator who encourages this quest would aspire to help us identify and cultivate the stranger in oneself common to all.

"The Politics of Recognition" opens with an explanation of why self-knowledge is currently at stake in various political movements against social discrimination. These all feature the demand that the self-image of a constituency of society be properly recognized.

> . . . [This] demand for recognition . . . is given urgency by the supposed links between recognition and identity, where the latter term designates something like a person's understanding of who they are, of their fundamental defining characteristics as a human being. The thesis is that our identity is partly shaped by recognition or its absence, often by the *mis*recognition of others, and so a person or group of people can suffer real damage, real distortion, if the people or society around them mirror back to them a confining or demeaning or contemptible picture of themselves. Nonrecognition or misrecognition can inflict harm, can be a form of oppression, imprisoning someone in a false, distorted, and reduced mode of being.[3]

The thesis of Taylor's essay is that my self-understanding, for example, is determined not only by my own image of myself but also by the image that others recognize in and communicate to me. If there is an incongruity between these images because others fail to recognize or misrecognize the self-image that I recognize, and if these others have the power to influence me, then my self-understanding could become seriously distorted as I accept features of the image that the others project. Such features could reduce the image that I recognized in myself, thus crippling my potential to flourish in or improve my world. The vulnerability, then, of our self-knowledge to the effects of another's misrecognition makes it something that can be attacked and defended, and so the stake of a politics.

> Thus some feminists have argued that women in patriarchal societies have been induced to adopt a depreciatory image of themselves. They have internalized a picture of their own inferiority, so that even when some of the objective obstacles to their advancement fall away, they may be incapable of taking advantage of new opportunities. And beyond this, they are condemned to suffer the pain of low self-esteem. An analogous point has been made in relation to blacks: that white society has for generations projected a demeaning image of them, which some of them have been unable to resist adopting. Their own self-depreciation, on this view, becomes one of the most potent instruments of their own oppression. Their first task ought to be to purge themselves of this imposed and destructive identity. Recently, a similar point has been made in relation to indigenous and colonized people in general. It is held that since 1492 Europeans have projected an image of such people as somehow inferior, "uncivilized," and through the force of conquest have often been able to impose this image on the conquered.[4]

Before considering Taylor's recommendation that a good way to combat such destructive misrecognition is through education, we should try to get a more perspicuous picture of why the demand for recognition is so crucial to self-knowledge. I may grant that the other's accurate recognition of my image of myself is crucial to fair and constructive communication between us, but why cannot I deny that such recognition makes much difference to that self-image? The self that I expect the other to recognize is presumably already constituted, therefore it is not clear why any subsequent recognition or misrecognition should affect the fact that I already know who I am. We may want to claim that we are entitled to more considerate recognition for other moral reasons, but to maintain that what is at stake in this argument is self-knowledge would seem to be a mistake.

To block this criticism, Taylor supports his thesis with both a historical and a theoretical argument. The former illuminates a significant change that occurred in the way we understand ourselves, a change in our self-knowledge caused by being recognized in different terms. (This argument is filled out in considerably more detail in his book *Sources of the Self*.)[5] It explains how the struggle that transformed feudal societies into modern democratic ones transformed our identities as well. The transformation started to emerge clearly in eighteenth-century Europe and had two components.

The first caused us to identify ourselves less as social superiors or inferiors and more as equals. Taylor describes this shift as a

> collapse of social hierarchies, which used to be the basis for honor. I am using honor in the *ancien regime* sense in which it is intrinsically linked

> to inequalities. For some to have honor in this sense, it is essential that
> not everyone have it. This is the sense in which Montesquieu uses it in
> his description of monarchy. Honor is intrinsically a matter of
> "préférences."[6]

This collapse changed the way we recognize each other, drawing attention to
what we all possess.

> As against this notion of honor, we have the modern notion of dignity,
> now used in a universalist and egalitarian sense, where we talk of the
> inherent "dignity of human beings," or of citizen dignity. The underly-
> ing premise here is that everyone shares in it. It is obvious that this
> concept of dignity is the only one compatible with a democratic society,
> and that it was inevitable that the old concept of honor was superseded.
> But this has also meant that the forms of equal recognition have been
> essential to democratic culture.[7]

Taylor points out that the struggle against feudal hierarchies which stood in
the way of democratic institutions understandably led to a struggle against
the notion of honor supported by these hierarchies. To oppose that notion
there arose the demand that the dignity of each one of us be universally and
equally recognized. This demand that we know ourselves as every citizen's
equal, that we understand ourselves in new terms, thus became an intrinsic
element of the modern demand for democratic social reform.

Alongside the former demand emerged the other component of the shift,
one which also opposed the determination of our identities in terms of
honor. We started to know ourselves instead as original individuals. Taylor
traces this shift to the work of Jean-Jacques Rousseau and Johann Gottlob
Herder; they are prophets of what Taylor calls the ideal of authenticity.

> There is a certain way of being human that is my way. I am called upon
> to live my life in this way, and not in imitation of anyone else's life. But
> this notion gives a new importance to being true to myself. If I am not, I
> miss the point of my life; I miss what being human is for me.[8]

To find myself and to stay true to who I am, I need to turn my attention to an
inner voice already deep inside me. Like the previous shift, this one subverts
the idea that I should be identified by a place in a hierarchical social structure I never made.

> This new ideal of authenticity was, like the idea of dignity, also in part
> an offshoot of the decline of hierarchical society. In those earlier soci-
> eties, what we would now call identity was largely fixed by one's social
> position. . . . The birth of a democratic society doesn't by itself do away
> with this phenomenon, because people can still define themselves by
> their social roles. What does decisively undermine this socially derived

> identification, however, is the ideal of authenticity itself. As this
> emerges . . . it calls on me to discover my own original way of being. By
> definition, this way of being cannot be socially derived, but must be
> inwardly generated.[9]

This ideal challenges us to recognize the self underneath inauthentic honors,
one growing in response to its own natural, independent predispositions. It
lent itself as well to the demand for democracy.

From the notion that our identities are determined by a feudal hierarchy
of honors, then, there is a shift on the one hand to the notion that they are
determined by a system that respects each self's equal dignity, and on the
other hand to the notion that they are determined by authentic self-discovery and self-cultivation. Both of these latter notions supported the general
shift to modern democratic societies. This historical account begins to
answer the objection that one's demand for recognition should make little
difference to one's self-knowledge. It contends that an idea of the self's equal
dignity or its authenticity is not first and naturally pregiven to us and only
secondarily made the focus of a possible demand for recognition. It rather
suggests that these ideas of our selves got hammered out piece by piece in
the course of a contingent political struggle, one that was motivated not only
or even primarily by a need for a new self-image. Before the struggle, we
were relatively content to know ourselves in terms of preferences. After a history of antagonizing events provoked the struggle for democratic rights and
redresses, we found ourselves only half-intentionally having to define ourselves in other terms.

Even if Taylor's historical account is accurate, however, it remains uncertain whether the link between shifts in the terms by which we ask for
recognition and shifts in our self-understanding is really a causal one or
merely one of coincidence. To establish that it is the former, Taylor develops
a theoretical argument that the quest for self-knowledge has a dialogical
character. He derives this character from the crucial role that language learning plays in self-definition.

> We become full human agents, capable of understanding ourselves, and
> hence of defining our identity, through our acquisition of rich human
> languages of expression. For my purposes here, I want to take language
> in a broad sense, covering not only the words we speak, but also other
> modes of expression whereby we define ourselves, including the "lan-
> guages" of art, of gesture, of love, and the like. But we learn these
> modes of expression through exchanges with others. People do not
> acquire the languages needed for self-definition on their own. Rather,
> we are introduced to them through interaction with others who matter
> to us—what George Herbert Mead called "significant others." The gene-
> sis of the human mind is in this sense not monological, not something
> each person accomplishes on his or her own, but dialogical.[10]

Taylor reasons as follows: First, he observes that I can define myself, either to myself or to others, only in the terms of some language. Second, he observes that nobody, including myself, is born knowing how to use a language; I must learn that skill from another language user. Third, there is the observation that this language learning requires a process of dialogue between myself and a teacher. These premises entail fourthly that I can define myself only on condition of having learned how to use a language of self-definition from an accomplished language user through a process of dialogue. Our self-understanding depends on dialogue with others who teach us the terms by which that self could be recognized. Thus our willingness to entrust ourselves, our very recognizability to ourselves, to these particular others and their language, makes them significant indeed.

It may appear that Taylor is describing a learning dialogue that occurs only so long as the child lacks a language of self-description. Once she or he has acquired that language, presumably there would no longer be any need for this kind of dialogical recognition; she or he would be able to understand the self's authentic inner voice on their own. But Taylor resists the idea that the dialogue has a terminal point; he insists that the need for it is lifelong.

> Moreover, this [dialogical character] is not just a fact about *genesis,* which can be ignored later on. We don't just learn the languages in dialogue and then go on to use them for our purposes. . . . We define our identity always in dialogue with, sometimes in struggle against, the things our significant others want to see in us. Even after we outgrow some of these others—our parents, for instance—and they disappear from our lives, the conversation with them continues within us as long as we live.[11]

Because we internalize, in a Freudian sense, those significant others, if we are to remain a self with integrity we need to stay true to, and so in touch with, all of those voices of our personal histories. Conversely, the authentic self does not emerge freely out of my inner depths, as Rousseau and Herder believed, but must be drawn out of those depths by the significant others on whom I remain, to some extent, heteronomously dependent. The inner voice I heed belongs to them.

According to Taylor, the reason that the quest for self-knowledge depends on the dialogical recognition of others is because the self can only be recognized in a language that is learned. To learn that language, I must enter into a dialogue with a significant other; as I adopt the terms of that other to define myself, that other becomes an internalized part of my self. I can then be authentically true to myself only by staying in dialogue with this partner who is either an embodied person or an element of my psyche. This theory of dialogical recognition, then, supplements the historical account of the transformation of our self-understanding with an explanation of how that transformation was caused.

No wonder the philosophical quest for self-knowledge has a political dimension. And no wonder that a primary site of concern for this politics of recognition is education. Taylor's arguments show that my very self-understanding depends on the language I learn and the teachers I incorporate into myself, a language and teachers that are historically rooted in a particular culture. What if that culture is antagonistic to other, closer languages and teachers I embody? What if the ideals promoted by its language and its teachers urge me explicitly or implicitly to devalue other ideals rooted in my familial culture? In response to this challenge, Taylor affirms attempts to criticize and open up "the canon" in university humanities programs and to set up Afrocentric secondary schools. He supports such curricular reforms less because he thinks that students should become more broadminded for its own sake, and more because he wants to combat the anti-democratic tendency of hegemonic cultures to instill a sense of inferiority in those they have colonized, and to give due recognition in compensation to violated cultures and subcultures.

> The reason for these proposed changes is not, or not mainly, that all students may be missing something important through the exclusion of a certain gender or certain races or cultures, but rather that women and students from the excluded groups are given, either directly or by omission, a demeaning picture of themselves, as though all creativity and worth inhered in males of European provenance. Enlarging and changing the curriculum is therefore essential not so much in the name of a broader culture for everyone as in order to give due recognition to the hitherto excluded.[12]

Our multiculturalist initiatives in education should be principally concerned with exposing and criticizing images and terms that stunt possibilities for self-definition, particularly for members of cultures that already suffer from a history of discrimination. These initiatives should strive to replace such images and terms with more promising ones that can evoke the potential for growth and achievement in all. Such an education could thus help prevent the seeds of monocultural domination from taking root in our diverse youth.

For the most part, Taylor's account of how our identities are vulnerably formed, and how educators could help protect us from abuse of that vulnerability, speaks to my experience. But it contains at least two disturbing tensions. One, which Taylor acknowledges, is between a democratic politics of recognition that is multiculturalist and one that is more traditionally liberal and universalist. This tension is rooted in the way that the two forms of democratic recognition, one focusing on dignity and the other on authenticity, lead social reform in different directions.

The recognition of dignity calls for a politics of commonality. Taylor observes that "with the move from honor to dignity has come a politics of universalism, emphasizing the equal dignity of all citizens, and the content of this politics has been the equalization of rights and entitlements."[13] This politics encourages me to recognize how alike I am to my fellow citizens.

The recognition of authenticity, in contrast, focuses on a self which is original and individual. It calls for an appreciation of the features which differentiate the self from others; such a recognition contrasts with the recognition of features which liken the self to others of equal dignity. The stage is set, then, for a politics of difference.

> With the politics of equal dignity, what is established is meant to be universally the same, an identical basket of rights and immunities; with the politics of difference, what we are asked to recognize is the unique identity of this individual or group, their distinctness from everyone else. The idea is that it is precisely this distinctness that has been ignored, glossed over, assimilated to a dominant or majority identity. And this assimilation is the cardinal sin against the ideal of authenticity.[14]

A multiculturalist politics, accordingly, would be a politics that promotes the recognition that members of different cultures each have unique identities, ones which ought not to be assimilated to some dominant commonality. It would be distinct from the politics of equal dignity, and so would be liable to enter into occasional conflict with that politics. Indeed, although both forms and politics of recognition have historically tended to promote democratic societies, the distinction here enables Taylor to identify a significant, built-in equivocation in such societies.

> For one [mode of politics], the principle of equal respect requires that we treat people in a difference-blind fashion. The fundamental intuition that humans command this respect focuses on what is the same in all. For the other, we have to recognize and even foster particularity. The reproach the first makes to the second is just that it violates the principle of nondiscrimination. The reproach the second makes to the first is that it negates identity by forcing people into a homogeneous mold that is untrue to them. That would be bad enough if the mold were itself neutral—nobody's mold in particular. But the complaint generally goes further. The claim is that the supposedly neutral set of difference-blind principles of the politics of equal dignity is in fact a reflection of one hegemonic culture. As it turns out, then, only the minority or suppressed cultures are being forced to take alien form. Consequently, the supposedly fair and difference-blind society is not only inhuman (because suppressing identities) but also, in a subtle and unconscious way, itself highly discriminatory.[15]

This is an insightful elucidation of how the aspirations of multiculturalism may clash with those of liberalism. Taylor holds out the hope that each of these can be eventually reconciled with the other. I remain uncertain, however, about the way he formulated this clash. Shortly, I shall explore whether a multiculturalist politics that acknowledges more fully the implications of dialogical recognition might not be a universalist one as well.

Besides this tension between the two forms of democratic recognition, there is another that could seriously damage the coherence of Taylor's account: namely, that between the multiculturalist politics of recognition and the philosophical quest for self-knowledge. On the other hand, Taylor affirms the above politics because it respects and supports my or anyone else's quest for self-knowledge, protecting such a quest from being unduly constrained by the misrecognition of others. On the other hand, this political sensibility makes it easier for me to react to anything that questions my current self-image as a misrecognition of that image by an antagonistic party. As long as cultural differences are stressed, this inherent antagonism appears bound to perpetuate itself, because it is unlikely that anyone who comes from a "radically other" world could ever recognize me in the way I see myself or my familiars see me. In such a suspicious and defensive posture, I would be disinclined to learn philosophically from strangers how to describe myself and my world differently and perhaps more inspiringly, and so my possibilities for self-understanding would be constrained after all. Conversely, my chances for succeeding at the philosophical teaching I described at the outset of this essay would be severely handicapped.

Let me respond to this second tension first. For the multiculturalist politics of recognition and the philosophical quest for self-knowledge to support each other harmoniously, it has to be possible for me to learn about who I am from a stranger, from the foreign terms by which such a person recognizes me, without fearing that I am thereby internalizing a reductive image of myself, particularly when that image conflicts with the self-image I already have. Is this possible? I think it is if we revise Taylor's idea of "authentic self-understanding."

Taylor usefully identifies my self-understanding with the statements that I make about who I am, statements that start to develop my proper name into a clear and distinct idea. As I reflect on those statements, and on how they are influenced by internal and external dialogues with various significant others, I can determine whether they are relatively coherent and so authentic. Thus take the case where I suddenly realize that the things I say about myself are contradictory and inauthentic. How would we describe this realization? We might say that I have come to understand that my self, the integrity of my being, is something that eludes the inauthentic words of recognition I have learned to use, words that express conflicting identities. My authentic self now appears to be an unrecognizable stranger, a being that neither I nor my significant others can clearly and distinctly define. It bears a cryptic proper name. But if this authentic self cannot be recognized, how do I know that it exists at all? I know this because I am able to recognize that there is something wrong with the contradictory things I say about myself and the self-images I affirm only by invoking this better self as a regulative ideal.

Most of us would consider such a realization to be an exceptionally aporetic moment that spurs us to search for a more coherent understanding and recognition of our authentic selves. If this aporia were not a means to such self-knowledge, then we would consider it simply destructive. Not only would it fail to issue in a better self-understanding than the one with which we started, but it would leave us without any reliable identity with which to cope with the demands of living. It would be a train of thinking that evidently lacks pragmatic value.

Yet what do we do about the propensity of the quest for self-knowledge to put the politics of recognition and philosophical learning in tension with each other? What I would like to suggest is that educators might be able to mitigate this tension if they reduced our investment in recognizable terms of self-understanding, making such terms less worth fighting over. And they can reduce this investment in turn by appreciating and cultivating aporias of self-understanding not as preliminary moments on the way to a clearer, more authentic definition of ourselves, but as themselves more authentic, honest ways of acknowledging the mystery that we are—that we exist. A mystery inscribed in each of our proper names. The aporetic realization that our recognizable selves leave something to be desired would no longer be the problem that authentic self-understanding is supposed to solve, but would be a way to understand why, at some level, our selves must be indefinite. And this understanding would be pragmatically valuable because it addresses the problem of the above tension and of cultural conflict in general.

This suggestion comes to me from what I have understood and appreciated of the critical practice known as "deconstruction." Jacques Derrida and allied thinkers have taught me that it is possible to read the history of philosophy not as a united inquiry progressing toward universal truth but as an ever-renewed conversation, drawing in all sorts of different characters, that is provoked by and that reproduces the thrall of aporia in language. These thinkers invite us to balance the "scientific" tendency in philosophy to value the features of language that promote ideal clarity, verified communication, and committed consensus, with a "literary" appreciation of those features that disclose material opacity (particularly of the signifier), unconscious signification, and undecided possibilities of interpretation. They demonstrate that language should not be assumed to be a negligible medium for one's own self-conscious thinking, but rather should be acknowledged as the necessary material and conventional support of thought, one which at the same time, however, impedes that thought from being completely defined by anyone, including its "author," and exposes it to what stays unthought. Accordingly, their own philosophical discourse that discloses these linguistic features involves us in indefiniteness.[16] Now when I look at the history of philosophical inquiry in the light of this linguistic shadow, I see that although philosophers continue to spin discourses in order to defer indefiniteness, this indefiniteness, like a force of nature, is bound to come back and haunt terms in the discourse. Once altered and alienated from their context, these now questionable terms stand to provoke new mouths to unweave the old discourse and another generation of pens to declare their independence from its terms. So philosophy perpetuates itself. Yet so too does indefiniteness, which remains the condition for the possibility of calling different thinkers into the conversation that keeps philosophy alive.

I believe that the discourse of self-definition, with which we in large part engage in dialogue with significant others, has this aporetic nature as well. From some such others, for example, I have learned to call myself "male," "Asian," "teacher," "healthy," "kind," etc. Yet at any moment in discourse, one such term or another is liable, for one cause or another, to appear suddenly questionable to me. What does it really mean to be "male," and do I want to identify myself with the characteristics that inform this term? Is "Asian" a term which defines a race or a culture, and for whom and for what purposes does it serve as a definition? What is "virtue?" At such moments, I am apt to appeal to the others from whom I learned these terms, in the hope that they can relieve my anxiety. But in the face of it, these others may admit that they too are not sure if these words have any definite meaning after all. What was it, then, that I learned from them? What becomes of the meaningful, *authentic* self I learned to recognize in myself in their terms? Who were those people, who once were so significant to me? Whom do I now want others to recognize? Who am I?

Like them, like you, I am a stranger—recognize me!

Can this reply suffice for all practical demands? Can it, for instance, serve as an intelligible locus of job responsibilities that co-workers can rely on? No, it cannot. To carry on in a fairly predictable way in many settings, each of us must assume one or another practical role, identity, for much of our lives. Still, we are bound to wonder about what it is that assumes these identities, particularly when they clash. I am arguing that the most honest name we have for that thing is the indefinite, mysterious self. This self has no positive features, and so cannot be judged to be "authentically truer" than other "fictive" identities we assume. But we must acknowledge its existence in order to see the lifeline on which these identities are strung.

The society most congenial to an acknowledgment of this self is a multiculturalist democracy. Such a society fosters the likelihood that each one of us will have to face the cultural stranger whose alternative terms of self-definition expose our self-knowledge, our recognizability to ourselves in certain terms, to indefiniteness. Because we want to respect and nurture the indefinite self, therefore, we would support a politics that promotes such a society. And this support would be based on a reason different than Taylor's respect for the unique features of one's cultural identity.

Of course, exposure to indefiniteness without any direction at all is less likely to bring selves together than to open up a divisive abyss of disorientation, fear, and antagonism. Hence the task for a multiculturalist education is to turn the instability of identity into a supple celebration of what eludes identification, to defamiliarize the self. Such an education would aim to direct us from a recognition of and respect for the cultural identity of the stranger, to a recognition that one's own cultural identity is likewise indefinite and self-estranging, to a recognition that this indefiniteness broaches a shared discourse. In such a discourse, we may learn that we are all strangers to ourselves, together cast into an unfamiliar, *unheimlich* home. In such a discourse, a politics sensitive to cultural differences would meet a politics that finds in these differences the natural limit of our intelligible identities; an incongruous mix of cultures would thus yield a common sense of strangeness. And so is born hope for a new politics of commonality, one grounded in nature conceived not as an intelligible (to some privileged cultural language) cosmos but as the withdrawing source of language and linguistic beings, the mysterious X. Such a politics would be guided by a discourse of universal rights for a multicultural society. It would mitigate the first tension in Taylor's account discussed above: that between the two strands of the democratic politics of recognition.

How could a multiculturalist education encourage such self-defamiliarization for democratically constructive purposes? It could do this by focusing classroom discourse on two kinds of curricular material. On the one hand, the teacher would present students with images of otherness drawn from history, anthropology, and the arts, and would press them to think again before taking the intelligibility of the stranger for granted. Like Taylor, I want to prevent cultural images from being given stultifying interpretations. On the other hand, the teacher would simultaneously treat these images as spurs to a questioning of the terms of the students' own sense of their identities, in order to bring to light latent, compelling, and alienating aporias. The fact that we can discuss these questions and aporias seriously and sincerely should then suggest to all in class that on the deepest level we are in touch with, and kin to, the cultural alien. It should discourage us from thinking that we need to distinguish ourselves invidiously and antagonistically from others, and encourage us instead to learn from those others about how to live with this dimension of ourselves. To develop this kind of questioning, philosophical literature is invaluable.

If we read such literature in the light of deconstruction as one that calls attention to the ineliminability of indefiniteness, then the history of philosophy affords us an important moral about human nature: that of our infectiously shared vulnerability. The appearance of indefiniteness calls philosophers into dialogue about what their self-knowledge is exposed to. To the extent that it has this power of a calling, indefiniteness evokes and extends the community of those threatened by it. Yet as the meaning of the terms it haunts withdraws into obscurity, it brings to light the meaning of a common concern, of a certain kind of friendship, of *philia*. And for these friends who in dialogue learn to appreciate their internally shared identity, their bonds of affection, this indefiniteness may then turn into a disarming source of good to be celebrated, a *sophia*. It gives the gift of intimacy. Thus *philosophia* could be transformed from a project to eliminate or reduce indefiniteness, from an epistemological project, into a giving thanks for how the return of indefiniteness reminds us of our awful and awesome, sublime communion with indefinite Being (ontologically different, as Heidegger shows, from culturally defined beings).[17] It could become a pacifying meditation on the night out of which we were born and to which we will mortally return, the night that draws us together.

Rimbaud blazed a trail in the arts with his declaration: "Je est un autre" (I is an other). I believe that the time is ripe to respond to divisive suspicions about who *we* are—does your *we* include my *we?*—by affirming that we *all* are other to ourselves. Such an affirmation marries a pacifistic rather than antagonistic politics of recognition to a multiculturalist education in self-defamiliarization as well as self-definition. This affirmation also sheds new light on the value of philosophical learning in a culturally diverse context. It suggests that we might appreciate philosophy less for its power to reach conclusions than for its power to unsettle presuppositions, less for its capacity to reduce differences to a single argument than for its capacity to use multiple perspectives to raise questions that put everybody, teacher, student, and surprised onlooker, at a loss for an answer. In the silence that ensues, we may then remember that before we are anything, we *are,* mysteriously side by side.

NOTES

1. See, for example, Stanley Cavell, *Conditions Handsome and Unhandsome: The Constitution of Emersonian Perfectionism: The Carus Lectures, 1988* (Chicago: The University of Chicago Press, 1990) and *The Voice of Liberal Learning: Michael Oakeshott on Education,* ed. Timothy Fuller (New Haven: Yale University Press, 1989).

2. In *Multiculturalism and the "Politics of Education,"* ed. Amy Gutmann (Princeton: Princeton University Press, 1992).

3. Ibid., 25.

4. Ibid., 25–26.

5. Charles Taylor, *Sources of the Self: The Making of the Modern Identity* (Cambridge, MA: Harvard University Press, 1989).

6. Taylor, "The Politics of Recognition," 26–27.

7. Ibid., 27.

8. Ibid., 30.

9. Ibid., 31–32.

10. Ibid., 32.

11. Ibid., 32–33.

12. Ibid., 65–66.

13. Ibid., 37.

14. Ibid., 38.

15. Ibid., 43.

16. See Jacques Derrida, *Speech and Phenomena and Other Essays on Husserl's Theory of Signs,* trans. with an intro. by David B. Allison (Evanston, IL: Northwestern University Press, 1973) and Jacques Derrida, *Limited Inc* (Evanston, IL: Northwestern University Press, 1988).

17. In this spirit, I am glad to acknowledge the example of Martin Heidegger's meditative thinking, particularly as he practices it in Martin Heidegger, *What is Called Thinking?* trans. by J. Glenn Gray and F. Wieck (New York: Harper and Row, 1968). For his explanation of the ontological difference between Being and beings, see, among other works, Martin Heidegger, *Identity and Difference,* trans. with an intro. by Joan Stambaugh (New York: Harper and Row, 1969).

14

Narrative in Philosophy of Education: A Feminist Tale of "Uncertain" Knowledge

Lynda Stone

Over the past decade or so, narrative has assumed an important place not only overall in educational research and practice but also increasingly in Philosophy of Education. There are several reasons: A general move in the academic disciplines toward interpretation; the development in education of qualitative forms of inquiry as response to narrowly-construed and positivistic quantitative forms; growth of a research field on teaching and attention to teachers' lives; and, a larger societal, romantic longing for community and for stories that no longer seem to count. As two devotees explain:

> Stories and narrative, whether personal or fictional, provide meaning and belonging in our lives. . . . The story fabric offers us images, myths, and metaphors that are morally resonant and contribute both to our knowing and our being known.[1]

An additional factor influencing this turn to narrative, one primary for this chapter, is from feminisms' theorizing in all areas of intellectual pursuit, including education.[2] More on this shortly.

The strong turn to narrative has been in intellectual disciplines not generally associated with its form, not in the arts and poetics. This means that a

173

shift of emphasis has occurred in Charles Taylor's two meanings, Jerome Bruner's two kinds of knowing, and C. P. Snow's two cultures.[3] No longer, as over the past three hundred years (save for the flowering of nineteenth century Romanticism), is analysis (science) rather than art, dominant.

The lengthy preeminence of science and analysis and explanation is understandable when within philosophy extremes are presented "for argument's sake." Narrative is delirium—light-minded, "pure imagination unconditioned by structures," and irresponsible. Analysis is hysteria (but only when as Freud asserted undertaken by women), serious-minded, systemic (not dogmatic nor rigid), responsible, and the positing of truth.[4] This caricature has fallen away as analytic philosophy has been influenced by European social theory. Knowledge is acknowledged as socially constructed if not altogether non-objective and the quest for certainty has been given up. Philosophy has become *more like* literature.

Enter increasingly, women philosophers and those with feminist orientations: Stories are alternative discourses—and these theorists have searched for and utilized alternatives. This is because across the academy as within philosophy women have felt left out. Their life experiences, their meanings, and their forms of communication have not been traditionally present. Stories matter, asserts critic Carolyn Heilbrun (herself a writer of mysteries):

> We can retell and live by the stories we have read and heard. . . . [They are] like the murmurings of our mothers, telling us what conventions demand . . . [and] they are what we must use to make new fictions, new narratives . . . [and new lives].[5]

Like their women/feminist academic counterparts, educational philosophers are employing narrative in their writings, variously in function, form, and scope.[6] Illustrative is pioneer Maxine Greene for whom literature manifests philosophic meaning. Her metaphoric use of authorial reference, particular story and criticism has paved the way for others to use. Likewise Nel Noddings' recent narrative phenomenology introduces significant, new philosophic method. Some connect narrative in personal and fictional forms to other disciplinary perspectives. Madeleine Grumet and Jo Anne Pagano, so-called "curriculum reconceptualists," employ phenomenology and psychoanalytic theory (among influences) to tell their educational "stories." Deanne Bogdan expertly weaves literary theory and criticism into philosophic pedagogical accounts. Finally, Susan Laird and Margret Buchmann have used fiction in varying degrees in their philosophic writings for analytic purposes.[7]

A summing point: Like the academy in general, narrative is increasingly important in Philosophy of Education. Here as elsewhere the work is both systematic and rigorous and seriousminded; its proponents are not (as one feminist aesthetician put it) "mere experience freaks."[8] For the field, narrative now represents a genuine alternative and significant addition to traditional method and content. In the following, a fictional letter is used to do Philosophy of Education, to frame and advance explanation through description of women's lives, The story becomes one of four women, two who never lived and two who have.

> Dear Ms. Bâ:[9]   December 1992; January 1994
>
> As you began a fictional letter, I now begin one to you. "I take a deep breath" because I too am speculating. I take a chance with this letter to seek reception as if we might have been friends, with no assurances of either reception nor friendship. My letter is in the tradition of western feminisms; it is as personal and political as it is academic and educational. It has politics just as your work. In my undertaking I have you as fellow author, and your fictional friends, Ramatoulaye and Aissatou, as models. I take heart and I continue.
>
> I begin by positioning us—may I call you Mariama?—as authors.[10] You are identified as a "pioneer of women's rights" committed to the eradication of inequalities between women and men in Africa. I am a white, North American academic and educator. I, as you, have taught school; we are both middleclass in our respective societies. We are in times of change but ones with important distinction: African nations continue to throw off the residues of an external colonialism, and to move for better or worse from traditional into modern/postmodern times. North American nations, it might be said, retain some internal colonialism against minorities as times become postmodern. In spite of some similarities, we are to my mind, significantly different. This is the difference that I want us to retain yet communicate across.
>
> To advance your feminist project, you write a fictional letter between friends who out of childhood similarities and adult differences remain close. Across our differences, I write a letter to you in order to put your important literary accomplishment to new ends, those within philosophy of education. Were you to know of my task, I hope that you would approve.

A Senegalese schoolteacher and inspector by profession, Mariama Bâ wrote the novelette, *So Long a Letter* because she wanted to strike out "at archaic practices, traditions, and customs that are now a part of [her] precious cultural heritage." After a long illness, Bâ died in 1981 just prior to the appearance of a second novel. This first book, the letter, was translated from French into sixteen languages and was awarded the first Noma Award for Publishing in Africa.[11]

The thesis of the present fictional letter—based as it is upon another[12]—concerns the lives of women as they experience certainty and uncertainty. The point is paradoxical: For many women what is certain about their lives is its uncertainty. This uncertainty manifests itself in three dimensions—tied specifically to Bâ's letter. These are agency, essentialism, and friendship. The first takes up the concept of human action from traditional, male-defined discourse and questions whether it is "natural" to be certain. The second connects as an exploration into what difference in women's lives means and how this influences agency. The third risks working through women's differences to suggest that friendship can occur. A founding irony: That uncertainty names the present era of postmodernism may mean that females—as they are used to uncertainty, tentativeness, and ambiguity—may be able to live psychologically better today than some (many?) of their male counterparts. If the norm of certainty is replaced by a norm of uncertainty, the question of who best fits the times takes on new meaning.[13]

The times suggest, and the present analysis posits, that the era is increasingly one of uncertainty. Themes of change rather than continuity, of transition rather than stability, permeate most descriptions of everyday life. To get at the era theoretically, a kind of dialectic is needed. This is to see description of experience as related to explanation and explanation as related to experience. One way to do this is to recognize that all private experience is potentially public (and its communication *is* public) and thus political. As feminisms' initial tenet asserts: the personal is political; the distinctions between private and public realms of experience are collapsed. Theory takes up the personal for non-personal exposition. Literary critic, Nancy Miller names one form as "personal criticism:"

> Getting personal in criticism typically involves a deliberate move toward self-figuration, although degree and form of self-disclosure vary widely . . . There is self-narrative woven into critical argument . . . [and] the insertion of framing or interstitial material . . . [As well, it] can take the form of punctuating self-portrayal . . . [or the portrayal of "intimate" others.] . . . [it is] confessional, locational . . . anecdotal . . . All function as a kind of internal signature or autographics.[14]

In sum, feminist writing (and increasingly other genres) is on occasion highly private and personal in order to further public/political/professional purposes. This is more than—although an extension of—consciousness raising. [Developing out of yesterday's revolutionary Chinese practice called "speaking bitterness," consciousness raising was an initial sharing of information for common purposes.][15] Today's academic practices also pose shared aims but with a much more thorough understanding of the uncommon ramifications of such endeavors.

Now a turn to the letter within this letter, to Mariama Bâ's account of Ramatoulaye and Aissatou and what they tell us about women's lives.

> Mariama, I return:
> I begin with the question of what women know of their actions in the world. What is certain for them? Out of my own experience and from

the stories of others, I take it that a norm among us exists of uncertainty. This is not to say that what we set out to do is never accomplished, it is. But it is to say something about norms. My view is that in spite of past successes, of beliefs and convictions, we never know if our actions will be realizable. And, even within the relatively privileged confines of some of our lives, often we are "reminded" of uncertainty and of our lack of control. I further suggest that this standard differs for many if not most men. Furthermore many of us know that actions we take out of this condition, and those taken by others for us, are not in our own best interests. We take this for granted: this is "as it is,"—is just part of life or "the system." It is, if we were all granted safe spaces to reflect, other than what we desire.

You write of uncertainty of action when describing the funeral and mourning arrangements of Ramatoulaye's dead but estranged husband, Modou. Ramatoulaye explains that by Islamic tradition,[16]

> the share of each widow [of the familial estate] must be doubled, as must the gifts of Moudou's grandchildren, represented by the offspring of all his male and female cousins.

> Thus, our family-in-law take away with them a wad of notes, painstakingly topped, and leave us utterly destitute, we who will need material support (p. 7).

> This is the moment dreaded by every Senegalese woman, the moment when she sacrifices her possessions . . . and worse still . . . she gives up her personality, her dignity in becoming a thing in the service of the man who has married her [and of his famililies] (p. 4).

What seems certain for Ramatoulaye and her friend Aissatou is that the actions of men in their lives determine their "destinies," and thus constitute the uncertainty that I explore. In each case, young lovers become loved and loving husbands, who decide in their middle ages and through the manipulations of others, to take new and much younger second wives. Ramatoulaye and Aissatou take different paths in response. Here there is self-determined action but within limiting societal conditions. Aissatou, proud daughter of a goldsmith divorces her husband, the son of royal blood; she cannot condone polygamy. Ramatoulaye's "choice" is for estrangement rather than divorce as she learns of the deeds of a greedy mother-in-law. The latter's actions (one wonders at her autonomy) devastate more than one life as children and a hapless second bride are implicated. All of this "ends" in the premature death of Moudou—taxed beyond endurance by financial burden. Ramatoulaye's decision is to live alone—and in a very "modern" decision to reject a new but unsuitable suitor.

Times of personal crisis and transition mirror those of a society. Ramatoulaye and Aissatou are fortunate in many ways, as part of an emerging middle-class. They are also somewhat economically self-supporting as graduates of the teacher training college. Ramatoulaye recalls to her friend, the experiences and purposes of their earlier years:

> We were true sisters, destined for the same mission of emancipation.
>
> To lift us out of the bog of tradition . . . to make us appreciate a multitude of civilizations without renouncing our own, to raise our vision of the world . . . [and] to strengthen our . . . qualities . . . for the promotion of black women (pp. 15–16).

As you know, Mariama, as times change so do traditions. In a rare victory, Ramatoulaye wins some recognition as a first wife in a legal fight over the distribution of her late husband's assets.

Women such as Ramatoylaye and Aissatou explain their choices and actions in two commonsense dimensions, one with regard to tradition and custom and the other with regard to other persons with whom they are in relation. Here heteronomy (meaning dependence) is the norm—and for many women (and some men) this standard is natural, certain and good. In contrast, "good" human action has been defined by western philosophers (until very recently men) in terms of autonomy meaning independence, and of free will, and of rationality. Certainty of action then occurs as rational persons exercise their free will to make choices and decisions of action. The dominant rhetoric is that if one wants to do something strongly enough, if one plans rationally to do it, if one examines possible choices of actions and consequences, then the act can be done. This conception plays out, importantly, whether one's act is conducted as planned (is successful) or not. Human action or agency is voluntary and able to be rationally justified.

This picture of agency, what feminists often write about as subjectivity,[17] has been criticized by them (and by others such as post-colonial theorists). Their critique arises, as indicated in the present story, because throughout history most women's lives have been constrained and circumscribed; they have acted "autonomously" as men have. However, that they have not acted freely and individually is *not* just an empirical matter. Were this the case, acting and active women today would change tradition and custom and this change would in turn change the possibilities of action. This has of course occurred over time. However, this view is insufficient as it denies the bases for tradition and custom, first in religion and second in philosophy.

In western philosophy, beginning with Aristotle (and to a different degree with Plato) women are defined as inferior to men in terms of rationality—all this founded in an unequal biology.[18] The initiating norm is that men are the generators of life and women the passive carriers. The latter as a result are less powerful and are identified with the body; in opposition, men are more powerful and identified with the mind. In society and throughout history this has meant that women are denied realms in which mind—rationality—counts, i.e., in the public sphere. In relegating them to the private sphere, to the home, women are denied contributing access to culture and to citizenship. As classic feminist analysis puts this, a hierarchical dualism is established in which women are assigned emotionality rather than rationality and, according to basic philosophic dogma, submission to men.[19]

As indicated, emotion plays a special role in the philosophic scenario. This is because it is defined as tied to passion and thus to *irrationality:* when passion is aroused, forces "conspire" to block rationality. A long history shrouds women in emotion and as objects to be dominated by strong subjects—by thinking male persons. This domination is important too so that women do not tempt men to be irrational. A connection to western religious litany is obvious.[20]

The feminist philosophic response is varied and evolving. One step is to argue for women as rational persons, capable of utilizing the same minds as men. Another step is to argue for the value of emotional aspects of all lives and thus to elevate the value of emotion. Still another is to argue for separate forms of female and male living, action, and decision-making. Finally two of the most recent are to break apart the monism of concepts such as rationality and emotionality. Added to rationality, still of particular importance, is the idea of "unconscious" contributions. And, incorporated into both women's and men's rational processes are the differences of power, of race and class. Agents or subjectivities are now multiple both within each person and across societies.[21]

One other element mentioned above concerns agency. This is autonomy, that is, individuality-collectivity and its related aspect, independence-dependence. Enter here women's historical experience as private members of families and through men of communities; enter here the historical primacy of women's relation to children for whom they have been principal caretakers. While debates have concerned the influences of nature or nurture on the gendered roles of women, no one can deny the centrality of dependence and collectivity. Feminist analyses have thus pointed to a significant contradiction for women's rationality, as contrasted with standard dimensions of individual autonomy. This is tricky: traditionally men acted alone and brought their families along with them; women acted in concert with their families, often putting the needs, desires, and purposes of others before their personal ones.[22]

A summing point is in order. Uncertainty of women's actions in the world devolve from two realms, one of experience and the other of explanation. In this regard, however, all women's experiences have not been the same—and relatively recent feminist theorizing emphasizes this.

> Hello again, Mariama:
>   I want to take up with you the matter of difference that I pointed to initially. For us, as feminists, this is known as the problem of essentialism. Difference, as Ramatoulaye and Aissatou demonstrate, is connected both to personal circumstances and societal situations. A set of rhetorical questions begin this part of our communication: Will you agree that personal differences are more easily accepted and worked through when women are of the same culture? Will you agree that these become complicated as factors of status and power—of tribal affiliation, of occupation, of racial/ethnic identity, and of social class intervene? Will you

agree that they become difficult, sometimes unresolvably so, when these last structural features (and associated life experiences) create distant "others?"

Ramatoulaye and Aissatou share common cultural beginnings and lifelong friendship as a result. The former reminds her friend of "[walking] the same paths of adolescence to maturity" (p. 1). Schooling is the same; then career paths diverge and there are different responses to marriage difficulties. Ramatoulaye writes,

> [Books] enable you [Aissatou] to better yourself. What society refused you . . . [initially as a "working class" woman,] they granted: examinations sat and passed took you also to France. The School of Interpreters . . . led to your appointment into the Senegalese Embassy of the United States. You make a very good living. You are developing in peace, as your letters tell me (p. 32).

Aissatou's struggle through divorce and career are not without painful consequence in times of transition. Such struggles are easier for Daba, Ramatoulaye's oldest daughter. It is she who fights for her mother's inheritance. Her married life differs from that of her mother and family friend.

> Daba does not find housework a burden. Her husband cooks rice as well as she does. . . . [He states boldly], "Daba is my wife. She is not my slave, nor my servant."
>
> I sense [Ramtoulaye continues] the tenderness growing between this young couple. . . . They identify with each other, discuss everything so as to compromise (pp. 73–74).

More choices are available to Daba than to her mother. But even for Daba's generation transition continues. Here is her statement of present politics and her "relative" power:

> In a political party it is rare for a woman to make an easy break-through. For a long time, men will continue to have the power of decision. . . . I prefer my own association, where there is neither rivalry nor schism. . . . [Therein] each of us has an equal opportunity to advance her ideas. . . . [We] work towards the progress of women . . . mobilized . . . [by] a healthy militancy (p. 74).

The daughter experiences a greater equality in marriage and a public solidarity among women that is denied her mother. Given her own societal situation, Ramatoulaye's actions to choose an independent life are indeed courageous. Her actions, common sense dictates, are not solely her own but undertaken by other brave women also. What is her own—through your voice, Mariama—is the public expression.

As the story of Ramatoulaye, Aissatou, and Daba indicates, significant differences surround the lives of women within any culture and across cultures. This problem of difference is known in feminist theorizing as "essentialism." The term has broader application beyond feminism: it means any explanation and valuation of "totality, singularity, sameness or oneness."[23] As explanation it conflates and reifies individual experience and by definition posits something as "alike" for all persons. Examples abound in modern philosophy's search for certainty, such as objectivism, foundationalism, and universalism.[24] Objectivism is the claim for an external explanatory matrix, foundationalism is the claim for a spatial or temporal initiating point, and universalism (often applicable when looking across cultures) is the claim for commonality of traditions and customs. Various explications of feminist essentialism concern universalism and also another form, structuralism.

Univeralism as applied to the experiences of women posits an innate femininity.[25] Such an assertion is not surprising given the standardization of traditional women's roles in reproductive and familial capacities. The issue is whether these are innate—biological or "god given." Or, whether these are the same for all women. Essentialism in feminist theorizing also incorporates the latter in a structuralism that focuses on influences of race and class on gender. Common sense turns to the experiential lives of women have dictated these new theorizings that applaud women's differences.

As Ramatoulaye, Aissatou and Daba exemplify, within a culture positionings (recall the authors' location in society) help "determine" individual paths. Their stories show that sometimes agency "intervenes" in structure so that particular persons "break out of their molds." This, as is well-recognized, is unusual and possible perhaps only in times of change. While the liberal hope has been and is for equality of opportunity, worldwide evidence of this remains rare.

From various feminist positions, writers take up structural issues of class and race, and explore matters within the "uncommon" struggle among women. Such a term names difference in contrast to the essentializing sameness of past "common" struggles. Marxist (now usually Socialist) feminists consider the various dimensions of social class location on equal opportunity—on home, occupation and education, on productive and reproductive capacity. Their basic point is to dismantle the hegemony of women's double lives as both mothers and workers. Difference from men is the key here. But there is more since it matters whether women are working or middle class: whether they have always worked outside of the home, whether they have choice in reproductive control. In this regard, Multicultural feminists consider the influences of race location on opportunity. They point out the privileging in the west of white, middle class women and the dangers of "inclusion" within a structural hegemony. For example, look at the implications of naming some different persons as others (as different *from*); look at the implications of majority as against minority labeling.[26]

Explicating the uncommon struggle among women relates, of course, to their differing relationships to men and to the centrality of power. Feminists of many varieties today inquire into the structures and increasingly the "poststructures" of power. Postmodern, poststructural feminists are attempting to "give up" the theoretical determinism of structures such as class and race in their move to particularism. But, a danger exists here. This is that moving attention away from matters of race and class as they influence gender may mean reinscribing past essentialisms (in new disguises). A return to a liberal feminist individualizing is not the answer as it neutralizes within a societal androgeny and even further separates women in their political (power) struggles.

Finally, one important aspect of *non-essentialism* within feminism is to rename the inquiry itself as "feminisms." This accounts for the recent and healthy proliferation of theoretical positions such as liberal, radical, Marxist, socialist, postmodern, poststructural, and multicultural. Others are also vibrant: black feminism, African-American feminism, womanism, lesbian feminism, lesbian separatist feminism, psychoanalytic feminism, and even (as vantaged from the left) new-traditionalism, and conservative or essentialist feminism. There are still others.[27] The point here is that within feminist theorizing, essentialism has particular meaning as women struggle to claim their own voices and multiple identities; to work through the power problems of their uncommon struggle, and yet retain some semblance of their overall and initiating project. Today this means achieving solidarity through differences—if only for a time.

> Dear Mariama, one last time:
> I end this letter by turning to the matter of friendship. You recall that at the outset I wrote of the risk in this, of seeking intimate connection across our differences and across the essentializing practices of white feminists. I want to explore the possibility of friendship in our continuing uncommon struggle as well as our common one. Why friendship you might ask.
> It seems to me that friendship is one realm of women's lives that has always thrived in spite of patriarchal domination. You write in Ramatoulaye's letter to Aissatou of their beginnings together:
>
>> Your presence in my life is by no means fortuitous. Our grandmothers in their compounds were separated by a fence and would exchange messages daily. Our mothers used to argue who would look after our uncles and aunts. As for us, we wore our wrappers and sandals on the same stony road to the koranic school. . . . [I still keep intact my memories . . . of us. . . . My friend . . . I call . . . you] (p. 1).
>
> In this beginning you offer traditional dimensions of friendship in common backgrounds—living in the same neighborhoods, attending the same schools, knowing the same people, living very similarly. The lives of childhood friends sometimes diverge as did those of Ramatoulaye and Aissatou; but significantly, friendships do survive these divergences.
> One reason for the survival of women's friendships has been (even if it differs now) solidarity, their joining together against oppression. About this, Ramatoulaye says,

> My heart rejoices each time a woman emerges from the shadows. I know that the field of our gains is unstable, the retention of conquests difficult: social constraints are ever-present, and male egoism resists.

> Instruments for some, baits for others, respected or despised, often muzzled, all women have almost the same fate, which religious or unjust legislation have sealed (p. 88).

A brief but important digression: Your book reminds me that life conditions of women around the world differ greatly. My own relative privilege lulls me sometimes (and more often those younger than I) into believing that things have changed. Yes, they have and even for you and yours. However, even with these changes there still remains a need for memory and for diligent attention to continued discrimination. This attention can transcend differences and facilitate mutual action for common purposes. And, through working together a move toward friendship.

Returning to the point, the friendship of Ramatoulaye and Aissatou models a significant aspect. This is that the connection transcends personal differences. Friends are openly critical of each other but in supportive ways. They discuss differences in ideologies and differences in daily practices and they do this without anger. But, even if anger erupts—a miscommunication taken too seriously—friends do not allow it to destroy. They reestablish warm intimacy often by laughing at themselves. Ramatoulaye expresses this acknowledgement of difference as well as the continuity of connection:

> [Aissatou,] Will I see you tomorrow in a tailored suit or a long dress? . . . Used to living far away, you will want . . . [a] table, plate, chair, fork? . . . But I will not let you have your way. I will spread out a mat. On it there will be the big steaming bowl into which you will have to accept that other hands dip.

> Beneath that shell that has hardened you . . . perhaps I will feel you vibrate. I would so much like to hear you . . . encourage my eagerness . . . to see you take part in . . . [my] new way.

> I warn you already, I have not given up wanting to refashion my life (p. 89).

Feminist theorists are presently struggling with the problem of essentialism, first to describe it as above, and second to overcome its limitations for association. One suggestion has been to posit a politics of difference, that is one that allows for very different women to put their differences aside for a time, to work together for common purposes and then to separate. Iris Marion Young's model is an enlightened pluralistic society offering the best of modern city life. She states:

> If we take seriously the way many people live their lives today, it appears that people enjoy cities, that is places where strangers are

thrown together. . . . [They exhibit] a temporal and spatial differentiation that . . . produce[s] an experience of *aesthetic inexhaustability*. . . . This
is an experience of difference . . . not planned and coherent . . . [of] always
having a sense of beyond . . . [and never grasping] the city as a whole.[28]

Such a position appears to facilitate women's politics but more is perhaps
needed. This is because a set of conditions is necessary for the coming
together in the first place: conditions that allow for the trust and communication necessary for effective political activity. This is where the idea of
friendship comes in.

The present proposal then is for adopting the memory of friendship among
persons who are not now friends, who might never be friends—or who just
might be. This is the attitude of *as if friends*. Very different persons, even
those distanced from one another, act *as if friends* if they exhibit openness to
different opinions and perspectives, if they demonstrate humility about their
own views, and if they try out trust of the other. This attitude means putting
each other in the best light possible within a climate of generosity.

Openness, humility, and trust—to return to the central theme of this
essay—all work from an initial position of uncertainty. Here uncertainty does
not mean hesitancy in action; in fact it suggests just the opposite. This is to
proactively assert the attitude of *as if friends*. Here uncertainty means accepting as natural the tentativeness, ambiguity, fluidity of all of life and
particularly of the beliefs and desires, knowledges, and actions of persons.
This uncertainty moves from a negative characteristic of women's lives to one
that is positive. The pardox is that something uncertain assumes a
certainty—a new kind of knowledge of self and others.

Openness to different opinions and perspectives entails four dimensions:
receptivity, listening, tolerance, and suspension of judgment. Receptivity is
required for openness as its initiating state and to be open one must "open
oneself up" to something new and different. This means in a positive rather
than a negative way, one of anticipation rather than antipathy. Following
receptivity comes "really listening." Perhaps this means assuming a stance of
sympathy for the different view—not taking hold of it totally but of considering it. The "real" dimension is significant because the listening must itself be
genuine and continue its positive orientation. Next is tolerance, an important
move. This means acknowledging difference and even disagreement but
agreeing that this is all right. Finally there is the temporary suspension of
judgment, suspension for the duration of the association. Such suspension
means that one may "get caught in one's own tolerance,"[29] in having to support ideas that are antithetical to one's own. What may occur over time,
however, is that the suspended negative judgment becomes a positive and
supportive one for new reasons—from new understandings.

Humility to one's own view is also essential for the attitude of *as if friends*.
Three of its dimensions are scepticism, playfulness, and ego-distancing. An

attitude of scepticism or continual doubting must permeate the interaction. Doubt here is directed *not* at the other but at oneself. This does not mean lacking self-assurance but rather it means always recognizing one's own limitations. Playfulness enters as each participant sees limitations in general, in human failures and foibles. In terms of ideas this means realizing that even the best ones have short lives. Finally, it seems to me, ego-distancing is crucial. This means putting one's ideas out in front, of attempting to separate temporary beliefs from one's emotional stake in them.[30] New ideas and practices develop far easier in a climate of reflection in which individual ownership is not the issue.

Lastly, trying out trust is the culmination of the effort of *as if friends*. Friendship is based on mutual and continuing trust that must begin at some point. In actual intimacies, this occurs most often over time and without a naming: in *as if friends,* this means a kind of pretense. The pretense is a positive one, and as sum, of putting the other in the best light possible from a perspective of generosity. One important element here, it seems to me, is to allow the trying out to take time and to incorporate mistakes. Friends do make mistakes, miscommunicate, and even hurt each other sometimes; as if friends will also do this.

What theoretically emerges from the attitude of *as if friends* is a new ethic of uncertainty. This ethic, based as it is on many/most women's experiences, helps women who are different, distanced, and "other" to each, potentially join together. It accomplishes within the uncommon struggle of women today what was the hope of solidarity of the common struggle of yesterday.

It allows for authors Mariama Bâ and Lynda Stone to communicate, to undertake endeavors for mutual benefit, to live well and in a specific sense with their uncertainty, and to share a kind of friendship. This surely, for women, is useful knowledge.

Maxine Greene posits: "It may be that education can only take place when we can be the friends of one another's minds."[31]

As an exemplar of doing Philosophy of Education—largely for an Anglo-American audience—this essay has utilized a narrative written by a late African feminist, Mariama Bâ. It is a special story, one that resonates with the experiences of many women (and some men too). It has been appropriated (the author hopes with the same spirit and honesty) to work through problems of women's agency and difference. Written a decade ago, it is still a story of the moment.

This essay does more than exemplify current feminisms' theorizing and issues. It explores the use of different methodologies for doing philosophy and Philosophy of Education. Such explorations are becoming commonplace in educational research. Indeed this seems an "era of narrative."[32] However, use requires caution.

The dangers of story, of local and particular tales, are twofold. The first is the potential for essentializing discussed in this essay. That is, to generalize out of narratives as formerly out of analyses, and to claim that there is underlying sameness in people's lives. The point, of course, is not that people do not live similarly, but to assert this as lawlike and natural. The second danger is the potential for a conservative romanticizing of particularity. This too is a kind of essentialism if one's own story is privileged over that of someone else. Both dangers, I believe, are remnants of modernity that need to give way in postmodernity.

Once again here is a return to tentativeness, to uncertainty, and difference. In postmodern, poststructural theory there is attention to the societal context out of which individuals' experiences occur—to matters, for instance, of race, class, and gender. But these structures are worked through in each theorization, in each account at each historicist moment. They are tentative, uncertain, and different not only from each other but in each telling and reading. Significantly, the particularity of narratives remains both intact and ethical. What does this last mean? Specific stories tell us only of their specificity but this is not unimportant. Importance lies in avoiding the dangers of reinscribing past essentialisms and discriminations and in attempting to avoid present and future harm through merely asserting difference for difference sake. Here one difference all too easily assumes dominance over another. The use of narratives then is an ethical undertaking, related surely to the central aim of education. This finally is to create a world in which fictional and actual persons, women like Ramtoulaye and Aissatou, and Mariama Bâ, can live lives free from harm. Exploring this aim is doing philosophy that has vast social and educational implications.[33]

NOTES

1. See Carol Witherall and Nel Noddings, *Stories Lives Tell: Narrative and Dialogue in Education* (New York: Teachers College Press, 1991), p. 1.

2. Lynda Stone, ed., *The Education Feminism Reader* (New York: Routledge, 1994).

3. Two traditions of human knowing have been present across the millenia. See Charles Taylor, "Language and Human Nature" in *Human Agency and Language: Philosophical Papers I* (Cambridge: Cambridge University Press, 1985), pp. 217–47; Jerome Bruner, "Narrative and Paradigmatic Modes of Thought," in E. Eisner, ed., *Learning and Teaching the Ways of Knowing* (Chicago: National Society for the Study of Education, 1985), pp. 97–115; and earlier, C. P. Snow, *The Two Cultures and the Scientific Revolution* (Cambridge: Cambridge University Press, 1959).

4. I have taken liberally here from David Hall's discussion of irony in *Richard Rorty: Prophet and Poet of the New Pragmatism* (Albany: State University of New York Press, 1994), beginning p. 139.

5. Carolyn Heilbrun, *Writing a Woman's Life* (New York: W. W. Norton, 1988), p. 37.

6. This is my interpretation of the perspectives within "education feminism" held by my colleagues.

7. See Maxine Greene, *The Dialectic of Freedom* (New York: Teachers College Press, 1988); Nel Noddings, *Women and Evil* (Berkeley and Los Angeles: University of California Press, 1989); Madeleine Grumet, *Bitter Milk: Women and Teaching* (Amherst: University of Massachusetts Press, 1988); Jo Anne Pagano, *Exiles in Communities: Teaching in the Patriarchal Wilderness* (Albany: State University of New York Press, 1990); Deanne Bogdan, *Re-Educating the Imagination: Toward a Poetics, Politics, and Pedagogy of Literary Engagement* (Portsmouth, NH: Boynton Cook Publishers, Heinemann, 1992); Susan Laird, "The Concept of Teaching: Betsey Brown vs. Philosophy of Education?" in J. Giarelli, ed., *Philosophy of Education: 1988* (Normal, IL: Philosophy of Education Society and Illinois State University, 1989), pp. 32–45. While not about women's lives, see Margret Buchmann, "Teacher Thinking, Teacher Change, and the 'Capricious Seamstress—Memory,' in H. Alexander, ed., *Philosophy of Education: 1992* (Urbana: Philosophy of Education Society and the University of Illinois, 1993), and Lynda Stone, "Contingency: The 'Constancy' of Teaching," *Teachers College Record, 94,* (1993) 4: 815–35.

8. This term was quoted by Meike Bal. The point is that attacks on feminist and other non-mainstream scholarship are still generalized in terms of poor scholarship.

9. Mariama Bâ, *So Long a Letter,* trans. M. Bode-Thomas (Oxford: Heinemann, [1980] 1989). Others using letters include the classic from Virginia Woolf, *Three Guineas* (San Diego: Harcourt Brace Jovanovich, [1938] 1966), and a recent example from Dianne Smith, "'Why Do We Have to Read About Girls Living in Australia and London?' Reflections from a Womanist Theorist on Critical Education," in L. Stone, ed. *The Education Feminism Reader,* pp. 328–335.

10. Positioning de-privileges "author-ity" by making each writing particular and historicist. Each person writes only for herself and speaks for no others.

11. This account is taken from the forepiece to Bâ's book, making some aspects of her exemplification autobiographical.

12. Clarifying the narrative and analytic structure of this account is vital: Bâ's novelette is in the form of a letter from Ramtoulaye to Aissatou. Sections here are marked off, first, in the form of a letter from Lynda Stone to Mariama Bâ, and second, in analysis and explanation that follows.

13. This is not to essentialize all female experience with males nor among males themselves but rather to focus on women's lives and begin empirically: given male dominance across virtually all societies in the past, the places of females have been derivative, "other," and less secure.

14. Nancy Miller, *Getting Personal: Feminist Occasions and Other Biographical Acts* (New York: Routledge, 1991), pp. 1, 3, 2.

15. A brief classical account is from Hester Eisenstein, *Contemporary Feminist Thought* (Boston: G. K. Hall, 1983), beginning p. 35.

16. All intertextual references are taken from Bâ, *So Long a Letter*. For convenience pages are cited in the text itself.

17. Examples are Susan Hekman, "Reconstituting the Subject: Feminism, Modernism, and Postmodernism," *Hypatia, 6*(2), 1991:44–62, and Lorraine Code, "Taking Subjectivity into Account," in L. Alcoff and E. Potter, eds., *Feminist Epistemologies* (New York: Routledge, 1993), pp. 15–48. Also from Europe see Rosi Braidotti, "The Female Feminist Subject, or: From 'She-self' to 'She-other'," in G. Bock and S. James, eds., *Beyond Equality and Difference: Citizenship, Feminist Politics and Female Subjectivity* (New York: Routledge, 1992), pp. 177–92.

18. Susan Okin, *Women in Western Political Thought* (Princeton: Princeton University Press, 1979).

19. There is an extensive literature devoted to a feminist critique of rationality—and thus of agency and personhood. See as examples, Genevive Lloyd, *The Man of Reason: "Male" and "Female" in Western Philosophy* (Minneapolis: University of Minnesota Press, 1979); and Moira Gatens, *Feminism and Philosophy: Perspectives on Difference and Equality* (Bloomington: Indiana University Press, 1991).

20. Nel Noddings, *Women and Evil* (Berkeley and Los Angeles: University of California Press, 1989).

21. Particularly helpful here is the post-colonial literature. See Trinh Minh-Ha, *Woman, Nature, Other: Writing Postcoloniality and Feminism* (Bloomington, Indiana University Press, 1989); and Gayatri Chakravorty Spivak with Elizabeth Grosz, "Criticism, Feminism, and the Institution," in *The Post-Colonial Critic,* ed., S. Harasym (New York, Routledge, 1990).

22. As Carol Gilligan and Nel Noddings have so powerfully theorized, this is caring. See their classic works: Gilligan, *In A Different Voice* (Cambridge: Harvard University Press, 1982), and Noddings, *Caring: A Feminine Approach to Ethics and Moral Education* (Berkeley and Los Angeles: University of California Press, 1984).

23. Lynda Stone, "The Essentialist Tension in Reflective Teacher Education," in L. Valli, ed., *Reflective Teacher Education: Cases and Critiques* (Albany: State University of New York, 1992), pp. 198–212. Most "isms" are either essentialist or in danger of becoming so; working with this contradiction—of potentially unifying particulars—is part of postmodernism.

24. I like David Hall's comment on this: "As a practical matter the appeal to transcendent others to secure and legitimate ourselves and our values hasn't worked." See Hall, *Richard Rorty: Prophet and Poet of the New Pragmatism,* p. 173.

25. Theresa de Lauretis, "Feminist Studies/Critical Studies: Issues, Terms, and Contexts," in *Feminist Studies/Critical Studies* (Bloomington, Indiana University Press, 1986), p. 2.

26. See Elizabeth Spelman, *The Inessential Woman: Problems of Exclusion in Feminist Thought* (London: The Woman's Press, 1988), Patricia Hill Collins, "The Social Construction of Black Feminist Thought," *Signs, 14*(4), 1989: 745–73; and Nancie Carraway, *Segregated Sisterhood: Racism and the Politics of American Feminism* (Knoxville: University of Tennessee Press, 1991). See also many of the

writings of bell hooks, among them *Talking Back* (Boston: South End Press, 1989).

27. A recent list is found in Sue Rosser, "Are There Feminist Methodologies Appropriate for the Natural Sciences and Do They Make a Difference?" *Woman's Studies International Forum,* 15(5–6), 1992: pp. 535–50.

28. Iris Marion Young, "The Ideal of Community and the Politics of Difference," in L. Nicholson, ed., *Feminism/Postmodernism* (New York: Routledge, 1990), pp. 300–23.

29. Thanks to my friend Anne Phelan for conversation about this idea.

30. I think this is similar to Paolo Freire's "mediation on the world;" see *Pedagogy of the Oppressed* (New York: Continuum, 1971).

31. Maxine Greene, Forward to Carol Witherall and Nel Noddings, *Stories Lives Tell,* p. xi.

32. Examples from the narrative literature in education are Ivor Goodson and Rob Walker, *Biography, Identity and Schooling: Episodes in Educational Research* (London: Falmer, 1988); and William Schubert and William Ayers, eds., *Teacher Lore: Learning from Our Own Experience* (New York: Longman, 1991). See also Susan Douglas Franzosa, "Authoring the Educated Self: Educational Autobiography and Resistance," *Educational Theory,* 42(4) 1992: 395–412.

33. Thanks to Wendy Kohli for very helpful editing, and to Harvey Siegel for critique.

15

Knowledge and Certainty; Feminism, Postmodernism, and Multiculturalism

Harvey Siegel

The provocative essays of Lynda Stone and René Vincente Arcilla are challenging on several levels: not only do they question the conventional understandings of the notions of knowledge and certainty as they have been developed in traditional, "modernist" epistemology; they also interrogate the presuppositions which underlie much of modernist epistemological discourse. It is with pleasure that I respond.

As both Arcilla and Stone do, I begin by situating myself: I am a white, male, analytically trained philosopher, who writes philosophy and Philosophy of Education in the dominant (but no longer hegemonic) analytic style. My main philosophical preoccupations concern some of the issues long regarded as central to epistemology: issues concerning justification, truth, rationality, and relativism. I believe that these issues are of central importance for Philosophy of Education; in particular, I (along with many others) have advocated rationality as a fundamental educational aim or ideal. Since my understanding of that notion, and my advocacy of it as a fundamental educational ideal, rest squarely on the modernist epistemological tradition within which I work, the interrogations of that tradition presented in the target essays interest me greatly.

Our mutual task in these essays is to dialogue across our differences, in a spirit of mutual respect and understanding. I accept these terms. But "conversation" and "dialogue" do not betoken only sweetness and light: in engaging in dialogue with those with whom one has differences, one is not limited to agreements with and compliments of one's partners in the dialogue. So when, in what follows, my comments are critical, I hope that it will be possible for the reader, as well as my dialogical partners, to receive them in the spirit in which they are intended: as honest furtherings of the conversation.

Lynda Stone

Lynda Stone's essay insightfully explores the role and relevance of *narrative* for Philosophy of Education. In this respect the form of her contribution, as well as its substance, reflects her commitment to feminist theorizing. I attempt in what follows to understand and critically consider the implications of her narrative for the epistemological questions she confronts.

Stone's understanding of "knowledge" and "certainty" joins these two notions together; her concern is not with knowledge and certainty but with "certain knowledge." According to Stone, for women, only one thing is known with certainty—namely, that their lives are uncertain: "For many women what is certain about their lives is its uncertainty."[1]

> [For women] in spite of past successes, of beliefs and convictions, we never know if our actions will be realizable. And, even within the relatively privileged confines of some of our lives, often we are "reminded" of uncertainty and of our lack of control. I further suggest that this standard differs for many if not most men. Furthermore many of us know that actions we take out of this condition, and those taken by others for us, are not in our own best interests.

The object of knowledge here is *action,* and "action", Stone suggests, has different meanings for men and for women. The "norm of certainty" which from Stone's view characterizes traditional epistemology and theory of action is a *male* or masculinist epistemological norm: for men but not for women, actions have the expectation of realization, of success; action understood as autonomous, freely chosen, and guided by reasons—that is, action as it is characterized in the Western modernist philosophical tradition—is decisively masculinist in its conception. Moreover, actions performed by males are at least typically in their own best interests. Not so for women, as the most recently cited passage indicates. For women, knowledge and action, as we have seen, are uncertain.

The philosophical importance of this uncertainty involves a rejection of essentialism (the idea that women share "an innate femininity") and a focus on differences, both of which are central to Stone's conception of philosophical feminism. She deplores an essentialism that "posits something as 'alike' for all persons" and which privileges the experiences and perspectives of white, middle class women. Stone applauds contemporary feminism's move "to rename the inquiry itself as feminisms" in order to emphasize the importance of avoiding a theoretically and politically debilitating essentialism. Her discussion of competing strands of feminist theorizing which struggle to formulate an adequate theory which rejects any difference-denying essentialism is both informative and inspiring. Feminists continue to be characterized by uncertainty, but the uncertainty here concerns not action but feminist theory itself.

Stone ends her essay by linking uncertainty with friendship, and proposing that women (and people generally?) adopt the posture of "as if friends":

> Very different persons, even those distanced from one another, act "as if friends" if they exhibit openness to different opinions and perspectives, if they demonstrate humility about their own views, and if they try out trust of the other. This attitude means putting each other in the best light possible within a climate of generosity.
>
> Openness, humility, and trust—to return to the central theme of this essay—all work from an initial position of uncertainty.

Such friendship, Stone demonstrates, involves receptivity, generosity, trust, humility, and an open acceptance of and commitment to work across differences. As Stone suggests, it is both theoretically and politically important to recast our philosophical musings so as to reject the traditional desire for certainty and to embrace as something positive—indeed, to accept as "a new ethic"—the uncertainty which characterizes women's lives and actions:

> Here uncertainty means accepting as "natural" the tentativeness, ambiguity, fluidity of all of life and particularly of the beliefs and desires, knowledges, and actions of persons. This uncertainty moves from a negative characteristic of women's lives to one positive.

Throughout her essay, Stone enjoins the reader to embrace the ideas that women's knowledge of their actions is uncertain, that it is crucially important to acknowledge differences, and that women who are different ought nevertheless to try and work across their differences, in the spirit of receptivity, generosity, trust, humility, and the hope of friendship. This is an inspiring vision for "these uncertain times"—for women and equally for men.

Nevertheless, I would like to make some observations concerning Stone's vision, and ask some questions concerning it. Most obviously, I suppose, are these: first, Stone's discussion of knowledge involves knowledge *of the outcomes of purposeful actions,* rather than knowledge in general. In this sense the focus of her discussion is rather more narrow than it may appear at first sight. Second, Stone's failure to distinguish between knowledge and certainty flies in the face of at least the great majority of the (male) epistemology of this century, which, at least since Peirce, has routinely rejected certainty as a condition of knowledge, and endeavored to develop theories of knowledge according to which knowledge need not be certain. In so rejecting certainty as a condition of knowledge, most contemporary epistemology unproblematically accepts Stone's "feminist" insistence on uncertainty as a characteristic of knowledge. Third, while Stone rejects essentialism within feminist theory, she seems quite happy to treat "male-stream" epistemology and action theory in essentialist ways, ignoring crucial differences which in fact define the contours of theoretical discussion within the Western philosophical tradition. I applaud Stone's rejection of essentialism, but I wonder why that rejection should not be extended beyond the bounds of feminism. I wonder also if Stone's rejection of essentialism ought to be somewhat more nuanced. Of course genuine differences should not be denied. But aren't differences sometimes properly deemed *irrelevant,* as when, for example, patriarchal oppression of women is deplored generally, whatever the differences may be among the victims of such oppression?[2]

In rejecting essentialism, Stone insists on acknowledging differences among women. If we acknowledge such differences, then shouldn't we be more cautious about regarding women as being correctly characterized by uncertainty? Won't some women enjoy more certainty in their lives than others? Moreover, don't most men also lack certainty in their lives? I wonder whether Stone's view is in the end quite essentialistic, despite her sincere rejection of it. Perhaps this is the most defensible position she can take: after all, there are samenesses as well as differences across women, across people, and across theories. But then her discussion ought to take this fact more adequately into account.

A final critical point: like many writers, Stone emphasizes the "situatedness" of knowledge and theory (I think problematically). All theorizing is situated, yes; but the relevance of any theorizing to any particular time depends on much more than the situation of its first being theorized. Theories developed and propounded from the vantage point of some particular situation and time are nevertheless often relevant to, and true in, other situations and times as well.[3]

In pointing to the uncertainty, and the unfairness, in Ramatoulaye's life, and in women's lives more generally, Stone teaches us a lesson of profound philosophical importance. Her vision of friendship is an inspiring one; it is a vision to which men (I hope) as well as women can aspire. Stone provides a clear, compelling feminist voice; a powerful one within contemporary Philosophy of Education.

René Arcilla

While Stone's essay is couched mainly in the voice of feminism, René Arcilla speaks in the voices of multiculturalism and postmodernism. His topic is self-knowledge, and he compellingly argues that recent educational interest in multiculturalism—in particular, in protecting and fostering cultural diversity—provides us with important new insights concerning the nature both of education and its philosophy.

Arcilla's view is developed by way of exposition and commentary on some recent works by Charles Taylor concerning the importance of dialogical interaction across cultures for the modernist quest for self-knowledge and self-understanding. Taylor's argument for multiculturalist education emphasizes the point that one's identity is constructed in part in terms of others' reflected images of oneself, and that incorrect, distorted, or demeaning images of oneself reflected back to oneself by others can have a disastrously negative effect on one's own self-image. As Taylor puts it:

> A person or group of people can suffer real damage, real distortion, if the people or society around them mirror back to them a confining or demeaning or contemptible picture of themselves. Nonrecognition or misrecognition can inflict harm, can be a form of oppression, imprisoning someone in a false, distorted, and reduced mode of being.[4]

Multiculturalist education, in Taylor's view, should have as one of its central tasks the resisting of this form of oppression. Arcilla reviews Taylor's complex analysis of shifting historical conceptions of selfhood, resulting ultimately in Taylor's view that "the quest for self-knowledge has a dialogical character," because of "the crucial role that language learning plays in self-definition." At this point a tension emerges between universalistic and individualistic conceptions of humans and human relations, and between "a democratic politics of recognition that is multiculturalist and one that is more traditionally liberal and universalist"—the common rights and entitlements of all must be honored, while at the same time honoring the unique identities of all, and resisting the temptation to ignore or deny differences. For Taylor, the important question is whether or not the drive for multiculturalist particularity and recognition of difference can be reconciled with modernist, universalist liberalism. For Arcilla, the important issue involves the way in which self-knowledge requires dialogical interaction with others. It is this interaction, Arcilla argues, which puts self-knowledge in jeopardy.

Taylor's argument for the necessity of dialogical interaction with others for the emergence of the authentic self concludes, as Arcilla reconstructs it, that "I can define myself only on condition of having learned how to use a language of self-definition from an accomplished language user through a process of dialogue. Our self-understanding depends on dialogue with others who teach us the terms by which that self could be recognized." Because, in the process of dialogue with significant others, those others become internalized parts of my self, "[m]y very self-understanding depends on the language I learn and the teachers I incorporate into myself." Arcilla argues that such dialogue is a necessary, and never-ending, condition of self-knowledge. Moreover, the moral imperative, noted earlier, of combatting the oppression which results from foisting upon marginalized others demeaning or distorted images of themselves, is in these terms fully explained and justified:

> Our multiculturalist initiatives in education should be principally concerned with exposing and criticizing images and terms that stunt possibilities for self-definition, particularly for members of cultures that already suffer from a history of discrimination. These initiatives should strive to replace such images and terms with more promising ones that can evoke the potential for growth and achievement in all. Such an education could thus help prevent the seeds of monocultural domination from taking root in our diverse youth.

Here the moral imperatives of avoiding injustice towards and oppression of members of marginalized cultures—imperatives fully endorsed by modernism—seem, to Taylor (and to me), to justify fully "our multiculturalist initiatives in education."

But, Taylor suggests, by endorsing and enacting such initiatives, that the way is paved for the emergence for all students of their authentic selves, and in so doing the possibility of their achieving genuine self-knowledge is kept open. Arcilla demures. He appeals here to Derrida and postmodernism, and suggests that Taylor's argument for the never-ending dialogical nature of self-knowledge misses a key fact about the *language* of such dialogue: the ineliminable possibility that the terms of the dialogue, and those of the mutual recognition which the dialogue fosters, can only be provisionally defined, and so are subject to being recurrently redefined—which keeps the dialogue inconclusive, and the need for it interminable.

The insight that Derrida provides is that of "the thrall of aporia in language." Arcilla's characterization of Derrida's findings concerning the "indefiniteness" of language and linguistic meaning leads him to characterize his own divergence from Taylor in similar terms:

> Although philosophers continue to spin discourses in order to defer indefiniteness, this indefiniteness, like a force of nature, is bound to come back and haunt terms in the discourse. Once altered and alienated from their context, these now questionable terms stand to provoke new mouths to unweave the old discourse and another generation of pens to declare their independence from its terms. So philosophy perpetuates itself. Yet so too does indefiniteness, which remains the condition for the possibility of calling different thinkers into the conversation that keeps philosophy alive.
>
> I believe that the discourse of self-definition, with which we in large part engage in dialogue with significant others, has this aporetic nature as well.

However, the bond between multiculturalism and self-knowledge which Taylor articulates becomes, in Arcilla's hands, a radical critique of the possibility of self-knowledge. For the indefiniteness, the aporetic nature, of the language of self-knowledge, forces the conclusion (according to Arcilla) that self-knowledge is a will-o'-the wisp—a goal which can never be attained. The indefiniteness and aporetic quality of language guarantee that our efforts to attain self-knowledge will inevitably fail. And this has a disturbing consequence for multicultural education: if self-knowledge is impossible, multiculturalist education cannot contribute to its realization, and so cannot be regarded as important for its contribution to that impossible-to-realize end. In this way, according to Arcilla, Taylor's justification of multicultural education fails.

But Arcilla offers a different reason for favoring multiculturalist education—"self-defamiliarization"—and on its basis revives a brand of universalism. Because of the aporetic nature of language and the indefiniteness of dialogically based meanings, he argues, our self-knowledge is fated to be tragically inconclusive and occasionally disrupted; but, a philosophy and politics of education can be fashioned which can serve to prevent this realization from fomenting political and social tensions. Since the indefiniteness and aporia which undermine our self-knowledge undermines *everyone's* self-knowledge, everyone is a member of the community of those whose self-knowledge is threatened. Consequently, we are joined together in community, and, rather than embarking on "an epistemological project . . . to eliminate or reduce indefiniteness," we can instead "giv[e] thanks for how the return of indefiniteness reminds us of our awful and awesome, sublime communion with indefinite Being." Education in a "multiculturalist democracy" can then be conceived as having a particular task:

> to turn the instability of identity into a supple celebration of what eludes identification, to defamiliarize the self. Such an education would aim to direct us from a recognition of and respect for the cultural identity of the stranger, to a recognition that one's own cultural identity is likewise indefinite and self-estranging, to a recognition that this indefiniteness broaches a shared discourse. In such a discourse, we may learn that we are all strangers to ourselves, together cast into an unfamiliar, *unheimlich* home. In such a discourse, a politics sensitive to cultural differences would meet a politics that finds in these differences the natural limit of our intelligible identities; an incongruous mix of cultures would thus yield a common sense of strangeness. And so is born hope for a new politics of commonality, one grounded in nature conceived not as an intelligible (to some privileged cultural language) cosmos but as the withdrawing source of language and linguistic beings, the mysterious X. Such a politics would be guided by a discourse of universal rights for a multicultural society.

The vision Arcilla here articulates, albeit an undeniably heady one, raises some obvious questions. How are we to understand the "indefinite Being"? Isn't this, too, a culturally bound conception? And is it likely that members of different cultures, or of any culture, would recognize the philosophical discourse extended by such an education as "sublime"? I worry about the wisdom of a social/educational agenda which rests upon, or has as its aim, the universal appreciation of a peculiarly *philosophical* understanding, however sublime it may appear to some to be. Moreover, I don't see why the indefiniteness and aporia which (according to Arcilla) undermine the modernist quest for self-knowledge don't also impinge upon, and undermine, the positive social/educational vision that Arcilla recommends—for that recommendation appears to depend upon the definite establishment of the indefinite (to wit: "I, Derrida, have definitely and firmly established, in language, that all language and meaning—and therefore knowledge—is indefinite").[5] This leads to some general queries I have concerning Arcilla's discussion of aporia.

First, consider the basic form of Arcilla's argument:

1. Language is provisional and indefinite.
2. Therefore, dialogue is interminable.
3. Therefore, self-knowledge, which depends upon dialogue, is indefinite, inconclusive, and subject to disruption.

The first, fundamental premise is that which expresses Derrida's claim concerning the aporetic nature of language. Should this premise be accepted? Not without qualification. Qualification is required because, unqualified, the claim it expresses is subject to a damning difficulty: if language has only provisional meaning, and is indefinite, then the premise expressing the claim is itself only provisional and indefinite. But if so, the claim is at least to some extent undermined, because its grand pronouncement about the nature of language is (to say the least) significantly limited. In other words, if language and meaning are, in general, provisional and indefinite, then so is the language expressing, and meaning of, the Derridean claim itself. But if so, then, first, neither (2) nor (3) above follow from it; and, second, it is incapable of undermining either the possibility of self-knowledge, or Taylor's justification of multicultural education in terms of the enhanced prospects for genuine self-knowledge of members of marginalized cultures, whose prospects for such knowledge are harmed by the absence of multicultural education. The fact that Derrida's thesis concerning aporia applies to itself undermines its ability to do the work Arcilla counts on it to do.

Second, the self-applicability of Derrida's thesis raises another difficulty. Do we *know* that language is aporetic? How could we, if language is in fact aporetic? This depends, of course, on what is meant by *knowledge*. If the thesis is that one understanding of language is as good as any other, then we can't know any claim expressible in language; this of course applies to the thesis itself as well as to everything else. This is a recipe for epistemological scepticism, based on a Derridean linguistic scepticism concerning meaning. (I won't pause here to consider the merits of such skepticism.) But the thesis needn't be read in this stark way; it is more plausibly understood as recommending a form of fallibilism rather than scepticism: since language is subject to aporia, it is always possible that what we think we know (e.g., to take Arcilla's example, that I am male) we may at some point decide that we don't know. Given the ever-present possibility of new insights, new theorizing, new evidence, and new alignments of meaning, we must always hold open the possibility that putative knowledge-claims, including self-knowledge claims, can be revised. That knowledge is in principle revisable in this sense does not lead to scepticism, but only to fallibilism. In this sense we can know, fallibly, that language is aporetic. (Whether we *do* know this is of course another question.) But this is only possible if we don't hold that one understanding of language is as good as any other; but, rather, that the Derridean understanding of language as aporetic, while in principle open to revision, is the best understanding we currently have. Here knowledge, understandings, and meanings admit of evaluations in terms of better and worse. This sort of fallibilistic but non-sceptical interpretation is the one Derrideans, including Arcilla, require, if their arguments about anything are to rest upon the Derridean premise. But if so, then, that premise is actually much weaker than it appears at least at some points in Arcilla's discussion. Indeed, no mention of the premise is required: we are all fallibilists now, and have been since Peirce; Derrida's discussion and thesis, understood fallibilistically, contributes nothing. Understood sceptically, it defeats itself and so also contributes nothing. Either way, then, the Derridean thesis is a lot less impressive than it appears at first blush.

I have been arguing that Arcilla's Derridean aporia entails not scepticism about self-knowledge, but only fallibilism; and that such fallibilism is completely consistent with Taylor's "liberal" reconciliation of the universal and the particular, and his equally liberal justification of multicultural education. That is, Taylor's justification of multicultural education succeeds, once the limitations of Derridean aporia are clearly apprehended and appreciated. (I note in passing that if self-knowledge is in this way rescued from postmodern, skeptical oblivion, then so too is knowledge of others, and other sorts of knowledge as well.)

Despite my unwillingness to embrace fully either the Derridean premise upon which Arcilla's argument rests, or his positive conclusion that the indefiniteness of language dooms self-knowledge to instability, which in turn harbors the possibility of a universal recognition of that instability as a gift which can put us in "sublime communion with indefinite Being," Arcilla's analysis of Taylor and Derrida is careful, clear, and challenging; his positive resolution of the difficulty he raises for multicultural education is original, radical, and challenging in the extreme. While the worries rehearsed above lead me to refrain from embracing Arcilla's vision wholeheartedly, it nevertheless seems to me that he has demonstrated decisively the contributions that postmodernist and multiculturalist voices can make to our collective conversation. For that we—that is, all of us, but especially the modernist laggards among us (among whom I of course include myself) are in his debt.

Concluding Conversation

In my discussion of both Stone's and Arcilla's essays, I have urged that we sharply distinguish knowledge from certainty. However uncertain these (or any other) times are, there is nevertheless in them all the room we need for (fallible) knowledge. And it is a good thing that there is, if we want to do justice to the important insights of feminism, postmodernism, and multiculturalism which Stone and Arcilla insightfully bring to our attention. While we might argue about exactly what those insights amount to, and about how deeply they challenge important strands of modernism, I think it clear that the feminist, postmodernist, and multiculturalist streams in Stone's and Arcilla's thoughts promise to replenish and energize the too frequently stagnant waters of Philosophy of Education. This, it is clear, is a major contribution to a field such as ours.

Kohli, the editor of this collection, poses the question: Who/what counts as a philosopher of education, and why? Stone doesn't answer this question directly; Arcilla regards the answer as necessarily indefinite. My own answer is that a philosopher of education is one who worries about fundamental philosophical questions concerning education—what are the aims of education?; how can such aims be justified?; what moral and intellectual considerations rightly guide and constrain educational activities?; what duties and obligations must educators and educational institutions meet?; how should we understand key educational notions, and key philosophical notions which are intimately related to education, like "teaching", "learning", and "knowledge"?; how is the curriculum best understood and designed?; and a host of other such questions—and worries about these questions in a way which is methodologically sophisticated and which is informed by past efforts to come to grips with them. This locates Philosophy of Education in a tradition, to be sure; and some may wish to reject that tradition. But *informed, credible* rejection requires a nuanced understanding of the tradition being rejected, and a detailed, careful articulation of one's reasons for rejection, which reasons can themselves withstand critical scrutiny; and that tradition itself encourages its own critical self-scrutiny—indeed, it encourages its own rejection, if such rejection is warranted. In so far, the philosophical tradition in which contemporary Western Philosophy of Education finds itself embedded welcomes the critical initiatives of feminism, postmodernism, multiculturalism, and other challenging new avenues of thinking about the philosophical dimensions of education.[6] That tradition is open to—indeed strives for—growth, correction, and improvement; and advances may be prompted in all sorts of ways. The tradition stands always in need of challenging criticism and insightful guidance from all quarters. It needs the help of these "isms". A panoply of outstanding philosophical questions central to Philosophy of Education—problems involving knowledge, justification, rationality, essentialism, domination, marginalization, universality, particularity, and many more—equally require that help. So I end by expressing my gratitude for the fact that Philosophy of Education can conduct the conversation, the dialogue across differences, that involves the many distinct voices that this volume brings together. To see how it turns out: stayed tuned to the conversation. Even better: join in![7]

NOTES

1. All citations to Stone are to her essay in this volume.

2. See here my "Gimme That Old-Time Enlightenment Meta-Narrative: Radical Pedagogy (and Politics) Requires Traditional Epistemology (and Moral Theory)", *Inquiry: Critical Thinking Across the Disciplines* (May 1993) 7(4): 1, 17–22.

3. This point is developed at greater length in my essay "'Radical' Pedagogy Requires 'Conservative' Epistemology," in *Journal of Philosophy of Education,* 1995, in press.

4. All citations to Arcilla are to his essay in this volume.

5. The relation between language and meaning, on the one hand, and knowledge, on the other, is less clear than Arcilla acknowledges. Does "language and meaning are provisional" entail "knowledge is provisional and indefinite"? Not obviously. It is not even clear what the latter claim comes to—does it assert fallibilism, or scepticism? I regret that I can't pursue this point systematically below, although it is addressed briefly in what follows.

6. See my "Gimme That Old-Time Enlightenment Meta-Narrative."

7. I am grateful to Wendy Kohli for helpful suggestions and advice.

16

Educating for Public Life

James M. Giarelli

Although we both study educational theory for our livelihood, when our daughter came of school age, my wife and I began to take the real-world problems of schooling seriously for the first time. Students of the public system from grade through graduate school and strongly committed to ideals connecting democracy with public, universal schooling, we counted ourselves advocates for public education. However, as we examined the alternatives available for our daughter, a more complicated picture and set of choices emerged.[1]

The public school system where we live in the suburban Northeast United States is widely considered to be a "good" school system. Cited as evidence are the high test scores students receive, graduation and college admission rates, special placement, honors, and individualized programs and curricula, and marketability of graduates. In brief, this system is considered "good" because it is thought to effectively prepare children with the skills, attitudes, and dispositions required for success in the workplace. This public school is considered effective because it prepares children for successful individual competition in the private economy. In substance and aims, it is *private* schooling.

We wondered, then, in what sense could this be counted as public education? As we looked further, we identified a school, The Friends School, a private school operating roughly on the Quaker philosophy, whose aims and programs were more in accord with our own vision of public education. In this school, a premium is placed on non-differentiation into age, gender, or ability groups. Instead, teachers, students, parents and interested community members struggle to work across lines of difference and hierarchy. The curriculum is schoolwide, thematic, derived from discussion among those involved and linked as much as possible to interests and as little as possible to measured ability. This school measures its effectiveness in terms of its ability to form communities of learning, relations of cooperation, dialogue, and engagement. This school's effectiveness is assessed against an ideal of full, free, communal sharing of knowledge, interests, and materials in service of associated development. In aims and substance, it is *public* education.

The contradictions, or at least problematics, present themselves. The public school, supported by local and state tax monies, takes as its purpose and standard the ideals of private education, while at least this private school, supported by tuition and philanthropy, takes as its purpose and standard the ideals of public education. Put more pointedly, the best "choice" for parents like us who are interested in their children receiving a public education is the private school rather than the public, state-supported school.

One obvious implication is the economic. The Friends School, dependent upon tuition, is unavailable to the great majority of residents, including our family. And since the state, public school has little interest in public education, this means that *a public education in any substantive, intentional sense is unavailable to most children.*

While these economic questions are always important, what my wife and I drew from this real world lesson is the absolute necessity to problematize the language of public educational discourse, to look to consequences rather than causes and to assume that language, on its face, serves to cover more than it reveals.

In this spirit of scepticism, in the remainder of this essay I will try to put the very title of this chapter up at issue. What might we mean by educating for public life? Is the alternative educating for private life? What place does schooling play in either of these possibilities? What is the relationship between public and private, schooling and education? What is the role of the state? Does the very language of public and private education play off more basic, perhaps pernicious, distinctions between public and private spheres, and with that, gender-based hierarchies which valorize some lives while belittling others?

I will take up these questions, not through an analytical, linguistic clarification of terms, although at times this could be helpful, but rather through a critical examination of some recent literature in the Philosophy of Education. In the United States in the 1980s, a healthy debate has re-emerged around the aims of education, centrally concerning the relationship between schooling and education and the alleged requirements of public and private life, the national and international marketplace, and the community of citizens. These "views from the 1980s" will be the central concern of this essay. Finally, I will return to my opening story, our choices as parents, the choices for our daughter, in the hope that this will open another, too long neglected, lens through with these issues can be discussed.

Education and Schooling, Public and Private: Voices from the Tradition

Of course, much of the classical literature in the Western intellectual tradition concerns the aims and forms of educating for public life. One quickly thinks of Plato's argument in *The Republic* for a differentiated education which would link innate differences in individual nature with the differentiated roles necessary for a just polis as an attempt to reconcile public and private.[2] In *Emile,* Rousseau also attempts to link public and private, the state and individual personality, through a particular form of education.[3] Dewey's consequentialist treatment of the public and private provides a powerful analytical tool for conversations about educating for public life.[4] For Dewey, since the distinction between public and private turns on an analysis of the sphere of perceived consequences of interaction, rather than on appeals to motives, human nature, or inherent qualities, the "public" or "private" qualities of any institution or interaction are always a subject of continuing inquiry. Thus, for Dewey, it is perfectly sensible to inquire into the ways in which institutions of private schooling may result in public education, while institutions of public education may result in private schooling.

Many more contributors to the classical literature on public and private, schooling and education, could be cited. However, this essay will focus on more contemporary variants, many echoing these classical positions.

Educating for Public Life: Voices from the 1980s

In the United States, the 1980s turned out to be a time of vigorous, broad-based, public, sometimes even philosophical debate about education and schooling, the public and the private. While centered on some common concerns about the relationships between democracy, schooling, and the education of citizens, this debate also produced distinct positions. I have discussed these views elsewhere as alternative public philosophies of education and suggested some thematic continuities and differences.[5] (In this essay, I want to return to some of the main varieties of the 1980s' debates, with particular attention to alternate treatments of the relations between education and schooling for public and private life.)

Limit Positions: R. Freeman Butts

In 1980, the noted educational historian R. Freeman Butts argued that the civic purpose of schools, their role in educating for public life, is their "most fundamental purpose." In several sources,[6] Butts presents a conceptual foundation to ground this view and a set of detailed specific pedagogical practices by which it might be achieved.

In brief sketch, Butts believes that "the goal of civic education for American schools is to deal with all students in such a way as to motivate them and enable them to play their parts as informed, responsible, committed, and effective members of a modern democratic political system. This . . . should include the three basic aspects; political values, political knowledge, and the skills of political participation needed for making deliberate choices among real alternatives."[7] At the core of all three basic aspects are consensually held civic values. Butts argues that "the fundamental ideas and values upon which our constitutional order is built should be the core of sustained and explicit study . . . from kindergarten through high school."[8]

Butts devotes a great deal of attention to an argument for ten specific political values of central importance to American society. Five of these values: justice, equality, authority, participation and personal obligation for the public good, concern the *unum,* the unitary tendencies; while five others, freedom, diversity, privacy, due process and international human rights, support pluralism, the goals of *pluribus.*

For Butts, these core values define the American ethos, while political knowledge defines the essential features of constitutional democracy. While Butts is certainly aware that his decalogue of core values is the beginning, rather than the end, of civic debate, he has no fundamental doubts about the aims of education. For Butts, there is a foundation of consensually held, communal beliefs and enabling institutions which bind American society into a community. The formation of an educated public requires that the community learn these beliefs and be initiated into these institutional practices. This is the fundamental purpose of public education and the fundamental role of public schools and teachers.

Limit Position: Alasdair MacIntyre

In a 1985 lecture, "The Idea of an Educated Public," later published in 1987, Alasdair MacIntyre rejects this foundationalist perspective and offers a radically different historicist account.[9] "Teachers are the forlorn hope of the culture of Western modernity. . . . For the mission with which contemporary teachers are entrusted is both essential and impossible. It is impossible because the two major purposes which teachers are required to serve are, under the conditions of Western modernity, mutually incompatible."[10]

For MacIntyre, these incompatible purposes are, first, "to shape the young person so that he or she may fit into some social role and function," and second, to teach "young persons how to think for themselves, how to acquire independence of mind, how to be enlightened."[11] In MacIntyre's view, the culture of modernity forecloses the possibility of achieving either of these purposes. First, thinking, at least in the Enlightenment tradition, requires some notion of rational justification or rational objectivity. No standards of rationality, no coherent notion of independent thought or enlightenment. And with no agreement on what standards for rationality are, no possibility of a culture whose initiation into or mastery of could be justified. For MacIntyre, "modernity excludes . . . the possibility of the existence of an educated public" and thus excludes the possibility of a justifiable system of public education in which the twin aims of socialization and individuation can be compatible.[12]

With the very idea of an educated public incoherent in modernist culture, what can public schooling be about? For MacIntyre, public education without an educated public becomes a mechanism to promote private consumption. "Take away such a public with shared standards of justification, with a shared view of what the point of the society of which it is a nucleus is, with a shared ability to participate in common public debate, and you reduce the function of the liberal arts and sciences . . . to the provision of a series of passively received consumer products."[13] No amount of internal tinkering can "reform" such a system. MacIntyre continues: "The concept of an educated public has no way of taking a life in contemporary society. It is at most a ghost haunting our educational systems."[14]

These two views can serve as limit positions in our consideration of the questions surrounding educating for public life. Butts's view that there exists some identifiable set of beliefs, values, and institutions which provide a foundation from which educators can begin to develop curricula and methods for the educational initiation of the young into a public is directly countered by MacIntyre's historicist reading that these foundations have been irrevocably destroyed in a modernist culture and that, since there is no educated public, there is no possibility for a coherent, substantive sense of public education.

While Butts's view seems to make too little problematic, MacIntyre leaves us, as educators, with only forlorn hope. But even MacIntyre recognizes that the idea of an educated public, this ghost haunting our educational systems, is "none the less . . . a ghost that cannot be exorcised."[15] To struggle on in the face of what we know, MacIntyre writes, would require teachers to seriously take up the requirements of inventing or reinventing a kind of community which does not or no longer exists. How can this kind of community be conceived? Where can we look for answers?

The next section considers three views from the 1980s which chart a course between the Scylla of Butts's sanguinity and the Charbydis of MacIntyre's forlornness. Robert Bellah, et al. in *Habits of the Heart*, E. D. Hirsch in *Cultural Literacy* and Henry Giroux in *Schooling and the Struggle for Public Life* all engage the problems attendant to educating for public life in cultures of modernity.[16] In their views, echoes of the responses to both the classical literature and the contemporary limiting positions are found.

Educating for Public Life: Views from the 1980s

Robert Bellah, et al. in *Habits of the Heart* take up the central questions concerning the public and private and educating for public life: What are our "habits of the heart," our "character," and how do we define ourselves and our lives with others? What do our signs and symbols mean to us? Do they give our lives meaning or fail it? At the core of the problem Bellah, et al. find an ideology of individualism whose pernicious effects threaten democracy, freedom, and the very idea of a public community. In response, they offer not so much a philosophical analysis, as a kind of public knowledge, which they call social science as public philosophy. In their inquiry, social science is wedded to normative concerns with the aim, not of objective knowledge, but of telling a story of the characters, myths, and dramas that mark the sense contemporary Americans make of their own lives. And finally, they look not to the state or government, but to local associations and face-to-face institutions of relation—marriage, family, therapy, civic, and voluntary associations—as the sources of these meanings.

Bellah, et al. share some of MacIntyre's scepticism about modernity. While cognizant of the historical prejudices of earlier traditions, they wonder aloud if the only effective counterforce to a fragmented culture of possessive individualism is some version of a telic tradition, a tradition which could supply a vision of the meaning of life as a purposeful striving for some "Good," some higher, larger, more general, perhaps more objectifiable moral purpose.

What is important is the contribution *Habits of the Heart* makes to the problem of educating for public life. Bellah, et al. argue that educating for public life requires some notion of a shared, substantive, common good transcending private choices. Communication alone is not the answer; appeals to a received tradition are impossible. Some new form of integration, which they call a social ecology, and discuss in terms of a culture of coherence and communities of memory, must be achieved through a social and educational movement. For Bellah, et al. there *is* a paideia, a configuration of educational institutions that teaches an intellectually and morally intelligible way of life, but it persists too often apart from the "first language" interchanges of state institutions, such as schools, and the sphere of acceptable public discourse. It is in the "second language" discourse of wider associations that we encounter and employ traditions that *begin* with consensus, instead of free, isolated individuals and thus start with some shared assent to the possibility of a common good.

These second languages, traditions of shared memory and purpose, can then serve as the starting points for public education. It is not enough to have one's tradition re-told in the first language of public discourse and become another item for consumption, enjoyment, or disparagement. For Bellah, et al. it is essential that one's story be re-told in the language in which it was lived and through the practices that define its community or tradition. In this way, we all may enter a tradition, enter a world in which it is sensible to talk of a coherent public and a meaningful purpose for public education, not by initiation or induction through a canonical past, but rather through dialogue and association. In this way, we can show serious concern for the idea of the public, provide access to a range of powerful public counter-spheres of meaning to resist the privatized anomie of modern culture, while still rejecting the efforts of those such as Butts to ground public life in the abstractions of constitutional language and those such as MacIntyre to rule out the very possibility of an educated public.

While deeply flawed in its design, *Habits of the Heart* poses a set of important questions. Does educating for public life require some shared sense of the aims of public life? Does this require an answer to what is arguably the oldest question in philosophy—Is there a "Good" and can it be taught? Is the idea of a "Good" required for a coherent, justifiable public education or inimical to it? The next view alleges that answers to these questions are unnecessary and that a justifiable system of public education can be based on the fragmented culture of modernity itself.

Just as Bellah, et al. fret the decline of a public and the loss of a civic community grounded in some sense of shared meanings, E. D. Hirsch in *Cultural Literacy* believes that a substantive sense of public education must be based on a view of literacy which is more than a technical facility at decoding symbols. For Hirsch, true literacy, the kind that enables communication, understanding, civic life, and the achievement of shared purposes, requires an initiation into knowledge of the background information, schemata, and taken-for-granted assumptions that give symbols their wider cultural and public meanings. Hirsch is worried about declining test scores, but even more he is worried that the loss of a tradition of cultural literacy threatens democracy, civic institutions, the economy, ideals of equality, equal opportunity, social mobility, and the nation-state itself.

Hirsch offers a critique of modern educational theorists, erroneously lumping Rousseau and Dewey together, who have provided a rationale for a content-free, abstracted curriculum which encourages psychological development at the expense of knowledge acquisition and mastery. In contrast, Hirsch argues that "only by piling up specific, communally-shared information can children learn to participate in complex cooperative activities with other members of the community"[17] and that "the basic goal of education in a human community is acculturation, the transmission to children of the specific information shared by the adults of the group or polis."[18] Where Bellah believes that the second languages of historical traditions and communities of memory might give normative grounding and substance to communication, Hirsch believes that there is a specifiable body of cultural knowledge which can be identified by the culturally educated which everyone must know to be literate, and that it is the primary purpose of public schools, their civic aim, to transmit this information through direct instruction.

Hirsch offers a straight-forward agenda for accomplishing this. First, panels of experts, such as textbook publishers and educators will decide on the contents of the national vocabulary—that background information, specific fragments of national culture, into which the young need to be inducted by direct transmission. This specific cultural content, what Hirsch calls an extensive national curriculum, will be the stuff of public schooling. It will provide the schemata, what Hirsch calls in other places, stereotypes, forms of mental shorthand, organizing tools, for processing the intensive curriculum of everyday experience through contexts of accepted cultural meaning. These items of cultural literacy will provide the categories by which experience can be encoded into habitual meanings that have been useful in the past; they will conserve the traditions of the civic community as expressed in the symbols of the educated cultural elite. Finally, general knowledge tests will be developed to assess the efficacy of such learning.

For our purposes, the primary question concerns the tension in Hirsch's work between the descriptive and prescriptive. For example, some may find Hirsch an echo of Butts' position that there is a normative, political community and debate over its fundamental beliefs and values should ground the substance and aims of public education. However, Hirsch waffles on the normative status of his project. He writes that "cultural literacy is represented not by a *prescriptive* list of books, but rather by a *descriptive* list of the information actually possessed by literate Americans."[19] In another place, he argues that the tension between diversity and community, the one and the many, can only be resolved by a cultural division of labor. At one level, there is a need for a kind of civic religion, a value-laden set of beliefs about the normative purposes and ends of the public community. At another level is culture itself, directed by civil religion but in constant development of content through debate and intellectual exchange. And finally, there is a civic vocabulary, that value-neutral set of symbols and consensually held meanings which allows debate in the other two realms. Hirsch holds that his list of cultural literacy, value-neutral and descriptive, falls into this domain. Yet, in other places Hirsch is deeply conflicted over this issue. He quotes Plato approvingly that there are "good reasons for being concerned with the specific contents of schooling, one of them ethical . . . whether a person is to be good or bad."[20] Hirsch writes of how cultural literacy places "higher value" on national than on local information and conceptual knowledge over practical knowledge. Unless Hirsch is committing some gross form of the naturalistic fallacy, deriving an "ought" from an "is", the claim that because there *is* shared cultural content, then we *ought* to induct the young into it, it is clear that Hirsch's cultural fragments are both descriptive and prescriptive. Hirsch's list of "what Americans know" can equally be labeled, for Hirsch, "what Americans ought to know." And while such prescriptivity may well be necessary, Hirsch's reluctance to provide a normative grounding for his pre-scription is a serious failure. In fact, the normative power of Hirsch's prescriptions lies in appeals to authority—the authority of experts, book publishers, the cultural elite, and ultimately, the nation-state. In the name of educating for public life, Hirsch would compel children to be inducted through the piling up of information into a prescriptive vocabulary and stereotypical schemata whose justification is no more than the coercive authority of compulsory, state schooling. And far from acting as a unifying or integrating force, Hirsch's attempt to compile an itemized list of cultural liter-acy *mirrors* the fragmentation of cultures of modernist, possessive individualism. Culture is not a list of items any more than a public is a list of individuals.

While Hirsch's view of educating for public life turns out to be a distorted, commercialized mechanism for authoritarian state schooling, he does raise, without answering, serious questions about authority and the "good." As he writes, "The question 'who is to say what the content shall be?' must not be allowed to serve its traditional role as a debate stopper."[21] Hirsch believes (and I agree) that his work "presents a broad challenge: to bring the hidden curriculum out in the open where it belongs and to make its contents the subject of democratic discussion."[22]

The next, and final contemporary view on educating for public life we will consider, the work of Henry Giroux, takes up this challenge directly.

Henry Giroux is committed to seeing that the question, "Who is to say what the content shall be?" is not a debate stopper. Like Hirsch, Giroux is interested in bringing the hidden curriculum out in the open and making its contents the subject of democratic discussion. Unlike Hirsch, Giroux does not back away from or vacillate on the central ethical decision that taking these interests seriously would entail. For Giroux, if the links between schooling, literacy, justice, and political democracy are taken seriously, then debates about public education must be explicitly normative and centered on the pursuit of a specific form of political community.

For Giroux, schools serve not as vehicles of mechanical state solidarity or as training grounds for consumer culture and corporate capitalism, but rather as contested terrains where the meaning of public and private, school-ing and education, are constructed in the nexus of power, history, identity, and interests. Central to Giroux's view is the inevitability and educative potential of struggle and conflict, an active reconstruction in which public spheres are created and democracy and political community are reinvented. Citizenship is an achievement grounded in a historically-informed agency sit-uated both in discourses of critique and opposition and discourses of possibility and hope. Education for public life in a democracy must be distin-guished both from state schooling and from functional preparation for competition in the private market economy. Thus, citizenship education cannot consist of the piling up of elite cultural knowledge or the initiation into a prescribed list of foundational ideas. Rather, education for public life "becomes a process of dialogue and commitment rooted in a fundamental belief in the possibility of public life and the development of forms of solidarity that allow people to reflect and organize in order to criticize and constrain the power of the state and to 'overthrow relations which inhibit and prevent the realization of humanity.'"[23] For Giroux, education for public democratic life requires the promotion of a kind of active agency which could critique and eliminate the "ideological and material conditions that promote various forms of subjugation, segregation, brutality, and marginalization, often expressed through social forms embodying racial, class, and sexist interests."[24]

Public education, in this view, as the empowering of counterpublic spheres of resistance and public re-invention, focuses on strengthening the "horizontal ties between citizen and citizen," rather than the hierarchical relations between citizen and the state, market, and cultural elite.[25] In this view, public schools serve as alternative public spheres in which the borders that distinguish groups and individuals provide the educative occasions for the reconstruction and validation of authentic difference and enabling solidarity.

At the core of Giroux's work is the effort to address directly the imperative of prescriptivity while avoiding both relativism and authoritarianism. Is there a democratic form of authority, a way to talk of the common, public good without imposition, a way to advance a *particular* ethical and political view of democratic community and democratic public schools without indoctrination? Is there any way to avoid the imperative of prescriptivity?

For Giroux, if all educators have either an implicit or explicit vision of who people should be and how they should act within the context of a human community, the basis of authority through which they structure classroom life is ultimately rooted in questions of ethics and power. Theorists of public education express a continuum of views on authority. Cultural conservatives, such as Hirsch, locate educational authority in the unproblematic reproduction of dominant culture. Liberal theorists also locate authority in tradition, although tradition itself is characteristically seen as conflicted, as in Butts's decalogue of *pluribus* and *unum* political values and Bellah's appeal to the practices and memories of second languages which compete with public speech for legitimacy. MacIntyre's deep pessimism about the possibility of locating *any* source of public educational authority in modernist culture is strongly echoed by many leftist or critical educators who view all authority as authoritarianism and thus are unable to defend any notion of a public education.

In *Education and the Struggle for Public Life,* Giroux offers an explicit alternative view of educational authority. For Giroux, drawing directly from the work of Kenneth D. Benne,[26] authority can be grounded in rules, expert knowledge, or the ethics of a democratic community. These alternate sources ground competing models of teaching, schooling, and public education.

Rule-based authority depends ultimately on state power for enforcement and thus supplies the logic for state education. In this view, teachers are technicians of the state's ideological apparatus and educating for public life is, in practice, a functional preparation for the existing normative and political order. Authority based on expertise depends ultimately on epistemic claims, themselves deeply implicated in relations of power and interests. In this view, teachers are autonomous professionals, teaching is a service industry where knowledge is exchanged as a commodity to learner/consumers for a fee in markets called schools. Educating for public life in this view either falls away in favor of something called "choice," or is construed as effective preparation for national and international consumer culture.

For Giroux, neither of these positions can sustain justifiable practices of democratic public education. In contrast, educational authority based in the morality of a democratic community, what Giroux sometimes calls emancipatory authority, rests not on appeals to state power or epistemic privilege, but rather on the educational practices which encourage and allow "strong democracy," itself marked by a "citizenry educated by public thinking, political judgment and social action."[27]

In this view, teaching is a form of public, intellectual practice, legitimated not by its endorsement by the state or claim to veridicality, but by bringing critical knowledge to bear in creating discussion of social freedom and public transformation. Teachers are not state technicians or autonomous professionals, but rather public educators; and educating for public life, while always grounded in the problematic contests and relations of real experience, is synonymous with schooling itself.

One central aim of this essay has been to problematize the question of educating for public life. As this brief review of views from the 1980s has shown, almost any agreement on a common vocabulary, set of starting points or ends-in-view for a broader alternative is unavailable. Indeed, the fundamental terms of the question seem forever trapped in the hermeneutical circle.

In the last section of this essay, I will return to the beginning story about our daughter's education as an opening into another, perhaps most central, problematic, the role of gender.

Overcoming the Tradition:
Education, Gender, and Public Schooling

The last thirty years of research on, about, and for women has taught us that it is no longer acceptable in rigorous scholarship to talk of persons in the abstract, apart from their location. Thus, it is important to recall that the "child" in my opening story was a daughter, a young woman, a female. What does educating for public life mean for *her*?

Another central element in that same scholarship on women has been a fundamental questioning of the concepts and categories around which male-dominated, academic disciplines have been constructed. Jane Roland Martin writes: "Since the 1970s, research has documented the ways in which such intellectual disciplines as history and psychology, literature and the fine arts, sociology and biology are biased according to sex. This work has revealed that on at least three counts the disciplines fall short of the ideal of epistemological equality for women: they exclude women from their subject matter, distort the female image according to the male image of her, and deny value to characteristics the society considers feminine."[28] Political and educational theory have not escaped this scrutiny or indictment.

At the core of this feminist work within political and educational theory has been a reassessment of the ideas of the public and private, productive and reproductive, spheres. In Jean Bethke Elshtain's analysis of the classic statements of the Western political tradition, she finds the public and the private as basic "guides to our orientation in the world."[29]

For some political theorists, "the public and private recedes into the background of analysis . . . because the existence of these spheres is simply assumed." Others believe "that the private should be integrated fully into an overarching public arena," while others call for the "privatization of the public realm with politics falling under its standards, ideals, and purposes," and still others call for a "rigid bifurcation between the two spheres with the private realm conceived instrumentally, treated as a necessary basis for public life but a less worthy form of human activity."[30] For Elshtain, these ways of distinguishing the public and private are "unacceptable as the basis of the reconstructive ideal,"[31] as part of the effort to recast "public and private boundaries to preserve each yet reach towards an ideal of social reconstruction."[32]

The suggestion that political theory, and for our particular purposes, educational theory, by focusing exclusively on received notions of the public is sexist, is addressed in others forms by feminist philosophers of science and social scientists. Sandra Harding writes that the focus on men and men's activities as universal subjects "leads us to ignore such crucial issues as how changes in the social practices of reproduction, sexuality, and mothering have shaped the state, the economy, and other public institutions."[33] Marcia Millman and Rosabeth Moss Kanter note how a focus on "public, official" role players and situations and neglect of the "private . . . informal, local structures in which women participate most frequently" results in a failure to understand "the interplay between informal, interpersonal networks and the formal, official social structures."[34] Heidi Hartmann views the family, the paradigmatic "private" sphere, as a "location where production and redistribution take place. As such, it is a location where people with different activities and interests often come into conflict with one another."[35]

This and much other scholarship clearly demonstrates how traditional distinctions and valorizations of public and private, the productive and reproductive, are enshrined in our political and social theory and how these distinctions reflect and support gender-biased descriptions of the world and the possibilities for action within it. It is precisely for these reasons that "educating for public life" must be made problematic and looked at anew.

After an illuminating analysis of the classics in Western educational theory with special focus on the public role afforded to women and women's education in these theories, Jane Roland Martin suggests a new theory of educational practices that moves toward a reconstructive ideal. For Martin, the fallacy of the false dilemma, education for public *or* private life, education for productive *or* reproductive functions, education based on gender *or* education having nothing to do with gender, "is a natural consequence of our ignorance of alternative ideals of the educated woman."[36] For Martin, the proper construction of educational theories, for men and women, requires that equal due be given to the historically-defined productive realm-preparation for citizenship and the workplace—*and,* the reproductive realm, which Martin describes to include "not simply conception and birth, but the rearing of children to more or less maturity and associated activities such as tending the sick, taking care of family needs, and running a household."[37]

What would inquiry into educating for public life become if we seriously followed the idea that an educational theory was a theory or theories of the "doings" that prepare one for conduct as a member of community, that education itself is the paradigmatic mode of socially established, cooperative human activity through which we attempt to systematically extend all varieties of human powers and excellences, and that these doings and excellences do not come neatly packaged in gender-driven categories of public and private, productive and reproductive?

I think a good conversational beginning is to engage in dialogue about what excellence means in common sense terms, where we take common sense literally as the sense it takes to live in a commons. With this in mind, in conversation it quickly becomes clear that when we consider the people we respect, love, are glad to get to know, and have as neighbors, work with, and so forth, we do not think of these people solely, if at all, in school-based categories of cognition and symbolic literacy or in theoretically-driven categories which distinguish between public and private. We might know some people we would go to hear a speech or for heart surgery, but not go hiking with or invite to our birthday parties. That is, we build our publics over a spectrum of competencies and qualities that people display in their lives and bring to ours. In other terms, we operate publicly in terms of a system of multiple excellences as Maxine Greene says, about which we make sophisticated, finely-honed comparative judgments.[38] The ability to make these judgments, to bring the skill, know-how, know-that, empathy, and imagination to bear in recreating a world, is a large part of what it means to be educated. In this process, the walls between public and private, productive and reproductive, are collapsed. That is, we see quickly how so-called public virtues and competencies such as efficiency and rationality are desiderata in some activities of the private world, while so-called private virtues and competencies such as nurturance and courage are requirements for an enabling and generous public life. If the aim of public education is educating for public life, forming and re-forming publics, then the purpose of schooling is to prepare people in the multiple excellences that give a public its quality, distinctiveness, and solidarity. And it is in large part the discourses of the private, reproductive practices that give public discourse its substance and its possibilities for education.

Conclusion

Every distinction, and perhaps especially that between private and public, productive and reproductive, masks power and claims of privilege. Feminist scholarship has shown both the distorting consequences this has had in theories of public education and opened a lens on a reconstructive ideal in whose light our daughters, and sons, may, in Dewey's terms, "learn to be human."[39]

NOTES

1. While I was attending a seminar on the Psychology of Love led by Carol Gilligan in 1986, one of the participants (I'm sorry I forget her name) remarked in one discussion, "Men are such bastards, they refuse to use their own children in their arguments." This remark struck me deeply and I have struggled ever since to keep it in my mind and heart as I try to write philosophy. This opening story is an effort in that direction.

2. *The Republic of Plato,* trans. by Francis W. Cornford (London: Oxford University Press, 1973).

3. J.J. Rousseau, *Emile, or On Education,* introduction, trans., and notes by Allan Bloom (New York: Basic Books, 1979).

4. John Dewey, *Democracy and Education* (New York: Free Press, 1966) and *The Public and Its Problems* (New York: Henry Holt, 1927).

5. James M. Giarelli, "Public Philosophies and Education," *Educational Foundations,* 4 (Winter 1990): 7–18.

6. R. Freeman Butts, *The Revival of Civic Learning: A Rationale for Citizenship Education in American Schools* (Bloomington, IN: Phi Delta Kappan Educational Foundation, 1980) and *Teacher Education and the Revival of Civic Learning,* Seventh Annual DeGarmo Lecture (Society of Professors of Education, 1982).

7. Butts, *Revival of Civic Learning,* p. 123.

8. Butts, *Teacher Education,* p. 14.

9. Alasdair MacIntyre, "The Idea of an Educated Public," in Graham Haydon, ed., *Education and Values* (London: Institute of Education, University of London, 1987).

10. Ibid., p. 16.

11. Ibid.

12. Ibid., p. 17.

13. Ibid., p. 29.

14. Ibid., p. 34.

15. Ibid.

16. Robert Bellah, et al., *Habits of the Heart* (Berkeley and Los Angeles: University of California Press, 1985); E. D. Hirsch, *Cultural Literacy* (Boston: Houghton Mifflin, 1987); Henry Giroux, *Schooling the Struggle for Public Life* (Minneapolis: University of Minnesota Press, 1989).

17. Hirsch, *Cultural Literacy,* p. xv.

18. Ibid., p. xvi.

19. Ibid., p. xiv.

20. Ibid., p. xvi.

21. Ibid., p. 144.

22. Ibid., p. 145.

23. Henry Giroux, *Schooling and the Struggle for Public Life,* p. 6. Giroux's internal quotation is from Douglas Kellner and Harry O'Hara, "Utopian and Marxism in Ernst Bloch," *New German Critique,* 9 (Fall 1976): 22.

24. Ibid.

25. Ibid., p. 30.

26. Kenneth D. Benne, "Authority in Education," *Harvard Educational Review,* 40 (August 1970): 345–410.

27. Ibid.

28. Jane Roland Martin, *Reclaiming a Conversation* (New Haven: Yale University Press, 1985): 6.

29. Jean Bethke Elshtain, *Public Man, Private Woman* (Princeton: Princeton University Press, 1981): 3.

30. Ibid., p. 4.

31. Ibid., p. 342.

32. Ibid., p. 4.

33. Sandra Harding, ed., *Feminism and Methodology* (Bloomington: Indiana University Press, 1987): 4–5. Emphasis in original.

34. Marcia Millman and Rosabeth Moss Kanter, "Introduction to *Another Voice: Feminist Perspectives in Social Life and Social Science,*" in Harding, *Feminism and Methodology,* p. 32.

35. Heidi I. Hartmann, "The Family as the Locus of Gender, Class, and Political Struggle: The Example of Housework," in Harding, *Feminism and Methodology,* p. 111.

36. Jane Roland Martin, *Reclaiming a Conversation,* p. 176.

37. Ibid., p. 6.

38. See Maxine Greene, "Excellence, Meanings, and Multiplicity," *Teachers College Record* 86 (1984): 283–97.

39. John Dewey, *The Public and Its Problems* (Chicago: Swallow Press, 1954): p. 154.

17

Education for Citizenship

Kevin Harris

John Stuart Mill saw it as an "almost self-evident axiom . . . that the State should require and compel the education, up to a certain standard, of every human being who is born its citizen" (Mill 1964, p. 160). And while many might see such an axiom requiring some justification, rather than relying on its allegedly self-evident nature, few apart from extreme anarchists are likely to disagree with the fundamental substance of Mill's claim.

This claim, however, like so many which are largely unproblematic when considered in broad terms, tends not to reveal that it is both built upon and contains within it issues of extreme complexity and controversy, and that once unpacked it more closely approximates the proverbial can of worms. Immediate issues arise, such as what is meant by "education", what standard should be set, how is a citizen defined, and so on. These lead to further questions such as who should determine the content of education, how can compulsion be secured, how can standards be set and maintained; and from there on the worms keep wriggling and wriggling.

For my contribution to the conversation in this collection I shall warily open the can I have displayed, but I shall be neither ambitious nor foolish enough to expect to monitor or control all the wriggling that will result. Instead, I shall simply examine certain aspects surrounding one of the first issues to crawl out as soon as the lid is removed; namely the role of State-provided or State-sanctioned education in preparing people to become active citizens of the State.

Picking up on Mill I have deliberately continued to use the word "citizen". When human beings are first born we tend not to regard them as functioning citizens. We expect, however, that after a period (today commonly set at eighteen years) the original twenty-one inch alimentary-canal-on-legs, which seemed capable of little more than emitting disruptive noises at one end and unpleasant smells at the other, will now be able to function as an integral contributing member of a complex social organisation. It is expected that such a person will have learnt sufficiently to participate in and contribute to the society's economy, culture, and politics; in short to its overall development as a society or State.

Maturation alone will not bring this about. Rather a deliberate teaching/learning process is required. But this does not necessarily call for State involvement, or for systems of State-provided public schooling as we know them. Mill himself was not advocating universal compulsory State schooling. He regarded the obligation for educating children as a "sacred duty" of parents; and for Mill the State's requirement and compulsion regarding education was more the establishment of a point where the buck stopped. The State was to step in and school, as one model among many competing models, where parents either failed to do their duty or else could not afford to educate their children properly. Today, however, at least in the developed world, the State has taken its "requirement" and "compulsion" to educate in a different light. In times much changed from Mill's it is now usually the case that State-provided or State-sanctioned schooling is offered universally and on a compulsory basis, as the legitimated formal context in which education ostensibly takes place; and that parents who wish to carry out their children's education themselves have to make the case to the State to do so.

The Content and Purpose of Schooling/Education

Learning sufficiently in order to participate meaningfully in the economic, cultural and political life of the State can result from experience, both within and outside of schooling, with infinite permutations and combinations of content. Thus in any complex society there could be a vast variety of possible curricula that its future citizens might encounter. But two features could be expected to be constant; namely the attempt to instill the dominant value and belief systems of the society in question—values and beliefs which direct the society in pretty much the way in which it is going—along with, for each particular society, the transmission of specific content judged necessary for that society's survival and furtherance.

It is in this way that all socialisation, including the production of the future citizenry, is conservative, in the literal sense of seeking to conserve and maintain the dominant value systems and the bodies of knowledge and belief deemed to have brought the status quo into being. It then follows that, in so far as schooling is concerned with socialisation, to that extent schooling is conservative. And schooling as required, provided or sanctioned by the State is even better placed to be conservative given that no State would consciously and deliberately foster a universal compulsory institution that openly challenged its dominant value, belief and knowledge systems; or set up and/or sanction an institution likely to produce the kind of future citizens who might overthrow the very State that formed or socialised them.

The idea, then, of schooling as a form of indoctrination for citizenship emerges as a real possibility, and examples of this are very easy to find. One thinks immediately of Nazi schooling, Stalinist schooling, schooling under China's cultural revolution, and some fundamentalist religious schooling. But all of these are instances of schooling and socialisation in societies that are variously monistic and which forbid criticism and even open debate of prevailing values and beliefs. Could it possibly be argued that schooling and socialisation in modern liberal democracies is similarly conservative and functions generally to produce citizens who will uncritically reproduce the social order?

Three matters immediately confront such a position. First; liberal democracies, in the very declaration of their liberal and democratic standpoints, indicate dissatisfaction with imposition and monism, and thus a consequent desire to promote plurality and freedom of belief. Secondly; the dominant discourse relating to schooling in liberal democratic societies proclaims that schooling is charged not just with socialisation but also with educating the future citizenry, and speaks of producing not compliant uncritical party and dogma-following citizens but rather autonomous citizens. Thirdly; modern complex societies are concerned with development and positioning for the future, rather than with strictly reproductive conservation in the way (say) the Boro Indians have conserved their lifeways for more generations than history can trace. It would appear, then, that modern, complex liberal democratic societies seeking to educate autonomous citizens are, at the most, minimally conservative; holding on to only those things that liberal experience and democratic debate have established to be worth retaining.

A delicate balance, however, must still be maintained. A liberal democratic State becoming too liberal and insufficiently conservative runs the risk of licensing either the extreme form of liberty advocated by Mill, or the extreme form of individualism promoted by Rousseau and often partially incorporated into forms of progressive schooling (Rousseau 1966). On the other hand, a State becoming too conservative and insufficiently democratic runs the risk of approximating Plato's ideal, where education was designed both to liberate the minds of the intellectually elite *and* to ensure that everyone happily stuck to their place, so that cobblers cobbled contentedly and left running the State to the wise (Plato 1986; Books 2–4).

Modern liberal theory avoids both extremes largely through the discourse of *liberal rationalism* which concentrates heavily on rationality, community, and justice. Individuality is still celebrated but is recontextualised in terms of autonomous citizenship; and freedom of individual action is proscribed within a social context in which autonomous agents rationally accept the need to live in a just, rule-governed society which operates in the interests of all while promoting maximum acceptable diversity. John White, a prominent proponent of liberal rationalism, suggests that "in a liberal-democratic society the proper task of government is to promote the well-being of all citizens by equipping them with the conditions of an autonomous life" (White 1988, p. 229), and the government is to do this through providing education which acquaints pupils impartially with a whole range of different ideals of the good life while not steering them towards any ideals in particular. Within such a frame of discourse government, liberalism, autonomy, choice, pluralism, tolerance, democracy, participatory citizenship, schooling, and education all lie together in apparent relative comfort.

This all sounds very different from the idea and practice of schooling seeking to conserve the status quo; and in a very real sense it is difficult to level the charges of conservation, indoctrination, and the promulgation of specifically selected values and knowledge at schooling in ostensibly liberal democratic pluralist societies. To make the charge even viable, let alone make it stick, we would have to establish how such a thing could be achieved, and also account for why it is being sought. Recalling that no State would consciously and deliberately institute a form of universal compulsory schooling that openly challenged the dominant value, belief and knowledge systems of that State, I am going to attempt to provide this account by applying a neo-Marxist analysis to both the role of schooling in society and the notion of conservation.

According to Marxism the State, although commonly identified in national and geographical terms, is properly recognisable as State Power (Marx 1971; Marx and Engels 1976; Engels 1975), and this power is exerted through offices or, as Althusser has termed them, apparatuses, which function to secure and serve the ruling interests in a society (Althusser 1984, pp. 15–22). Also according to Marxism, the central identifying feature of a social formation is not its political mode, whether it is democratic or totalitarian; but rather its dominant mode of production, whether it is feudal or capitalist or socialist. It then follows that what State Power seeks to legitimate, secure, and conserve in any society is basically the conditions or *relations of production* which will secure the dominant mode of production and continue to serve the ruling interests—the interests of the class which owns and/or controls the means of production. This, will, of course, have much to do with knowledge and values; but for "conservation" in Marxist terminology read "reproducing the relations of production that secure the dominant mode of production."

If this much is accepted, the question of "why" is easily settled. Universal compulsory schooling is established to transmit and legitimate the knowledge and values which are to preserve the ruling interests and to secure the reproduction of the dominant means of production. Thus, in a capitalist society State-provided and State-sanctioned schooling serve, conserve, and secure the interests of the capitalist class by legitimating and promoting that knowledge and those values perceived to be well placed to serve the interests of capital.

The more difficult and complex question is How is this achieved?; and Marxism answers: largely by ideology; by making things appear differently to the way they are (Marx and Engels; 1976).[1] In order to illustrate this I am going to consider six issues relating to education and citizenship in liberal democratic States, but more importantly I am going to consider them as *illusions;* and as illusions which do not readily appear as such because they also function clearly as *allusions.* As Althusser again has indicated (1984, p. 36), if such illusions didn't key into or allude to our experience of the world they would all too readily be recognised as illusions. The fact that they allude in some cases, or are presented in theoretic contexts in which they appear to naturally or logically allude to experience, helps create the illusion that they apply universally and accurately describe the world. (Before beginning, however, I must offer the important warning that the following account will be qualified after its completion. I therefore beg the patience of those who find what follows bordering too closely on crude reproduction theory or conspiracy theory.)

First; there is the illusion of education itself, or more exactly the illusion that schooling is primarily concerned with educating. The allusion works here both through the everyday linguistic nexus between schools and education, and in that schools *do* offer educative activities, and they certainly do educate large numbers of people to varyingly high levels. But schools also act as agents of social control, and in doing so instill into a large part of the future citizenry the knowledge, skills and attitudes that will make them more or less compliant people well placed to contribute to reproducing the means of production. Although the development of critical thought has constantly been on the overt agenda for school curricula, it less commonly happens in practice. In today's schools people are learning more than ever before, but in these recessionary times when schools are becoming more directed to providing employment skills rather than developing critical thought, students are hardly being introduced to those reflective practices that can free them from being bound by their ideological context. Sociology, anthropology, philosophy, and political economy are studies kept for those levels of higher education by which time the large majority of the population has dropped out or been ushered out, and even then the content of these subjects is controlled in ways

---

1. This is a most complex and contested issue. For useful introductory discussion see Larrain (1979).

likely to promote existing legitimated dominant values, rather than form a basis for becoming critical of them. It is easier to absorb what is offered at school and higher education than it is to become seriously critical of it. Students have enough on their plate trying to meet their basic requirements; and there is little if any time or space or opportunity both to master the orthodoxy and develop and expound a critical view of it. Also, when the aim of studying is to gain good grades in order to get a job, especially in times of high unemployment, schooling, or the period of formal education, might wisely be spent learning the ropes rather than devoting time to the risky and unprofitable task of trying to untie them and discover who is holding them.

The indication, above, that curricula content is controlled to promote certain knowledge and values, leads directly to the second illusion; namely the illusion of the neutrality of knowledge. This is supported by the allusion that some knowledge appears to be unquestionably neutral—two plus two equals four; Washington is the capital of the USA; ammonia consists of sodium, oxygen and hydrogen; the Battle of Hastings was fought in 1066; and Mt Etna is an active volcano—regardless of whether one is a Republican, a Democrat, a Marxist, black, white, gay, straight, male or female. It is also supported by one of our dominant theoretic contexts, going back to Plato, that real knowledge (as distinct from belief or opinion) is apprehension of eternal unchanging truths which are untrammelled by our personal predilections and which are basically unaffected by limits or restrictions on the way we see things (Plato 1986, Book 7). This view legitimates school knowledge as a neutral revelation of the world; and it is often further claimed that, notwithstanding that knowledge is infinite and school curricula must be selective, selection of curricula content, or that knowledge which "is of most worth", is also made on neutral epistemological and/or pragmatic grounds. Knowledge, however, is never theory-free or neutral; and that which is included in school curricula is a very specific selection. Not everybody's knowledge, way of seeing the world or priorities of concern get on the agenda. If we think of human knowledge as the sum of the utterances the whole of humanity has come to make about the world, it is clear that only a few voices (even from our own society) are heard in school curricula, and even less of those are legitimated. This leaves pupils in an unequal relation to school knowledge; and points to the third illusion.

This is the illusion of equality of educational opportunity and mobility. The allusion here is that all children, regardless of gender, race, creed, colour, religion or class are offered a place in school, are offered more or less the same curricula (more so with the advent of national curricula), much the same access to teachers and other resources, and at certain points are all confronted with more or less the same testing and sieving devices. No set of opportunities could appear more equally offered. And yet the reality of it is that schooling within societies recognised as liberal democracies systematically discriminates against females, people of colour, certain ethnic groups, certain minority groups, and children of the working class, and of the less wealthy. Part of the reason for this is that it is not their knowledge and their experience that schooling fosters, transmits, and legitimates. In fact it is often the case that schooling denigrates this, and in doing so reinforces a sense of inferior or marginal social location among such groups. But some of these children do, of course, succeed; many against the odds and many positively helped by understanding teachers and other school personnel. This then provides the allusion for the myth of mobility. While it is the case that schooling provides the means for some to rise quite dramatically through the social ranks (an achievement which tends to be disproportionately heralded) it has again been shown almost universally that, as the Coleman Report put it, "schools bring little influence to bear on a child's achievement that is independent of his [sic] background and general social context" (Coleman 1966, p. 325). It is more the case that schooling reinforces children's social locations rather than promotes mobility; and once parents reproduce their own kind schooling reproduces the relations of production in society from the appropriate progeny. There are distinct advantages in being the white Anglo-Saxon heterosexual son of wealthy professional or business-connected parents.

Now, moving a little beyond schooling, there is the fourth illusion; of autonomy. This is secured in the undeniable allusion that within liberal democracies people do have real choices and options, along with certain rights and controls over their own lives. It is revealed as an illusion, however, when we recognise the lack of power that we have over the basic structural matters that shape our individual and social lives and the conditions within which we can make our choices. The freedom and autonomy we do have lies in being able to make limited adjustments to actions and decisions made by governments, banks, and huge business enterprises. Consider, for instance, the current situation in which all of us are presently exercising differing levels of freedom and choice in adjusting our lives to the effects of a global recession. This recession, however, is not the natural or inevitable cyclic thing it is often portrayed as being, and it is not the result of actions "ordinary citizens" are commonly blamed for, such as buying too many imported goods or seeking crippling wage rises. It is, in fact, the structural outcome of certain actions very few of us made, and hardly any of which most people were capable of preventing. A clear specific example in this regard can be seen in the actions of the German Bundesbank increasing interest rates in August 1992 to counter inflation brought on by problems in assimilating those who had come from the East to the new unified Germany. This action of a mere seventeen people in turn precipitated a massive outflow of funds invested at lower interest rates in other countries, and this, in conjunction with other factors associated with present moves towards developing a form of unified Europe (moves which few governments have given the people a voice in through referenda) brought about sharp decreases in the value of a number of major currencies. The result of the German bank officials' actions, and of those chasing maximum capital gains, was to plunge entire countries deeper into the recessions they were struggling to emerge from, and to seriously affect the lives of hundreds of millions of people—people whose freedom and autonomy nevertheless rendered them powerless spectators to the process.

It might be argued, however, that we have the freedom and the mechanisms to force governments to alter policy, to put governments out of office and to call banks and businesses to account. This is the fifth illusion; the illusion of democracy and power, and it too has its allusion. In liberal democracies all citizens are entitled to vote for their representatives in governments every so often; all banks and businesses are accountable to their shareholders who meet regularly; and it is not uncommon for governments and boards of directors to be voted out of office. Clearly people do have power and access to decision making (although it could be argued that Republicans are the same as Democrats while capitalism remains). The point is citizens don't have it where and how it really counts. A vote for a representative every four years is hardly a voice in the government of the country, as Kozol (1985, p. 94) has so poignantly shown; and often a vote for a party is by no means support for policies that party either takes to the polls or later puts into operation. Not everybody who voted Republican in the 1960s and 1970s supported America's involvement in the Vietnam war; just as not everybody who voted for the Conservatives in the UK in 1992 supported Britain's acceptance of the Maastricht Treaty. Governments of the people in liberal democracies may be elected *by* the people; but they do not necessarily govern *for* the people in the sense of representing the people's wishes when they act.

None of the above, however, is to suggest that people have no power to effect change in society. Clearly standards of living and social values have changed such that the working class, along with people of colour, women and gays are generally better off than they were a hundred years ago. We must be careful not to belittle the enormous efforts that have gone into bringing about such changed conditions, or even the propensity to effect change itself. But we must also recognise that it has taken enormously disproportionate effort, not to mention blood, to secure even a modicum of rights for *majority* groups; and that even though some of these people may never have had it so good, they still suffer comparatively badly within their own liberal democratic societies. While the rich are getting richer and some of the poor are getting rich, the number of the poor are increasing, as is the extent of their poverty and their chances of ever gaining access to wealth and power. The underclass is growing and the struggle for racial and gender equality is by no means successfully completed.

This leads nicely to the last illusion: the illusion of liberalism. Here again the allusion holds. More alternatives are now offered and tolerated, restrictions almost everywhere are being relaxed, and speech seems freer than it has ever been. In fact, anti-establishment commentary is often not merely tolerated but even celebrated, as liberals boast of their penchant to fight to the death to protect the rights of others to say things they themselves disagree with. It will be pointed out yet again that I am free to write this stuff, whereas such a foray in a non-liberal society would quickly land me in a mental institution or the legendary salt mines. Two other things, however, are not so readily pointed out. The first is that, while in a liberal society radicals may not have to suffer to the lengths of a Sakharov or a Solzhenitsyn, they come by recognition the hard way, and all too often find jobs, audiences, promotions, and especially consultancies denied to them. The second is that even the most liberal of societies can have the stoppers put back on very quickly by those who actually hold power. Positions won after decades of bitter mass struggle can be swept aside in an instant by the few who have the power to do such simple things as make a single appointment to the Supreme Court. In practice liberal democracies tend to be not too tolerant, or liberal, about things which threaten the conditions for reproducing the relations of production and the dominant mode of production.

The discussion above might leave us with a pessimistic conclusion regarding education for citizenship; namely that education is primarily directed to conservation, in the sense of reproducing the relations of production, and thus its purpose is to provide differentially-skilled compliant citizens willing to reproduce the existing relations of production. That, however, smacks too much of the crude reproduction theory some of us promoted in the 1970s (Bowles and Gintis 1976; Harris 1979, pp. 140–4), and of the conspiracy theory many of us wanted to deny at the same time (Harris 1979, pp. 67–9). But even though there is now good reason to support a conspiracy theory, the reproductive aspect of the above case is too easy, too crude.

Can Schooling be Transformative/Revolutionary?

The preceding argument fails to take adequate notice of two major points; namely that schools can be sites of resistance, and that *education* is by its nature critical and transformative. It is the level of resistance, along with the presence of education, that distinguishes schooling in liberal democracies from that in totalitarian regimes.

Resistance is the lesser of the two issues; although it was the one the early critics of crude reproduction theory mainly called attention to. It is, of course, the case that things do not go along nicely and smoothly either in schools, or in society at large. Positions tend to be contested, and at times the contest can be severe and messy. Anyone who has ever taught in schools or fought a local issue or a more general cause would know of the contest and the mess. But in schooling children are younger, relatively powerless and more compliant, and although they might not meekly accept all that is laid before them they are well placed to assimilate or just recognise as legitimate the values and knowledge passed on there. This would also be exacerbated in times of recession and high unemployment, where credentialling becomes more eagerly sought and highly prized, and where schooling thus functions even more powerfully as an agent of social control.

Transformative critical education is the larger issue, and not withstanding the conservative nature of schooling it is not a foregone and hopeless cause. Students and teachers do not come to school out of a vacuum, but rather carry the baggage of their beliefs and experience with them; and it is possible, even likely, that there would be a proportion within the school who would bring the weapons of criticism and the desire to transform to the educative exchange. There are, however, a number of difficulties associated with this; and three ought at least be mentioned.

First; engaging in critical transformative education requires recognition of how people (citizens) are constituted as ideological subjects, how naturalisation and illusions are created, and how critical perspectives can be established. It also requires the educator, himself or herself a product of schooling and wider socialisation, to have recognised and overcome the very process of constitution as an ideological subject. Neither recognition is impossible to achieve (Harris 1992).

Second; critical education entails the enormous difficulty of attempting to be critical of, and transform, the very system one is working within. This basically requires using the elements of that system against itself, which can be more difficult than might first appear. For instance, there are school structures, texts, curricula, and power relations that have to be followed and employed in the very act of attempting to transform both those things directly and what is instantiated in them. This can cause contradictions in practice, and failure to achieve both the legitimated goals (which for the current students' sake must still be pursued) and the critical goals. As Aronowitz and Giroux have noted (1985, pp. 23–45) transformative intellectuals (teachers) occupy contradictory, paradoxical and tension-filled roles in schools; and for their extra pains suffer de-legitimation within their own field as the more accommodating teachers gain praise, success, and promotion.

Third; the critically transformative teacher, like all teachers, is in a privileged position with regard to learners, but as a critically reflexive person may be loathe to exploit this privileged position (Bereiter 1972, p. 26; Lankshear, 1987, p. 240). Here the teacher might do well to take a leaf from the State's book, for exercise and exploitation of privilege is what the State, as State power does. However a critically educative teacher would need to avoid not only making children the "walking wounded" of a cause, but also merely replacing one form of indoctrination with another. Such a person would have a lot of listening to do in school, and a great deal of reflexive knowledge to acquire outside.

Conclusion

I want to conclude my part in this conversation by replying to things that have been said to me in other contexts and which could easily be said in reply here: namely that I am simply reacting to an imperfect system of liberal democracy. No liberal seriously believes that we have presently achieved truly representative government; that our schooling system is perfect; that we have fully succeeded in achieving the conditions for affording equality and full autonomy to all; and so on. They might even see these as historically evolving processes, and chide me for mistaking moments in a developing process as structural barriers. My last word on this, then, is to stress that the issue as I see it is not the relative perfection or state of evolution of liberalism and democracy; but rather socio-political requirements in States where capitalism is the dominant mode of production. Capitalism undoubtedly benefits many, and in its historical development there will be continuing changes in whom it benefits and to what degree. But it is also a mode of production which, throughout all forms of its historical development, exploits and structurally disadvantages others. While the propensity to benefit some entrepreneurs through structurally disadvantaging other people remains, capitalism can easily contain central tenets of liberalism, but it cannot function in conditions which allow for real equality, real autonomy, and real democracy. Thus, while the State is a capitalist State, manifested in the exercise of State power operating to secure and protect the interests of capital and the capitalist class, its apparatuses will simultaneously legitimate the discourse of liberalism, create the sorts of illusions illustrated above, and seek to deny to its citizens the critical faculty, level of autonomy and those elements of democracy which could seriously endanger the process of reproducing the relations of production through which the State defines itself, and in terms of which it seeks to conserve itself.

BIBLIOGRAPHY

Althusser, L. (1984). *Essays on Ideology*. London: Verso.

Aronowitz, S. and Giroux, H. (1985). *Education Under Siege*. Boston: Bergin and Garvey.

Bereiter, C. (1972). "Moral Alternatives to Education," *Interchange,* 3(1).

Bowles, S. and Gintis, H. (1976). *Schooling in Capitalist America*. New York: Basic Books.

Coleman, J.S. et al (1966). *Equality of Educational Opportunity*. Washington: US Government Printing Office.

Engels, F. (1975). *The Origin of the Family, Private Property and the State*. New York: Pathfinder Press.

Harris, K. (1979). *Education and Knowledge.* London: Routledge and Kegan Paul.

Harris, K. (1992). "Schooling, Democracy and Teachers as Intellectual Vanguard," *New Zealand Journal of Educational Studies,* 27(1): 21–33.

Kozol, J. (1985). *Illiterate America.* New York: Anchor and Doubleday.

Lankshear, C. (1987). *Literacy, Schooling and Revolution.* Lewes: The Falmer Press.

Larrain, J. (1979). *The Concept of Ideology.* London: Hutchinson.

Marx, K. and Engels, F. (1976). *The German Ideology.* Moscow: Progress Publishers.

Marx, K. (1971). *The Early Texts* (ed. D. McLellan). Oxford: Oxford University Press.

Mill, J.S. (1964). *Utilitarianism, Liberty and Representative Government.* London: J.M.Dent and Sons (Everyman's Library).

Plato (1986). *Republic.* Harmondsworth: Penguin Books.

Rousseau, J.J. (1966). *Emile.* London: J.M. Dent and Sons.

White, J. (1988). "Two National Curricula—Baker's and Stalin's. Towards a Liberal Alternative," *British Journal of Educational Studies,* XXXVI.

18

Education for Citizenship: Obstacles and Opportunities

Patricia White

One way of arriving at a considered view of the form education for citizenship should take in a democratic society is to consider obvious obstacles to such an education in imperfectly democratic societies with which one is familiar. Proceeding in this way can have a number of advantages. It can, for a start, avoid the rather overblown, rhetorical stance which sometimes characterises writing on the aims of education for citizenship. Not because it avoids the need to have a conception of the aims of citizenship education—how otherwise would the obstacles be identified as such?—but because it can help to make the, perhaps implicit, conception one is working with more precise. In so doing it can provide a usefully specific focus for educational effort at the broad policy making level and at classroom level.

Two Views of the Obstacles to Education for Citizenship

In their discussions, Kevin Harris and James M. Giarelli both identify major obstacles to the realisation of their conceptions of education for citizenship in a democracy.

For Harris capitalism is the major obstacle, since it cannot allow for "real equality, real autonomy and real democracy." A capitalist state will always operate "to secure and protect the interests of capital and the capitalist class." Current capitalist states, however, (Harris's examples are drawn from Western Europe and the USA,) do not do this in any nakedly obvious way. They "legitimate the discourse of liberalism" and create the illusion that they are liberal democratic states. They do this, inter alia, by fostering a number of illusions: namely, that schools are educating students, the knowledge taught is neutral, students enjoy equality of educational opportunity, and citizens exercise autonomy, whilst living in a democratic and liberal society.

In this situation teachers, as "transformative intellectuals," need to recognise the ways in which they have been constituted as ideological subjects, learn how to establish critical perspectives and educate their students to do the same. Doing this within a capitalist education system will not be easy and the teacher will need to avoid "replacing one form of indoctrination with another."

For Giarelli it is not clear that education for public life is possible at all in the USA in the last decade of the twentieth century. His overview of a broad spectrum of views in the first part of his paper leads him to conclude that "almost any agreement on a common vocabulary, set of starting points or ends-in-view . . . is unavailable."

But then it seems that the dismantling, or perhaps the revision, of certain distinctions may offer a way forward. These are, according to Giarelli, the "traditional distinctions and valorizations of public and private, the productive and reproductive, . . . enshrined in our political and social theory and how these distinctions reflect and support gender-biased descriptions of the world and our possibilities for action within it." These distinctions "mask power and claims of privilege," as every distinction does.

Removing this obstacle means, for Giarelli, collapsing the walls between the public and private, the productive and the reproductive and then educating people in "multiple excellences" drawn from these spheres.

Getting Clear About the Obstacles

Identifying obstacles to education for citizenship can bring a desirable precision to the whole enterprise. For it to do that though, the characterisation of the obstacles needs to be exact and concrete and precisely why they constitute obstacles to desirable states of affairs needs to be examined in careful detail.

According to Harris's account, the capitalist state operates to protect the interests of the capitalist class. In any extended version of this conversation, Harris would need to offer a more precise and detailed analysis of the nature of the capitalist state in advanced industrial societies in the late twentieth century. Is Harris's view that the state is a direct instrument of class rule—"the executive committee of the bourgeoisie," as in traditional

Marxism? His claim that "there is now good reason to support a conspiracy theory" would tend to suggest this. On the other hand, much of his analysis suggests that he, in line with other critics, sees the state sandwiched between contradictory influences. It is buffeted on the one side by organised labour and socialist political movements, demanding the extension of citizenship rights, and on the other by private and corporate capital whose owners want to resist government attempts to procure income to provide community services supportive of those rights. Getting the analysis right, whether it approximates to one of those just mentioned or is different again, is crucially important for education for citizenship. For instance, taking the first view might lead to the conclusion that the way forward is to destroy the capitalist class and build a new kind of economic order and society. This would require an account of the way in which the capitalist class is to be dispossessed, a careful delineation of the new order—including an account of "real equality, real autonomy and real democracy"—as well as a defence of any proposed wholesale construction of social institutions against "utopianism". Alternatively, if, as Harris seems to, one accepts that power and privilege have yielded to political pressure in the past and could continue to do so, then a rather different citizenship education is required. Certainly recent evidence seems to suggest that "economic development contributes most to welfare when guided by an effective public authority that guarantees civil, political and social rights to all and is thus open to pressure by effective political mobilisation" (Doyal and Gough 1994; see also Doyal and Gough 1991). So perhaps on this analysis citizenship education should have in view a mixed economy with appropriate employment, health, educational, and arts policies.

Giarelli's major obstacle, too, needs a more probing analysis before one can judge what, for him, stands in the way of education for citizenship. Giarelli talks of the traditional valorization of public and private, the productive and reproductive spheres. Concretely for citizenship education we need to know if he has in mind, for instance, the designation of some tasks as private unpaid tasks—bringing up children, looking after the house, looking after sick members of the family—whilst other tasks are public and have a renumeration attached to them. Or is the crucial obstacle the linkage of this distinction with the idea of gender-specific roles, with which it has been linked historically but from which it is separable? Questions about the best ways of raising children, equitably distributing housework have occasioned lively and ingenious contemporary debate which clearly bears on citizenship education (see eg. Okin 1989; Nussbaum 1992; Delphy and Leonard 1992).

What is at issue in these and other writings is a revisionary look at who does the work in the public and private spheres and how that work is regarded and valued. That seems clearly different from a wholesale collapsing of the public/private distinction which it seems Giarelli may have in mind at the end of his paper when he claims that every distinction masks power and claims of privilege. But is that so? Fruit and vegetables? Deciduous and ever-green trees? And if it is often the case with social categories at least, does it follow that all such distinctions should be collapsed? What of those cases where the distinctions are designed to privilege the unfortunate and the weak in the distribution of some benefit—food in times of rationing, seats on trains? In the case in point, the public/private distinction, what would a collapsing of the distinction entail? Would it mean the end of any notion of a private sphere at all—the end of intimate friendships and private diaries as well as private fishing rights or private slaves? A private sphere may be necessary to support some of the most cherished goods in human life. It may also serve to hide some of the worst abuses. An investigation is needed which indicates how we can have the one without the other.

This leads to a puzzle. Giarelli draws attention to the difficulty of establishing an education for citizenship in a society which has divided starting-points and aims. What is unclear to me is how a collapsing, or even a revision, of the public/private distinction is going to help here. Any attempt to redraw the public/private distinction is likely to cut across the values groups within the society place on family life or local loyalties, thus producing more discord.

Obstacles, Evils, and Pessimism

Harris and Giarelli depict the obstacles standing in the way of citizenship education as large-scale and general—capitalism and a division of life into spheres to shore up privilege and power. This has several effects. It leads to a conception of citizenship education as at best a struggle for victory over great evils, and as, at worst, impossible. It leads to understandable pessimism about this area of education, since it seems the school can do little, except make its students aware of the situation in which they find themselves. Since this is a task requiring a sophisticated understanding of social and political arrangements it can only come in the later years of schooling. In the early years, for Harris as for Giarelli, there seems to be no possibility of citizenship education.

But perhaps the situation is not so stark and thus the outlook not so bleak. Perhaps closer inspection of the obstacles can give grounds for realistic hope. It can encourage a political attitude that aims "not at ending evils, but at preventing their victory" (Seneca, quoted in Nussbaum, 1990, p. 213). This is not to say that it is an attitude which is *tolerant* of evil but it is one which stresses the importance of fostering what good there may be. To that end it cannot rest with large abstractions: it has to try to see more of the detail of our political and social life to foster the good in the face of the pervasive obstacles to it.

Opportunities and Democratic Dispositions

Contemporary liberal democracies are, as Harris allows, different from totalitarian governments. There are, as Giarelli accepts, some possibilities for virtue in some areas of life. I want to argue that the institution of the school needs to exploit these opportunities to establish its own ethos, supportive of the basic dispositions underlying democratic citizenship.

Democrats certainly need considerable knowledge and understanding of their situation, as Harris rightly emphasises, but they also need to be certain sorts of people. We all develop an array of dispositions—to be kind or spiteful, lethargic or enterprising, tolerant or bigoted, tidy or untidy and so on—in all kinds of combinations and to all kinds of degrees. With education for public life in mind, therefore, teachers from the first school onwards need to look at the part the school might play in shaping the dispositions democratic citizens require (See Callan 1994, for a similar view which sees the cultivation of civic dispositions, like "emotional generosity," as a viable and wise alternative to a sentimental civic education or alienated scepticism).

A full treatment of this topic, covering the great range of relevant dispositions (self-respect, tolerance, honesty, hope, courage, patience) is impossible in this context but let me try to make some specific remarks about what, for me, would be one of the "multiple excellences" Giarelli refers to as necessary to a public. For the way forward, it seems to me, is via the concrete and specific.

Let me focus on trust, which I have discussed in detail elsewhere (White 1993). Trust, both personal trust in other people and social trust in institutions, is vital to human life (see Gambetta 1988). Indeed Baier (1985) has suggested that a moral theory (or family of theories) that made trust its central problem might be a way of bringing together the insights of those currently alternative theories which put obligation and caring at the centre of consideration.

In a pluralist multicultural society, in particular, the school has a major role to play in helping students to become trustworthy, to learn to trust others, and to have a proper trust and distrust of institutions.

Trust involves the belief that you can rely on someone (specifically, their beliefs, dispositions, motives, good will) or something (an institution or a piece of equipment) where there is a greater or lesser element of risk. One may or may not be conscious of the trust relationship and it will involve varying degrees of personal commitment.

Learning to trust another person typically has no definite beginning and grows slowly. By contrast, trust relationships can be destroyed by a single action and are not easily repaired, for those wronged are likely to be resentful, disappointed, and suspicious. Both Baier (1986, p. 238–9) and Luhmann

(1979, p. 74–5) have sensitive treatments of the supporting attitudes needed to maintain and repair trust relationships. Between them they stress, for instance, self-confidence, tact, delicacy of discrimination in appreciating *what* one is trusted with, good judgement as to *whom* to trust with *what* and a willingness to forgive and admit fault.

Schools can do much to help children to form, maintain and, when necessary, repair trust relationships. In many inner city schools in the U.K. some children come to the first school already disposed to be distrustful of other groups and so a sensitive building of trust has to start from the outset. Without such bonds of trust neither fullhearted tolerance nor any bonds of civic friendship will be possible.

No society, much less a pluralist democracy, could survive simply on the basis of personal trust between individuals. It requires a basis of social trust. By analogy with personal trust, citizens need to believe that they can rely on the institutions within which they are living to be informed by goodwill towards all members of society. It seems to be a necessary condition for social trust that citizens do not regard their society as structurally unfair (Dunn 1988, p. 77). Concretely they need to believe that the society's legal, economic, and political rules and procedures are fair, being fairly applied and that if the system breaks down there will be swift redress for any wrong.

At this point the wide-ranging critiques of contemporary societies Harris and Giarelli have offered might suggest that social trust in such societies would be sparse. Distrust amongst the majority of the population as well as amongst minority groups would be likely to be widespread. Is the role of the school here to attempt to paper over the cracks and encourage social trust in institutions operating, for instance, in class-biased, gender-biased and ethnically-biased ways?

The short answer is no. The school, along with other major institutions, will be encouraging a judicious distrust of the system. As Luhmann (1979) and others (eg. Shklar 1984, p. 185, 190) have noted, a political system which will promote the well-being of all its citizens must have institutions into which distrust as a protective device has been built. Democracies have a legal opposition, an independent judiciary, independent commissions of inquiry into matters of public concern, a free press and, if educators have done their work, a vigilant public who will judge the government by what it does rather than its rhetoric.

Schools will be introducing their students in this context to the possibility of fundamental and procedural distrust. Fundamental distrust is directed to the aims or ends of a system or institution, procedural distrust to means and procedures. Institutions can tolerate large amounts of procedural distrust if their basic aims are accepted but fundamental distrust is a powerful destructive force. A nuanced political education will introduce students to both of these notions via work on, for instance, reasons for trusting democratic systems in general and specific versions of democracy in particular. If the ends and/or procedures of these were changed, it might be asked, might they merit greater trust? In addition it will encourage students to examine the criteria citizens might employ to judge how far they should trust parties, politicians or specific institutions within a system—again focussing on ends and procedures.

But this is just to scratch the surface of the complex issues involved in encouraging personal and social trust in school in the contemporary situation. It is a topic which clearly merits further wide-ranging investigation as well as careful treatment in teacher education. Several teachers have pointed out to me that in a situation where social trust may be breaking down, the common school can offer a unique forum where young people can be encouraged rationally to take stock of whether distrust of some, most or all of our current institutions should be fundamental or whether repair and reform is the path more likely to produce more good than harm. The school occupies this privileged site because it is in a position to foster personal trust between students from different groups so that debate and dialogue take place between people who have come to see each other as trustworthy, even if trustworthy advocates of radically opposed viewpoints.

I have chosen to focus on trust because it seems to me that much of the analysis of Harris and Giarelli would support the view that in many of the older and newer aspiring democracies there is, for very good reasons, a crisis of trust in the system; I hope I have shown however, that even in this unpromising situation the school need not be powerless to educate for public life. It can promote personal trust between its members and it can encourage a thoughtful analysis of social trust and how it might be maintained, repaired or restored. It can focus here both on the wider society and also, importantly, because it can serve instructively as a responsive model, on the school itself.

In order to deal with the topic with the specificity and concreteness I have urged is required, I have had here to concentrate on just one aspect of the way in which an attention to relevant dispositions can contribute postively to citizenship education. Linked to trust are connected dispositions, like hope and self-respect, which the school can seek to encourage in all its pupils (see White 1986, 1991 for detailed treatments). On hope, for instance, if any worthwhile change is going to be possible, people have to feel realistic hope (rather than have, say, be in the grip of apathetic cynicism or wishful thinking) and they have to feel that they are able to bring about such change. (Beyond this, I can do no more than gesture towards a growing body of work, both by philosophers of education and philosophers with other interests, on the specific dispositions which teachers and schools might be encouraging: Baier (1986, 1990) on trust and honesty; Bok on honesty and secrecy, (1978, 1984); Callan (1993) on patience and courage; Nussbaum (1993) on mercy; Rorty (1986) on courage; and Taylor (1985) on pride, shame, and guilt.)

Teachers, Democratic Dispositions, and Public Life

On a view which assigns particular importance to the fostering of democratic dispositions teachers have a crucial role. Encouraging children to be patient, courageous, merciful, and honest "at the right times, with reference to the right objects, towards the right people, with the right motive, and in the right way," in Aristotelian fashion, requires careful, perceptive attention to individual children and their attitudes, actions and situation as well as to the school and the way its organisation and rules, intentionally or otherwise, shape behaviour.

It also requires of the teacher that she increasingly brings home to students as they get older, that on occasion life as a citizen in a democracy is not easy. The more successful the education in democratic dispositions and the more the student becomes a merciful, courageous person the more she will feel the tug of different values. In fact, the teacher will be encouraging this by typically saying in response to a remark which seems to be stressing one value in a situation to the exclusion of all other considerations: "But don't you think that it's more complicated than that?" A school student, for instance, may want to take a strong line on the importance of truth-telling at all times and in all circumstances. And although, in the U.K., recent curriculum guidelines on spiritual and moral education (1993) support this by referring to truth-telling as a moral absolute, any teacher worth her salt should draw attention to the possibility that other values which the student also holds dear may sometimes prove weightier than honesty. Where others' well-being is seriously at risk, for instance, reticence (pace Kant) may be wiser than the whole truth.

I have focussed in my part of this conversation on obstacles to education for democratic citizenship and the light they can throw on the aims of citizenship education. What I see as one of the greatest obstacles to education for citizenship is the teacher who is committed to a single value, or a fixed hierarchy of values, who is very clear about what is wrong with the world and how it can be put right and who sees it as her duty to encourage her students to see the world in this way. Democratic citizenship demands teachers who on occasion complicate matters for their students, who remind them that they are committed to a number of values; this fact makes the way forward more problematic than it might have seemed at first. The skill is to do this in such a way that students see that democratic citizens should not be paralysed in the face of competing commitments, but that they need to judge and act in the light of them. This may mean that they attempt to effect a compromise. It may mean sometimes that they, regretfully, are simply not able to satisfy a particular moral concern. The "regretfully" is very important here because it registers the commitment to the value which has had to be overridden. As Bernard Williams puts it, it "embodies a sensibility to moral costs" (Williams 1978, p. 65). Conveying to students a lively appreciation of the idea of *moral* costs should be a central aim in any education for democratic citizenship.

I am left with a puzzle. Would such a teacher be one of the "transformative intellectuals" or would she constitute an obstacle for them?

BIBLIOGRAPHY

Baier, A. (1985). "What Do Women Want in a Moral Theory?" *Nous.* 19(1): 53–63.

Baier, A. (1986). "Trust and Antitrust," *Ethics.* 96: 231–60.

Baier, A. (1990). "Why Honesty is a Hard Virtue" in O. Flanagan and A. R. Rorty eds. *Identity, Character and Morality: Essays in Moral Psychology.* London: MIT Press.

Callan, E. (1993). "Patience and Courage." *Philosophy,* 68(266).

Callan, E. (1994). "Beyond Sentimental Civic Education." *American Journal of Education,* February 102(2): 190–221.

Bok, S. (1978). *Lying: Moral Choice in Public and Private Life.* Hassocks: Harvester Press.

Bok, S. (1984). *Secrets: On the Ethics of Concealment and Revelation.* Oxford: Oxford University Press.

Delphy, C. and Leonard, D. (1992). *Familiar Exploitation: A New Analysis of Marriage in Contemporary Western Societies.* Cambridge, England: Polity Press.

Doyal, L. and Gough, I. (1991). *A Theory of Human Need.* London: Macmillan.

Doyal, L. and Gough, I. (1994). "Socially Regulated Capitalism Does Best." *The Guardian,* 21 February 1994.

Dunn, J. (1988). "Trust and Political Agency" in D. Gambetta ed., *Trust: Making and Breaking Co-operative Relations.* Oxford: Blackwell.

Gambetta, D. (1988). *Trust: Making and Breaking Co-operative Relations.* Oxford: Blackwell.

Luhmann, N. (1979). *Trust and Power.* Chichester: Wiley.

National Curriculum Council (1993). *Spiritual and Moral Development: A Discussion Paper.*

Nussbaum, M. (1990). *Love's Knowledge: Essays on Philosophy and Literature.* Oxford: Oxford University Press.

Nussbaum, (1992). "Justice for Women!" *The New York Review of Books,* 8 October 1992.

Nussbaum, M. (1993). "Equity and Mercy," *Philosophy and Public Affairs,* 22(2).

Okin, S. M. (1989). *Justice, Gender and the Family.* New York: Basic Books.

Rorty, A. R. (1986). "The Two Faces of Courage," *Philosophy,* 61(236).

Shklar, J. (1984). *Ordinary Vices.* London: Harvard University Press.

Taylor, G. (1985). *Pride, Shame and Guilt.* Oxford: Oxford University Press.

White, P. (1986). "Self-respect, Self-esteem and the School: A Democratic Perspective on Authority." *Teachers College Record,* 88(1) Fall.

White, P. (1991). "Hope Confidence and Democracy." *Journal of Philosophy of Education,* 25(2).

White, P. (1993). "Trust and Toleration: Some Issues for Education in a Multicultural Democratic Society" in J. Horton ed., *Liberalism, Multiculturalism and Toleration.* London: Macmillan.

Williams, B. (1978). "Politics and Moral Character" in S. Hampshire ed., *Public and Private Morality.* Cambridge: Cambridge University Press.

PART THREE

EXPANDING/
EXPLODING
THE "CANON"

CULTURE, ART, AND REPRESENTATION

19

Textuality and the Designs of Theory

Suzanne de Castell

> At one point, I thought there was a real need to examine certain things because there was so much hypocrisy. But it really broke down, especially after Watergate. Everybody now knows what's happening. They might not want to see it, but certainly things are very much in the open and you don't have to keep examining everything to see how it works. People know that the CIA has done a lot of chemical warfare testing, they know how things work now; they just don't give a damn. The society's totally disintegrating. We're wallowing in our own fucking nihilism. . . . We're wandering around and we don't know what to do, living in a sort of hell with AIDS and crack and everything else. It always is a guerrilla warfare, so you do have to look at context, the culture, what's happened, to see what makes sense at the moment.
>
> —Kathy Acker, *Hannibal Lecter*

This is a time at which, for many of us, the practice of philosophy of education* has become, increasingly, impossible. It is a practice which, (to appropriate Acker), for many of us, just seems not to "make sense at the moment . . ." This essay, then, tries to sketch out the way a *textual economy and politics of truth,* may be brought to bear, as critique, on the (dis)articulation between the traditional culture of philosophy of education, and the contemporary cultural context within which it is embedded. The term "culture" in

---

*Throughout this chapter, Philosophy of Education is not capitalized by choice of Suzanne de Castell.

this essay, I should point out at the outset of the discussion, is being used in the sense of a (forward looking) *cultivation,* rather than of a (backward-looking) *invocation,* of cultural heritage (Williams 1976).

Representing Philosophy of Education

A 'crisis of representation', in the double sense referring both to *who* is represented/representative, and to *how* representation is enacted—enunciates the failures of modernism: in particular the enlightenment project with its "interests in the universal" (Bourdieu 1990, p. 33)—the impacts of poststructuralist critiques of subjectivity, of individuality, of the very idea of 'human rights', of rationality, of the very idea of knowledge . . . All these present to the discipline, and to its practitioners, formidable intellectual challenges. More deeply disturbing yet than these are the material realities of the everyday: while career-theorists spout exhortatory platitudes about the "wonderful world of education",[1] the actual material and ideological conditions of public education (including the institutional status of philosophy of education itself), render public education, in any sense worth defending, implausible at best. Philosophers of education confront at this time, then, a set of theoretical and practical dilemmas of critical urgency and importance for the profession, which has, sadly, so far been disconcertingly silent on this range of questions—questions which are surely both terribly difficult and terribly serious. It is the argument of this essay that the time for "business as usual" is over.

Matters of Form/Politics of Theory

Theory at its best, Foucault has argued, is a struggle against power, against the weight of tradition, the force of ideology, the inertia of habit, the strength of conviction. At its worst, says, Foucault, "theory is an instrument to obstruct, prohibit and invalidate the practical knowledge of those who struggle against the arbitrary imposition of power . . ." (Foucault 1977, p. 209).

It is well worth asking—and indeed this essay will later ask—where philosophical theories of education fit along this continuum. But before we even begin to interrogate the subjects of our theory, we need I think to question, to challenge and finally to disrupt the hegemony of its representational forms, for it is within these very forms that invisibility, privilege, silence, censorship—all sanctioned "in the name of the profession" (see also Bourdieu 1990; also, less directly, Lacan 1966)—first take their shape as textual practices of exclusion, of oppression, of violence.

We have, I think, a good deal to learn from postmodernism, naming as it does a position from which cultural forms of representation have shifted from text to image, from linearity to simultaneity, from coherence to rupture, from argument to story, from the universal to the particular, from the "voice of authority" to populist heteroglossia. What would it mean for philosophers of education to take this shift seriously? How would our professional theories and practices need to be transformed in order to explode fixed conceptions both about subject matters/disciplinary boundaries, and about the very subjects of our theorizing? How, in short, can we be "true" to our subject/s?

It is from the standpoint of this question that I want to engage with questions about representation, asking first about the cultures by whom and for whom such representations are accomplished, and asking, secondly, about the arts by means of which such representations have been and might yet be undertaken. This second question about the manufacture of representation requires that we consider what I'm calling the *'designs'* of theory—and to consider 'design' in two distinguishable but related senses. Interrogating the 'designs of theory' in the first sense takes up the question of how technologies of representation shape and constrain what can be represented; in the second sense it takes up the question of 'design' conceived as artifice, distortion, misrepresentation. In both senses, it should be noted, 'design' effects a reconfiguration. The central argument of this essay is that 'design', so understood, effects a reconfiguration of the domain—the goals and practices—of philosophy of education.

Representing the Subject . . . 'Others' in 'Our' Discourse

> The fact is . . . that *writing* can no longer designate an operation of recording, notation, representation, "depiction" (as the Classics would say); rather, it designates exactly what linguists, referring to Oxford philosophy, call a performative, a rare verbal form (exclusively given in the first person and in the present tense), in which the enunciation has no other content (contains no other proposition) than the act by which it is uttered . . . (Barthes 1977, p. 146–7).

Although it's surely more important to examine current professional discourses than those of the past, it's nevertheless worth taking some time to recall that we who have been initiated into this discipline by means of what are today of course decidedly dated writings have assimilated, as Wittgenstein would say, not only concepts, but concepts inseparably associated with judgments. The discourses by means of which we, as a "professional culture", a "community of practice", (Lave and Wenger, 1991) have internalized our discipline, by means of which we have, that is to say, ourselves become *participants* in these specific socio-cultural practices of philosophy of education, constitute "philosophy" for us as a form of life within which are embedded a set of assumptions, a set of 'certainties' (Illich, 1988). These 'certainties' define philosophy of education itself in terms of concepts and practices which are both narrowly gendered and extensively exclusionary. It is important to remember that this is what we have learned with our very first words as speakers in this discourse, this language in which we have all been such willing and able pupils. . . .

That professional socialization into discourses of exclusion begins, conceptually if not temporally, with the practice of defining 'education' by reference to the concept of 'the educated man', such that, as Hirst and Peters point out in their 1970 classic, *The Logic of Education,* (the textbook in the field for some years not only in Britain, but as well in North American introductory courses):

> Nowadays . . . the concept of an educated man has very much taken root. It is natural, therefore, for those working in educational institutions to conceive of what they are doing as being connected with the development of such a person. . . . In brief, because of the development of the concept of an 'educated man', the concept of 'education' has become tightened up because of its natural association with the development of such a person (Hirst and Peters 1970, p. 24–5).

What sort of a 'person' is this, then? Explain Hirst and Peters, besides the 'everyday' concept of a person, there is what they call a ". . . richer sense as when we demand 'respect' for persons. This use of 'person' is connected conceptually with having what might be called an assertive point of view, with evaluation, decision and choice, and with being, to a certain extent, an individual who determines his own destiny by his choices. . . ." (p. 53) ". . . by speaking of individuals as persons", they go on, "we draw attention to a group of characteristics that animals do not share with human beings, which are connected with having an assertive point of view" (p. 91). Assertiveness, the ability to evaluate, to decide and choose, to determine one's own destiny. . . . Who is the subject of these sentences? Who is being spoken of here?

As they expound further upon the "excellences which are intimately connected with being a person," Peters and Hirst rightly, I think, observe that "there are no general 'powers of the mind' that can be exercised in a vacuum. They are rather adverbial to activities and modes of experience . . ." (p. 54). But whose activities and modes of experience are the basis for defining "powers of the mind"? Even the most cursory analysis of discourse in the principle generative (or what are always termed the 'seminal') texts in philosophy of education reveals without much doubt that the subject of this discourse is male- and not just male, but male and of a particular race, class, and culture.

To protest that these texts' persistent deployment of 'he' by no means justifies such an accusation, because 'he' is generic in English is of course from a linguistic standpoint simply false. To argue the more specific and at least potentially adequate case that, *within those texts,* 'he' was used (according to the fashion of those times) *as if it were generic* is equally false. Gender is pronominally coded in these texts, but it is coded in such a way as to privi-lege a particular identity position (which, remember, is not only sexed, but raced, and classed as well), and to subordinate others. A re-read of *Philosophy of Education,* for example, the -seminal- Oxford University Press collection edited by Peters, reveals a grand total of three non-masculine pronouns: the first referred to a typist (p. 59), the second to a prostitute (p. 67), and the third to "the housewife". As for the rest of the text, 'man' was utilized not only in the definition and justification of education, but in the definition of rationality, human excellence, even personhood.

There was in this collection one reference to non-dominant cultural identi-ties—a dismissive remark by David Hamlyn about the need to determine with respect to generalizations about learning "whether what is true of John and Mary is also true of Fritz, Ali, and Kwame . . ." (212–3) And there were numerous, if veiled, references to class, primarily in disdainful comments about "bingo"—a pastime enormously popular in lower working class com-munities, and an extensive discussion of the distinction between 'work' (into which 'education' properly 'fit') and "labour" (within which it did not.) John Austin, in *How To Do Things With Words,* drew attention to the perfomative function of utterances: "The issuing of the utterance", he wrote "is the per-forming of the action" (Austin 1962, p. 6). My argument here is concerned with the performative dimension of discourse in philosophy of education, and how these discourses function, as Barthes (1977) reminds us, *performa-tively* as accomplishments of exclusion, enacting rhetorically a set of integrated acts of dominance and subordination.

Often the (ostensible) propositional content of such discourses may be directly contradicted by their performative effects. The Greek conception of a liberal education, for instance, on Hirst's classic account of it, was "liberal" first "because it was the education of free men rather than slaves." (Hirst 1973, p. 89) (*But who among us as philosophy students did not know that Aristotle lumped together the capacities of slaves with the capacities of women?*) And second, says Hirst, the Greeks "saw it as freeing the mind to function according to its true nature, freeing reason from error and illusion, and free-ing man's conduct from wrong." Now if a liberal education aims at the mind functioning according to its true nature, and mind is the essential distin-guishing characteristic of man, must it not follow in one fashion or another that it is 'man', first and foremost that liberal education is about? But no, we've been told, its *rationality* which is the focus. ". . . the mind, in the right use of reason, comes to know the essential nature of things [including, pre-sumably, that the essential nature of man is rationality] and can apprehend what is ultimately real and immutable (p. 101).

Such is the God's eye view, the "view from everywhere and nowhere" (Haraway 1991) which informs philosophical discourses. But taking serious-ly the observation of Peters and Hirst that powers of the mind do not exist in abstraction, but are "adverbial" to specific experiences, specific practices and forms of life, we can't really accept such a characterization. This view is indeed from somewhere, even if it does not know or want to know that it is. And where is it from? Consider this 'generic' discussion of how 'a man's rationality' works, and within what practices and forms of life. The first, from Peters' discussion of activities engaged in "for their own sake" in his essay "The Justification of Education": "A man [and do just try to read this as generic] who wants to give equal expression to his passion for golf, gardening and girls is going to have problems, unless he works out his priorities and imposes some sort of schedule on the use of his time" (249). And later, my own personal favourite, from the same essay discussing a concluding problem, the problem of why, even though a man can only become educated if he pursues worthwhile activities, should he, once having become educated, persist in such activities. "Why," Peters asks, "should not an educated man settle for an undemanding job which allows him plenty of time for playing golf which is the one activity he really enjoys apart from eating, sunbathing, and occasionally making love to his wife." And Peters goes on to explain of this generic subject of philosophy of education that "He is not philistine; neither is he particularly instrumental in his outlook. He just loves his game of golf more than any of the more intellectually taxing types of pursuits. Golf is to him what he presumes science is to the other fellow" (p. 265).

Now it would be nice to imagine that that was then, and this is now, and we don't do it like that anymore. Sadly, this is far from the truth, notwithstanding the popularity of what's mistakenly construed as "gender-inclusive" language and the addition of "women's ways"—(but only *some* women's ways, of course!). As Judith Butler (1990) reminds us, the strategy here is to construct the kind of subject one is prepared to admit into discourse, and only then to grant that subject "equal rights." But this is in no way either to acknowledge or to accept difference.

One example of this is the way contemporary philosophy of education, considered in terms of its discourses and its practices, attempts to accommodate "difference" in relation to gender. There are three ways: it 'adds women' as a sex, but without that addition making a difference to the discourse—the modernist solution. It constructs women (as caring and connected)—the liberal constructivist solution. Or it appropriates and deploys 'feminist critique' as a way of understanding *itself* better—the "learning-more-about-the-self-by-learning-about-the-other" solution offered by critical theoretic conceptions of gender. Note that all of these solutions construe 'gender' in terms of 'women' and preserve the discourse with merely surface-structural modifications and refinements. And so-called postmodernist attempts to deal with difference—I think here particularly of Henry Giroux and company, and the essay on "dialogue across differences" by Burbules and Rice (1991), construct postmodernism as a continuation (with criticisms appended) of modernism, and persist in emphasizing 'similarities' as a means of de-emphasizing difference. But no amount of sophistical sleight of hand with the concept of the same—which is in any case as we well know a systematically ambiguous concept—will make the problem disappear. It's not so easy as that, not any more.

But consider what *might* be the consequences for philosophy of education were gender, (to continue with this particular example of 'difference'), to be taken explicitly and seriously into account. What this could NOT mean, it should by now be clear, is any kind of "add women and stir" approach, from which is formulated a 'new' conception of education based upon the 'educated woman' instead of upon the "educated man". Such a response seems scarcely to constitute an advance, either conceptually or methodologically. Conceptually, such a response is doomed to be both essentialist and exclusionary: essentialist, insofar as it reduces 'gender' to 'sex', and 'women' to a small sub-set of people—white, heterosexual, above working-class—biologically designated as 'female', and exclusionary because of all the people this reductiveness would of necessity leave out of account. Methodologically, such a strategy leaves intact the inherited apparatus of inquiry which is itself just as problematic, as its conceptual superstructure—and for the same reasons.

Difference/Distance

> . . . it seems to us that it is time to recognize that, in a deep sense, Blacks in L.A. live in a different world from whites, in something like a different nation. They and the police are like foreigners to each other. And understanding this distance means comprehending relations, not according to norms of universal equality and equal treatment, but as the rules of one community over another. (Crenshaw and Peller 1993, p. 69)

What difference might be made to philosophy of education by taking "difference" (explicitly) into (its) account(s)? This is the question we must begin to take seriously, and from the first moment of its asking, the tremors begin and the edifice starts to crumble.

We scarcely know, from this position, what questions to ask, and this uncertainty I think is [certainly!] all to the good. Having finally to confront head-on the epiphenomenal character of theoretical questions, and to reconceptualize questions as derivative from actual material conditions and relations among actual human communities renders us unable to continue in the old ways, to ask, for instance, ask what 'we' mean, or even what 'is' meant by 'education', since we would have to recognize from the outset the diversity of things which would be meant. With this understanding comes the realization that our foundational questions are now dissolving into dust, that we do not even know (or perhaps do not care to know) any longer who "we" are, except that we are no longer who "we" were. Instead of the exhortation to discover whether our generalizations about learning cover not only John and Mary but also Fritz and Ali and Kwame, presuming as that question does that everyone's experience is in principle accessible to the investigator, one preliminary question might be, "How can valid abstract generalizations be produced when one not only does not know about others' experience, but indeed **cannot** know what such experience is like." (Ellsworth 1990). The radical theoretical uncertainty entailed by accepting the limits imposed upon us by a recognition of difference plays an ironic counterpoint to the painful clarity of the material conditions in terms of which relations of ruling are established and maintained by one community over another. There are substantial ethical/epistemological implications of such recognition. For instance it would then make far more sense, instead of asking what knowledge is needed in order to "free a man's conduct from wrong" (Hirst 1973, p. 89), to ask, instead, how we can go on living in the full knowledge of the inevitability of our own complicity in evil, and what education might be able to do to address the impossibility of innocence, the tragic inescapability of unethical conduct, given how the very artifacts and practices we value most have been produced and continue—even in this very moment in our own practice—to be produced in and through the oppression and exploitation of others. In the case of our professional practice as philosophers of education, consider, with respect to the material actualities of our annual conferences, the women of colour who come early each morning to clean for us, who work in the background away from the illuminated center of our discourses to feed and water us, to tend to our grosser bodily functions—and consider all the other people whom we make invisible but upon whose backs we very directly and very hypocritically "work". Or the teachers and students and un-named Others who function as the always-silent referents of our discussions, the always-grateful beneficiaries of our—always only textual—conclusions? What would it be, what would it make of our discipline if we were honest enough and courageous enough to bring these 'others' into our consciousness, into our practice? And lastly, recalling as I wrote this paper what it was like for me to read these texts for so many years, and later to write them, trying, struggling, and failing, to make meaning out of what was I now see not so much as intellectually difficult to grasp, but simply so relentlessly and unutterably *boring* (Frigga Haug, 1992) so terribly alienating, so diminishing for me as a human subject rendered invisible and indeed inhuman by these discourses, what would it be to construct discourses which did not alienate and exclude readers whose subject-positioning was other than central, other than dominant? What would it be to cultivate philosophy as a field of inquiry which did *not* require that those not from positions of dominance must go back to these old relics, these alienating texts, these conceptual dinosaurs, and require that they be studied and learned as a condition of entering into that professional culture?[2] What would it mean to learn to read and write philosophy of education differently? Could we write at all? Would there remain any such thing as philosophy of education?

Writing and Representation: Questions of Textuality

> The true historical significance of writing is that it has increased our capacity to create totalistic illusions with which to have power over things or over others as if they were things. The whole ideology of representational signification is an ideology of power. To break its spell we would have to attack writing, totalistic representation and authorial authority . . . (Taylor 1988, p. 131).

Central to this essay's discussion of design in terms of representation is the fact that philosophy of education is principally a *textual* practice (de Castell 1989), conducted within a particular kind of professional/expert community. This textual community forms a peculiar kind of cultural context, a very particular "community of practice" (Lave and Wenger, 1991).

Consider first, then, text as a kind of technology. Text is, after all, an artifact, and it is the material means by which *philosophical* thought is produced, or so runs a now well-rehearsed argument advanced by classicist Eric Havelock. (1963; 1986) In his *Preface to Plato* (1963), Havelock considers in depth and detail the transformations of mind from Homeric (oral, poetic) to Platonic (literate, prosaic) thought. He argues that philosophical work, "philosophy" itself, can be seen as a by-product of writing, an epiphenomenon of literacy. Havelock offers us a detailed working out of the ways in which the use of writing for speculative (as opposed to documentary) purposes altered the character of speculation itself, as orally told, poetically-preserved myths and stories constitutive of Greek culture gave way to textually-preserved theoretical propositions generative of Greek history, philosophy, and then science. To illustrate the epistemological impacts of the technology of writing, Havelock focuses on the first such use about which much is known—the philosophical writings of Plato. Havelock describes Plato as a writer who sought to organize "once and for all a prose of ideas; who would expound once and for all in writing what the syntax of this prose should be, and who could explore the rules of logic which should govern it" (p. 305). Writing, because it enabled the separation of the utterance from the speaker and from the particular circumstances of that speaking, made it possible—and for the first time, so the argument goes—to constitute knowledge as an object, and to classify, subdivide and systematize it into distinctive disciplinary domains.

Havelock's contention is that it was the technology of writing which made these intellectual developments not only possible, but indeed unavoidable, as soon as writing began to be used as a tool for thinking with. It seems important to recall, however, that the earliest uses of writing, which appear to have been in Sumeria, circa 3500 BC, were for account-keeping: imaginative and speculative uses appear much later (Goody 1986).

Havelock characterizes the transformation of mind from 'Homeric' to 'Platonic' in terms of a movement from the world of actual particulars, of which directly referential 'accounts' can be rendered, to the abstract realm of general ideas, populated by 'universal' forms. In the writings of Plato, philosophy's "Father", we are urged to discard the accidents and incidentals of time, place, and circumstance and to focus instead on what is absolute, enduring, universal, and necessary. For this purpose, explains Havelock, a thing "must somehow be isolated from its setting in the great story, set itself by itself, and identified *per se*." And so, says Havelock, the Platonic pages are filled with the demand that we concentrate not on the things of the city, but on the city itself, not on a just or unjust act, but on justice, by itself, not on noble actions, but on nobility *per se* (Havelock 1963, p. 217).

David Olson, whose concern is with contemporary rather than classical investigations of the cognitive consequences of literacy, takes Havelock's work as his point of departure. "The Greek alphabet," he writes, "with its ability to record exactly what is said, provided a tool for the formulation and criticism of explicit meanings" (Olson, p. 180, in Kintgen et al., 1988). Writing systems make possible the development of systems of classification, intellectual 'genres' differently capable with respect to representational effect.

The material technology of writing, Olson then suggests, was in these ways critical to the development of objective knowledge. It

> permitted the abstraction of logical procedures that could serve as the rules for thinking . . . [thus] written prose led to the development of abstract categories, like the genus/species taxonomies so important not only to Greek science, but also to the formation and division of various subject-matter areas. Much of Greek thought was concerned with satisfactorily explaining the meanings of terms—an essentially literate enterprise (Olson 1988, p. 181).

In speaking of what he called "our intellectual debt to our scripts," Olson goes on to argue that "We introspect on language and mind in terms of the categories prescribed by our writing systems."

What did this novel form of literate intellectual labour amount to? Here's Olson again:

> The Greeks, thinking they had discovered a method for determining objective truth, were in fact doing little more than detecting properties implicit in their native tongue. Their rules for mind were not rules for thinking, but rather rules for using language consistently; the abstract properties of their category system were not true or unbiased descriptions of reality, but rather, invariance in the structure of their language . . . (p. 181).

As Havelock had put the point earlier on, this was an error of misreading the properties of their grammatical system for the "deep structures" of objective external reality—recall here Wittgenstein's characterization of pseudo-problems as "language gone on a holiday . . ."

Significant challenges have been made to the implicit technological determinism in Havelock's and Olson's accounts of the dependence of particular—and especially "philosophical"—forms of thought on writing. And certainly as literacy studies have proceeded, what's been termed the "literacy hypothesis", the "general theory" of literacy that claims for literacy transformative effects upon individual and cultural capacities, has had to give way to a series of particular theories which recognize that what literacy makes possible is far more than it makes necessary, and that it is particular social conditions, particular "communities of practice" *in their specific relations to* particular representational technologies, which have regulated the concrete articulations and uses of particular forms of thought.

The Bears in Novaya Zemlya . . .

"In the far north, where there is snow, all bears are white. Novaya Zemlya is in the far north, and there is always snow there. What colour are the bears there?"

"There are different sorts of bears"

[the syllogism is repeated]

"I don't know. I've seen a black bear; I've never seen any others . . . Each locality has its own animals: if it's white, they will be white; if it's yellow, they will be yellow."

"But what kind of bears are there in Novaya Zemlya?"

"We always speak only of what we see; we don't talk about what we haven't seen . . . What I know, I say, and nothing beyond that!"

And the Soviet psychologist Alexander Luria goes on to ask on the basis of many similar exchanges with illiterate Russian peasants, "What exactly is the structure of the derivational and inferential processes among people whose life rests upon concrete practical activity?" (Luria 1979, p. 102). Whereas for a long time, these interviews have been taken as illustrations of the kinds of cognitive deficiencies remediable by the acquisition of literacy, more recent scholarship has begun to investigate the extent to which such forms of thought are not necessary evolutionary accomplishments, "higher" forms along a universally applicable developmental scheme, but contingently developed and quite particular forms of thinking as dysfunctional and poorly suited to some circumstances as they are facilitative in others—forms of though which are, as Peters might have said "adverbial" to particular activities.[3] This is I think the gist of the notion of "situated cognition", which varies according to its location within particular "communities of practice".

Such insights have formed the basis of the important observation by literacy researchers Scribner and Cole that much of what we have taken to be features of the human mind turn out to be by-products of particular, contingent practices of formal schooling. Comments Luria, "It is of considerable interest that this shift and the capacity to perform 'theoretical' operations of formal and discursive thinking appear after relatively short-term school instruction" (1979, p. 133). In other words, we have tended to mistake the cultural specificities of institutional schooling for formal and invariant features of thought. The particular kind of language and thought encouraged and developed by the practices of formal schooling is abstract, theoretical, decontextualized, paradigmatically syllogistic reasoning. Practical reasoning, that is, thought and language specific to and embedded within students' particular concrete circumstances in communities outside the mainstream, accordingly, are consequently disvalued, discouraged, even pathologized. Hence teachers will engage children in theoretical discourses on, for instance, whether *it is right* to discriminate against others "simply because of the colour of their skin," but classroom discussion will not extend to explicitly asking them why *they themselves are* cruel to one particular child in their class, or why they physically violate another . . . Which form of thought, then, is "higher", which is more "developed"? In the face of actually occurring everyday instances of discrimination, it would be at least plausible to argue that it is the latter, and not the former.

As philosophers of education, we need to ask what practices our own distinctive disciplinary forms of thought are "adverbial" to.

Technologies of representation as systems of cultural practice

Ursula Franklin (1992) profoundly challenges technological determinism, by conceptualizing technology, not as artifact separable from its contextual conditions, but construing technology, instead, as a situated practice, as a "system of practices". She writes "Technology is not the sum of the artifacts, of the wheels and gears, of the rails and electronic transmitters. Technology is a **system.** It entails far more than its individual material components. Technology involves organization, procedures, symbols, new words, equations, and most of all, a mindset." For Franklin, technology has to do with "the organization of work and of people. . . . [it] includes ideas and practices; it includes myths and various models of reality, . . . [it] changes the social and individual relationships between us. It has forced us to examine and redefine our notions of power and of accountability" (Franklin 1992, p. 12).

Ever since Plato's Socrates proclaimed that "It's not who said it, but what was said, that matters," the distinctively literate accomplishment of separating the speaker from the speech and the circumstances of speaking is a rupture that has been semantically preserved in philosophical discourse by means of what Eric Havelock called an "anthropological grammar" (Havelock, p. 224 in de Castell et al., 1988). It is preserved in the taken-for-granted parallel distinction Franklin here emphatically *rejects*, between tools and practices, between "technology" and "technique", between artifacts and the situated and embodied competences involved in their operation and use.

Franklin's perspective invites us to explore the ways all of these elements are connected, the ways activities are dependent upon and defined by particular technologies (just as teaching used to be inseparable from the chalkboard, psychoanalysis from the couch, or the way education is nowadays inseparable from books). This permits us to explore the way identities and communities are defined in relation to particular, technologically-mediated activities. Franklin points out that

> Looking at technology as practice . . . links technology directly to culture, because culture, after all, is a set of socially accepted practices and values. Well laid down and agreed upon practices also define practitioners as groups of people who have something in common because of the way they are doing things, out of this notion of unifying practice springs the historical definition of "us" and "them". I think it is important to realize that the experience of common practice is one of the ways in which people define themselves as groups and set themselves apart from others. "Around here, this is how we do things" a group will say, and this is their way of self-identification, because "others" may do the same thing differently (p. 15).

It becomes possible to see, in these terms, how within the professional community of philosophy of education, identity, technology, culture, and practice are intertwined.

This is the standpoint from which it has seemed to me terribly important to ask how it is that *philosophical* practice is defined for us, in terms of how such definition is accomplished. (Another way of approaching this question is to ask what it is discursively which makes a particular text or argument "philosophical"?) As Franklin points out:

> It becomes so easy and seemingly objective to define the content by the way something is being done or prescribed to be done. Teaching, for instance, is now a clearly circumscribed activity that takes place in a particular location and is conducted by particularly trained or ordained practitioners, and whatever somebody may teach you in working together with you, it isn't the kind of learning for which you ever get a credit. (p. 17)

It's worth wondering what is it we miss out on when we define philosophy of education as we have traditionally done, and it becomes particularly interesting to investigate what it might mean for philosophy of education if our discourses and practices were truly to be redefined in relation to the contemporary material and social conditions within which and in relation to which they are currently being carried out.

In an extensive review of literature on "text and textuality", W.F. Hanks concludes that the fundamental contribution of textual analysis to contemporary scholarship is the challenging of disciplinary discursive formation. "Textual studies," he points out, "have shown that the analytic enterprise is itself a species of textual practice, and therefore must be evaluated accordingly" (Hanks 1989, p. 119). No small part of this evaluation for philosophers of education must surely be the consideration that, in a post-modern, post-literate world in which although far more intellectual work is produced and published than ever before, far more people are 'educated' than ever before, fewer people actually read in any extended sense, far fewer write much, and far fewer yet can find significance, can find their experiences and their voices represented in the textual forms upon which our profession places almost exclusive reliance. What, then, are our goals? For whom do we work?

Of no less importance, surely, is that although the primary medium of philosophical theorizing is the written word, pedagogical practice is still very much an affair of speech (Barthes 1977, p. 190–215). And speech (after Austin, Searle, and Habermas) is interaction, is social practice. To whom, then, do we speak?

The central question for philosophy of education, I have tried to suggest, has to do with the forms, the traditional textual forms in which we represent ourselves, about who and what thereby become subjects of philosophy of education, and about who and what is obscured, occluded, rendered silent and invisible by means of these traditional forms of representation.

And I have tried to show how these questions about representation can be seen to be, at one and the same time, questions about professional identity and cultural stability. How can our professional culture stay the same, even as the world is changing everywhere else? Could it not be, in substantial measure, because in our dialogues and conferences and literary exchanges and lectures to the uninitiated, there is remarkably little difference between our contemporary practices and those of philosophers long dead. And is it really this we propose to continue doing into the future?

Re-Designing Discourse: Back to the Future?

By speaking of the 'designs' of theory, I have intended a double reference, a reference on the one hand to ways in which the traditional textual forms and situated practices within which the work of philosophy of education is done, operate to shape, constrain, bias, limit, and direct the human subjects and the subject matters which philosophy of education acknowledges and finds significant. At the same time, I've wanted to preserve and to explicitly acknowledge a sense of 'design' as artifice, fraudulence, deception, as evoking the "forging" of meaning and significance. To that end, I've tried to set out a conception of philosophical analysis as a peculiar kind of materially-conditioned practice, one whose continuation depends upon misrecognizing itself as an autonomous intellectual activity, and I've tried to consider some ways in which philosophy of education is itself a by-product, and epiphenomenon, of the technology of writing. ("Queen of the sciences" indeed!—in drag . . .) This is a perspective from which central philosophical problems must now be admitted to have been *"foci imaginarii"* (Rorty 1979)—a deflated and desiccated corpus of elaborate pseudo-problems, intellectual "simulacra" (Baudrillard 1988) whose primary purpose is to conceal the fact that there is, materially, nothing that this discourse is actually about. This, however, is the charitable view . . .

There is a more pointedly intentionalist thesis to be had here. As Cornell West reminds us, there are certain things we can no longer be permitted NOT to know, and a central one of these, for philosophers of education, is the impact of our own traditional rhetorical practices, our own inherited technologies of representation. In order to move forwards from here, we would I think do well to go back, if only for the briefest instant—back to the intents of philosophical inquiry, seen first and foremost as a "love of wisdom", and to recall that what Socrates did in his own practice was not to continue the traditions of the past, but to disrupt them; not to require his students to internalize the works of the old authorities—in his day, the poets—but to break with them, to repudiate their authority. Socrates exhorted his students to seek wisdom with all their hearts and minds, and to find it elsewhere than the places they had been told it must reside. This is what, at its best, a postmodern critique *which is not just a rehabilitated modernism* can do for philosophy of education today—to force the abandonment of what we "cannot not know" to be not merely inadequate but indeed corrupt, and to relegate the preservation of the antiquated texts and practices in which such inadequacies and corruptions reside to the historians, just as the history of biology, of mathematics, of every other discipline in which we have found growth and development to be possible, is the business, not of biologists and mathematicians, but historians. These are the long dead and dusty relics of a bygone era, and our business, as philosophers of education seriously concerned with the actually appalling conditions of peoples' lives in the present, lies elsewhere.

NOTES

1. These memorable words were enunciated by a currently eminent senior "educationalist" during his interview for the position of Dean in the faculty where I am, *mirabile dictu,* even now employed.

2. Nussbaum 1990, for instance, has provided extensive and important discussions of the intellectual/ethical constraints of traditional philosophical discourse. However, her analyses remain persistently tied to canonical texts, and this produces a curiously myopic species of insight, certainly problematic from the standpoint of this essay.

3. See also Wertsch, 1991, pp. 93ff.

BIBLIOGRAPHY

Acker, Kathy (1991). *Hannibal Lecter, My Father*. New York: Semiotext(e).

Aronowitz, Stanley and Henry Giroux (1991). *Postmodern Education*. Minneapolis: Minnesota University Press.

Austin, John (1962). *How to do Things With Words*. Cambridge, Mass.: Harvard University Press.

Barthes, Roland (1977). *Image/Music/Text*. Translated by Stephen Heath. New York: Hill and Wang.

Baudrillard, Jean (1988). *Selected Writings*. Translated and edited by M. Poster. Cambridge: Polity Press.

Bourdieu, Pierre (1990). *In Other Words: Essays Towards a Reflexive Sociology*. Translated by Matthew Adamson. Stanford: Stanford University Press.

Burbules, Nick and Suzanne Rice (1991). "Dialogue Across Differences: Continuing the Conversation" *Harvard Educational Review*, 61: 400–23.

Butler, Judith (1990). *Gender Trouble: Feminism and the Subversion of Identity*. New York: Routledge, Chapman and Hall.

Crenshaw, Kimberle and Gary Peller (1993). "Reel Time/Real Justice" in R. Gooding-Williams, ed., *Reading Rodney King*.

de Castell, Suzanne (1989). "On Writing of Theory and Practice." *Journal of Philosophy of Education*. 23: 39–50.

Ellsworth, Elizabeth (1990). "The Question Remains: How Will You Hold to the Limits of Your Own Knowledge?" *Harvard Educational Review*, 60: 397–405.

Foucault, Michel (1977). *Language, Counter-Memory, Practice*. Translated by D.F. Bouchard and S. Simon. Oxford: Basil Blackwell.

Franklin, Ursula (1992). *The Real World of Technology*. Concord: Anansi Press.

Giroux, Henry (1988). "Border Pedagogy in the Age of Postmodernism." *Journal of Education*, 170(3): 162–81.

Gooding-Williams, Robert, ed. (1993). *Reading Rodney King: Reading Urban Uprising*. New York and London: Routledge.

Goody, Jack (1986). *The Logic of Writing and the Organization of Society*. Cambridge: Cambridge University Press.

Hamlyn, David (1973). "The Logical and Psychological Aspects of Learning" in R.S. Peters, ed., *The Philosophy of Education*. Oxford: Oxford University Press.

Hanks, W.F. (1989). "Text and Textuality." *Annual Review of Anthropology,* 18: 95–127.

Haraway, Donna (1991). "Situated Knowledges . . ." in *Simians, Cyborgs and Women.* New York: Routledge.

Havelock, Eric (1963). *Preface to Plato.* Cambridge, Mass.: Harvard University Press.

————. (1986). *The Muse Learns to Write.* Binghamton: Vail Ballou Press.

————. (1988). "Instruction of Preliterate Cultures," in Suzanne de Castell et al., *Language, Authority and Criticism.* London, New York, and Philadelphia: Falmer Press.

Haug, Frigga (1992). "The Hoechst Chemical Company and Boredom with the Economy" in *Beyond Female Masochism: Memory-Work and Politics.* Translated by Rodney Livingstone. London, New York: Verso.

Hirst, Paul and R.S. Peters (1970). *The Logic of Education.* London: Routledge and Kegan Paul.

————. (1973). "Liberal Education and the Nature of Knowledge" in R.S. Peters, ed. *The Philosophy of Education.*

Illich, Ivan and Barry Sanders (1988). *A.B.C.* New York: Vintage.

Lacan, Jacques (1966). *Ecrits,* Paris: Le Seuil.

Lave, Jean and Eugene Wenger (1991). *Situated Cognition.* Cambridge: Cambridge University Press.

Luria, A.R. (1979). *Making of Mind.* Cambridge, Mass.: Harvard University Press.

Nussbaum, Martha (1990). *Love's Knowledge.* New York: Oxford University Press.

Rorty, Richard. *Philosophy and the Mirror of Nature.* Princeton, NJ: Princeton University Press.

Williams, Raymond (1976). *Keywords.* London: Fontana Paperbacks.

Wertsch, James (1991). *Voices of the Mind.* Cambridge, Mass.: Harvard University Press.

West, Cornell (1987). "Postmodernism and Black America" *Zeta Magazine* 1(6): 27–29.

20

Beyond the Formal and the Psychological: The Arts and Social Possibility

Landon E. Beyer

Recent theoretical and practical work in education and the arts promises to significantly alter the ways aesthetic experience and its role in classroom life are understood. Critiques of traditional understandings of the aesthetic suggest possibilities for the transformation of aesthetic education in the schools, and more generally for new meanings from which altered social practices may spring.

Art of some kind, perceived along certain lines, and valued in particular ways, has probably been a central part of every civilization and culture. This points to the fact that the term "art" has itself frequently been used in an honorific sense—as naming something intrinsically valuable, to be admired by the members of that culture. At the same time, of course, there have existed vastly different objects and experiences, and equally multitudinous ways of perceiving and understanding them, that have been labeled as art and seen as valuable for the aesthetic experiences which they generate. Indeed, this open textured quality of the arts and aesthetic theory has been pointed to as an important defining feature of these domains (Weitz 1956).

Still, throughout the history of art appreciation and aesthetic theory, schools of thought have developed that have been more or less dominant as they guided people's interactions with works of art: the search for the "essence" of the art object in Platonic thought, the fascination with Beauty as the central component of works of art, a commitment to Significant Form as the defining feature of the arts, and a concentration on the psychologically distanced sort of perception and understanding that contributes to a "presentational aesthetic" (Beyer 1979a). While no one approach to the arts or aesthetic theory has been able to maintain its dominance over the long haul, there have been significant periods of time within particular societies in which people's understanding of the value and place of art has been shaped by such traditions.

The first part of this essay explores some of the more mainstream ways in which aesthetic experience has been understood, while the final portion addresses the possibilities of constructing an aesthetic theory in accord with which a critical consciousness can be promoted that will help propel social change. I am especially concerned with the possibility that the arts may further ways of life and meanings that are not yet widely practiced, as they contribute to our moral and political undertakings.

Behind the ideas and issues discussed in this essay is an essentially moral commitment to changing the current realities of schooling. The tendencies of schools to emphasize intellectual apathy, linear thinking, respect for authority, isolated and individualizing work, ideologically impregnated views of what it means to be "human," and interpretations and meanings of events that are often partial and ideologically useful in maintaining forms of cultural hegemony, for example, have been well documented (Jackson 1968, Vallance 1977, Apple 1979, Sirotnik 1983, Cuban 1992). This is not to suggest that schools uniformly do this, or that teachers have consciously sought to provoke such outcomes, or even that conscious attempts to do these things are always successful. The work of many dedicated, hard working teachers has provided evidence of the possibilities of education reversing the tendencies toward intellectual apathy and linear thinking (Beyer forthcoming, Berman and La Farge 1993). Yet the dominant structures and processes of schooling—whose knowledge gets taught there, what kinds of evaluative practices and social relations are promoted, the traditions on which we have relied in thinking about curriculum and pedagogy—has often served to promote perspectives and values that reproduce these larger cultural and social phenomena (Beyer and Apple 1988, Beyer 1989). This essay seeks to aid in the process of resisting the tendencies toward passivity and submergence, as we formulate alternative visions and practices in the arts that can alter the current realities of school life and the personal, social, and cultural contexts in which they reside.

Limiting Theories of Aesthetic Experience

An often cited shortcoming of analytic philosophy and Philosophy of Education is the removal of analysis, representations, and judgments from the larger contexts in which thought and action take place—and the very dissociation between thought and action to which this leads. One of the consequences of this, as Suzanne de Castell notes, is the inability to recognize how cultural codes—for example, those reflecting gender, racial, class, sexual, age-related, and other identities and ideologies—become embedded in forms of language and modes of representation. These tendencies have been especially pervasive in aesthetic theory and, as a result, in many approaches to aesthetic education.

Yet I do not share the view as de Castell does that "it's more important to examine current discourses rather than those of the past." "The past" is, at least often, still with us, and cannot be categorically separated from current situations and future possibilities. Nor do I believe that whatever canon has been thought to exist in philosophy or Philosophy of Education consists exclusively of "old relics" or "conceptual dinosaurs" that can therefore be ignored or discarded. I would argue, on the contrary, that works like Plato's *Republic* are still valuable in Philosophy of Education, even though I disagree with most of the substantive epistemological, political, and aesthetic directions outlined in that work. Part of the value of the *Republic* resides in a certain literary or aesthetic style, partly because, as de Castell notes, "Socrates exhorted his students to seek wisdom with all their hearts and minds, and to find it elsewhere than the places they had been told it must reside." This strikes me as excellent contemporary advice for our students. In addition, Plato's mistakes and omissions are often quite instructive, as can be seen, for example, in the critique of Jane Roland Martin (1985).

There may be few philosophical questions older than those concerned with the nature of "art" and its defining characteristics. Departing from the concerns of ancient philosophers, the advent of a more individualistic modern age gave credence to assumptions that were quite different from those previous approaches to art that emphasized the discovery of an artistic "essence." The dispositions or state of mind of the person involved in art appreciation might now define the status and very possibility of engagement with the arts. Indeed the historic movement from "art object" to "aesthetic experience" can be understood as a concern for the quality of *experience* made possible by a psychologically guided perceptual interaction with an object, rather than for the characteristics of the art object per se.

However, the possibility that art might be considered more wholistically as giving rise to experiences involving general human concerns and interests, was to be thwarted. A central factor involved in this thwarting of wholism, and the divorce of aesthetic from other, allegedly more mundane experiences, was the emergence of *attitude theories* of aesthetic experience.[1]

There are four sets of ideas that are especially relevant to the aesthetic attitude tradition, and that have been influential in helping shape our culture's receptivity to art. These include: aesthetic disinterestedness; psychical distance; aesthetic perception; and aesthetic formalism. A brief look at these four ideas will be useful in understanding the ways in which the arts were to become separated, within the dominant traditions in aesthetic theory, from everyday life (see also Beyer 1984).

First, borrowing from certain theological traditions involving the proper attitude to be taken in the worship of God, we are aesthetically disinterested when our attention is focused on the "excellence of the object" before us, apart from whatever *consequences* it may have for us individually or collectively. One contemporary advocate of this perspective has commented that our appreciation of a work of art, "cannot be disinterested unless the spectator forsakes all self-concern and therefore trains attention upon the object for its own sake" (Stolnitz 1961, p. 107). As aesthetic participants, we should concentrate simply on reading the poem, viewing the painting, or hearing the music. In paying attention to the poem or painting itself, we are not concerned with the consequences it may have for us after the experience is concluded. To accomplish this, second, we must psychologically distance ourselves from the work of art. This basically involves putting art "out of gear" with our other interests and actions, so that art is not connected with "practical concerns." The basic presumption is that any object or event—even one usually signaling fear, attraction, or some other emotionally charged reaction—can be approached and appreciated aesthetically if we disconnect it from our usual affections, feelings, and expectations. To be engaged in a truly aesthetic experience, therefore, we must dislocate our more typical, instrumentally-guided way of attending to events, bracketing out our typical dispositions and proclivities. In this way we will be able to see art, this tradition tells us, "as it is"—unclouded by personal sensibilities and predispositions (Bullough 1912).

Third, the aesthetic attitude tradition places central emphasis on the *perceptual* qualities of art. This means that art should be seen as its own end, and train attention on the perceptible qualities it displays. As one writer has expressed this point, "on occasion we pay attention to a thing simply for the sake of enjoying the way it looks or sounds or feels. This is the 'aesthetic' attitude of perception" (Stolnitz 1960, p. 34). Within aesthetic perception, the art object becomes individuated and autonomous, cut off from connections with other objects, people, and events. Perceived as a work of art, the object becomes an island unto itself.

These three emphases lead naturally to a fourth component of the aesthetic attitude tradition. By making our attention disinterested and psychologically distanced, thereby ensuring the autonomy of art, we are drawn to the internal qualities and structures of the art object under observation—the qualities of shading, color, brush stroke, contrast, etc., in painting. In an important sense this is the only domain still open to us as appreciators, since the art object's connection to personal sentiments, social values, and future aims is thwarted when we take the "proper" aesthetic attitude. We thus tend to focus on "the looks of things" in aesthetic encounters. "What makes appreciation aesthetic," one writer asserts, "is that it is concerned with a thing's looking somehow without concern for whether it really is like that; beauty we may say, to emphasize the point, is not even skin deep" (Urmson 1968, p. 367). An abiding interest in an object's form, and the appearance of various schools of Formalism, is thus encouraged (see Parker 1920, Pepper 1949, Beardsley 1958, and Gotshalk 1962).

Attitudinal theories of aesthetic experience remove art—through the development of a particular way of perceiving and understanding sensory input from art objects—from historical and social contexts (see Beyer 1979a). As well, such theories place the appreciator's ideas, experiences, and actions outside the realm of aesthetic contemplation. "Art" in this theory names an abstracted, autonomous, purified or exalted domain. Perhaps no single passage in the recent history of aesthetic theory better captures this point of view than the words of Clive Bell:

> To appreciate a work of art we need bring with us nothing from life, no knowledge of its ideas and affairs, no familiarity with its emotions. Art transports us from the world of man's activity to a world of aesthetic exaltation. For a moment we are shut off from human interests; our anticipation and memories are arrested; we are lifted above the stream of life. (1913 p. 25)

While Bell's remarks may be thought of as hyperbole, they are in keeping with the central tenets of the aesthetic attitude tradition. They represent the pursuit of art as a special, removed, spiritual realm, the mysteries of which are only accessible to those with the proper set of dispositional tendencies.

It is this point of view that has prodded one proponent of aesthetic education, Harry S. Broudy (1977), to remark that our experience of art involves only "the realm of appearance for its own sake, [and consequently] demands no commitment to action" (p. 7). Similarly, Broudy (1972, p. 48) has cautioned that, "it is naive to believe that art cannot endanger morals. It can if the viewer is unable to perceive art objects aesthetically, and the untrained perceiver is likely to have this infirmity." Clearly, on this view, art is to be kept safe from the possible taint of politics, social action, and moral discourse.

While such theoretical traditions may be challenged from a variety of perspectives, and on several grounds (see Casebier 1977, Dickie 1977, and Beyer 1988), it is the understanding of art that derives from them that is of central concern. Attitude theories, in accentuating the presentational, distanced, formal qualities of art, reduce our attention to the surface features of the object, while trivializing its content. Moreover, aesthetic representations on this model tend to be the plaything of an elite. No longer a part of the ebb and flow of human and social experience, art becomes something to behold and exalt on special occasions, in contexts removed from daily life, utilizing a form of attention that makes the domain of art by definition "impractical" and intimidating for many, to be enjoyed and appropriated by those social groups with the requisite leisure, wealth, and some elusive (and often snob-bishly perceived) dimension of "taste."[2] The view of art as abstracted, isolated, and socially epiphenomenal, mandating the creation of a peculiar set of psychological propensities, certainly contributes to the sense that "art" is for the privileged and advantaged. An absorption in the phenomenal field of art sanctioned by the aesthetic attitude gives the appearance of apprecia-tion as not only highly impersonal and abstract, but essentially a matter of discovering appropriate mechanisms of aesthetic sensitivity through the cul-tivation of taste.

The emphasis on psychological bracketing, the perceptible qualities of objects viewed disinterestedly, and the proliferation of a variety of Formalist schools of thought, have been rejected more recently by an alternative theory of art that emphasizes the role of subjective response, especially in literary criticism. For example, David Bleich in *Subjective Criticism* (1978) challenges the philosophical tenets of attitudinal theories in aesthetics and the episte-mological assumptions on which they are based. Unlike attempts to dismiss the personal sentiments of art viewers, Bleich says that "facts can acquire meaning only as a function of someone's subjectivity"; further, "to make a distinction between the interpretive and quantitative sciences is no longer possible. The subjective paradigm suggests that knowledge in general comes through synthesized interpretations" (p. 33). It is through the interaction of some person—with a specific biography, set of emotional tendencies, inter-personal history, and so on—with the aesthetic object that meaning is constructed. Instead of insisting on the bracketing of perception and distanc-ing of art, this theory emphasizes the subjective motivations, associations, and dispositions of the participant as these are crucial ingredients in the development of all knowledge.

Using psychoanalytic theory as a model for subjective knowledge that is authoritative, Bleich further develops his theory of the subjectivity of aesthet-ic experience: "Like the interpretation of dreams, the interpretation of an aesthetic object is motivated not by a wish to know the artist's inten-tion . . . but by the desire to create knowledge on one's own behalf and on behalf of one's community from the subjective experience of the work of art" (1978, p. 93). Aesthetic interpretation, like its counterpart in psychoanalysis, is on this view deemed correct, appropriate, or compelling to the extent that the reader's subjective response is found personally or psychologically useful. "The fundamental act in the recording of response is shifting the mind's objectifying capacity from the symbolic object to one's self, the subject" (Bleich 1978, p. 151).

Like the psychologist concerned with the articulation of therapeutically beneficial interpretations, the participant in subjectively-oriented literary encounters is led to develop responses that are psychologically useful. For example, after reading D. H. Lawrence's *Lady Chatterley's Lover,* one partici-pant compares Mellors to a former boyfriend in high school. In commenting on this reaction, Bleich says that parts of her response "suggest forms of disappointment in herself that are related to disappointments first in Clifford, then in her grandfather, but perhaps offset through identifications with her father" (Bleich 1978, p. 186).

The theoretical perspective developed by Bleich forms an interesting counterpoint to the attitudinal tradition of aesthetic experience. The author is suggesting that aesthetic value is determined by the subjective motives and associations of the perceiver. The resulting aesthetic knowledge is controlled by the maintenance of a "psychological homeostasis" in which psychologically disturbing experiences are translated through interpretation so as to ameliorate their disturbing qualities. Aesthetic experience is therefore valuable to the extent that it is therapeutically soothing.

Yet there are problems with this emphasis on subjectivity that have a bearing on the very question of the value of art. As a form of subjectivity, art becomes a healing psychoanalytic tool, serving only to make more manageable the psychic conflicts of the perceiver and encouraging emotional adjustment. Insofar as this approach is privatized and individuated, it may overlook larger realms of meaning provided by moral, political, and ideological matrices. Even when the aesthetic interpretations produced are discussed within a community, as Bleich suggests, their value as psychoanalytic tools may delimit the possible moral force of art. If the effort is to ameliorate psychic disturbances, clarify autobiographically-related episodes, and enhance one's self image, the morally critical edge of art is likely to be denied. Since the aim of aesthetic experience so construed is something like emotional harmony, the possibility of art challenging and helping reformulate our personal, moral, and political assumptions seems unlikely to be realized. In those cases where art embodies ideas and allusions that challenge our beliefs and commitments, and thereby produces emotional disharmony, such challenges become reduced to emotional disturbances to be ameliorated by psychotherapeutically soothing interpretations. In the process any personally and socially transformative role of art is put in jeopardy. To be a liberating, moral force, art must be capable of critiquing, and at least occasionally transcending, those very psychological strains that Bleich seeks to ameliorate with the aid of a subjective theory of art (see Beyer 1979b).

Both the attitudinal approaches that characterize modern aesthetic theory, and the psychoanalytic emphasis within subjectivist theories of art, are partially responsible for the ambiguity which our culture exhibits with respect to art. The former approach displaces art from the realm of everyday action, personal involvement, and life choices, emphasizing instead the perceptible, decontextual nature of art involving absorptive exaltation by and for an elite. The latter perspective, in psychoanalyzing aesthetic response, discounts the critical edge of aesthetic value that might propel transformative personal and moral possibilities. Both traditions serve to demean the possibility of art as a life force.

Aesthetic Experience and Moral Imperatives

I fully agree with de Castell that philosophers of education need to ask ourselves "how we can go on living in the full knowledge of the inevitability of our own complicity in evil, and what education might be able to do to address the impossibility of innocence, the tragic inescapability of unethical conduct, given how the very artifacts and practices we value most have been produced and continue to be produced in and through the oppression and exploitation of others." What sort of aesthetic theory and education will help us see the connections between the arts and the elimination of evil, the interconnections between art and ethical conduct?

A variety of alternative perspectives and actions, of ways of seeing and doing, have emerged that seek to open new conceptual and political ground in educational, social, and cultural theory. The current climate may provide a moment for some synthesis or integration of divergent possibilities where this is of value, knowing that difference is a value that frequently makes a difference. Or perhaps the politics of a "radical pluralism" that respects difference, but that appropriately values a synthetic vision that allows for alternative possibilities built upon the possibility of collective interests, may in some way be the only real option we have in a world in which security and certainty are exposed as deception and dishonesty (see Plotke 1989).

In *A Room of One's Own,* Virginia Woolf (1929) wanders through the apparently pacific environs of "Oxbridge University," appreciating both the natural and cultural wonders that comprise that environment. She recalls essays on the works of Milton and Thackeray that suggest not a single word could be changed for the better in these classics. She considers whether, contrary to such views, any changes in the original manuscripts might actually have been made by either author, and decides to investigate, realizing the library in which these texts are housed is only a few hundred yards away. Upon discovering that entrance to this library is prohibited to those unaccompanied by a Fellow of the College or a letter of introduction, Woolf is forced to leave. She writes:

> That a famous library has been cursed by a woman is a matter of complete indifference to a famous library. Venerable and calm, with all its treasures safe locked within its breast, it sleeps complacently and will, so far as I am concerned, so sleep for ever. Never will I wake those echoes, never will I ask for that hospitality again, I vowed as I descended in anger. (Woolf 1929, pp. 11–12)

Later that day, after having the kind of luncheon normally reserved for the privileged, and having considered the value of libraries, churches, food, and wealth, Woolf reconsiders what she has seen and heard; she wonders,

> . . . what effect poverty has on the mind; and what effect wealth has on
> the mind; and I thought of the queer old gentlemen I had seen that
> morning with tufts of fur upon their shoulders; and I remembered how
> if one whistled one of them ran; and I thought of the organ booming in
> the chapel and of the shut doors of the library; and I thought how
> unpleasant it is to be locked out; and I thought how it is worse perhaps
> to be locked in. . . . (Woolf 1929, p. 40)

Instead of seeking an assumed safe haven, set off from the world of ugliness, manipulation, and mechanical repetition that comprises a seemingly ever larger portion of our daily lives, philosophers of education must recontextualize the aesthetic as a material and personal force, existing within the intersections of familial, social, ideological, and historical currents and actions that comprise central elements of our actual and possible lives. Yet how to overcome or enlarge the legacy of modernism is not at all obvious.

One of our problems involves how to develop a language to substitute for the masculinist views of detachment, objectivity, and neutrality that have shaped our modern understanding of art through such mechanisms as attitude theories of aesthetic experience. In *Sex, Class, & Culture,* Lillian S. Robinson (1978) discusses what it means for an idea to be "bourgeois" in more or less traditional Marxist terms, citing *The German Ideology* as explaining how the strands of power intersect within a class that rules in both an ideational and a material sense. She follows this citation with the observation that

> Italian adolescents have expressed the same view somewhat more colorfully: "How could a young gentleman argue with his own shadow, spit on himself and on his own distorted culture while using the very words of that culture?" (Robinson 1978, pp. 5–6)

We have tried often to utilize the meanings, images, and metaphors of the ways of thinking we seek to transcend within the very act of criticism. Our own language can indeed be a powerful prison house. Such is the situation in a good deal of current writing in educational and cultural theory, and one that may be mitigated, at least in part, by a feminist aesthetic.

There are several important respects in which work in feminist aesthetics has altered our understanding of the value of the arts. Not the least of these is the extent to which the historical exclusion of women's (and other marginalized groups') art, and the misrepresentation of women and others, either through silence/absence or more overt means, has been recognized and responded to. In terms of realizing the potential of a feminist aesthetic, one course of action involves recognizing this potentially liberating potential of women's expression.

This concern for recognizing women's art is related to the question, explored by Rosalind Coward (1980), of whether *women's* works of art are necessarily *feminist* works of art. As Michele Barrett asks,

Is the recovery of women's artistic work of the past an integral part of our developing feminist project, or merely a sentimental resuscitation of marginalia better left in the obscurity to which establishment criticism has consigned it? What do we gain by elevating traditional crafts such as embroidery and knitting to the status of art objects and hanging them in galleries? What is the meaning of an art exhibition where the objects displayed are kitchen utensils or the careful record of a child's upbringing? How should we react to art that claims to be based on a "female language" or on an artistic rendering of the female body and genitalia? In what sense might these various imaginative comments on women's experience be seen as "feminist" art? Is a work of art feminist because the artist says it is, or the collective who produced it announce their feminist principles of work? (Barrett 1982, pp. 42–43).

The study by Judy Chicago, "The Dinner Party," perhaps epitomizes some of the questions surrounding the questions posed here. For Barrett, the Chicago exhibit in its portrayal of Virginia Woolf, for example, is less than illuminating:

> There [Woolf] sits: a genital sculpture in deep relief (about four inches high) resting on a runner of pale lemon gauze with the odd blue wave embroidered on it. Gone is Woolf's theory of androgyny and love of gender ambiguity; gone the polemical public voice; gone the complex symbolic abstractions of her writing. I found this exclusive emphasis on genitalia, and the sentimentality of the trappings, a complete betrayal . . . (Barrett 1982, p. 45)

Unlike Coward, however, Barrett concludes that while not all women's art is feminist art, whatever feminist art is must be a subset of women's experience—a shared experience of patriarchal oppression.

A second possibility for understanding and valuing a feminist aesthetic entails recognizing the double-sided partiality in male views of the canon, and suggests that we need to reconsider more generally the basis of aesthetic significance and its gender determinants. Such an approach promises to significantly widen what is considered art, and to the extent that it is successful could reform both aesthetic sensitivities and aesthetic education. This seems to be a guiding perspective in Andreas Huyssen's (1986) essay, "Mass Culture as Woman." In considering the problems associated with "saying I" for the woman writer, Huyssen says,

> Given the fundamentally differing social and psychological constitution and validation of male and female subjectivity in modern bourgeois society, the difficulty of saying 'I' must of necessity be different for a woman writer. . . . The male, after all, can easily deny his own subjectivity for the benefit of a higher aesthetic goal, as long as he can take it for granted on an experiential level in everyday life. (Huyssen 1986, p. 190)

In redefining subjectivity and recognizing the gender determinants of varieties of it, the definitions of valued art that center on masculine cover-ups of a subjective objectivity are challenged. In recognizing the socially constructed "I," moreover, we go beyond the psychologism noted in Bleich's (1978) notion of subjective criticism.

Yet a third possibility for a feminist aesthetic is one that raises questions about the very nature of "an artistic tradition," and the basis upon which only some creative actions are labeled "art." This provides a more fundamental challenge to mainstream assumptions about art, as it undermines the hierarchical structures upon which artistic canons must depend. Yet the problem with such a view is the tendency to deny any criteria with which works of art might be distinguished as to their value—however that might be conceptualized and in spite of the intellectual and practical difficulties of coming to some agreement on what this value might consist in.

In terms similar to those just utilized in considering the possible value of a feminist aesthetic, Elaine Showalter (1985) summarizes the varieties of feminist criticism:

> The intellectual trajectory of feminist criticism has taken us from a concentration on women's literary subordination, mistreatment, and exclusion, to the study of women's separate literary traditions, to an analysis of the symbolic construction of gender and sexuality within literary discourse. It is now clear that what we are demanding is a new universal literary history and criticism that combines the literary experiences of both women and men, a complete revolution in the understanding of our literary heritage. (p. 10)

The threat of homogenization and marginalization is always present in any reputedly universalizing theory, as many people writing within postmodernism have pointed out (see, for example, Foucault 1980, Giroux 1988, Rorty 1989, and Ellsworth 1989). While such threats are real and must be continually guarded against, responses to questions about "our own complicity in evil," and the need to confront "unethical conduct," according to de Castell, must be rooted in social and political activities that attack injustices; these require some form of political solidarity. To the extent that postmodernism fosters an insularity of discourse and a particularity of knowledge, it undermines efforts to act in the name of social justice—efforts that require concerted, collaborative actions combining global and local sensitivities (Beyer and Liston 1992). These efforts can be enhanced, as well, by emphasizing the integration of aesthetic and other activities, necessitating what Judith Barry and Sandy Flitterman-Lewis (1988) describe as "the need for a feminist reexamination of the notions of art, politics, and the relations between them, an evaluation which must take into account how 'femininity' itself is a social construct with a particular form of representation under patriarchy" (p. 87).

This understanding of a feminist aesthetic raises the crucial question of cultural politics and its role within feminist criticism and practice. Simply put, what are the politics of cultural production, distribution, and appreciation and what is the connection between feminist art and politics?

I would argue, with Barrett, that while not all women's art is feminist, all feminist art is related to a common experiential background. The question of cultural politics is then immediately complicated by the realities of class, ethnicity, race, sexual orientation, and so on. That is, if feminist art is necessarily based upon the socially constructed experience of being a woman, how divergent can that experience be (given membership in other groups, differing value commitments and priorities, a range of historical situations, and so on) and still be identified as essentially *women's* experience? Under what circumstances, within what contexts, and utilizing what theoretical perspective does gender have the centrally organizing role in the experience of women? What do we do with experiences that involve women but not centrally as gendered subjects, or that involve men as something other than subjects who are fundamentally gendered, but where there are other, perhaps compelling similarities, commonalities, and possible political alliances, for example, those surrounding race, ethnicity, age, or class (see McCarthy and Apple 1988).

It may be possible to construct a critical aesthetic theory that, in including several strands within its boundaries, does not homogenize the important differences among them, but that can serve as a force for political action. Such a cultural politics must be able to move toward social and cultural transformation, and this certainly assumes a commonality of purpose among the protagonists that always poses a threat to diversity and authenticity among "the others" (Beyer and Liston 1992).

Cultural Politics and a Materialist Aesthetic

One problem with basing any approach to the arts on a particular fund of experiences—even if we can decide what the elements of commonality are to be that create such experiences—is that such an approach, if left unexamined and unclarified, can easily become an individualistic, essentially psychological domain. Left out is a consideration of the structural pressures that shape and reshape that experience. An awareness and critical understanding of such structures is essential if we are to develop a critical aesthetic that carries with it the possibilities of social change. As Barry and Flitterman-Lewis explain:

> In evaluating . . . types of women's art, our constant reference point will be the recognition of the need for a theory of cultural production as an armature for any politically progressive art form. . . . Every act (eating

an orange, building a table, reading a book) is a social act; the fundamentally human is social. Theory enables us to recognize this and
permits us to go beyond individual, personally liberating solutions to a
"socially" liberated situation. . . . Theory, as a systematic organization of
the range of cultural phenomena, can produce the tools for examining
the political effectiveness of feminist art work. (1988, p. 88)

The authors go on to develop a four-part typology of women's art that is
interesting and useful. This typology identifies art works: 1) that assume a
female essentialism, and result in the "glorification of an essential female art
power" (Barry and Flitterman-Lewis 1988, p. 89), for which the Judy Chicago
exhibit provides one example; 2) that view "women's art as a form of subcul-
tural resistance" (p. 91), which would include typically women's crafts as a
kind of counter-culture; 3) that are submerged in or entirely outside of patriarchal forms of expression—including women artists who see themselves as
"separatists," and those who are nonfeminists, seeking acceptance from patriarchy; and 4) that situate "women at a crucial place within patriarchy which
enables them to play on the contradictions that inform patriarchy itself" (p.
94). This final segment of women's art recognizes the socially constructed
nature of "woman" and "women's art," the role of discourse in those processes
of production, and the intersection of multitudinous social practices.

> Activism alone in women's art has limited effects because it does not
> examine the representation of women in culture or the production of
> women as a social category. We are suggesting that a feminist art
> evolves from a theoretical reflection on representation: how the repre-
> sentation of women is produced, the way it is understood, and the
> social conditions in which it is situated. (Barry and Flitterman-Lewis
> 1988, p. 94)

This effort to produce a dialectical, participatory, situated feminist aesthetic
"implies a break with the dominant notion of art as personal expression,
re-situating it along the continuum connecting the social with the political
and placing the artist as producer in a new situation of responsibility for her
images" (Barry and Flitterman-Lewis 1988, p. 97). This sort of feminist art,
then, moves us beyond the categories of disinterestedness and ideological
isolation, and also provides clues to what might be central to such art beyond
its being a part of collective "women's experience." It also distinguishes itself
from other sorts of feminist aesthetic theory—the study of women's exclusion
from the canon, the development of women's own artistic traditions that dismiss canonical views altogether—as it seeks to understand the situatedness
of art so that it can further the alteration of those very situations.

An emphasis on the socially constructed nature of art, and its links with
other institutions and actions, lies close to the center of a materialist aesthetic. A materialist theory of aesthetics informed by feminism, and a feminist

theory of aesthetics informed by a non-reductionist social theory, provide a possibility for personal and structural transformation through the arts.

This view is based upon the belief that an organic unity that gives voice to aesthetic value, political possibility, and personal liberation is theoretically defensible and practically feasible. Such a unity must transcend the often critiqued but still deeply embedded dichotomies of reason/emotion, objective/subjective, public/private, and productive/reproductive that are inherited, in part, from patriarchy. Two propositions are especially important: first, that in representing or expressing situations or themes, all art contains within it an at least implicit way of seeing, constructing, and making sense of the world, of communicating a vision of what life is or could become—and therefore both hides and discloses political and social visions. In the words of some critical educational theorists, the arts may be both productive and reproductive (Apple 1982). Such visions may be harder or easier to discern, given a particular work's complexity and its use of symbolic notation, and the extent to which the members of the audience share symbolic and experiential reference points, and are open to aesthetic forms that challenge conventional ways of seeing. Second, no liberation movement can be totally or exclusively personal, individuated, or psychological, as important as these elements frequently are. Nor can "the social" and "the personal" be conceived as separable, reified categories, with an autonomous existence and point of reference. If "art" and "politics" cannot be isolated, neither can "personal" and "social" change which the arts can help forge. As one commentator on Marx has argued with respect to the former claim:

> Vulgarized dogmatic views on the character of the link between art and politics are profoundly alien to the Marxist-Leninist understanding of art. A truthful and diversified representation of reality cannot be replaced by any didactic illustration of political slogans. Such substitution cannot but lead to a belittling of artistic truthfulness and hence undermine art's social impact. (Zis 1977, p. 66)

Similarly, the possibilities of structural transformation must be rethought, recognizing that such change has personal meanings that may be ambiguous, and aware that personal and familial changes, in order to become implanted, often must be accompanied by larger alterations.

The sort of critical aesthetic theory that is consistent with an integration of the personal/political, and of art/politics, sees the arts as an important aspect of social and personal life, connected with material, structural, and personal relations that are complex, dialectical, and sometimes oppositional—relations that extend well beyond the encounter with a particular work of art. By locating women's experience within this complex set of constructs, and seeing the arts as a basis for both understanding and transforming the socially constructed definitions of woman, art, and politics, a critical theory of aesthetics may be realized that can help alter our consciousness, our schools, and our social situations.

In rejecting the notion of art as socially removed, ideologically neutral, and impersonal, we challenge some of the most important of the dominant traditions in European, male-dominated aesthetic theory. As a project with politically transformative possibilities, the construction of a critical, socially conscious alternative theory of aesthetics must be able to promote collaborative, collective pursuits that work toward the overthrow of relations of dominance in a society characterized by oppressive and unequal relations of power and domination; such an aesthetic theory must also be broad enough, and open enough, to foster the personal expressions of people denied a voice in society and the mainstream artistic community, as we generate a different sort of community within which diversity and points of intersection are respected. We cannot afford people who are "locked in" or "locked out." If the arts divorced from a social context are empty, the aesthetic without a sensitivity to personal voice must surely be blind.

What does this perspective imply for the recreation of aesthetic education that is tied to the development of a critical consciousness and to social change? There is an array of cultural, ideological, and social realities within which students (and adults, too, of course) develop their orientations and values, which often conflict with the very values and practices required for the development of a critical consciousness that can be furthered by a reconceived aesthetic. The treatment of women and girls in a variety of texts and institutions; the violence depicted on television and other media (as well as the violence witnessed by many children everyday, as they make their way from home to school and back again); the racism in open view in many families, neighborhoods, and communities; and the systemic nature of the oppression visited on the poor, people of color, and women, may well affect the forms of consciousness that students bring to schools. And these forms of consciousness will also shape the very student interests that progressives have long thought central to include within the curriculum. Bombarded by ideologically-laden representations that reflect dominant social interests and often become sedimented into students' consciousness, the resulting hegemony may create interests that, when expressed, encode sentiments and priorities that are the very antithesis of what is required for significant social change.

Ignoring those hegemonic beliefs and practices is not possible. Pretending that such beliefs are inconsequential results in superficial forms of student participation within which significant educational experiences do not take place, since ideas remain disconnected from those core values and perceptions that affect the meaning of school and social life. Even when students listen attentively to teachers' and texts' discussions of the horrors and injustices of racism, for example, their commitment to racial equality, social justice, and sensitivity will be only apparent or verbal if we do not help them make connections between their own experiences and beliefs and the possibilities for equality. This is a fundamental problem associated with the use of textbooks and other sanitized and dislocated forms of knowledge, inquiry, and curricula.

One of the things that is required in order to respond to this problem is the incorporation of forms of popular culture—television programs, movies, music, video productions, comic books, and so on—into the curriculum so that developing an understanding of the meaning and influence of such works becomes an important part of what schools are for. Helping students develop a critical, analytical, reflective attitude toward those forms of popular culture in which they are caught up, but which are not often analyzed, and are usually seen as non-academic or otherwise inappropriate for the public schools, is central to encourage not just the *expression,* but the *critical evaluation,* of those forms. At the same time, an emphasis on certain moral values—equality, tolerance, respect for human life and the need for peace, a commitment to some notion of a common good, for example—will not be significant for students unless they can come to understand the meanings of such lofty ideals within their own day to day lives. To facilitate some notion of an ethical culture in schools to which an altered form of aesthetic education might powerfully contribute, it is important that the personal, social, and political implications of moral values for our lives and actions, in and out of school, become a part of the curriculum. This might be encouraged by the production of student forms of popular culture that connect what are often considered more distant moral imperatives and the real life, flesh and blood experiences of children—in and out of school. The arts, as these capture both the meaning of common events and the possibilities for alternative ways of life, might well make lasting contributions to this effort.

Conclusions

In an indictment of the dominant traditions in aesthetic theory, Raymond Williams (1977) says, "we have to reject 'the aesthetic' both as a separate abstract dimension and as a separate abstract function. We have to reject 'Aesthetics' to the large extent that it is posited on these abstractions" (p. 156). Developing a materialist theory of cultural forms that includes the arts, and that discloses their potentially liberating political and social affects for human life, helps make clear the ways in which the arts are a *productive* force. In an earlier work, Williams (1961) discusses the ways in which the arts of a period help construct a "structure of feeling" that gives shape to, and helps reveal, social processes, objects and relationships, and ways of life; this structure of feeling is "the culture of a period: . . . it is the particular living result of all the elements in the general organization. And it is in this respect that the arts of a period . . . are of major importance." In the arts, "in the only examples we have of recorded communication that outlives its bearers, the actual living sense, the deep community that makes the communications possible, is naturally drawn upon" (p. 48).

The arts can do more than document the "actual living sense, the deep community that makes communications possible." They can, through the imaginative rendering of people, events, values, places, feelings, and ideas, help disclose worlds that are not yet in place, and thus serve as a force to bring about their creation. This is the political promise of art, a promise not to be fulfilled through a narrow instrumentalism, but through its efficacy in helping us reflect on, and transform, our ways of life, our personal and social being. This is only a potential value of the aesthetic experience, of course, and not one that is currently widely held. If it is to become a reality, we must continue to develop a theory of the aesthetic that goes beyond an abstracting Formalism and an isolating psychologism—one that places the arts as a material, productive force, within the moral values, everyday lives, and personal and social interactions of people. Such a theory, and the experiences it makes possible, might indeed help us respond to the evils in the world.

NOTES

1. I use the phrase "attitude theories" generically to cover a variety of specific positions in aesthetics. All of these theories share, however, the view that it is something about the *attitude* of the participant that is definitive of aesthetic experience. For a more detailed account of these theories, see Parker 1920; Pepper 1949; Beardsley 1958; Stolnitz 1961; Gotshalk 1962; Bullough 1912; Stolnitz 1960; and Urmson 1968).

2. The study by Laura Chapman (1982, pp. 170–71) highlights the elitist nature of the fine arts in contemporary American culture. For example, the median income of those who visit art museums is some $3,500 higher than the national average, while for opera goers the differential is $6,500. Similar discrepancies are reported when one considers the educational level of the art audience. There exists, in short, a cultural elite, whose income, status, and education clearly demarcate them.

BIBLIOGRAPHY

Apple, Michael W. (1979). *Ideology and Curriculum*. London: Routledge & Kegan Paul.

Apple, Michael W. (1982). *Education and Power*. Boston: Routledge & Kegan Paul.

Barrett, Michele. (1982). "Feminism and the Definition of Cultural Politics," in Rosalind Brunt and Caroline Rowan, eds., *Feminism, Culture and Politics*. London: Lawrence and Wishart.

Barry, Judith, and Flitterman-Lewis, Sandy. (1988). "Textual Strategies: The Politics of Art-Making," in Arlene Raven, Cassandra L. Langer, and Joanna Frueh, eds., *Feminist Art Criticism: An Anthology*. Ann Arbor: UMI Research Press.

Beardsley, Monroe C. (1958). *Aesthetics: Problems in the Philosophy of Criticism*. New York: Harcourt, Brace, & World, Inc.

Bell, Clive. (1913). *Art*. New York: Frederick A. Stokes Co.

Berman, Sheldon, and La Farge, Phyllis, eds. (1993). *Promising Practices in Teaching Social Responsibility*. Albany: State University of New York Press.

Beyer, Landon E. (1979a). "Aesthetic Theory and the Ideology of Educational Institutions," *Curriculum Inquiry, 9*(1).

Beyer, Landon E. (1979b). "Cultural Forms as Therapeutic Encounters," *Curriculum Inquiry, 9*(4).

Beyer, Landon E. (1984). "What Role for the Arts in the Curriculum?" in Carl Grant, ed., *Preparing for Reflective Teaching*. Boston: Allyn and Bacon, Inc.

Beyer, Landon E. (1988). "Art and Society," in William F. Pinar, ed., *Contemporary Curriculum Discourses*. Scottsdale, Arizona: Gorsuch Scarisbrick.

Beyer, Landon E. (1989). *Critical Reflection and the Culture of Schooling: Empowering Teachers*. Geelong, Victoria: Deakin University Press.

Beyer, Landon E. (forthcoming). *Education for a Revitalized Democracy: Teachers' Voices on Values and Politics in Schools*.

Beyer, Landon E., and Apple, Michael W. (1988). *The Curriculum: Problems, Politics, and Possibilities*. Albany: State University of New York Press.

Beyer, Landon E., and Liston, Daniel P. (1992). "Discourse or Moral Action? A Critique of Postmodernism," *Educational Theory, 42*(4).

Bleich, David. (1978). *Subjective Criticism*. Baltimore: The Johns Hopkins University Press.

Broudy, Harry S. (1972). *Enlightened Cherishing: An Essay in Aesthetic Education*. Urbana: University of Illinois Press.

Broudy, Harry S. (1977). "The Whys and Hows of Aesthetic Education." St. Louis: CEMREL, Inc., 1977.

Bullough, Edward. (1912). "Psychical Distance as a Factor in Art and an Aesthetic Principle," *The British Journal of Psychology*, Volume V.

Casebier, Alan. (1977). "The Concept of Aesthetic Distance," in George Dickie and Richard J. Sciafani, Editors, *Aesthetics: A Critical Anthology*. New York: St. Martin's Press.

Chapman, Laura H. (1982). *Instant Art, Instant Culture: The Unspoken Policy for American Schools*. New York: Teachers College Press.

Coward, Rosalind. (1980). "Are Women's Novels Feminist Novels?" *Feminist Review, Number 5*.

Cuban, Larry. (1992). *How Teachers Taught: Constancy and Change in American Classrooms 1890–1980,* second edition. New York: Teachers College Press.

de Castell, Suzanne. (in press). "Textuality and the Designs of Theory," in Wendy Kohli, ed., *Critical Conversations in Philosophy of Education*. New York: Routledge.

Dickie, George. (1977). "All Aesthetic Attitude Theories Fail: The Myth of the Aesthetic Attitude," in George Dickie and Richard J. Sclafani, eds., *Aesthetics: A Critical Anthology*. New York: St. Martin's Press.

Ellsworth, Elizabeth. (1989). "Why Doesn't This Feel Empowering? Working Through the Repressive Myths of Critical Pedagogy," *Harvard Educational Review*, 59(3).

Foucault, Michel. (1980). *Power/Knowledge: Selected Interviews & Other Writings 1972–1977*. Edited by Colin Gordon. New York: Pantheon Books.

Giroux, Henry. (1988). "Postmodernism and the Discourse of Educational Criticism," *Journal of Education*, 170(3).

Gotshalk, D. W. (1962). *Art and the Social Order*. New York: Dover Publications, Inc.

Huyssen, Andreas (1986). "Mass Culture as Woman: Modernism's Other," in Tania Modleski, Editor, *Studies in Entertainment: Critical Approaches to Mass Culture*. Bloomington: Indiana University Press.

Jackson, Philip W. (1968). *Life in Classrooms*. New York: Holt, Rinehart and Winston.

Martin, Jane Roland. (1985). *Reclaiming a Conversation: The Ideal of the Educated Woman*. New Haven: Yale University Press, 1985.

McCarthy, Cameron, and Apple, Michael W. (1988). "Race, Class, and Gender in American Educational Research: Toward a Nonsynchronous Parallelist Position," in Lois Weis, Editor, *Class, Race, & Gender in American Education*. Albany: State University of New York Press.

Parker, De Witt. (1920). *The Principles of Aesthetics*. Boston: Silver, Burdett, and Co.

Pepper, Stephen C. (1949). *Principles of Art Appreciation*. New York: Harcourt, Brace, & World.

Plotke, David. (1989). "Marxism and Democratic Theory," *Dissent*, Summer.

Robinson, Lillian S. (1978). *Sex, Class, & Culture*. New York: Methuen.

Rorty, Richard. (1989). *Contingency, irony, and solidarity*. New York: Cambridge University Press.

Showalter, Elaine. (1985). "The Feminist Critical Revolution," in *The New Feminist Criticism: Essays on Women, Literature, and Theory*. New York: Pantheon Books.

Sirotnik, Kenneth A. (1983). "What You See Is What You Get: Consistency, Persistency, and Mediocrity in Classrooms," *Harvard Educational Review*, 53.

Stolnitz, Jerome. (1961). "On the Significance of Lord Shaftesbury in Modern Aesthetic Theory," *The Philosophical Quarterly*, 11(43).

Stolnitz, Jerome. (1960). *Aesthetics and Philosophy of Art Criticism*. Boston: Houghton Mifflin Company.

Urmson, J. O. (1968). "What Makes a Situation Aesthetic?" in Francis J. Coleman, ed., *Contemporary Studies in Aesthetics*. New York: McGraw-Hill Book Company.

Vallance, E. (1977). "Hiding the hidden curriculum: An interpretation of the language of justification in nineteenth-century educational reform." In Arno A. Bellack and Herbert M. Kliebard, eds., *Curriculum and Evaluation*. Berkeley: McCutchan.

Weitz, Morris. (1956). "The Role of Theory in Aesthetics," *Journal of Aesthetics and Art Criticism,* 15.

Williams, Raymond. (1961). *The Long Revolution.* London: Chatto and Windus.

Williams, Raymond. (1977). *Marxism and Literature.* Oxford: Oxford University Press.

Woolf, Virginia. (1929). *A Room of One's Own.* New York: Harcourt, Brace and Company.

Zis, Avner. (1977). *Foundations of Marxist Aesthetics.* Moscow: Progress Publishers.

21

The Difference We Make: Philosophy of Education and the Tower of Babel

Kal Alston

> Like all simple and unsophisticated peoples we Americans have a sublime faith in education. Faced with any difficult problem of life we set our minds at rest sooner or later by the appeal to the school. We are convinced that education is the one unfailing remedy for every ill to which man is subject, whether it be vice, crime, war, poverty, riches, injustice, racketeering, political corruption, race hatred, class conflict, or just plain original sin. We even speak glibly and often about the general reconstruction of society through the school. We cling to this faith in spite of the fact that the very period in which our troubles have multiplied so rapidly has witnessed an unprecedented expansion of organized education. This would seem to suggest that our schools, instead of directing the course of change, are themselves driven by the very forces that are transforming the rest of the social order.[1]

George Counts here offers a manifesto calling for the Progressive and socialist revolution of society beginning with educators. He sets off to identify, and to prescribe remedies for, the fallacious thinking that he believed kept even those with progressive intentions shackled to the past. He also, as in the paragraph above, suggests that American society is both enlivened and enervated by its faith in schools as catalysts of change. We rely (too) completely on education as a means of ameliorating what ails us. This faith is part superstition, part religion, part willed ignorance, and part motive optimism. Counts, at the end of the day, wants us to remain faithful to our ideals, but to submit them and ourselves to the purifying fires of scepticism, self-criticism, renegotiation, and renewal. Educators, he posits, are in positions of enormous social power, except that they are too acquiescent to other economic, political, and cultural forces. By continuing the mythical power of the school to provide moral and cultural correctives for American society, educators obscure the revolutionary and transformational possibilities of visionary educative practice. To limn those possibilities, to make schools "really effective, they must become centers for the *building,* and not merely for the contemplation, of our civilization."[2]

Beginning with this passage from Counts seemed appropriate here because I am investigating the question of what Philosophy of Education can say in the ongoing conversations about the so-called "multicultural education." Counts's position is apropos insofar as it, first, frames notions of American secular faith in societal reconstruction. While we may now rely on RICO statutes[3] to deal with racketeers, faith in education has expanded schools' responsibilities beyond the traditional Three Rs to curricular and student services that encompass an enormous range. It is in this context that "multicultural education" emerges as a new wave of reform, renegotiation, reclamation—three new Rs.

Second, Counts opens the question of how our understandings of knowledge, power, and ethics are fragmentary and problematic at the same time as they are indispensable to formulating progressive educational practice. I will suggest that much of the discussion on "multicultural education" exposes the partial nature of those understandings. Third, Counts makes it clear that the philosophical contribution to schools, insofar as schools take up the challenge to act on and with society, cannot be purely contemplative. Philosophy of Education, if it wishes to contribute to the efficacy of education, must have a view of itself as dynamic, participatory, and in the thick of the problems that schools face. In short, Counts answers for me the question of whether philosophers have an abiding interest/obligation to enter the fractious debates in schools of all sorts over "difference." Where, how, and from which positions we do this are explored, at least in a preliminary way.

Multiculturalism as Myth: Faith of Our Fathers *or* It's a Small World

Chatter, chatter, liberty, equality, fraternity, love, honour, patriotism and what have you. All this did not prevent us from making anti-racial speeches about dirty niggers, dirty Jews and dirty Arabs. High-minded people, liberal or just soft-hearted, protest that they were shocked by such inconsistency: but they were either mistaken or dishonest, for with us there is nothing more consistent than a racist humanism since the European has only been able to become a man through creating slaves and monsters.[4]

Clearly, the term *multicultural education* means different things to different people. The only common meaning is that it refers to changes in education that are supposed to benefit people of color.[5]

It's a world of laughter, a world of tears
It's a world of hopes and a world of fears
it's so much that we share
That it's time we're aware
It's a small world after all!

Sleeter and Grant originally published their combination literature review and new typology of "multiculturalism" in 1987. Whatever the virtues of either of those efforts, it is fair to say that their most lasting insight might be that multicultural education has no one meaning (in theory or in practice) that is coherent and consensual. Nevertheless, Grant and Sleeter's one hundred and twenty-seven referenced sources (on K–12 American schooling) seem paltry compared to the masses of articles, curricular materials, books and other publications on the subject that have appeared since 1987. And it is certainly no more clear in 1993 that multicultural education has a commonly understood meaning.

These new multicultural enthusiasms have appeared in diverse arenas, from state legislatures to school boards, from college curriculum committees to teacher in-service training. The various manifestations of multicultural education have caused fractious dissent and heated confrontation as well as some fruitful and not so fruitful change. Regardless of the problems that the various debates have generated and uncovered, the discourse of multicultural education continues because of two connected varieties of American faith: faith in schools as arenas for social change and faith in the mythos of equality.

American public schooling has, whatever its failings, been sustained through its ethos of equal access and opportunity. Schools as institutions could be counted on to reflect a balance between the interests and values of a local community (for example, in fiscal and personnel allocation, control, and prioritization) and the goals of a national common culture (manifest in efforts to produce adjusted and productive workers and citizens). The maintenance of that balance relies in part on broad, even if sometimes coerced, consensus that those two sets of cultural norms are by and large understood, accepted, and compatible. This consensus is being challenged by the various manifestations of the multicultural education debates. Further, while faith in the efficacy of this balance opens up some possibilities of conversation about how schools themselves can change to meet changing populations and needs, faith may also in some instances impede critical examination of the basic assumptions that have contributed to the development of current problems.

Rather than using the typology offered by Sleeter and Grant, I want to look for evidence of the "faith problem" in four arenas: pre-collegiate education, post-secondary education, curriculum, and community. These arenas are sites of contestation that are contiguous and connected yet differentiated and dynamic.

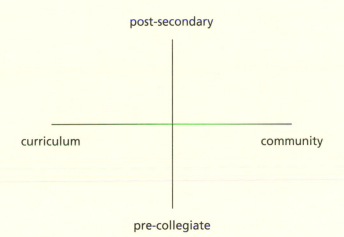

Figure 1: The four arenas of education

By looking at the four points of the axes, the interstices, and the continua, places in which faith may be shored up and those in which it might well be excised can be discovered.

This Pie Has Four Wedges

Wedge the first

curriculum

pre-collegiate

In pre-collegiate education, schools are having to respond to legislative parental, and other pressures to include materials on "historically underrepresented" or ignored groups, particularly in history and social studies curricula. In Illinois, for example, state legislators began in the late 1980s to require school districts to provide curricular content on African-Americans, women, and the Holocaust.[6] In New York, the Regents appointed a panel to make recommendations about how to change the high school social studies curriculum, statewide, to acknowledge both new knowledge and new populations in New York State.

The New York Committee members "were mindful of" several trends that they acknowledge in the opening of the ninety page document: although ever more aware of the "global village," American schools' primary goals must remain nation-building and citizen-molding; contemporary ethnic minorities, unlike their predecessors, are "determined" to maintain their cultural stakes in public spaces and institutions; social studies, as the traditional vehicle for "civics," must accept the burden of teaching about diversity and of addressing the gaps in the traditional curriculum; and, finally, since the real goal of education should be the development of academic skills and intellectual habits, any lapses or lacks in *content* should not be grounds for criticism of the curriculum.[7]

In effect, the Committee lets itself off the hook before the document itself begins. The responsibility of public schooling, though challenged by noisy and unwilling-to-go-quietly-into-that-great-melting-pot ethnic groups, is to build "the attitudes, knowledge, skills and understandings essential to continuing national cohesion and viability."[8] In these initial paragraphs the struggle between the one/unum and the many/pluribus, is a theme that persists throughout. And despite the goal of this committee to address the "problem" of forging a unified curriculum in the face of ever more diverse claims on resources, attention, and truth itself, the Committee continues to assert the traditional, hegemonic discourse of nation building as the core of social studies education.

In order to re/produce this traditional discourse without recognizing the deep contradictions embedded in the project, the Committee relies upon three fundamental beliefs: the meaning of multiculturalism can be limited to new representations (both more and better) of historically oppressed ethnic and racial groups; that given the ethnically changing populations of school-age children, curricular changes will both shore up students' pride in their identity and reiterate the common culture of the United States; and rational discourses about diversity have the capacity to change students' intellectual habits as well as their social and moral ones.

The view of multiculturalism in the Report is one in which the "multi" represents the "minority" outsiders who desire inclusion in the narratives of social studies. History and geography have been mono-vocal discourses, but in the new order, new voices can be added to the oration. This additive view of "cultures" does acknowledge that allowing more than one perspective may add to the richness of the accounts of the past and the present. Yet, the Report cannot resist the impulse to limit and to domesticate those voices and perspectives. For example, gender, class, and religious interests, as well as those of other socio-cultural groupings, have been glossed over or suppressed.[9] According to the manuscript, this was a matter of "fairness" since no curriculum could address all of these groups, so the decision was made to concentrate on those ubiquitously underrepresented ethnic and racial minorities (African-American, Latino, Asian-American, and Native American). The co-chairs of the Committee made special mention of the disposition of gender issues: important though they are, they are best served as providing context for broader cultural considerations. In fact, they suggest, if gender issues were brought into consideration, "the sexism question [would dominate] discussion and action."[10]

It becomes clear that the terrain of "difference," broadly construed, will not be traversed here, but that multiculturalism will be the rearticulation of strategies of cultural containment. The melting pot will be reconfigured with less of an assimilationist cast; schools must find a way to acknowledge, even celebrate if need be, these groups with unspoken histories. Yet, they must also keep the factions harmonious enough to coexist peacefully in the "common culture." Although the most vociferous dissenters on the "unum" side continue to worry that "every viable nation has to have a common culture to survive in peace"[11] and that the Report promotes the increase of the "fragmentation, resegregation and self-ghettoization of American life,"[12] they, like the Report itself, fail to define adequately "common culture"[13] at the same time as they ignore the insistence of the Report on the centrality of national identity. Nevertheless, their fears point to something that Nathan Glazer develops in his additional comments: that the Report allows for a very essentialist and fixed notion of race and ethnicity. He at least wants to suggest a continued dynamic and critical approach to identity that is missing not only in this Report but in the multicultural education discourse overall.[14]

The third of the beliefs cited above, faith in rationality to change hearts as well as minds, is also stated explicitly in the report from the co-chairs.

> We want our students to become thinking participants in, rather than trained validators of, decisions concerning the affairs of the nation. Such richly intelligent beings are very likely to recognize and respect the important things that we share in common as well as the unique things that make us different.[15]

This article of faith assumes that schools have the capacity to produce "richly intelligent" beings—at the same time that even those who believe that they know what such a being would look like and how to measure it are convinced that schools have for the most part *failed* to produce such creatures. This article of faith assumes that, evidence to the contrary, schools are aiming to produce lovers of knowledge and devotees of learning—at the same time that the adoption of more universalized and comprehensive assessment tools

would seem to make those goals even more unrealistic (and less cost effective) than ever. This article of faith assumes that the more students learn
about persons other than themselves, the more likely they are to embrace
both commonality and difference—at the same time that it appears that the
struggle for identity/ies in America will be ongoing for all self-reflective people and that this struggle is not necessarily made shorter or less fraught by
more knowledge and more intellective skill. These articles of faith may in fact
lay a heavier burden on the schools than they could ever hope to fulfill in
any meaningful way. The distance between faith and reality needs critical
evaluation and pragmatic bridge building.

Wedge the second

community

pre-collegiate

The call for separate academies for African-American males represents a
challenge to the faith in the separate capacity of public schools to address
social inequities. It also provides a story that connects curricular and community problems. These proposed and implemented programs[16] offer a
critique of the failures of forced desegregation and the goal of social integration as a means to ending racism. The State and its agents cannot, on this
account, change the unequal distribution of social goods (wealth, education,
racial tolerance) simply by putting black and white children in the same
schools. At least, it is empirically the case that the legacy of *Brown* is limited
in the extreme: court-ordered desegregation took place primarily in the
South, and the methods of implementation placed the burdens of busing disproportionately on black children, and integrated school enrollments do not
prevent both the social and academic segregation of students *within* schools.
Further, in urban centers in which the vast majority of public school students are non-white, the absence of metropolitan-wide busing (busing
beyond city limits) ensures that most schools will remain segregated in fact.[17]

The NAACP's opposition to some of these academy programs seems a reaf-
firmation and justification of its position in the frontlines of legal battles to
remove barriers to entry and integration. However, some spokespersons from
the NAACP and the Urban League seem also to be worrying about the consequences of a loss of faith and hope in a changing society.[18] Conversely,

according to the advocates of the various programs, the reliance on the traditional liberal (or even progressive) solutions to the panoply of social and economic problems assailing Black communities around the country is naive at best and pernicious in reality.

The abandonment of progressive faith is, of course, not total. While parents and educators in Detroit and Milwaukee are demanding radical change in the schools, they clearly retain their belief that schooling has the capacity, if appropriately executed, to change the lives of their children. Further, while they are suggesting radical changes in the content and delivery of education, Milwaukee's proposal,[19] for example, continues to make a direct link between school achievement and success in the adult world of America.

Multiculturalism, in this account, is about articulating the "culture" of African-American children in the context of historical oppression as well as past and present triumphs. This account brings to light some raw power conflicts that often remain occluded at the same time it must insist on a different kind of cultural hegemony. This account takes up quite seriously certain aspects of gender conflict but also squashes challenges to its particular interpretation of the gendered history of race relations in this country.

The curricular aspects of the Milwaukee Plan are plotted in very similar language to the New York Report; however, the Plan ups the ante by making explicit its goal to introduce Afro-centered materials at all levels of the curriculum. Molefi Kete Asante, a scholarly proponent of Afrocentricity, has made it clear that his support is for curriculum change that "means treating African people as subjects instead of objects, putting them in the middle of their own historical context as active human agents. It is not the implementation of a particular world view as if it is universal."[20]

Asante's efforts to reposition Africa without advocating separatism have not always been successful. Afrocentric approaches to curriculum run the risk of repeating the errors of "Eurocentric" curricula in refusing to submit to self-criticism and emphasizing the "centric" rather than Asante's "contextual" perspective. Correctives to the elisions of the past may not necessarily take the form of providing a distinct (and inwardly-gazing) curriculum to children already alienated from the culture of power. Yet, there is a hint in these proposals that its proponents are aware that simply adding more and diverse perspectives to the traditional contents of the curriculum will not suffice. Structural changes in the management of school districts and buildings as well as bringing teachers into the classroom with diverse backgrounds are also being proposed. The question of how to connect the content of the curriculum to the subjectification of African-Americans (and other "others") will, nevertheless, be difficult to answer in the the face of the derisive charges of "ethnic cheerleading" on the one side and defensive "nation"-alistic retorts on the other.

The demand that the "community" be educationally self-determining exposes both a history of broken promises and the power relations woven into schooling. The history includes laws banning teaching slaves to read, the establishment of normal and manual training schools, the revocation of separate-but-equal, and the realization that desegregation did not necessarily mean the achievement of either social integration or educational quality. The power relations that get illuminated revolve around issues of local control of schooling and how community and personal identity are negotiated. Local control is part of the American educational/political folk wisdom. The vaporous quality of local control has traditionally come to light when a community seeks to deviate in some extreme way from the "normal" path of schooling regulation and/or content.[21] The appearance versus the reality of the locus of control has been deeply felt in urban communities; Chicago, for example, finally decentralized much of school regulation, but arguably only after the schools had reached physical, academic, and emotional bottom. The plans in Detroit and Milwaukee represent demands not only that parents contribute their time and energy to their children's education, but that the community's adults, its teachers and its business and political leaders, take back the schools from bureaucrats and reformers whose vantage points are too distant from the immediacy of the lives of *these particular children*.

At the same time, this reclamation of power, this call to self-determinacy, requires the specific marking of communal boundaries. Because power and sovereignty are at issue here, new practices of solidarity are called for in order to create a separate and separable identity turf for the community. These iterations of the values, histories, characteristics, and ideologies of the community provide the grounds for solidarity at the same time as they provide the ground from which insiders can negotiate, bargain, and fight against those on the outside. The comfort, material and psychical, derived from community belonging comes often at the cost of having to view identity as static and subject to tests of authenticity. And it would be a mistake to assume that the essentializing and hegemonic values of this once-oppressed community could not be repressive to individuals within it.

In the case of the Afro-centered male academies, the question of racial identity has been bound to a particular view of black manhood. The historical and sociological accounts of the "disappearing black male" and the resultant focus of the academies on a revitalized notion of the transition to manhood mean that gender difference is part of this schema. Yet the themes of male bonding and challenging peer culture woven through many of these programs do not even make a show of looking deeply at intracommunity gender relations. The mothers who protested their daughters' exclusion from these academies were silenced by charges of cooptation and betrayal. In Detroit, as in New York State, (female) gender interests were described as conflicting with racial claims.

> These [boys and girls] are children whose life chances are conditioned on the same material circumstances: the same homes, the same poverty,

the same cultural temptations and difficulties—as well as the same potential for hope. To suggest, even implicitly, that schooling as it is is healthier for girls, or that the success of girls is conditioned on the failure of boys, is unconscionable. Further, to suggest that mothers, grandmothers and other women, such as teachers, who are responsible for the raising of these children are insufficient role models for males potentially creates a schism that school cannot heal.[22]

So the problems of balancing faith and scepticism are not relieved simply by changing the contours of the group or the educational strategy.

Wedges the third and fourth

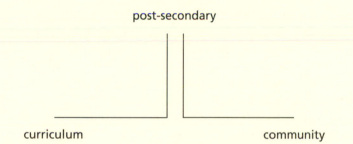

post-secondary

curriculum   community

The university has been an important site of the "culture wars."[23] Rather than rehearse the battles in truncated form, in this section I will tell two stories of things I have observed at institutions I know well and love (upon occasion). These stories are by no means complete, but they highlight the faith question at the post-secondary level. One story takes place at a Big Ten university in the Midwest (the U) and the other at a midsize Ivy League college (the C).

At the U, the curricular issues of multicultural education have been woven through departmental debates, hiring and promotion decisions, and the U's campus-wide transformation of the undergraduate general education requirement. Professors have been encouraged to consider how to add/infuse race, class, and gender into courses for undergraduates. As with many campuses, since the mid-1980s, there has been at least the perception of an increase in the number of bias-related incidents: name-calling, property defacement, personal, confrontations in person and in print, and the like. Meanwhile, as denizens of a large research university community, many faculty have taken up various positions on the barricades of the "culture wars." And, finally, the financial pinch, while not as desperate as on some campuses, has meant that state legislators, agencies, and U's administration have had to come up with plans to scale back programs and offerings. This last happenstance has tended

to force units to defend themselves and to point out the vulnerables elsewhere to anoint as sacrificial lambs.

Two highly respected professors in the humanities presented a conference
in the spring of 1993, "Higher Education in Crisis."[24] They invited scholars
from around the country, including the leadership of organizations created or
revitalized around the idea that recent events in the world of ideas and the
material world are potentially threatening to life in academe. Almost every
speaker over the three-day event invoked some notion of multiculturalism—speaking of diversity, difference, identity politics, or universalistic
humanity. Yet, the nature of the belief structure, assumptions, and anxieties
of this group seemed to be quite different from those of K–12 educators as
they talked about multicultural education.

First, the culture at stake in the battles elucidated at the conference is the
culture of the university. While the Regents in New York hold public schools
accountable for the production of citizens and the building of nations, the
university's mission, when read from these debates, is the production of
knowledge, knowledge industries, and knowledge workers. The "multi" in
multicultural education is not totally inscribed on those historically under-
represented/oppressed groups, but is expanded to encompass the ideological
identities assumed by scholars from the various camps.

The U, then, is the site of the canon wars, which intersects with, but does
not encompass the meaning of "multiculturalism." The fights over whether
first-year students at Stanford or Princeton or the University of Illinois *ought*
to read Shakespeare and Plato or Alice Walker and Sappho are virtually
meaningless when read as debates over the old or the new received wisdom
or over control over syllabi. The debates take on layers of meaning when
they are read as representations of multiculturalism rather than "the thing
itself." The debates do not constitute *the* crisis in higher education, but intersect with other manifestations of crisis: threats of lowered funding; public
suspicion of the elite/intellectual functions of the university (and of the professions); the loss of civility and sense of community in campus life as clashes
between groups and individuals become more common.

Yet, the central fallacy of the conference was the notion that the humanities
scholars in the room had captured the crisis—a fallacy that simultaneously
reinforces the idea that these rational discourses about diversity (read: intellectual turf) can change the perception of the university both from the inside
and the outside, and the idea that the bureaucrats who set the course of the U
will really be moved by these discussions so far removed from real discussion
of real power relations. (Should we, for example, raise taxes to pay higher
salaries to professors? Imagine having to explain that to constituents who
pour concrete or empty bedpans or type the professors' "divine" utterances.)
What is needed is for those who believe in the vital contributions of the U to
the world outside of the U to transform these internicine battles over the
authority of the one and the many into a battle for a legible, legitimized, and

enlivened connection between knowledge and "living well" or to abandon the battlefield.

The second parable is one about family values. When students hear about the C, they are told about the wondrous communion of the "C family." The C, for many years, had the highest percentage of its living alumni contributing to its annual giving campaign. The student body and the faculty have remained relatively small, allowing a comfortable and familiar community on campus that interacts constantly with the off-campus extended family. This has been no mere public relations metaphor, but a kind of living image that provided a special metaphysical comfort zone. There is not space here to tell the detailed story of the last twenty-five years at the C.[25] Nevertheless, the highlights include the decision in the late 1960s to increase recruitment of black male students, the decision to "return" to the C's original mission of educating Native Americans, the decisions to admit women and subsequently to open equal access.

Interestingly, coeducation was probably the most culturally disruptive phenomenon of the recent past. The fiercest struggles were between the traditionalists, who wanted the C to stay the "same" with some girls attending classes, and the progressives who felt that the C's continued academic and cultural significance relevance required systematic and systemic transformation into an educator of men and women. The former opposed equal access admissions which would (and did) lower the number of men admitted to each class as the number of women rose. The latter campaigned to change the words of the alma mater ("stand as brother stands by brother" became "stand as sister stands by brother") There was a concerted effort made on the part of the progressives to ensure that women would not be marginalized in this transformed family culture.

If the 1970s were the turbulent transition years, the early '80s were perceived as a time in which the C was in a healing mode and a time in which the traditionalists fought back by bringing a national spotlight on the trials of the C. While the attention was largely negative, it also shed some light on the paradoxes of the C family/community paradigm. There are, on the one hand, those whose belief in the C family is offended by phenomena like a Gay and Lesbian Alumni association and "the black tables" at the dining hall. (Separatism is ungrateful, at best, when practiced by minorities but thoroughly unremarkable when practiced by the football team or sorority members). There are, on the other hand, those whose wish for inclusion in the community has been stymied by stigmatizing, stereotyped, and marginalizing discourses. Both groups operate with an assumption that some version of the "community"—either restored or transmuted—can provide intellectual, social, economic, and/or moral security. Difference can, on the one hand, become insignificant within the elite—at least for those persons who are willing to accept and benefit from the (metaphoric and actual) family identity whatever the cost to their bonds to other communities and families. On the other, difference is a double-edged sword for those who both see clearly the ways in which their existence in the family is tolerated only under certain conditions and see difference as a crucible for a dynamic and radical assertion of personal identity. This last struggle matters because these students (and others) recognize that this family is a non-compulsory unit, that is, the C is quite different from pre-collegiate schools which are compelled to deal in some way with the varieties of students who are themselves compelled to attend. The students at the C may find themselves at various points struggling with choosing their battles: getting the legitimacy and power that comes with the education and degree from the C; making the institution respond to needs that either were not present or went unacknowledged in the past; engaging in their own young adult struggles to understand and accept themselves. The C family metaphor is at once the prize and the punishment. The faith in the family under the best of circumstances impels its members to continue conversations about its problems, but at its worst, in the fear of its rejection, the family becomes a bludgeon with which to compel conformity and silence.

A critical and serious examination of multicultural education at the C has the possibility to change the eternal "nature" of liberal education, the unity of the C family, and the tone of the "diversity" discourse. This examination would entail an honest evaluation of the power relations that play out in a community that relies on alumni, students, faculty, staff, and administration for its continued survival. Each of those communities is itself diverse and participates in its own rites of legitimation and authorization, and without clarifying those relations and distinguishing between them, the blind faith of the family cannot be replaced by an enlivened and participatory understanding of the C's mission and future.

Philosophers of Education—The Rescuers Down Under

As far as ends and values are concerned, the empirical material that is necessary to keep philosophy from being fantastic in content and dogmatic in form is supplied by the ends and values which are produced in educational processes as there are actually executed. What a philosophy of education can contribute is range, freedom and constructive or creative invention. [A]ny one is philosophical in the degree in which he (sic) makes a consistent effort in [the] direction [of seeing] life steadily and [wholly].[26]

[T]his imperious being, crazed by his absolute power and by the fear of losing it no longer remembers clearly that he was once a man; he takes himself for a horsewhip or a gun; he has come to believe that the domestication of the "inferior race" will come about by the conditioning of their reflexes. But in this he leaves out of account the human memory and the ineffaceable marks left upon it; and then, above all there is something which perhaps he has never known: we only become what we are by the radical and deep-seated refusal of that which others have made of us.[27]

You make a few distinctions. You clarify a few concepts. It's a living.[28]

Schooling at every level is beset with wearying, frustrating problems. At the risk of being corrected by my colleagues in the field, I would venture to say that some of those problems seem highly unlikely to be made better through the intervention of philosophers. I am willing to accept, however, that this claim may well be wrong because it is difficult to think of a problem that could not benefit from the illumination of educational ends and values. As Dewey says, those ends and values are generated in practices themselves, not simply in ideas and wishes. But philosophers of education can bring, as Morgenbesser suggests, a clarifying vision and a capacity to distinguish. We can invoke, as Sartre demonstrates, dark and ineffable powers of the will and spirit; and, we can question the costs and joys of faith in education. Philosophers, if we wish to contribute to the building as well as the contemplation of education and society, can bring a wholesome perspective and vision to the project.

Taken at face value, Morgenbesser's characterization of philosophy could be viewed as either glib or damning. On the one hand, Morgenbesser is winking at his audience: You know that we are uncovering the great mysteries here in philosophy, but since we all know that it is the great work of great men, I can afford to be clever and off-hand about it. On the other hand, those who are not in on the joke about greatness understand that, clever or not, Morgenbesser has perhaps exposed philosophy's dirty little secret. To wit, it is not brain surgery; it is not even carpentry or bread baking. If a bunch of nerds want to get in a sweat over the difference between "society" and "culture," it won't rock the world one way or the other.

Neither the self-congratulatory nor the irrelevancy reading of making distinctions and making clear should be allowed to ride, however. It is one thing to enjoy free play with one's colleagues, battling back and forth over the hotly-contested turf of Philosophy of Education. It is quite another to assume that these tussles will, in and of themselves, signify the world. Those Morgenbessian tasks can be intellectually challenging; yet that quality says nothing about whether distinguishing and clarifying will be self-reflexive or illuminating projects. As reflexivity, these tasks are the foundation of terra firma of life among those who speak the same language (at least vaguely) and are recognizable to their fellows (through a glass, darkly). It's a living, but is it a living well? As illuminating tasks, clarifying and distinguishing became situated in the realm of practice where there are multiple tongues and many peoples.

Dewey, of course, saw the organic nature of the world and of philosophy. He believed that we could overcome our bifurcating tendencies in philosophy if we developed his steady and wholesome gaze. This integrative view may seem distant from one that prizes making distinctions, but the distance is illusory because Dewey's take on bifurcation is a cautionary tale about the evils of oversimplification and lazy thinking. In *The Child and the Curriculum*,[29] he chastises both the child-centered and curriculum-centered educators. While each faction may have its own failings and salvations, both have missed the point. They have divided up the world into us and not-us. In doing so they establish neat boundaries and can feel free to spin argument after argument based on their own internal logics. This leaves both sides, Dewey posits, short on the possibility of an integrated sense of identity and position. It is not the drawing of distinctions that troubles Dewey here but the truncating of distinctions that cuts off the ability to see these two opposing arguments as part of a larger encompassing argument about the relationships, of teachers, learners, and learning—an argument with many nuances and difficulties. That larger, more textured canvas can be ignored by taking sides in a well-marked battleground.

Making (real) distinctions is a philosophical enterprise insofar as it gets beyond the simple-minded dualisms that enable the cutting off of debate rather than its continuation. One good recent example is offered by Nel Noddings in *The Challenge to Care in Schools* (1992). Leaving aside the backdrop of care, Noddings offers up a radical notion to schools: that they *genuinely* provide a place and time for the nurturance of all human capacities, not only the intellectual. While it may be true that schooling institutionally serves broad social ends, the tangible rewards in schools are given for individual academic achievement. In following Noddings's line, educators acknowledge that: we have been making distinctions between students based on a single, linear standard; therefore, there are "good" and "bad" students within that standard; challenging that single standard entails differentiating interests, dispositions, capacities in ways that may not be as easy to measure/evaluate as the acquisition of academic skills and knowledge; in bringing artful distinctions into play (ones that may pertain within one person as well as in a school population), whole new ranges of difference may come into play at the same time that the simplistic and hierarchical differentiations may break down.

I do not recall Professor Noddings getting a groundswell of support from philosophers of education when she offered a version of her argument at an annual scholarly meeting. And I shudder to think what reception she gets in audiences who genuinely believe that school improvement can be read, *tout cort,* in rising test scores and more knowledge—knowable and known. Here a philosopher suggests that parsing quadratic equations and sonnets may constitute truth and beauty for some of us, but that these activities are not all in the world that can be true and beautiful. There are many kinds of capacities and understanding that can be fostered in schools; we are tapping into a tiny fragment of human talent and interest and, at the same time, are punishing children who do not fit into that tiny corner.

In the Noddings example, her insights about certain kinds of distinctions are put in a context of her arguments about caring, vocationalism, and other matters. Whether or not one subscribes to the context, the insight itself suggests firstly that making distinctions, while it may lead to conceptual clarity, may also lead to confusion and complications in the practical realm. Secondly, it suggests that philosophical skills can interact dynamically with the realm of educational practice.

These two points can serve as a focus as we return to our central question: where, how, and from which positions may philosophers of education enter the debate over difference in the schools, a debate that has been played out most recently over multicultural education.

In the discussion of multiculturalism I suggest that the debate in its various guises could be challenged on the grounds of faith. I want to use faith as the frame for looking at snapshots of the "problems" of multicultural education.

- Faith in the power of new representations of (old) minorities groups
- Faith in the restorative value of curricular change
- Faith in rationality to increase tolerance and racial understanding
- Faith in the empowerment of localized communities
- Faith in the culture of the university to preserve
  - academic freedom
  - rationality and civility
  - the sovereignty of academe
  - the academic community as (surrogate) family

Embedded in these worlds of faith are the layers of dualisms that Dewey exposed and with which we still grapple: equity/excellence, tradition/nihilism, them/us. Educators seeking to meet the demands of the new multiculturalists face too many dualisms and not enough time. I would not suggest that philosophers can resolve the tensions of faith and scepticism but that they can enrich the texture of the debates by keeping the questions from being settled for once and for all.

Faith allows institutions and those who govern them to move forward, to articulate policy. Programmatic, curricular, and staff changes are made to respond to shifts in community perception. Now we "celebrate difference" rather than collude to eliminate it. Philosophers may respond by asking if this is not the language of surfaces, change upon occasions that require transformation in relations of power. They may point to the paradoxes and dilemmas in living well and honestly in a complex, variable, and unpredictable community that is ostensibly designed around pursuing the good for one group (students), through the labor and collaborative efforts of faculty, staff, parents, and the public. How can funding fiestas and Third World Centers and deans of multiculturalism move beyond symbolic acquiescence to newly vocal and powerful groups to transforming the world of school? Philosophers may suggest that those celebrations be used as a first step, rather than a last step, in changing the terrain of racial and ethnic discovery and identify formation. What is this thing called race? How can one hold on to a "minority" identity without capitulating to the damaging power relations that have inscribed that designation throughout living memory? How can taking on "race" encourage or provoke the non-raced (i.e., whites) to take themselves seriously as raced persons? How can difference here be used in its specificity to locate/defuse/refuse/detonate the power relations that in fact keep the schoolhouse or the campus running?

Philosophers can provoke questions about the claims about knowledge and truth that underlie the debate about multicultural education. Can the "truth" about multiculturalism be liberating? We may ask the question of how it is that "culture" and "multi," as reflections of particular notions of racial-ethnic group identity, are based upon a formal, partialized knowledge that does not yet reflect the phenomenal world of "being black," "living Jewishly," "putting on feminine drag." The common understanding of cultural identity rests on the narrowest band of categories possible so that one can be easily identifiable as "a" or "not-a," "b" and "not-b," by oneself and by others. The fixed categories of difference provide the vocabulary of the multicultural education discourse at the same time that they stifle resistance and refusal because the categories become the only language in which we can speak of ourselves. In an inversion of the Babel story, we used to know many tongues and ways of communicating but now have been reduced to one Ur-language that threatens us with its invitation to hubris.

Philosophers of education may say, "Be not afraid." We *can* understand multiple discourses, synthesize and disburse multiple phases of identity, distinguish seriously between multiple levels, essences, mirages, and experiences without going crazy or giving in the easy hierarchies and judgments. *Knowing oneself* in this context remains foundational to the philosophic project, yet rejects linear fixity and opens a panoramic, dynamic view of knowing, the knower, and what is known. Knowing oneself becomes an artful project, mixing science, history, metaphors, narrative, and experience. Multicultural education's epistemic foundations then do not have to rest on the ability of rationality to cure or kill disputes and differences. Rather, they may rest on an expansive notion of how various forms of knowledge can come into play and how they can infect the power relations and ethical understandings of the proponents and participants.

Philosophers of education, as they take up Counts's challenge to help make schools centers for building rather than contemplating society, can add positively to the case for a multicultural education. They can insist that as schools, at whatever level, contemplate curricular and structural change, they not get caught in either the additive/corrective strategy or crass political responsiveness. We may suggest that schools open up to the possibilities as well as the challenges of facing up to genuine difference—not just in race, class, and gender, but in temperaments, abilities, talents, dispositions. As that conversation unfolds, we may remember Noddings's diagnosis of moral bankruptcy in schools: We have acknowledged and accepted only one set of goals and standards for schools. When we have trouble meeting them we tinker with the means or the evaluative instruments of the ends. We could, instead, recognize that our ends are narrow, incomplete, and sometimes harmful, that our ends do not arise out of our practices and knowledge but are truncated by our paltry vision of *the* good life and *the* educated person—as well as *the* multicultural education.

Philosophers of education may themselves refuse to be locked out of these multicultural education debates, may refuse to be simply what we have been made (and what we have made ourselves): that is, silent and undisturbed. The self-referential debates must continually be aired and entered into over and over again in likely and unlikely settings. Conversations that may have seemed to have been over long ago about the ends of education can be reopened with contemporary purposes, revivified by the exposure of the lack of a fixed, final end point.

The scope of educative possibilities is reduced when the task becomes a simple matter of improving the existing mechanisms of schooling. In refusing simple reiteration and recapitulation, philosophers of education can engage the traditions of their practice in work that is critical and transformative.

> The movement by which, not without effort and uncertainty, dreams and illusions, one detaches oneself from what is accepted as true and seeks other rules—that is philosophy. The displacement and transformation of frameworks of thinking, the changing of received values and all the work that has been done to think otherwise, to do something else, to become other than what one is—that, too, is philosophy.[30]

The "multi" culture/language/vision of Philosophy of Education can potentially bring together distinction, clarity, difference, the one and the many, unifying wholesome visions, rationality, refusal, and multiple phenomenal worlds. Philosophers of education can invest the multi/cultural/education with the meaningful 'babel' of pastiche and collage that moves us beyond faith in schools as a cure to social ills to a multifaceted complex, illuminating vision of self, identity, and education that is alternately and simultaneously crystalline, opaque, and translucent.

NOTES

1. George Counts. *Dare the Schools Build a New Social Order?* (Carbondale, Illinois: Southern Illinois University Press, 1932), 3.
2. Ibid., 37 (my italics).

3. RICO statutes are meant to eliminate racketeering and criminal conspiracy. While the laws were passed to deal with organized crime, in recent years they have been used to pursue inside traders in the financial world as well as anti-abortion activists in their violent and non-violent obstructions of medical facilities and personnel.

4. Jean Paul Sartre, Preface to *The Wretched of the Earth,* by Franz Fanon. Translated by Constance Farrington. (New York: Grove Press, 1963), 22.

5. Christine E. Sleeter and Carl A. Grant, "An Analysis of Multicultural Education in the United States" in *Facing Racism In Education.* Nitza Hildalgo, Cesar McDowell, and Emilie Siddle, eds. (Cambridge: Harvard Educational Review, 1990), 153.

6. Note the bizarre non-parallelism here. It is not "Blacks, women, and Jews" or "slavery, first and second wave Feminism and the Holocaust," but a mixture of persons and movements. Also, ironically, in the early 1970s the state legislature had already passed a law requiring the teaching of "Black History." They probably forgot because of the effects of such a high rate of compliance.

7. New York State Regents Executive Summary. *Report of Social Studies Syllabus Review and Development Committee.* Executive Summary, June 13, 1991.

8. Ibid.

9. Economic and social class is covered in a section of the Report on Economic and Social Justice (21) in which the systemic and institutional imbalances of power and resources are supplanted by a more personal probing of how students themselves might address issues of fairness and equity in their own lives.

10. While there have been struggles between feminists and race activists, this account of how gender got left behind seems to suggest the zero-sum nature of the game here, promote escalations of those tensions and disagreements, and make women of color as well as others "choose" *one and only one* identity. Further, the idea that feminists hold enough power to control the discourse—as opposed to the power held by traditional forces of hegemony—casts the feminists as the villain(esses) staved off by the benevolent and protective father (who of course has only the best interests of the weak and defenseless Negroes [i.e., children] at heart).

11. Ibid., Kenneth T. Jackson, A Dissenting Comment, 80.

12. Ibid., Arthur Schlesinger, Jr., A Dissenting Opinion, 89.

13. Michael Berubé points directly to this failing in Schlesinger's longer work (*The Disuniting of America*) in his insightful and incisive piece "Disuniting America Again." In *The Journal of the Midwest Modern Language Association,* vol. 26. n.1 (Spring, 1993), 34–35.

14. I suggest some of the pitfalls to the articulation of a static identity even as a strategic position in the "Pragmatics and Politics of Difference," in *The Journal of the Midwest Modern Language Association,* vol. 26. n.1 (Spring, 1993), 58–74.

15. Report, 67.

16. Carole Ascher, School Programs for African American Male Students. ERIC Clearinghouse on Urban Education (May, 1991), Appendix.

17. Jennifer Hochschild, *Thirty Years After Brown,* (Washington, DC: Joint Center for Political Studies, 1985).

18. Ascher, 14.

19. Milwaukee Public Schools, African American Male Task Force, *Educating African American Males: A Dream Deferred* (May 1990).

20. Michel Marriott, Afrocentrism: Balancing or Skewing History? *New York Times,* 11 August 1991, p. A18.

21. See *Wisconsin v. Yoder,* 406 U.S. 205 (1972).

22. Kal Alston, "Community Politics and the Education of African American Males: Whose Life Is It Anyway?" In *The Politics of Education Association Yearbook: The New Politics of Race and Gender,* edited by Philip Zodhiates and Catherine Marshall (1993).

23. See Roger Kimball, Dinesh D'Souza, Diane Ravitch, Nathan Glazer, Gerald Graff, Arthur Schlesinger, Stephen Greenblatt. See *The New Republic, The Nation, The National Review,* and *The Chronicle of Higher Education.*

24. I want to thank them for doing all the work needed to arrange such a conference, and I want to make it clear that despite my criticisms (some of which I was invited to share at the closing session), I have the highest regard for these colleagues and respectful appreciation for their efforts. The criticisms elaborated briefly below are aimed less at this conference in particular than at a generally troubling discourse.

25. Of course, someone ought to do so, to counter both sentimentalized reminiscences and the baroque distortions fostered by Dinesh D'Souza 1981 and Charles Sykes in *Illiberal Education* and *The Hollow Men,* respectively.

26. John Dewey, *The Sources of a Science of Education,* 58.

27. Sartre, Preface, 14.

28. Sidney Morgenbesser, when asked his definition of philosophy, as quoted by Gerald Dworkin in "Sticks and Stones: Some Reflections on Campus Speech" in *Report of the Program for the Study of Cultural Values and Ethics,* 3 (November 1991, 15–20).

29. John Dewey, *Child and the Curriculum/School and Society,* (Chicago: University of Chicago Press, 1908).

30. Michel Foucault, "The Masked Philosopher," interview by Christian Delacampagne (Paris, 6–7 April 1980) in *Michel Foucault: Politics, Philosophy, Culture.* 330.

22

Postmodern Dilemmas

Svi Shapiro

Kal Alston's call for a Philosophy of Education that can challenge the grounds of faith in the discussions about multiculturalism is a compelling demand. She is right, I believe, in pursuing such challenges not only to expose the cogency and practical effectiveness of these "worlds of faith" but because they might facilitate a more genuinely transformative process of educational change. Such challenges might enable us, as she notes, to locate and destroy the power relations that suffuse school and campus. Or they might open up the possibility of a more deeply searching interrogation of hierarchy and differentiation as they are embedded in the schooling process. And with that a recognition of the pathetically narrow vision of human purposes instantiated in our curriculum. Or they might lead us to work out ways of validating human differences in life-affirming and generative forms without, as she says, "capitulating to the damaging power relations that have inscribed that designation throughout living memory."

What I want to do in this brief commentary is to pick up and continue this examination of our grounds of educational faith; to expose the assumptions and meta-level commitments that structure our arguments as philosophers and theorists of education, especially in those cases where these commitments are to a more just, equitable, and compassionate social order. I am especially interested in those "layers of dualisms" (as Alston refers to them) that are always insinuated into our narratives and that, whether explicitly or implicitly, we are inevitably forced to grapple within. While I am attempting to tease out some of the dualisms from Alston's own text, this is in no sense to be understood as a "picking apart" of a colleague's work. The dualisms, paradoxes, and ambiguities detected in this text *belong to us all.* In all of their uncertainty and contradictoriness they are the unavoidable epistemic foundations of critical intellectual work at this historical moment.

Moral Commitment or Discursive Closure: A Postmodern Dilemma

In a curious way postmodern theorizing has made possible a continuation of that very characteristic intellectual propensity for moral and political ambivalence. This is quite apparent in Alston's essay which is simultaneously both politically liberal and ethically postmodern in its scepticism towards those who would prefer "simple-minded dualisms that enable cutting off debate rather than its continuation"; or who are ready to ignore the "larger, more textured canvas" by "taking sides in a well-marked battleground." Of course liberalism and postmodernism arrive at this hesitation towards taking sides through quite different routes. The former preaches the desirability of impartiality and value-neutrality in the search for truth. It emphasizes reasoned debate and the quest for intellectual clarity unsullied by the bias of vested opinions or ideological commitment. Postmodernism, on the other hand, arrives at its disdain for ideological commitment through a deep pessimism that what we have to say can be anything but narratives dressed-up as truth. Some of its most noted proponents have held that the most influential of these in our historical epoch—the "grand metanarratives" have brought little but disaster to the human condition. They have little advanced human freedom, justice, or autonomy. So we must be extraordinarily wary about any whole-hearted stake in a particular set of moral principles or political and social visions. These, it is argued, represent not much more than a consoling saga for a world bereft of rationality or meaning—becoming little more than a club to beat those who would desist from their "truth" or accuracy. The writer's admonition against the taking of sides seems at times to issue from a well-ingrained liberal conscience in which open-ended debate must at all times be preserved, and, elsewhere, from a postmodern scepticism towards the possibilities of knowing the truth of anything. Paradoxically Alston is also a passionate believer in democratic values and the importance of validating human and cultural diversity. Somehow, (in ways not made clear) a deep commitment to the struggle for social change must be reconciled with a worldview that shrinks from a passionate taking of sides. Certainly there is a sense here in which the passionate quest for social transformation inevitably contains the impulse towards intolerant discursive closure, an epistemological absolutism, and an ideological agenda incompatible with a philosophy that values reason. Is it unfair to ask the real Professor Alston to stand up? Of course the task here is not a psychological inquisition into one individual's apparent intellectual inconsistencies. Nor is it to expose, in that time-honored ritual of academic life, the apparent flaws of a colleague's scholarship. Much more valuable, I think, is the way such conflicts, inconsistencies, or contradictions point to the deeper fault lines of our common intellectual and cultural life; fault lines which mark the tension-filled ground of ideas, beliefs and values upon which we *all* stand. In this sense the contradictions between the call for a socially transformative educational agenda, and, at the same time, warnings to stay clear of intellectual partiality begin to make more sense. Here, simply, is the wretched dilemma forced upon us as part of the condition of postmodernity. It is a state of intellectual and moral schizophrenia so cogently captured by the liberation theologian Sharon Welch in what she calls the dual contemporary imperatives of acting with "infinite suspicion and absolute commitment."[1] Welch's dilemma is arrived at in full recognition of the horrors of our world. While a third or more of humankind lives in unspeakable misery, when forty thousand children die every day of malnutrition and for want of basic medicines, are we to be temperate and open-ended in our commitments? Should we really make our arguments so that, God forbid, we do not close off the continuing debate? In the face of the appalling hunger, sickness and brutality that fills the world is not a militant partiality called for? Must we not display in all of our work an absolute and uncompromising commitment to what Michael Lerner calls *Tikkun Olam*—the repair of the world?

Yet our anguish is in the fact that as intellectuals, at least, we are now more the children of Foucault than Marx. Under the influence of Foucault we have been forced to face the full consequences of a world where our ethical and political commitments have been brutally cut loose from all claims to be anchored in some Archimedean point of knowing. For Foucault what determines "truth" is nothing but a preference about who we wish to stand with in struggle—whose side are we on socially, politically, and morally. All the "isms" of the modern epoch arrogate to themselves, more particularly to intellectuals who represent and live by them, the capacity to find what is true and real. Their premises are always one of epistemological certainty. In each there is the apparently clear distinction between truth and error, science and ideology. Each offers the promise of accurately and correctly knowing the nature of things. But from Foucault's point of view all that we ever get, whether or not something is declared as true, is a language and perspective that offers itself up as truth. If one discourse or language is given more value than another this is not because of its intrinsic character or "truth", but because of the way this particular version of reality organizes our perceptions and understanding of the world. And every such version of reality is tied in with the exercise of power by one group or another. Foucault's work brings us clearly to what Welch describes as the inevitable epistemological nihilism of the twentieth century. The events of this century, she asserts, "Make it impossible to honestly assert with any assurance the likelihood of certain knowledge."[2] There is no ultimate reference point for truth outside of a history that might make it become true. In a world where brutalities, injustice, and degradation demand resolute and determined human response there is the paradox of increasing uncertainty about what we know, and the ethical and political commitments that are consequent on this knowledge. If knowledge is always dependent on human interests who are we to believe? And on what basis can we act? A deep—indeed infinite—suspicion must settle over all our choices.

The Body in Revolt: Towards a Language of the Sensual

Of course such deep scepticism about how we know and understand our world has devastating consequences for something as epistemologically fragile as the categories that structure our notions of culture. The very delineation of identity, history, and geography are quickly thrown into a quicksand of shifting, and unsecured judgements. Indeed the imperative for an appreciation of cultural diversity and the recognition of hitherto invisible cultures is the consequence of the breakup of universal assumptions about knowledge, rationality, and values. Paradoxically it too is threatened by the relentless postmodern deconstruction of categories and identities. Alston's comments are very relevant here: "Multicultural education's epistemic foundations . . . do not have to rest on the ability of rationality to cure or kill disputes and differences." More accurately, I think, a postmodern world view has exploded the capacity of rationality to make sense of cultural identity at all. Certainly rationality is no match for the raging, existentially hungry, desirous being that now seeks to find a home in this world of such widespread banishment and exile. The insurgent forces of "identity politics" around the globe is powered by the body in revolt. A fact which, at the very least, challenges the adequacy of so much philosophical inquiry or intellectual analysis. To attempt to encounter this "body/subject" means reaching out to a language of the aesthetic which for many is both an uncomfortable and an unfamiliar terrain. Here the aesthetic refers to a discourse of the body which encompasses what Terry Eagleton has described as the whole region of human perception and sensation. Eagleton makes clear, in no uncertain terms philosophy's long exclusion of the sensate, of the body:[3]

> The distinction which the term "aesthetic" initially enforces in the mid-eighteenth century is not one between "art" and "life", but between material and immaterial: between things and thoughts, sensations and ideas, that which is bound up with your creaturely life as opposed to that which conducts some shadowy existence in the recesses of the mind. It is as though philosophy suddenly wakes up to the fact that

there is a dense, swarming territory beyond its own mental enclave which threatens to fall utterly outside its sway. That territory is nothing less than the whole of sensate life together—the business of affections and aversions, of how the world strikes the body on its sensory surfaces, of that which takes root in the gaze and the guts and all that arises from our most banal, biological insertion into the world. The aesthetic concerns this most gross and palpable dimension of the human, which post-Cartesian philosophy, in some curious lapse of attention, has somehow managed to overlook. It is thus the first stirrings of a primitive materialism—of the body's long inarticulate rebellion against the tyranny of the theoretical.

(Perhaps all this is more aptly summarized by the novelist Milan Kundera who notes that "*I think therefore I am* is the statement of an intellectual who underrates toothaches."[4]) Eagleton's comments are echoed by Sherry Taylor who has described the works of feminist writers who have attempted to "write the body."[5] This means, she says, including the knowledge of the body in the language of the mind. It means rejecting "fleshless" language and insists upon putting the feeling, breathing, living bodies of women back into language. She quotes Margerite Duras:

> "The capacity on which men judge intelligence is still the capacity to theorize. It has been under attack for centuries. It ought to be crushed by now, it should loose itself in a reawakening of the senses, blind itself and be still."[6]

Duras' anger, says Taylor, is directed towards the continuing use of the "old ways of theorizing"—ones that distance and objectify, and in which other forms of knowing are suffocated. These older ways of theorizing and knowing are structured preeminently by "seeing" not by feeling or by touch. Taylor notes that the "body subject" in rational discourse has suffered the effects of alienation in its denial of sensual existence and concrete social experience and it has truncated the knowledge of human experience in the separation of objective and subjective worlds. Few can have described this better than Andrea Dworkin who contends that it is the skin which "bears the content of our lives."[7]

> Everytime the skin is touched, one feels. All feeling passes through it, outside to inside . . . The skin is our human mask; it is what one can touch of another person, what one sees, how one is seen . . . It is both identity and sex. . . . What one is and what one feels in the realm of the sensual, being and passion, where the self meets the world—intercourse being, ultimately, the self in the act of meeting the world.

We will have to confront the often pathetic inadequacy of so much of our philosophical knowing and theorizing if we are to take seriously the region of sensual being and embodied existence. Certainly the world of the "multicul-tural" is little if it is not the terrain of resistance in bodily forms, the enfleshed expression of human marginality, indignity, and suffering. It is the space within which one may encounter the body's sometimes inarticulate rebellion against how one lives in the world. It is a place of gnawing desire, frequent pain, and occasional ecstacy; of touch, movement, feeling, and of death. Can our present philosophical discourse encounter life in this way?

This inadequacy of our present language is, too, echoed in the engagement with the question of identity. Alston here, also acknowledges an approach to knowing which crosses into less familiar discursive terrain: "Knowing oneself . . . remains foundational to the philosophical project." And such knowledge rests on an "expansive notion of how various forms of knowledge can come into play [that] . . . mixes science, history, metaphor, narrative, and experi-ence." Yet something more is required here also. In the attempt to sweep away all vestiges of essentialism in understanding the self (with its implica-tions of fixity in human nature), the conscious, intentional nature of human subjectivity has been derided or denied. The influential post-structural view is one in which the self is viewed as a fiction. Instead what exists is what Suzanne Moore has called a kind of cultural autism where the individual is emptied of any subjective center.[8] Human subjectivity becomes nothing more than a series of social positions which together form a devastatingly contra-dictory and wholly elusive notion of the self. Such a view fails to speak to the existential quality of human experience and choices. It leaves us without responsibility, conscience or hope. It fails to capture the quality of becoming as women and men project themselves forward in order to address the incompleteness of their existence, struggle for greater freedom or an expan-sion of justice in the world. It is a view of the self which seems to reflect and reinforce the separation of intellectual life from politics, of academic theory from the flesh and blood world of commitment, sacrifice, and struggle. If we are to have a meaningful discourse concerning multicultural education we must have a language that addresses in resonant terms human identity in all of its dimensions; that can speak to our embodied lives, and the passionate nature of human agency as it seeks recognition, dignity, and justice.

Transcending the Legacy of Rational Knowing

In realizing this possibility we will have to, also, break out of the debilitating legacy of rational knowing even in its critical, postmodern versions. The lat-ter's power to critically deconstruct knowledge and epistemological categories is, sadly, in inverse proportion to its capacity to generate an affirmative vision of human possibility—one that is surely crucial when we talk of the need for social change in the direction of more just social relations and an inclusive vision of cultural experience. It is perhaps worth noting here that the language of the political Right is effective precisely because of its capacity to mobilize popular support around moral claims. However disingenuously, it expresses criticism and resistance to the oppressive effects of society while unabashedly advancing its moral, cultural, and political vision of how the world needs to be. It offers more than the language of critique: it paints a powerfully resonant image of the future (which in the conservative case is, not surprisingly, evocative of the mythological past). As Stuart Hall, Cornel West, and others have pointed out, it is precisely in regard to this future image that the Left has failed so badly in recent times. Unlike the Right, the Left has either withdrawn from, or been unable to construct, the kind of moral vision which is capable of mobilizing a collective will and political agency in favor of emancipatory and radically democratic social change. Yet in developing this language the Left has suffered from the effects of their own successes as relentless deconstructors of transcendent truth claims and metaphysical narratives. The very stuff that constitutes compelling visions of change and transformation are blasted by our own critical philosophical discourse. Simply put, and to return to Sharon Welch's succinct formulation, how can we join our infinite cultural suspicions to an absolute moral commitment? How is it possible to constitute a moral and human vision in a language of universal and unconditional conviction—surely the necessary discursive form for a politics of struggle and hope—within an intellectual framework whose immanent logic compels us to see all such claims as contingent or arbitrary. Here, of course, critical thought's long marriage to modernism with its narratives that are so determinedly rationalistic and secular has brought knowledge and understandings that are resolutely distanced from issues of religious faith, and transcendent beliefs. It has discounted the centrality of such concerns to the life-worlds and energies of many people, and places itself at odds with many of the most powerful and moving discourses of freedom and resistance in the contemporary world. One thinks, for example, of the African-American struggle in the United States and its inextricable relation to the Black church and the vision of the social gospel. Or of the power of liberation theologies among the revolutionary movements of Central and South America. But to accept and include such discourse in its own language of transformation and change means to shed any remaining illusion about our capacity to describe the world as it really is, rather than in metaphors that offer resonant and evocative images concerning human existence and possibilities. To include the spiritual and the religious in our language of social or educational change is to acknowledge that political struggle is not so much about "truth" but about how we and others can image or re-image the world. It is about the way we can envision human possibility, identity and a meaningful life. While we have come to more clearly see the mass psychic impoverishment that is so pervasive in our culture, what is emphasized by intellectuals is often little more than the possibility of an endless transgression of cultural limits and the proliferation of differences among people. Yet for many people this "postmodern bazaar" is repulsive and terrifying. It is part of the problem not the solution. It offers little that validates tradition, that speaks of love, that connects human lives across time and space. And it says little about what might transcend the particular, the local and the contingent and be able to speak to the whole human condition. When we move from the analysis of education to the crucial question of how progressive change can and might be effective we begin to recognize the importance of what philosophy is so often scornful of—narrative, myth, and imagery. It is precisely through these—not the rational or analytic forms of knowing—that human beings are impelled towards the project of social transformation and cultural change. Stuart Hall has expressed this well. He notes:

> images are not trivial things. In and through images, fundamental political questions are being posed and argued through . . . The future has to be imagined . . . "imaged". . . . People make identifications symbolically through social imagery, in their political imaginations. They "see themselves" as one sort of person or another. They "imagine" their future within this scenario or that.

Becoming Public Intellectuals: Difficulties and Dangers

In this encounter with the question of images and the construction of a resonant vision for change one of the central concerns raised by Alston must be confronted—the triviality or otherwise of intellectual and philosophical work. Alston is right and honest to express her own disquiet around this issue. Does what we do have any meaning or significance beyond our ability to impress fellow intellectuals with our words, or the ability of our scholarship to display a lethal ingenuity vis-a-vis our fellow academics. Her own considerable ambivalence on this score is surely related to the question of our willingness or competence to be what Russell Jacoby calls "public intellectuals."[9] To be a public intellectual means to define the value of our work primarily in terms of its success at contributing to the formation and sway of public discourse and dialogue that has implications for public policy and social change. That so much of our work falls very far short of coming within that orbit must be confronted in an honest way. We must confront our own considerable stake in remaining within a narrow and esoteric realm of language. It is a stake dug deep in the ground of fear, egotism, and denial. There is, for one, the possibility of committing ourselves visibly to political or ethical positions which may run counter to our own career aspirations, or that may place in jeopardy our professional aspirations. There is, too, the possibility of forsaking the rewards of academic acceptance or celebrity by writing in the "wrong" places and in the "wrong" style. To confront the question of the triviality of our work means to fully acknowledge the increasing withdrawal of the university from any kind of a role as an institution committed to challenging or disturbing the fundamental premises of our public life, cultural values, and economic and political relations. A fact painfully obvious in the bureaucratic merger of public universities with their state's department of education or public instruction. Even when we appear to be acting in serious opposition to the dominant culture we must question whether our positions really are that threating to the practices, theories, and interests that hold sway. In this regard the recent embrace of multicultural goals within education may be something much less than a critical or transformative act. David Rieff has recently argued that far from being a radical threat to the hegemonic culture, multiculturalism's "silent partner" is the newly globalized consumer capitalism.

> The reality is that no serious player in the business world has anything but the most vestigial or sentimental interest in Western civilization as it is roughly understood by campus radicals and conservatives alike. What each side's argument fails to take into account is that capitalism is the "bull in the china shop" of human history. The market economy, now global in scale is by its nature corrosive of all established hierarchies and certainties up to and including—in a world now more than fifty percent non-White and in which the most promising markets lie in Asia—White racism and male domination. If any group has embraced the rallying cry "Hey, Hey ho, ho, Western culture's got to go," it is the world business elite. . . . Eurocentrism makes no *economic* sense in a world where within twenty-five years, the combined gross national product of East Asia will likely be larger than Europe's and twice that of the United States. In such a world, the notion of the primacy of Western Culture will only be an impediment to the chief goal of every company "the maximization of profits."[10]

Far from being a threat to the social order, argues Rieff, multiculturalism is driven, in the first place, by big business which has decreasing use for nation states and national boundaries. Financial and industrial capitalism are now multicultured and global in their operations bringing about a "multiculturalism of the market" not a "multiculturalism of justice." The collapse of borders, says Rieff, has turned out to be very far from the liberating event envisaged by academic multiculturalists.

Despite the very real dangers of intellectual incorporation described by Rieff, the meaningfulness of our work is only made possible where we are impelled by a clear moral and political commitment to relieve unnecessary human suffering and to advance the possibilities of a radically more democratic culture. As intellectuals we will have to pursue these goals in ways that may be described as whole-hearted and half-sure. That is to say, impelled with passionate conviction as well as by a critical suspicion towards all of our ideas and beliefs. This will mean, in the first place, that our work will unashamedly express what David Purpel calls a prophetic voice that would affirm the vision and possibility of a world constructed around the values of love, justice, peace, community, and joy.[11] Nothing short of this is capable of meeting and confronting the obfuscating moral discourse of the Right or of resisting and exposing the social purposes of the pervasive educational language of technique and instrumental rationality. It will mean working to offer a human vision that is able to construct out of a whole range of subjects and subjectivities, a collective will—what Gramsci called a "popular bloc," that sees itself similarly oppressed or thwarted from realizing a life of happiness and fullness. The emphasis here is on inclusivity *and* the widest possible affirmation of diverse subcultures and human experience.

Yet within this context of vision and affirmation we will also have to recognize and attempt to clarify the difficult tensions and ambiguities of our radical democratic project. (In that context it is worth noting that in the attempt to provide both theoretical clarification *and* to display a fiercely partisan position vis-à-vis political and moral struggle is not to play mutually exclusive roles, but represents the symbiotic characteristic of a committed intellectual life). Among such tensions the preoccupation with questions of cultural "difference" can reduce politics to the clamor of a warring tribalism. Far from a deeply communal or inclusive vision it may (and frequently does) produce a world balkenized into the endless proliferation of claims among those who assert a monopoly on oppression and victimization. Such oppression becomes a jealously guarded experience about which no one outside of its particular domain ought speak. The concern here is not to disregard "differences." The world, as we know too well, has been hideously deformed by the way whole groups of human beings have been silenced and made invisible through the power of other peoples discourses. Yet the validation of these disregarded voices is a necessary though insufficient condition for democratically-directed change. It too easily becomes a politics that divides and excludes people. It becomes a holier-than-thou sectarianism, very far from the image of a world in which we can all see ourselves as valued and loved. And while we emphasize irreducible differences and distinctions, the Right and the religious fundamentalists will bludgeon us into a "recognition" of our "common" heritage, tradition, and values. Despite the important and liberating assertion of multiple identities in modern (or postmodern) society, and the complexity of demands, claims, and needs that are consequent on them, we should not imagine that this lessens the significance of a morally and spiritually-rooted vision of global community as the leitmotif in the struggle for democratic change and renewal. The quest for an overcoming of social fragmentation and human separation must go hand in hand with the recognition and validation of cultural particularity. Similarly the world we have entered makes it harder to clearly identify some kind of "natural" Left constituency. Who are we to see as the victims of oppression and who the perpetrators? Who will respond with enthusiasm for an alternative educational discourse and agenda that concerns itself with issues of social justice and democracy. The shifting more fluid nature of identity in today's culture, and the multiple forms of suffering, indignity, and deprivation felt by human beings in the world makes the ground on which we struggle to banish or mitigate oppression a slippery surface which refuses any secure point from which we might situate ourselves, and understand who we are in relation to those around us. We slide quickly from roles where we exploit and dehumanize others to those where we ourselves are the objects of others exploitative attitudes and practices. There is no single axis around which all relationships of power and domination, struggle and resistance are plotted. There are instead a multiplicity of fields in which human beings struggle for freedom, justice, dignity, and a fuller realization of their lives. These fields overlap and cut across one another producing a complex social map of human aspirations and struggles. Such struggles have their own dynamic, character and set of possibilities. Families, schools, religious communities, neighborhoods, work places, cultural institutions, state institutions, sustain and focus deep, sometimes explosive, tensions. While such tensions are fueled by the unrealized aspirations and disappointed hopes generated from within the culture, they cannot easily be assimilated to one another, or reduced to one overarching problem that if resolved would herald a utopian transformation of the world. One that solves, at a single stroke, all our problems and concerns. Relinquishing such an apocalyptic tale of revolutionary change may be disappointing to those who hunger for the simple, the universal, and the either/or explanation of events. Yet nor should it diminish our sense of radical possibility and the hope of human transformation and social change. We have been relieved from the old Left fixation on finding the historically 'privileged' agent of social change, or the one real focus for radical struggle. Instead we can now open our eyes and see a world replete with human aspirations for fulfillment, plenitude, dignity, justice, compassion, love, and spiritual significance, and the multiple struggles to realize such possibilities, if only in a limited way, in the worlds we have inherited.

NOTES

1. Sharon Welch, *Communities of Resistance and Solidarity* (New York: Orbis, 1985).

2. Ibid., p. 14.

3. Terry Eagleton, *The Ideology of the Aesthetic* (Cambridge: Basil Blackwell, 1990), p. 13.

4. Milan Kundera, *Immortality* (New York: Harper Collins, 1992) p. 200.

5. Sherry Taylor, "Skinned Alive: Towards a Postmodern Pedagogy of the Body." in *Education and Society* 9(1) (1991). pp. 61–72.

6. Margerite Duras in Marks, E. and de Courtivron, I. (eds). *New French Feminisms,* (New York: Shocken Books, 181).

7. Andrea Dworkin, *Intercourse* (London: Arrow Books, 1988), pp. 25–26.

8. Suzanne Moore, "Gender, Postmodern Style," in *Marxism Today* (May, 1990).

9. Russell Jacoby, *The Last Intellectuals* (New York: Basic Book, 1987).

10. David Rieff, "Multiculturalism's Silent Partner" in *Harper's* (August 1993) pp. 62–72.

11. David Purpel, *The Moral and Spiritual Crisis of Education* (Westport CT: Greenwood, 1988).

23

Toward an Ecological Perspective

C. A. Bowers

Richard Rorty's description of the role of the philosopher in a "post Philosophical culture" seems to open the door to a field of inquiry that was becoming increasingly irrelevant to everybody except other philosophers. Foreshadowing what would later become a full blown epistemological/ideological position suited to meeting the contingencies faced by "ironist individuals" all over the world, Rorty re-defines in his 1982 collection of essays, *Consequences of Pragmatism,* the responsibilities of philosophers. Philosophers must no longer concern themselves with Truth or any other expression of a universal; nor should they adopt the position of going beyond the explanation of how "things hang together" by laying out a rational framework that can be used to justify how "things *must* hang together." The new role of philosopher in the post-philosophical culture would be that of the "all purpose intellectual," the "name dropper . . . who uses names . . . to refer to sets of descriptions, symbol systems, ways of seeing" (1982, pp. xxxix-xl). With so many promises of modernism now being contradicted by recent events, Rorty's vision of the philosopher as an ironist individual who demystifies the authority of all cultural patterns may appear as the model that educational theorists should adopt. But as Rorty himself retains key aspects of modern consciousness in his own thinking—namely, the assumption that change resulting from the ongoing relativizing of accepted beliefs is progressive, and the anthropocentric view of the world—I would argue that adapting his approach to the broad domain of education would further exacerbate the crisis that extends beyond modernism, and now confronts all forms of life on the planet (Bowers 1993).

While liberation from cultural patterns that "hang together" in ways that are socially and environmentally problematic is one of the most essential challenges we face, there is also the challenge of re-orientating cultural practices in a manner where what has proven ecologically sustainable is valued over what is new, experimental, and unproven. In effect, Rorty's approach, as well as that of educational theorists who see the challenge of modernism in terms of fostering a form of individuality identical to Rorty's ironist individual, addresses only one aspect of the crisis. If educational theorists do not address other aspects of the crisis, including the need for a worldwide recognition that Aldo Leopold's land ethic (or their own cultural version of it) is a universal that cannot be violated over the long term without leading to disastrous breakdowns in the sustaining capacities of natural systems, their well-intended efforts will further strengthen the modern patterns of consciousness that increasingly appear as ecologically unsustainable. Understanding the other challenges facing educational theorists is thus contingent upon a radical reframing of how the crisis of the environment is to be understood.

Except for people who are attempting to deal with specific environmental problems, like a toxic spill from a Maquiladora plant in Matamoras or the near total collapse of the cod fishery off Newfoundland, most North Americans learn about the extent of the ecological crisis through television, newspapers, and the vast literature published by environmental groups. The crisis is represented in the form of information such as: data on the amount of greenhouse gases released by a particular country or worldwide, number of children deformed by toxins released by a local industrial plant, number of species put at risk by destruction of primal forests. In addition, the information is usually framed in terms of steps that must be taken to protect the environment as a natural resource, such as enacting new laws and developing more efficient technologies. When represented as deleterious changes that are occurring in natural systems, it is difficult to recognize the implications that environmental abuse has for educational philosophers—beyond their personal attempts to live a life that minimizes the unnecessary use of nonrenewable resources.

But when framed in terms of what the ecological crisis really is, namely, a worldwide crisis that challenges the foundational beliefs of every cultural group, the range of issues needing to be addressed by educational philosophers becomes nearly overwhelming. In suggesting that educational philosophers have a responsibility for addressing a wide range of exceedingly complex issues I am fully aware of their dismal failure over the last decades to influence either educational policies or classroom practices, and that leading educational philosophers continue to exclude the human/habitat relationship from their formulations of how individual emancipation is to be understood (Bowers 1991, 1993). My task is to identify the areas that need to be addressed by genuinely radical thinkers who understand how the educational process and "individual" intelligence are deeply affected by the multiple ways a culture reproduces its symbolic foundations, the ideological roots of modernity, and that the human/culture relationship is part of a larger set of ecosystems. Given the fact that the parent field of philosophy has not awakened fully to the constitutive role that culture plays in shaping the epistemological orientation of philosophers, not to mention its near total silence on the ecological crisis, the above expectations for educational philosophers may seem unrealistic indeed. But I suspect the blurring of genres that now characterizes much of the insightful thinking within the field of education, including the editor's expectations for this book, may be a sign that a new type of educational theorist is emerging. Indeed, recent declarations by leading philosophers that the whole enterprise was wrongly conceived in the first place and is now moribund, might serve as an impetus for dropping the burden of being labelled an educational philosopher. This, however, is an issue that needs to be taken up in other forums. While I shall continue to refer to the responsibilities of the educational philosopher (mostly out of deference for the book's editor) I am really addressing the possibilities of a radically different way of thinking about educational issues.

Understanding the alarming imbalance between growing human demands and the declining viability of natural systems as basically a cultural problem helps to illuminate a range of issues that have direct implications for how the next generation of modern youth are to be educated. In order to put the issues in focus I would like to suggest two other ways of framing the nature of the ecological crisis that go beyond the information approach to changes at the micro and macro level of ecosystems. The crisis can be understood, firstly, as undermining the self-legitimating claims that have fused the Western approach to modernization with an ontological view of progress that supposedly transcends all cultural orientations. The paradox of progress (modernization) putting ecosystems increasingly at risk (e.g. influence of consumer-oriented cultures on the carbon cycle and the amount of toxins spread across the Earth's surface) suggests a second way of framing educational issues that will require an even greater ability to think against the grain of current orthodoxies. The critical question in this domain of inquiry is: What cultural patterns are ecologically sustainable over the long term? In the remainder of this essay I will lay out the issues that need to be addressed by educational theorists in each of the three ways of framing the human/environment relationship.

Framing the Ecological Crisis in Terms of Information

Information about the condition of natural systems is now an inescapable aspect of the educational experience of students who watch the television, read newspapers, and participate in class discussions in certain social science areas and most areas of the sciences. The authority of the medium of communication, however, is part of the message—including the visibility of experts who give legitimacy to the information. Computers are often a key aspect of this growing subculture of information. But at an even more basic level, what students are really learning about are the changes in the relationships that make up an ecosystem. The relationships are, in effect, being mathematized, translated into the language used for communicating information, and communicated to an anonymous public on the assumption that information is the basis of individual thought and action. In effect, the way of understanding and communicating about changes in life sustaining systems reflects an epistemological orientation that is both culturally and historically specific. As this epistemological/cultural orientation influences how students understand the most basic relationships between themselves, the environment, and their long term prospects, it would seem a legitimate area of critical concern for educational theorists. Here the challenge is to clarify how "things hang together"; that is, how does the scientific mode of inquiry reproduce the Cartesian epistemology that underlies other areas of modern cultural practice? Does the computer also amplify a cultural epistemology and ideology, and are they part of the solution to the problem of long term sustainability or part of the problem? What are the silences in the scientific/computer-based discourse, and can they be addressed in a way that allows the data on the condition of the environment still to be taken seriously in a way that allows the data to be understood as a symptom of deeper cultural patterns? Noel Gough's observation (1992) that the report of the World Commission on Environment and Development, *Our Common Future,* is "riddled with modernist assumptions emphasizing order, accountability, systematisation, rationalisation, expertise, specialisation, linear development and control" serves as an example of how information cannot be separated from the cultural reproduction process.

The well-intended efforts of scientists and others concerned with changes in the Earth's ecosystems need to be put into perspective by theorists who understand the political, economic, moral, and epistemological aspects of the human/habitat relationship now being packaged as "objective information." And these interpretative frameworks need to be understood as rooted in the deep symbolic foundations (metanarrative level) of a cultural tradition. The "symbol systems, ways of seeing," to recall Rorty's phrase, do not exist free of their originating cultural base, but instead represent a form of discourse that privileges certain interests over others. That is, they involve the exercise of power over the fundamental issue of whose way of knowing and being is to prevail, and thus are part of intercultural politics that needs to be addressed in a more honest manner. Within this domain of educational inquiry and demystification, Rorty's vision of the new breed of theorist seems to make sense. But when we turn to the other ways of framing how the ecological crisis must be understood, the critical role of the theorists needs to be complemented by an ability to recognize the common patterns in different cultural groups' ecological wisdom, and to clarify how this wisdom can be reproduced within the context of the student's own cultural form of learning. That is, the theorist must be able to ignore Rorty's injunction to treat all values and cultural norms as relative to the judgment of the ironist individual, and to affirm the authority of certain cultural values and practices.

Framing the Ecological Crisis in Terms of the Failed Promises of Modernism

A basic question that needs to be given serious consideration by every cultural group is whether the environment can survive the impact of modernization. While the question deserves book length treatment just to sort out what is meant by modernization, and how it is interpreted in different parts of the world, I think it is safe to make the generalization that in terms of North American cultures the assumptions and values that underlie a particularly environmentally destructive form of modernization serve as the dominant conceptual framework taught in the public schools. I think it is also safe to generalize that teacher education programs, in terms of their near total silence on the cultural roots of the ecological crisis, fail to provide teachers the conceptual frameworks necessary for understanding how the modern mind set is encoded in the language/thought process of the classroom. These programs also fail to provide a basis for recognizing alternative cultural patterns—particularly those based on metanarratives that represent humans as interdependent members of the biotic community.

I suspect the temptation on the part of some educational theorists will be to substitute modernity for capitalism as part of their ongoing critique of domination. This would be too simplistic, partly because there has not been any sustained effort to sort out the complexities of modernization and partly because these critics are themselves so wedded to the deep cultural premises of modernism that they cannot envision alternatives to them. Moreover, cultures that have resisted modernization by holding on to traditions that have enabled them to live in relative ecological balance would likely be viewed by these critics as oppressive and in need of the liberating power of a critical pedagogy. While it is now fashionable among certain Western intellectuals to turn against modernization as they know it, peoples in different cultures around the world are using aspects of modern consciousness to transform their own traditions. In some instances progress means embracing Western science and technology, free market principles, individualism, and the consumer life style. But in other instances they are borrowing modern beliefs and values relating to racial equality, freedom of inquiry, the rule of law, human rights, and political democracy. In Chile, Tunisia, and Kazakhstan, to cite just a few countries involved in the worldwide environmental movement, people are utilizing democratic practices as the basis for addressing environmental problems in their own regions. For most post colonial societies, grass roots political action directed toward solving environmental problems would not be possible without democracy. And their political efforts would not succeed without the information about the sources and consequences of environmentally disruptive practices obtainable through the use of modern science and technology. Additional examples of the Janus nature of modernity could easily be cited. The main point here is that modernization, particularly when considered within the context of cultural groups who are addressing the problematic aspects of their own traditions and bioregions, is too complex to be dealt with through the selective filters required by a categorical pattern of criticism and analysis. It is also too seductive and disruptive to be ignored.

What is needed from American educational theorists is a more careful mapping of the assumptions, values, and analogues taught as part of the explicit and implicit curricula—in the public schools and teacher education programs. Since the appearance of *Cultural Literacy for Freedom* (Bowers 1974), I have been arguing that the beliefs and values associated with modern consciousness have been framed in terms of anthropocentric metanarratives—narratives that treat the environment as an exploitable resource, and that key elements of this form of consciousness are communicated through the curriculum as the taken for granted reality. Michael Apple and others have illuminated how the curriculum reproduces class, racial, and gender biases. The task now is to expand on the efforts of another small group of educational theorist (e.g., Noel Gough, David Orr, Kathleen Kesson, Donald Oliver, Thomas Colwell, and others) who are helping us understand how the content of the curriculum (and other areas of professional discourse) relates to the ecological crisis. Textbooks, films, educational software, as well as the ongoing classroom discourse, need to be examined from an ecological perspective. If questions such as the following were used to foreground what otherwise is so taken for granted as to go unnoticed, we might have a clearer understanding of how schooling contributes to the double bind of a culture of progress that destroys the ecosystems upon which its future depends: What is the image of the individual that is represented in the curriculum, and how is success understood? What is represented as the central activities in people's lives? What forms of knowledge are represented as important, and what is the basis of their authority? How is community represented? What human relationships are emphasized? How is tradition understood, and what forms of tradition are given special visibility? How are humans viewed in relationship to the natural environment? What is the role assigned to science and technology, and are they treated as synonymous with social progress. What are represented as the limits that humans face? Is the individual's sense of responsibility represented as extending beyond self to include past and future generations? Questions such as these will help illuminate the deep cultural patterns that influence how many adults, even after they have forgotten the factual material they are tested on as students, will interpret an increasingly violent world.

The basic tenets of modernism, expressed in terms of how individualism, success, technology, work, science, and progress are understood, present educational theorists with a second challenge—to clarify both the historical/cultural origins of these typified ways of thinking (that is, what is encoded in iconic metaphors such as technology and progress) and how this aspect of the dominant cultural schemata relates to the problem of long-term sustainability. For example, the efforts of Lewis Mumford, Jacques Ellul, and Don Ihde to understand the cultural forces that influenced the mainstream approach to technology need to be expanded on by theorists who can clarify how different forms of technology select for amplification cultural orientations that contribute to the abuse of the environment. Eugene F. Provenzo Jr.'s study of the cultural values reinforced through Nintendo video games (1991) does not relate the cultural values and analogues to ecological issues, but it presents a major contribution to undermining the myth sustained by many educators that technology is culturally neutral. Other aspects of modern consciousness reinforced in public education, such as the current view of creativity, need to be examined from the perspective of meeting the test of ecological sustainability. The main point being made here is that the taken for granted assumptions and values given legitimacy by the myth of progress, and still taught to students in spite of spreading poverty and the increasing visibility of degraded natural systems, need to be radically reconstituted. What is to be substituted in the classroom curriculum and the professional education of teachers is a problem educational theorists have a responsibility for addressing.

The threat our particular form of modernization poses for the Earth has led to a number of distinct discourses that also need to be sorted out by educational theorists. Ecofeminists, social ecologists, deep ecologists, and the emerging discourse that goes by the name of ecosophy represent what can be interpreted as new expressions of grounded philosophical inquiry. Each discourse represents an attempt to recover or constitute metanarratives for clarifying both the root causes of our environmental dilemmas and the directions for future cultural development. With few exceptions these discourses have not dealt directly with formal education.

While the introduction of an ecological perspective into an analysis of the public school/modern consciousness relationship appears to make the domain of inquiry so broad that individual effort becomes futile, there is still the problem Rorty warns against getting involved with. Should educational theorists take a leadership role in identifying the cultural analogues, beliefs, values, technologies, and so forth that will contribute to a more ecologically sustainable world? As both silence (indifference?) and deliberate detachment end up reinforcing the existing cultural orientations, it is difficult to see how educational theorists can avoid taking a stance on how students understand the relationship between the patterns of their own lives and what is happening to the environment. As suggested earlier, all communication is about relationships: soils, water, air, plants, and animals are part of the complex information exchange networks that constitute our primary relationships of touching, seeing, smelling, hearing, and tasting (not to mention eating). The patterns that govern how we, as humans, experience these relationships, and even our awareness of them, are largely dictated by culture. In the same way that David Orr's statement (1992 p. 90) that *"all education is environmental education"* (that is, education cannot avoid reproducing the cultural patterns for understanding human/environmental relationships) all educational theory is environmental theory. But just as education can influence students to understand their relationship to the environment in terms of immediate self-interest and economic exploitation (which is proving to be a disastrous form of education) so educational theory can strengthen cultural patterns (ideologies, metanarratives, metalanguages) that fail to represent human interests within the context of the larger biotic community. But an approach to educational theory that is more conscious, even reflective, about the cultural patterns it reinforces needs to be supplemented (radicalized?) by an understanding (insofar as it is possible) of pre-modern forms of consciousness.

Framing the Ecological Crisis as the Loss of Ecological Wisdom: What Modern Students Can Learn from Traditional Ecologically-Centered Cultures

If the educational theorist approaches the question: "What is it that adults can teach youth that will not further jeopardize either their prospects as they become adults or the prospects of their progeny?" from an ecological perspective I strongly suspect that Rorty's guidelines for philosophers will have to be abandoned. In his 1982 essay, Rorty warns philosophers against taking positions on how things *must* be; and in *Contingency, Irony, and Solidarity,* he describes the ironist (the new philosopher?) as doubting the "final vocabulary she uses," and "does not think her vocabulary is closer to reality than others" (1989, p. 73). Furthermore, he argues that the orientation of a society inhabited by ironist individuals will be a liberal one "content to call 'true' (or 'right' or 'just') whatever the outcome of undistorted communication happens to be, whatever view wins in a free and open encounter" (p. 67). Rorty's fusing of reflective doubt, democracy, and social progress is shared by the emancipatory tradition of educational theorists that includes John Dewey, Paulo Freire, and the current advocates of Critical Pedagogy. The role of the educator in this tradition is to facilitate the process of questioning within a democratic framework. The result is that the knowledge of previous generations, if students encounter it at all, is to be subjected to the critical judgment of students. I strongly suspect that when the cultural assumptions legitimating the moral superiority of this "process" approach to education are examined from a perspective that takes account of how little critically reflective individuals know about ecologically sustainable practices, the "growth," "process," "critical reflection" approaches will be seen to be an expression of the Western cultural myth that equates life with linear growth, expansion of opportunities, and unending self-discovery.

Perhaps the most important aspect of the Western mindset the ecological crisis brings into question is the sense of temporality that influences the modern individual to view the past with suspicion, the present as an existential exercise in de-mystification, and the future as an every widening horizon of possibilities. I find John Berger's distinction particularly useful for illuminating the radical shift modern educators will be forced to make as the consequences of environmental disruption become more widespread. "Cultures of progress," he writes, "envisage future expansion. They are forward looking because they offer ever larger hopes. . . . A culture of survival envisages the future as a sequence of repeated acts of survival. Each act pushes the threat through the eye of the needle, and the thread is tradition" (1979, p. 204). The question of what knowledge adults should pass on to youth becomes somewhat easier to make sense of when we recognize that the impact of technology, life style expectations, and, now, sheer numbers of people who have yet to attain the minimum life sustaining quantities of protean, fiber, and fresh water, place all cultures in the survival category. So-called developed nations such as the United States, Japan, and Germany sustain the illusion of plenitude by mining the next generation's resource base—often in sites around the world not visible to the middle class whose major concern is with meeting the payments on the new car and their childrens' university education. To put it more succinctly, the only knowledge that morally can be passed from one generation to the next should meet the test of long-term sustainability. That is, education needs to be understood as a process of conserving cultural patterns that enable people to meet their material, communal, and spiritual needs without further degrading the habitat. If we use this criteria the anthropocentric conservatism of Allan Bloom, Mortimer Adler, and E. D. Hirsch Jr. will be seen as part of the problem (Bowers 1992).

As most of the public school curriculum is based on the assumptions underlying a culture of progress, the task of using schools as sites where ecologically sustainable traditions can be passed on (and improved) becomes particularly daunting. The problem is further complicated by the fact that while we have examples of still-existing cultural groups who have evolved along sustainable pathways, we do not have a clear understanding of what a modern sustainable culture would be like. The study of sustainable cultures not entirely overwhelmed by the pressures of modernization (Hopi, Koyukon, Australian Aboriginal groups) suggest that they evolved distinct ways of addressing relationships they all regard as primary to human life. A question raised by these cultures is whether a modern culture that provides for its members without diminishing the capacity of natural systems to sustain future generations can exist without evolving ways of understanding these fundamental relationships.

Characteristics of Primal Societies
That May Have Relevance to Modern Educators

As I have addressed elsewhere the possibility that the answers to our own ecological survival may, in part, have been worked out by premodern cultures (1992, 1993, also see Gough, 1991), I shall only summarize the shared characteristics of cultures that understand wisdom as living in balance. The term "characteristic" is not quite the right word here, as it can easily be interpreted to mean uniformity in cultural patterns—when in actuality there is wide diversity. But it is the best term for identifying what is shared in common between different cultural groups. Before the impact of modernization (literacy, individualism, consumerism, etc.) we can see in ecologically-centered cultures like the Hopi, Kwakiutl, Balinese, and Australian Aborigine the role metanarratives plays in providing a coherent view of reality—in all its dimensions: how things came to be, how things are today, and what the future holds. While the metanarratives are profoundly different from culture to culture they share the common characteristic of placing humans within a spiritual world that includes plants, animals, sun, rocks, and rain. In short, humans are not represented as separate, superior, and subject to a fundamentally different moral code. The fate of humans, in effect, is tied to a world of reciprocal relationships with other beings and forces that make up the life/spirit world. The metanarrative, whether it takes the form of The Dreaming, Spider Woman, or the three worlds that must be kept in balance through the strict observance of rules and ceremonies, represents community as inclusive of all forms of life. In turn, the languages of dance, music, and narrative represent the behaviors of animals and other natural phenomena as a source of analogues for understanding how to live in balance. Modern Western cultures which emphasize through their metanarratives the superiority of "rational man" have a much more restricted view of community and of moral relationships.

The metanarratives of ecologically-centered cultures also foster a way of situating oneself in time that is profoundly different from the view of time that serves as the most basic symbolic coordinate of modern consciousness. In these cultures, time is understood as cyclical rather than as linear and progressive. Whereas modern humans understand ourselves as moving away from the past, and thus no longer in need of the technical knowledge and wisdom that sustained past generations, ecologically-sustainable cultures understand the the past, present, and future as interconnected—and interdependent. The identity, responsibility, and authority of the person are framed by a sense of the past and future as being palpable, and to which they are accountable. Persons with special gifts grow in their ability to restate the tradition, to make it concrete and vital in the life of the inclusive community, and thus help to insure that the pathway taken by future generations remains coherent and viable. This is profoundly different from the modern individual whose power of expertise is gained by overturning both traditional technical knowledge and wisdom. Lastly, these cultures appear to share the common characteristic of giving more importance to developing the spiritual languages of art, music, dance, and narrative which are essential for connecting the person to a larger symbolic universe. These are languages that provide for participatory expression within the community and serve as a form of collective wisdom for how to live in sustainable relationships within the bioregion.

These characteristics of ecologically-centered cultures—metanarratives that do not represent humans as separate from nature and as uniquely privileged (i.e., being rational, possessing a soul), an inclusive sense of community that incorporates the rest of the biotic community into the moral order, the non-progressive and non-linear sense of time, and the emphasis on meeting non-material needs by stressing the development of spiritual languages—can easily be romanticized, and even treated as cultural packages that can be incorporated into New Age thinking. I have introduced them into the discussion of an ecological perspective for the purpose of suggesting that premodern cultures may enable us to see ourselves more clearly. They may also represent important sources of wisdom about how humans can define and meet their needs without destroying the environment in the process. The classroom implications are as varied as they are complex. For example, an understanding of the cultural messages encoded in a premodern form of expression (what moderns would term "art"), as well as how it allows for individualized participation in its expression, might help students recognize how the modern approaches to art reinforce the materialistic and relativistic sense of values associated with capitalism and an anomic form of individualism. The characteristics of premodern cultures may illuminate the role that elders play as bearers of folk knowledge that is tested and revised over time, and that the ways in which this knowledge is shared further nurtures relationships essential to a viable community. This pattern stands in sharp contrast to the experimental nature of expert knowledge, and the expert's relationship to the community. There are also differences between premodern and modern cultures in terms of how they understand the nature of technical knowledge, how premodern forms of knowledge are integrated into a highly sophisticated knowledge of the characteristics of the local habitat. A discussion of why modern societies have built barriers to learning about the cultural achievements of premodern peoples who constructed exceedingly complex symbolic universes might also occur in classrooms. The irony today is that what remains of premodern peoples who developed ecological cultures (in Bateson's sense of the term) are the only non-theoretical models we have. While we cannot copy them directly, we can still learn from them. The challenge for the educational theorist will be to use, without romanticizing, the analogues that have evolved from their experiences as a basis for illuminating the assumptions that underlie the content of the school curriculum, and for opening students' minds to new (and ancient) pathways.

Recognition of Minority Cultures as Sources of Ecological Wisdom

The tradition of viewing as inferior cultural groups who do not embrace the values and patterns of thought of the dominant culture, with its emphasis on technological progress, competition, individualism, and consumerism, may now be preventing us from recognizing the importance of these cultural groups to our future survival. These marginalized groups—American Indian, Hispanic-American, African-American, poor rural whites, and religious communities who have chosen to live apart from the materialism of mainstream culture—managed in varying degrees to sustain themselves as communities under difficult economic and political circumstances. In some instances members of these groups have tried to work out a form of dual cultural citizenship that would allow them to retain their ties to their original culture that provides the deepest sense of meaning and identity. If we can shift the focus away from the dominant question of why these groups, with some exceptions, are not equally represented in the highly technical professions and the managerial levels of corporate America, we may discover traditions of community life where the emphasis is on involvement in sustaining rich and complex community relationships rather than the acquisition of material goods. For educators concerned with introducing into the curriculum alternatives to the consumer/technological/human achievement ethos that now prevails in most classrooms, taking seriously the still meaningful cultural traditions of these minority groups may provide an important basis for curricular innovation and reform. But a great deal of work needs to be done before teachers will be able to frame for students how the various traditions of minority cultures may represent examples of ecologically sustainable patterns. We need to begin understanding marginalized cultural groups from an ecological perspective. This would include understanding how folklore, still viable metanarratives, institutions like the Black church, extended families, ways of communicating the specialness of social relationships, music, and so forth, help to sustain the community as a moral ecology that does not have a disruptive impact on the environment.

After we obtain a fuller understanding of the distinct cultural traditions of marginalized groups the challenge for educational theorists will be to clarify how these traditions should be introduced into the classroom as a deep cultural approach to environmental education. The suggestion that marginalized cultures should be kept in an impoverished condition because they have developed alternatives to the ecological pathologies of the dominant culture needs to be guarded against. There are also dangers connected with teachers introducing "information" about minority cultural practices without really understanding how different forms of knowledge are communicated, the profound differences that exist between spoken and written forms of discourse, how different cultural groups use metaphor to organize reality and to communicate about relationships, the differences between folk and modern technology, the nature and role of metanarratives, and the cultural/spiritual role of the arts. If teachers remain ignorant of these fundamental characteristics of cultural reproduction they will likely turn the curriculum, in spite of its minority cultural content, into another supermarket-type learning experience where students are more enticed by the packaging of the new learning products and by vague pronouncements about learning to appreciate cultural differences. Knowledge of minority cultures, knowledge of the dominant culture, and knowledge of the teacher's role as a mediator in the cultural reproduction process represent important areas of liminality where educational theorists must be prepared to step forward by taking a position on *what* "must" be done, and help to frame the larger discussion of *why* it must be done. Convincing social groups who now enjoy unparalleled economic benefits from cultural practices that are deepening the ecological crisis to wake up to the dangers of the myths they live by is certainly beyond the power of educational theorists. But it is not too unreasonable to expect educational theorists to take responsibility for illuminating how students can encounter a more sustainable form of education.

BIBLIOGRAPHY

Berger, John. 1979. *Pig Earth*. New York: Pantheon Books.

Bowers, C. A. 1974. *Cultural Literacy for Freedom*. Eugene: Elan Publishers.

———. 1991. "The Anthropocentric Foundations of Educational Liberalism." *The Trumpeter*. 8(3): 102–108.

———. 1993. *Education, Cultural Myths, and the Ecological Crisis: Toward Deep Changes*. Albany: State University of New York Press.

———. 1993. *Critical Essays on Education, Modernity, and the Recovery of the Ecological Imperative*. New York: Teachers College Press.

Gough, Noel. 1991. "Coyote, Crocodile, Chaos, and Curriculum: Premodern Lessons for Postmodern Learning." Clayton, Victoria, Australia: Unpublished manuscript.

———. 1992. "Narrative Inquiry and Critical Pragmatism: Liberating Research in Environmental Education." Clayton Victoria, Australia: Unpublished manuscript.

Orr, David. 1992. *Ecological Literacy: Education and the Transition to a Post Modern World.* Albany: State University of New York Press.

Provenzo, Jr., Eugene. 1991. *Video Kids: Making Sense of Nintendo.* Cambridge: Harvard University Press.

Rorty, Richard. 1982. *Consequences of Pragmatism (Essays: 1972–1980).* Minneapolis: University of Minnesota Press.

———. 1989. *Contingency, Irony, and Solidarity.* Cambridge: Cambridge University Press.

24

Whose Ecological Perspective?
Bringing Ecology Down to Earth

Madhu Suri Prakash

The ecological perspective of C. A. Bowers brings a crucial dimension conspicuously absent in the gender, race, class and other liberation pedagogies well known today. In extending his attempts to explode the canon of contemporary philosophy and education, I want to separate the grain from the chaff in perspectives ecological. I especially wish to distinguish perspectives that promote cultural diversity as well as gender and class liberation, from those that further exacerbate our academic "monocultures of the mind."[1]

From Professional Hegemony to People's Science

The discourse of ecology that dominates today reveals the birth of yet another modern science, perhaps the last. It is the latest addition to the academic empire of specialized professional discourses. Like contemporary Philosophy of Education, this professional "language game" is abstract and far removed from the conversations of ordinary people about the concrete problems of their local places, rapidly losing their natural or cultural diversity.[2]

More than a decade ago, Wendell Berry, Ivan Illich, and others forewarned us of this emerging environmental science. In *Gender,* Illich predicted the increased threat to women, culture, and nature posed by the promoters of "global order" and "global citizenship." Their "steady-state societies" will be nothing more than an "oligarchic, undemocratic, and authoritarian expertocracy, governed by ecologists,"[3] he concluded.

Recognizing the threat, many are attempting to salvage ecology from this doom. Emerging grassroots ecological perspectives mark the birth of the first *postmodern* science: a people's science, replete and rich with concrete knowledge—reflecting experiences drawn from women's lives, from cultures, classes, and persons silenced by the professional norms of modern science. This postmodern science of ecology is strengthening people's resistance to the increasingly oppressive eco-speak, the patriarchal powers and privileges of professional ecologists—now claiming to protect for all of us our planet in peril.[4]

The *modern* science of ecology dominated the global Earth Summit of Rio de Janeiro in 1992. The *postmodern* reaction to it expressed there and elsewhere by ecofeminists, deep ecologists, grassroots activists, and many others goes far beyond the conference.[5] I share their deep misgivings about the ecological perspectives of those who man the World Bank, NASA, the World Watch Institute, and other prestigious institutions, now generously funded for efficiently "managing" the whole planet. Equally disturbing are those who reconceptualize the earth as an "ecosystem", while threatening other cultural conceptions of nature and Creation. I also share the growing moral indignation provoked by the Global Environmental Facility, created in Rio, through which developed nations attempt to increase their control over the nature of the "less developed" cultures, under the pretense of protecting the planet from mismanagement. Alarming also are the bioengineering enterprises of universities and agribusiness enterprises, now promising new and sustainable "green revolutions" for mass manufacturing food, supposedly to end global hunger.

Ecological perspectives, it is clear by now, are as vulnerable to co-optation by oppressive modern institutions as any other epistemological enterprise— including the entire range of contemporary sciences and arts, legitimized and eulogized by professional educators for promising human liberation. In responding to Bowers' ecological perspective, I want to distinguish between the professional hegemony of ecology *qua* modern science and the cultural and gender liberation realized by ecology *qua* first postmodern science. The former destroys nature and culture, while successfully marketed today under the modern banner: we can have our cake and eat it too; enjoy a green planet along with economic growth for "the good life"—as defined by "developed", "First World" peoples. On the other hand, bringing us down to earth, ecology *qua* postmodern science represents real liberation: replacing destructive global interventions with local initiatives in the regeneration of nature/culture; transforming the transient, individualist, residents of national economies into the rooted dwellers of self-reliant communities; junking the endless needs of *homo oeconomicus* by promoting the virtues of soil; discouraging the pronouncements of global loudspeakers, while encouraging the authentic dialogues of local voices.

Race, Class, Gender and Ecology: from Accommodation to Liberation

As a "woman of color" observing the increasing global domination of Eurocentric perspectives on ecology and education, I see the real need to extend the hard-won successes of race, class, gender, and other liberation or critical pedagogies. Far from imposing a "digression," ecological considerations actually bring us to their "logical culmination." For the "mentality that exploits and destroys the natural environment is the same that abuses racial and economic minorities, that imposes on young men the tyranny of the military draft, that makes war against peasants and women and children with the indifference of technology. The mentality that destroys a watershed and then panics at the threat of a flood is the same mentality that gives institutionalized insult to black people and then panics at the prospect of race riots."[6]

This mentality is shaped by gigantic institutions and technologies that destroy the cultures of peoples who live on the human scale—the scale that accurately reflects our capacities to understand and take care of the consequences our actions have upon others. It is influenced by an education and economics that destroys communal self-sufficiency and cultural diversity, while promoting the exploitation of "Others." And it is the product of a politics that can hide or legitimize race, class, and gender oppression. These social institutions and technologies—educational, economic, political, and other—also prevent us from seeing how our high "standard of living" abuses the whole natural world; and in doing so, brutally exacerbates race, class and gender oppression. For every time we disregard the environment, we tend first to threaten the homes, health, and the autonomous livelihoods of those already most oppressed, silenced, and vulnerable—peoples we can avoid ever knowing or feeling for, since they live sufficiently far away.

While the hard-won successes of race, class, gender and other liberation pedagogies offer us important guidance in our adoption of perspectives ecological, their limitations in effectively exploding the academic canon are equally instructive. They reveal all the professional temptations to be resisted, if our ecological perspectives are to escape co-optation by leading modern institutions, curricula and pedagogies. As in all effective co-optations, the most damning failures lie well hidden under the guise of institutional success—the legitimacy and recognition gained within the very systems that these critical pedagogies are meant to challenge and change.

"Why doesn't this feel empowering?" asks Elizabeth Ellsworth in her struggles to escape the successfully institutionalized critical pedagogies.[7] Her answer reveals the co-optation that transforms "successful" critical pedagogs into the "intimate enemy": reembracing the highly abstract, utopian and global lines of theoretical inquiry we started out by challenging; reenacting the teacher-student, oppressor-oppressed relationships we are committed to demolishing in theory.[8]

A range of other failures mar race, class, gender, and other critical pedagogies—in large measure because they remain as divorced from ecological concerns as the patriarchal disciplines. For our contemporary successes as critical pedagogs do not bring us any closer to the earth: her soils and waters, her plants and creatures. Instead, they further feed our middle-class concerns that, observes Bowers, include "meeting the payments on the new car and [our] children's university education"—along with acquiring the manicured green lawn, the picket fence, the V.C.R. and the air-conditioned, four-wheel-drive automobile, to name only a few of the endless trappings of our middle-class standard of living.

That this standard is ecologically unsustainable and the source of the oppression of millions across the world seem not to be pressing issues for most liberation pedagogs. George Bush, it seems, spoke as much for today's successful critical pedagogs as he did for his conservative fans when he pronounced at the Earth Summit: "The American way of life is not up for negotiation."[9] To challenge this posture, Berry warns that each of us is implicated in the ecological crisis, and in the race, class, and gender oppression exacerbated by it. "A protest meeting on the issue of environmental abuse is not a convocation of accusers, it is a convocation of the guilty." For "every time we participate in our wasteful economy, and our economy's first principle is waste—we are contributing *directly* to the ruin of this planet."[10] And the first victims of this increasing ruination are the "underdeveloped", the "poor", and other oppressed peoples.

In overcoming the failures of contemporary liberation pedagogies to explode the academic canon, postmodern ecological perspectives must resist three temptations. These define contemporary academic success, and are also responsible for the failures of professional co-optation or accommodation. The three temptations include: abstract, global, utopian thinking and conduct—the products of large, impersonal institutions that delink themselves from the problems and predicaments of concrete places; the recreation of new disciplinary fiefdoms and specialties, following patriarchal principles; and the pursuit of the needs and wants of *homo oeconomicus,* that legitimize the growth of the economy, and jeopardize non-economic relationships. By resisting these temptations of our ecologically destructive and socially oppressive "education," critical pedagogs can really participate in the insurrection of the subjugated forms of knowledge, made evident by Foucault. To explode our professional canon, we must resist the global domination of modern professional ecologists. This means participating in the local dialogues that constitute postmodern ecology—a people's science.

A Postmodern Ecological Perspective: From Global to Local

Rorty's "all purpose intellectuals," anthropocentric and committed to "progress," are incapable of addressing the ecological crisis, Bowers rightly observes. For paving paths that lead beyond the achievements of contemporary liberation pedagogies, Bowers commends the earthy wisdom of primal, premodern and minority cultures. Their wisdom demands that we open our culturally blinded eye—the legacy we have inherited, along with stolen lands and waters, from our ancestor Christopher Columbus; a legacy faithfully perpetuated by our schools and universities, despite the recent multiculturalist peppering of their curricula.[11]

Clearly, cultures marginalized today by "developed" and "educated" peoples have nothing to teach us about global ecological perspectives—either of Columbus or of the contemporary proponents of "global citizenship". Today's globalisms make sense only to those indoctrinated to "belong" to such abstract entities as the modern nation state; or habituated to seeing the earth from satellites and spaceships—reducing her from up high into a little ball, a "bauble", a "Christmas tree ornament."[12]

"Planetary belonging" remains alien to the cultures of those "Others", who know their soils and waters, the plants and animals of their bioregions very intimately. This intimacy comes with the scale that encourages us to use our feet for transportation, and our communal hands to feed, clothe, and shelter ourselves, free from the blindness created by "opaque" industrial technologies. Content to "belong" on the human scale, those "Others" limit themselves to cultural spaces that are small, and can be taken good care of by their local communities. This means abandoning the aspirations of the "developed" to belong to and manage the whole planet.

Viewed from the modern mindscape with its Promethean overreach, these non-globalist perspectives appear pitifully parochial. Yet they teach the globalist, "discovering" descendants of Columbus how to overcome our ongoing exploitation of unknown places and peoples, redefining "the good life" or "human needs" so that these can be achieved in local terms.

Explaining why global perspectives simply exacerbate the diseases they pretend to cure, Berry cautions: "Properly speaking global thinking is not possible. Those who have thought globally have done so by means of simplifications too extreme and oppressive to merit the name of thought."[13] Challenging modern environmentalists' slogans to "Think globally, act locally," Berry clarifies why global thinking, in all its forms, is not just futile, but in fact impossible and dangerous: "You can't think about what you don't know, and nobody knows this planet. . . . The people who think globally do so abstractly and statistically, by reducing the globe to quantities."[14]

Opposed to such quantification, the cultural perspectives of minorities, nonmoderns, and other marginalized peoples forsake the arrogance to

"Think Big" or "think globally." They invite us to be humble, to "think little"—on the human scale; the scale of our local communities. By realizing that the right local questions will be the right global ones, we will conclude with Berry: "You can't do a good act that is global. . . . A good act has to be scaled and designed so that it fits harmoniously into the natural conditions and given of a particular place."[15] Local knowledge, local skills, and local love give substance and feasibility to socially just and ecologically preserving acts.

Local acts do have profound global implications. But unlike the acts of globalists, they are constructive rather than destructive. Observes Berry: "If we want to keep our thoughts and acts from destroying the globe, then we must see to it that we do not ask too much of the globe or any part of it. To make sure that we do not ask too much, we must learn to live at home, as independently and self-sufficiently as we can."[16]

A Postmodern Ecological Perspective:
From Residents to Dwellers

Most of the people who still live sustainably today own no diplomas. And those possessing all kinds of academic degrees are recklessly participating in the destruction of the planet. These degrees, these signs and symbols of modern success, sell so well because they promise us the liberation of "upward mobility": of the "'uprooted careerist', the 'itinerant professional vandal' devoid of any sense of place, the yuppie, the narrow specialist, the intellectual snob."[17] All these role models exemplify the knowledge and skills for supplying ourselves with consumables from "places around the world that are largely unknown to us, as are those to which we consign our toxic and radioactive wastes, garbage, sewage, and industrial trash."[18]

After observing the unsustainable lifestyle of global citizens "educated" for uprootedness, David Orr diagnoses the growth and pervasiveness of ecological illiteracy today. Year by year, he notes, the number of people educated through first-hand experience of the land dwindles. Our education compels us to embrace "the architectural expressions of displacement: the shopping mall, apartment, neon strip, freeway, glass office tower, and homogenized development—none of which encourage much sense of rootedness, responsibility, and belonging."[19]

Today's upwardly mobile graduates possess the attitudes and skills of a "resident": "a temporary and rootless occupant who mostly needs to know where the banks and stores are in order to plug in."[20] The resident is the successful "product" of an "educational" process, which is little more than "abstraction piled on top of abstraction, disconnected from tangible experience, real problems, and the places where we live and work."[21] Orr calls this education "utopian," which he notes literally means "nowhere." Examining the consequences of the utopian, de-placed and abstract teaching promoted in our "nice" campuses, Orr concludes that the "sum total of violence wrought by people who do not know who they are because they do not know where they are is the global environmental crisis."[22]

To undo the global damage perpetrated by ecologically illiterate graduates, Orr's educational curricula and pedagogies conscientize modern residents into becoming "dwellers". For dwelling teaches the rooted knowledge of caring "stewards"; of people who belong to the places that, in turn, belong to them. Roots grow as we learn to inhabit places long enough to develop affection and foresight—overcoming residents' indifference to and ignorance of the long term consequences of our choices and actions. Responsible, caring foresight requires us to live close to the sources of what we eat and wear, build, cultivate or manufacture with. The ecological literacy of dwellers is linked inextricably to the liberation promised by bioregional self-sufficiency.[23] With this autonomy, we can escape the traps and tyranny, the social oppression and ecological violence of rootless residents; of their goliath institutions—designed to fulfill the needs of *homo oeconomicus.*

A Postmodern Ecological Perspective: From the Needs of Homo Oeconomicus to the Virtues of Soil

From the perspective of *homo oeconomicus,* nature serves a crucial economic function: to sustain the flow of jobs and "goods"—the increasingly obsolescent commodities of the industrial economy. The growth of our economy requires that nature be "maintained." Viewed from this "ecological" perspective, nature is "unfinished"—a mere "resource" for the expansion of the manmade world.

Observing the terrible violence resulting from this modern perspective on ecology, Berry concludes that we are living in "the most destructive and, hence, the most stupid period of our species."[24] We eat, clothe, heat, house, heal, transport, and educate ourselves in order to prop and expand the industrial economy, while "abusing" and "raping" the earth as well as her nonmodern cultures. Practicing communal interdependence, these cultures successfully keep the economy marginal to their social and ecological relationships. The perspective of *homo oeconomicus,* in contrast, leaves us increasingly flooded with economic "goods", while wretchedly poor in the virtues essential to community and bioregional self-sufficiency.

Alisdair MacIntyre's *After Virtue* also reflects on the "institutionalized acquisitiveness" of *homo oeconomicus* and its destructive consequences for the virtues and moral norms of communities. "*Pleonexia,* a vice . . . is now the driving force of modern productive work: removed as it is from the moral constraints of household and local communities."[25] Preceding MacIntyre, while reminding us of Mandeville and others, Mumford described the modern "moral alchemy" that converts "the seven deadly sins (pride, envy, sloth, greed, gluttony, avarice, and lust) into economic virtues for the growing economy."[26]

After uncovering this dark underside of the modern "history of needs," Ivan Illich suggests escape from the work, schooling, and ecology of *homo oeconomicus*—all designed to gratify our manufactured needs.[27] He calls for replacing the abstract dominant discourse about "planet earth" with an ecological perspective that teaches us to enjoy the concrete "virtues of soil." For we "stand on soil, not on earth. From soil we come, and to the soil we bequeath our excrements and remains. And yet soil—its cultivation and our bondage to it—is remarkably absent from those things clarified by philosophy in our Western tradition."[28]

Descending from the ivory tower of abstraction and global eco-speak, Illich invites us to look "below our feet because our generation has lost its grounding in both soil and virtue." By virtue, Illich refers to the "shape, order, and direction of action" which is defined by local culture and bioregion: "informed by tradition, bounded by place, and qualified by choices made within the habitual reach of the actor."[29] The virtues require practices which are "mutually recognized as being good within a shared local culture," those that enhance our "memories of place." Abstract and utopian, controlled by the principles of economic growth, modern education destroys such memories by stripping us of our bonds to the soil, air and waters of our places. Nonmodern education strengthened these bonds through "labor, craft, dwelling and suffering supported, not by an abstract earth, environment or energy system, but by the particular soil these very actions have enriched."[30]

Illich's "philosophy of soil" demands a "disciplined analysis" of the experiences and memory of soil which support subsistence and virtue. With the abandonment of communities by people "educated" to be individualists, the communal memories needed for virtue disappear. The physical soil also departs. Desertification, pollution, and the other ecological ills follow. These "natural disasters" of modern ecology, for Illich and other postmodernists, are in reality the cultural and moral losses of craft, dwelling, labor, and the virtues of the soil. To liberate ourselves from the devastation brought on by the education of *homo oeconomicus*, we need ecological literacy—or education in the virtues of rooted dwellers.

Down-to-Earth Ecology and Education

This century's most well-known experiments in professional education, including those of Dewey, Neill, Freire, and other "radicals", are noteworthy for achieving ends *other* than those of rooted dwelling. In this section, I sketch two alternative experiments that seem to me to be particularly instructive for bringing ecology and education down to earth: liberating them from the hegemony of modern professionals, while recovering the cultures, gendered relationships and virtues of rooted dwellers. The first experiment comes from my own culture; the other is quintessentially American.[31]

Ecologically prescient that the "civilization" of *homo oeconomicus* would consume and devastate the entire earth "like locusts", Mahatma Gandhi initiated his radical educational experiments on the Tolstoy Farm in South Africa almost a century ago. In its scale, Gandhi's Tolstoy Farm exemplified an extremely modest local initiative, a very humble beginning to a project that was to become a global tumbling block, bringing down *the* colonial Superpower on which, it was boasted, the sun could never set.

Rich in lessons about living with full respect for all of nature, human and other, education on Tolstoy Farm was not conceived to teach ecology as a separate subject; nor to save the planet; not even to bring down an oppressive global empire. It was an attempt by Gandhi and a small group of other dissidents to regenerate their own "culture of silence"; to teach themselves and their children the knowledge and skills to be neither oppressors nor oppressed; to live simply so that others can simply live; to practice freedom through achieving self-sufficiency; to be autonomous in satisfying their basic human needs, intellectual, physical, emotional, and spiritual—all this through refusing to cooperate with the oppressive modern economy and educational system.

Children and adults started their day on the farm by working together in the field, pasture, workshops, kitchen or urinals of the community. The afternoons were concentrated on the 3 Rs and other theoretical inquiries that could be directly applied to understanding and improving the life of the community. Gandhian education "conscientized" human hands, head, and heart [his 3 Hs] with the theoretical knowledge and the practical skills of the indigenous, nonmodern cultures of the soil; of those who have for centuries sustained themselves and their bioregions by practicing the virtues of self-sufficiency. Their pedagogy demonstrated that we can meet all our basic needs by the labor of our own communal hands—thus liberating us from being oppressors or oppressed.

Inspired by Gandhian ideals and even more so by the virtues of soil practiced by Thoreau and other American thinkers, David Orr has initiated the Meadowcreek Project at Oberlin College in Ohio and Conway College in Arkansas. Not as daring or radical as Gandhi's, Orr's experimental curricula and pedagogies represent the pioneering attempts of our day to bring modern campuses closer and closer towards the virtues of dwelling in community.

All education is environmental education, Orr stresses, as he brings all the disciplines to bear on the careful study of our ecologically unsustainable lives and learning, on and off campus. This study begins with the "basics": food, for example. The entire campus community learns about its immoral, violent, and wasteful ways of feeding itself. Abandoning the criteria that define educational success today, Orr's education for ecological literacy focuses on reducing the unsustainable distances traveled by our food.[32] For these keep us ignorant of the enormous human oppression and violation of nature caused by our industrial eating. Campus waste, landscape, building architecture, and all other elements of local life are similarly studied with the aim that faculty, administrators, and students can start living in ecologically sustainable and socially just ways. Teaching us to think and act locally, on the human scale, on and off campus, Orr leads the way today in demonstrating that we can bring ecology down to earth by recreating sustainable communities—even on our campuses, controlled today by the industrial economy towards which its graduates are headed.

From Global Loudspeakers to Local Voices

While criticizing Rorty's "all purpose intellectual" and celebrating the ecological wisdom of nonmoderns, Bowers' proposes a radical departure from mainstream philosophy and educational theory. In the spirit of sharing his affirmations and proposals, I now wish to express two general reservations about Bowers' essay and my response to it. In doing so, I draw attention to the professional hurdles that most of us engaged in Philosophy of Education, including Bowers, need to overcome, if we are to achieve the educational aim of living and learning sustainably.

My first reservation is about the academic genre Bowers and I continue to employ here, even in a section of the book titled "Expanding/Exploding the Canon." This genre, it is all too clear, traps us within the confines of the disciplines that Bowers justifiably urges us to abandon. It makes our ecological perspectives inaccessible and irrelevant for the public, largely constituted by non-philosophers of education.

My second reservation is about content. Like our style, it is detached from ordinary life and language. Our philosophical discussions of nature are thoroughly dislocated or disembedded from the local spaces we inhabit. We analyze an abstract earth from a lofty academic tower. Following professional norms, we write principally as disembodied intellectual voices, and not as persons engaged in conversation with neighbors, families, and friends. Speaking impersonally through loudspeakers to other uprooted global citizens or all-purpose intellectuals, our writings say little or nothing about our own personal attempts at living and working, teaching and learning in ways that make more moral/ecological sense within our own local communities.

In fundamental contrast, the oral educational traditions of indigenous peoples, like the non-professional genres of Aldo Leopold, Wendell Berry, Wes Jackson, and other well-known "New American Prophets,"[33] richly reflect the concrete colors, textures, sounds, smells, flora and fauna of well-defined, intimately known and cared for local places. Today, there are also scores of grassroots publications that explore and celebrate local experiments in sustainable living. One example is *The Aisling Quarterly,* the journal of my colleague and friend, Dara Malloy. It regularly reflects upon the practical experiments of de-professionalized thinkers, educators, writers, and activists who are withdrawing from economic and other globalisms, becoming well-rooted in their own indigenous cultures, while relearning the ecological virtues of dwelling within their own communities.[34]

Inspired by these alternatives in writing, thinking, and dwelling, it seems only appropriate to end this essay with a brief personal note of my own local struggles to teach, learn, and live for ecological sustainability. My context is neither the Tolstoy farm nor Orr's small liberal arts college. It is the typical, mammoth, modern university, located in the heartland of rural Pennsylvania. Most teach at or graduate from this institution, ignorant about the ecology of this part of the country, and of its systematic destruction by our university, our school system, and by other local or transnational institutions.

During the standard academic year, I meet with approximately two hundred students, studying to become school teachers. My modest project is to try and make a small dent in our ecological illiteracy during the span of our fourteen short weeks together—experienced by learners and teachers alike as a mad scramble to fulfill the standard course requirements of an institution driven by the compulsion to generate credit hours. Infected by the maniacal frenzy of the typical semester on campus, most students graduate from my course hurriedly "banking" a few facts about the ecological crisis, their destructive daily lives essentially unchanged—accurate reflections of the unsustainable institutional culture that certifies them as "educated."

Every semester, I try not to be daunted by the challenge of developing the virtues of dwelling in social contexts where dwellers are an anomaly. It is a real struggle to design experiences that overcome the ecological destructiveness of professional credentialing. It takes a certain hope to live with the vast gap separating the reality of our institution with the theories we study. And every semester yields its small successes. There are students who complete the course more critically conscious of "the good life" guaranteed by our professional credentials; who see with new eyes previously hidden aspects of our unsustainable social reality: from our computer or toilet paper to our flush toilets, our disposable plates, diapers, and napkins, our cars, highways, refrigerators, air conditioners, lawnmowers, supermarkets, agribusiness corporations, hot showers, newspapers and computers. These cultural artifacts and institutions of our daily lives take on new meaning when reassessed by their implications for social oppression and ecological destruction, for decreasing personal autonomy or social justice. Every semester, some of us finish the course a little less addicted to these economic "goods" or "conveniences," and a little more skilled in the virtues of social justice and ecological nonviolence.

My failures have taught me that it is counterproductive to focus on grim environmental disasters, worse case scenarios, and "global issues," such as the size of the ozone hole, global warming, the greenhouse effect, or the loss of biological diversity. For these leave most students emotionally paralyzed and intellectually distracted from problems which we can practically address today. Equally problematic are de-contextualized conceptual analyses of ideas, like "sustainability," technological or ecological.

Constructive dialogue and action are most effectively stimulated by critical studies of ecological problems that lie close to our doorsteps; and, closer yet, to our mouths. These include the food we eat and the garbage we generate. How is our food grown? Who is oppressed? Who benefits from such food production? What is its impact on our intestines, our air, water, and soil? What is happening to our local community farmers? How are we oppressing them through the kind of food we purchase? How can we change our eating and consuming patterns to be less oppressive and oppressed, less ecologically violent? How much garbage do we produce and why? Where does it go? What does it destroy? What can we do to be less wasteful today? These questions direct us towards practical solutions for regenerating the destroyed ecology and cultures of our town.

But what does the unsustainability of our food, garbage, energy, and other ecological issues have to do with education in general and with Philosophy of Education in particular? Not surprisingly, this question troubles those who have been taught to systematically separate education from ecology, agriculture, waste management, town planning, and all other aspects of dwelling. The success of my course depends on the skill with which I build bridges between the writings of Dewey, Freire, Peters, Scheffler, and other philosophers of education with Frances Moore Lappe's *Diet for a Small Planet,* Rachel Carsons's *Silent Spring,* Wendell Berry's *The Unsettling of America: Culture and Agriculture,* and other writings on our unsustainable practices and institutions. There are endless possibilities for complementing the Philosophy of Education "canon" with books and articles that shatter its irresponsible silence on ecological destruction and regeneration.

Our theoretical in-class explorations are complemented with the study of local persons and community groups who exemplify eating, defecating, bathing, healing, and in other ways living, working, and teaching more sustainably. We share personal stories of ecological ignorance followed by conscientization; of modern "certainties" about efficiency and healthfulness transformed into shattered myths; of successful changes in daily behaviors and conduct that seemed at one time to be inconceivable or plain "primitive" and "backward." More real-life stories emerge from our research projects on local role models—those who are innovative, daring to dwell; empowering themselves and others through initiatives in community-supported agriculture, organic farming or growing kitchen gardens; those engaged in reducing, reusing, and recycling waste; in cleaning up local streams, lakes and ponds;

in resisting their neighbors' norms about dandelion-free lawns; continually discovering multiple uses for gray water, while engaged in "technofasting"; replacing "responsible reuse" for "convenience"; composting all organic materials at home, while creating dry latrines. All these local success stories give new life to our theoretical explorations of concepts like "virtue", "moral responsibility", "ecological literacy", and "education for a postmodern world." We part slightly better educated about of the ecological problems and prospects for our campus, township and bioregion. No longer does ecology remain a subject separate from education or philosophy for us. Informed by ecology, our philosophies of education compel us to abandon our roles *qua homo oeconomicus;* learning to tread less harshly on humans and others.

While every personal success in making daily changes, however minor, keeps us hopeful, it also continually reminds us how deeply implicated we all are in our unsustainable institutions and technologies. This recognition is essential for counteracting the pervasive tendency to distance ourselves from the social oppression and natural destruction entailed by our lives as ecological illiterates; to pass the buck; blaming, for example, the corporate world and corrupt governments for the current pace of environmental destruction. Locating the ecological crisis in hundreds of daily personal habits and decisions empowers and conscientizes us to make radical changes—beginning with "basics" like the food we uncritically consume several times a day. These basics, given their immediacy and concreteness in our daily lives, are essential to bringing ecology and educational philosophy simultaneously down to earth and close to home. This reduces their isolation not only from other professional disciplines like agriculture, but also from each other. This ecological perspective transforms the eating of industrial food, for example, pulling it out of the domestic or private domain into the arena of public morality and politics—as explosive as abortion or the issues of race and gender discrimination in textbooks.

My continued folly in accepting the university's competitive evaluations and grades does severely hamper my attempts to practice what I preach: to help create sustainable communities, grounded in the principles of learning to live simply. I am equally limited by my lack of courage in rejecting other academic norms, including those that socialize us to be "itinerant professional vandals": productive at participating in ecologically draining and polluting conferences; or in committee work and research that leave us no time to change our neighborhoods of uprooted transients into communities of dwellers.

In our explorations of marginalized ecological perspectives, the fact that I am "a woman of color" offers several advantages. These include first-hand experiences of living and flourishing in cultures with more sustainable patterns of daily living. These experiences are instructive and encouraging, however, only if they are presented with humility and tact. I am slowly learning the sensitivity it takes to introduce ecological perspectives which deconstruct the most cherished "truths" of learners: including the belief that we are technologically and culturally "developed;" that our politics, economics, and morality make us the most "advanced" people in the world.

There are also distinct disadvantages to being a "woman of color" teaching "White" people about the unsustainability of their way of life. To contend with all of the limitations of being an "outsider", I need to continuously remember and respect the clear line that separates critical pedagogs from oppressive professors who only reward students for agreeing with the perspectives propounded in class. Success in teaching radical ecological perspectives, it is clear, depends on giving learners the full powers of intellectual disagreement; in respecting their refusal to participate in their own culture's critiques; of never failing to affirm fully "the otherness of the other."

Finally, to promote ecological ways of living, it is crucial to celebrate what we love in nature, rather than by focusing exclusively on the destruction that frightens and dismays us. While waking us up to the awesome prospects that have come to haunt us, ecological perspectives are educative only when they continuously connect us to the natural world we know and cherish. Through these connections, we reeducate ourselves; learning to belong to places we have helped regenerate with affection, loyalty and care.

NOTES

1. Vandana Shiva. *Monocultures of the Mind.* (London: Zed Books, 1993).

2. For some examplars of ecology *qua* modern science, see: The World Commission on Environment and Development, *Our Common Future* (Oxford: Oxford University Press, 1987); and different issues of the *Bruntland Bulletin,* now renamed *The Bulletin—Quarterly Review of Progress Towards Sustainable Development,* Geneva: Centre for Our Common Future; Michael Keating, *The Earth Summit's Agenda for Change* (Geneva: Centre for Our Common Future, 1993); and Lester Brown, et al.'s annual *The State of the World* (New York: Norton, 1988); and of the subsequent years.

3. Ivan Illich. *Gender.* (New York: Pantheon Books, 1982), p. 19.

4. For some exemplars of ecology *qua* postmodern, people's science, see Vandana Shiva, *Staying Alive: Women, Ecology and Development* (London: Zed, 1989); "Whose Common Future," *The Ecologist,* 22, no. 4 (July/August 1992); Wolfgang Sachs, "Environment" in Wolfgang Sachs ed. *The Development Dictionary: A Guide to Knowledge as Power* (London: Zed, 1992). Also see Wolfgang Sachs, "The Gospel of Global Efficiency: On Worldwatch and Other Reports on the State of the World," *IFDA Dossier,* no. 68, (Nov./Dec. 1988); Tariq Banuri and Frederique Apfel-Marglin, *Who Will Save the Forests? Knowledge, Power and Environmental Destruction* (London: Zed Books, 1993); David Cayley, "The Earth is Not an Ecosystem," (Toronto: Canadian Broadcasting Corporation, 1992); and Ivan Illich, "The Shadow Our Future Throws," *New Perspectives Quarterly,* 6, no. 1 (Spring 1989). Wolfgang Sachs, ed., *Global Economy—A New Arena of Political*

Conflict (London: Zed Books, 1993). For the historical evolution of perspectives ecological, see Donald Worster, *Nature's Economy: A History of Ecological Ideas* (San Francisco: Sierra Club, 1977).

5. For another example of ecological perspectives that promote cultural diversity and gender liberation, see Vandana Shiva, "The Greening of Global Reach," *The Ecologist,* 22, no. 6 (Nov./Dec. 1992).

6. Wendell Berry, *A Continuous Harmony—Essays Cultural and Agricultural* (London: Harvest/HBJ, 1972) pp. 72–73.

7. Elizabeth Ellsworth, "Why Doesn't This Feel Empowering? Working Through the Repressive Myths of Critical Pedagogy," *Harvard Educational Review,* 59, no. 1 (February 1989).

8. For a rich analysis of how the oppressed become the intimate enemy, see Ashis Nandy, *The Intimate Enemy* (New Delhi: Oxford University Press, 1983).

9. "Whose Common Future," p. 167.

10. Berry, *A Continuous Harmony,* p. 74.

11. All of us, Indians as well as others, are by now his descendants, argue Z. Sardar, A. Nandy, M. Davies, C. Alvares, *The Blinded Eye* (New York: The Apex Press, 1993).

12. Wendell Berry, "Nobody Loves This Planet," *In Context,* no. 27 (Winter 1991): p. 4.

13. Wendell Berry, "Out of Your Car, Off Your Horse," *The Atlantic Monthly,* February 1991, p. 61.

14. Berry, "Nobody Loves This Planet," p. 4.

15. Berry, Ibid. p. 4.

16. Berry, "Out of Your Car," p. 62.

17. David Orr, *Ecological Literacy: Education and the Transition to a Postmodern World* (Albany: State University of New York Press, 1992), p. 100.

18. Orr, Ibid. pp. 126–127.

19. Orr, Ibid. p. 127.

20. Orr, Ibid. p. 102.

21. Orr, Ibid. p. 126.

22. Orr, Ibid. p. 102.

23. For his insightful discussions of the differences between residing and dwelling, see Orr, Ibid. pp. 102–103 and pp. 130–31, for example.

24. Wendell Berry, *What Are People For?* (San Francisco: North Point Press, 1990), pp. 61–2.

25. Alasdair MacIntyre, *After Virtue* (London: Duckworth, 1981), p. 211.

26. Orr, *Ecological Literacy,* p. 181.

27. Ivan Illich, *Toward a History of Needs* (Berkeley: Heyday, 1977). Also see, Ivan Illich, *Tools of Conviviality* (New York: Harper & Row, 1973); *Deschooling Society* (New York: Harper & Row, 1970); and *The Celebration of Awareness* (New York: Doubleday, 1970).

28. Groeneveld, L. Hoinacki, I. Illich, and friends, "The Earthy Virtue of Place," *New Perspectives Quarterly,* 8, no. 1 (Winter 1991): 59.

29. Groeneveld, et al., "The Earthy Virtue of Place," Ibid. p. 59.

30. Groeneveld, et. al., Ibid. p. 59.

31. For a further analysis of both these educational experiments, see Madhu Suri Prakash, "Gandhi's Postmodern Education: Ecology, Peace, and Multiculturalism Relinked," *Holistic Education Review,* vol. VI, no. 3 (Autumn 1993).

32. The typical mouthful of American food travels 2000 kilometers from farm to dinner plate. See L. Brown, et. al., *The State of the World 1991* (New York: Norton, 1991), p. 159.

33. This is the title of a course taught at The Pennsylvania State University by Prof. Barbara Anderson-Siebert. Its focus has been on the writings of Wendell Berry, Wes Jackson, and other significant thinkers exploring alternative ways of learning and living. This course is not only innovative in its content, but also in its pedagogy; it goes far in putting to practice the ecological/educational ideas of Berry, Jackson, et al.

34. For examples of such grassroots initiatives, promoting rooted learning and living, successfully bringing ecology down to earth, see *The Aisling Quarterly,* Inismor, Arainn, Co na Gaillimhe, Eire.

25

Matters of the Mind

Jo Anne Pagano

Not since Nietzsche wrote God's obituary has an announced death caused caused a major intellectual revolution. I refer, of course, to the much publicized death of the Author. While many have moved with alacrity to bury his sorry carcass, others, through prayer and devotion, look to the resurrection. The members of each of these groups may be characterized as belonging to competing narrative communities, as operating under opposing governing narratives. To borrow from Terrence Des Pres, the gravediggers subscribe to a narrative of power, while the worshippers subscribe to a narrative of knowledge. According to Des Pres, each of these governing narratives tells the story of its own hero—either the hero of power, often a trickster, or the hero of knowledge, the seeker of truth.[1] What we have here is yet another situation in which we are asked to choose one side or the other.

While postmodernism is the sexier of the two choices, it is not an altogether comfortable choice for feminists to make, and for the same reasons that make the priesthood an unlikely vocation. Both choices involve repudiation of the body, the body with which women have been identified. Moreover, the heroes of both of these narratives are solitary and singular selves, despite the postmodernist's claim to have disseminated selfhood, to have exploded the fiction of selfhood. In this regard, it has been noted that postmodern philosophies and literatures really say nothing new to women whose lives are defined by their positions in relationship to others, whose selves, to borrow the jargon, are always already disseminated. The fact of female Otherness, of the definition of women's lives in relational terms, defies the myth of the autonomous unitary subject who is the hero of the narrative of knowledge. It is precisely the selflessness of Otherness that feminist narratives contest, but not necessarily the particularity of selfhood.

Women's speaking and writing is one among many currents in contemporary Western cultures bearing thought toward rewriting the myth of selfhood. The ideal of selfhood and the drive to consensus articulated by Habermas and believers in the resurrection presumes a community of interest eyed with suspicion by those whose interests it has been in the community's interest to repress. Women and other outsiders must be suspicious of appeals to our "we-ness" knowing that *we* implies *they* with little benefit to *them*. This narrative of truth is a disguised narrative of power. Postmodern theories might appear to promise a friendly neighborhood for feminist theories to set up housekeeping in, beginning as both do with a critique of masterful meaning and of the self who is the master of meanings. And it is true that we could find worse neighbors, neighbors who would as soon drive us out of town. Still, I wonder about the terms of the mortgage. And I guess I'd like to consult a structural engineer.

Odysseus was a trickster, more clever by far than Polyphemos, the loutish cannibal Cyclops with "no muster and no meeting, no consultation or old tribal ways."[2] Odysseus told this monster Polyphemos his name: "My name is Nohbdy: mother, father, friends, everyone calls me Nohbdy."[3] When Odysseus took a torch and with it put out the light in Polyphemos' single eye, the Cyclops must finger "nobody" as the villain. This led his neighbors to withdraw with the advice that he should pray to Zeus since if nobody was responsible for his mutilation it must be an act of the gods. When the theorist argues the dissemination of "the personal agent of signification," otherwise known as the author, across a range of rhetorical and grammatical positions I wonder if he's just another Odysseus pulling the wool over the eyes of the one-eyed kings. The eyes/I's no longer have it. And despite my being a woman who gets to speak in public, I am still nobody.

The trick disguises, or perhaps represses, the wisdom of scepticism which is founded on the desire of the exile for the Garden of Eden or for the maternal body, depending on your preference in myths of origins. In this it is no *mere* trick. Postmodern theory returns us to repressed material through its own system of repressions. Religious authority forbids both knowledge and desire; scepticism attempts to accommodate philosophy to the limits of human knowledge; postmodern theory makes a virtue of necessity and sweeps away the knowing subject making of his objectless desire the definition of human existence—its essence. The trick of the postmodern turn, like the sceptical idealism that is its patrimony, represses the horror of the little boy in Freud's fantasy who knows that his mother is castrated and fears his own castration, who becomes aware of the possibility of castration at the same time that he becomes aware of himself as one who knows the other's difference. This trick only apparently diminishes the drive to masterful meaning for after all there are still things to be said and claimed and argued and tested. In the epistemology that flows from this trick, difference is asserted while its importance is denied. Barbara Johnson notes:

> What the transfer of personhood to rhetorical entities does enable de Man to achieve, however, is the elimination of sexual difference. By making personhood the property of an "it," de Man is able to claim a form of universality which can be said to inhere in language itself, and which is not directly subject to ordinary feminist critique, however gender-inflected language can be shown to be. The analysis of the rhetorical operations of self-resistance is, as de Man asserts, irrefutable in its own terms. But the question *can* be asked why de Man's discourse of self-resistance and uncertainty has achieved such authority and visibility, while the resistance and uncertainty of *women* has been part of what has insured their lack of authority and their invisibility. It would seem that one has to be positioned in the place of power in order for one's self-resistance to be valued. Self-resistance, indeed, may be one of the few viable postures remaining for the white male power establishment.[4]

It may be the only viable posture which secures to the male his continuing mastery. For if difference is assimilated to discourse, in many cases reduced to discourse, then the Otherness of the female subject becomes metaphorical merely and as immediately available to male as female. Difference is effectively denied and epistemological authority reinstituted in the regime of undecidability. The neighborhood appears less hospitable than it seemed at first. At the same time, as Jane Flax notes, feminist theories are postmodern philosophies and all postmodern discourse is deconstructive in its distancing us from received beliefs concerning knowledge, truth, self, and language. We must understand that speaking women speak from a place of contradiction necessarily and that our speaking must lead to a place of contradiction.[5] Our differences sustain our connections, and our connections are expressions of our difference. We cannot have one without the other.

I am suggesting that as feminists we can accept the death of *an* author, that is of a version of "author," by reconceptualizing authorship in the same way that we do selfhood. In acting as god's coroner, Nietzsche was not denoting an empirical fact. "God is dead" is a moral-epistemological premise from which follow certain attitudes towards knowledge and its uses. It carries us towards a sense of radical responsibility and implies a radical nearness to the world and to other people. If god is dead, and if, in some sense, everything is then permitted, how am I to choose? The necessity of choice in human affairs means that everything is not permitted. But without god, what then? The death of the author is just such a premise. It is a moral-epistemological proposition, but one that in some hands seems to propel us headlong toward a radical irresponsibility and a radical distance from the world and other people. In other hands, the premise may turn us to our own responsibility by turning us to the body that others are so quick either to inter or endow with magicoreligious properties.

Of course, the terms postmodernism, poststructuralism, and deconstruction are as misleading as the terms consensus epistemologies, pragmatism, praxis philosophy, or feminism. These terms suggest a unity of thought which simply does not exist, although each is, in a sense, part of the structure of the others. A fair representation would distinguish Derrida from say, Lyotard and Rorty. Unlike Lyotard and Rorty who reject the principle of reason, Derrida demands a reason for reasonableness. Similarly Lyotard and Rorty may be read as postulating consensus epistemologies, but their insistence on the "performative" effects of knowledge simply uncritically reaffirms the communal self-image and consensus of ideas of Eurocentered liberal intellectuals.[6] Certain feminists adopt both of these positions as others embrace Habermas' communicative reason versus the subject-centered reason of the praxis philosophies whose distortions he claims to correct and the postmodernisms which nourish the romance of subjectivity.

The choices as typically articulated are limiting and specious at a deep level. Whether we choose Lyotard's method of language game analysis, or Habermas' linguistic investigation of validity claims, or whether we choose for a self, disseminated among rhetorical functions, we remain very much victims of objectivity fetishism, a form of displaced eroticism, even as we celebrate at the wake of objectivity. These are all choices among idealisms, choices which betray a deep suspicion of the body and its attachments to the world. Skulking about in the cellars of all these formulations is a fantasy of unfettered mind, a mind free of the body and its sorrows and desires, a fantasy having its origins in infantile erotic desire.

Still, the discourses we have are the discourses we are born into and in which we learned to speak and write, the discourses in which we are schooled. The attraction for us of postmodern discourses is in their rejection of monistic theories, feminist and others, and their movement toward a proleptic and prefigurative significatory moment in an undesignated but richly possible future. In the decades since the Holocaust with the threat of nuclear annihilation, distance from received beliefs and suspicion of authority—political and scientific authority alike—is critical. Postmodernism is instinct with a deep suspicion of authority and of the scientific rationality which has unleashed the unthinkable and unspeakable on the world. But postmodern thought need not necessarily reject reason and authority. Habermas' procedural rationality is an attempt to save the appearances from seeming antirational or irrational schemes. I think the choice between reason or no reason, authority or anarchy, overlimits us by defining reason too narrowly and by assimilating it to a very few operations. The questions, as all admit, are questions of practice.

In postmodern educational theory, the teacher occupies the same rhetorical function as the author in literary theory or philosophy. The central moral-epistemological problem is one of authority. In classrooms, teachers have authority, power, the say-so, the power to say it is so. Like the author of a fiction or a philosophy, however, the teacher, like a self in Lyotard's language, doesn't amount to much. Teachers are positions at certain nodal points through which messages pass. The authorial and pedagogical "I's" are fictions functioning in literary or educational narratives as the ones with the say-so. This representation neglects the fact, of course, that teachers have real authority in a real world and their say-so has real consequences in real students' lives. Moreover, whether we conceive of education as the transmission across generations of that which is most valuable in a culture, as the domestication of a properly socialized and stratified workforce, as the constitution of consumers of surplus production, or as the initiation of persons into language games, we presume some sort of consensus and communal self-image.

If we take seriously the postmodern view of the self, a neat trick since it is scarcely imaginable to me that I am a fiction or a rhetorical function, it seems that education, as ordinarily conceived is inherently totalitarian. It is a narrative of power, necessarily. Or else it seems that teaching is simply some sort of antic entertainment never to be taken seriously. Deconstruction teaches us that the postmodern divided subject, the self which is not itself, is an artifact of the unitary subject. It is one of a pair of binary oppositions situated within a logic of domination and submission. The centrality and indurateness of the logic of domination in postmodernism is just what Habermas proposes to edge off the page with the force of the reciprocal actions of intersubjective communicative agents who proceed with respect for universalizable grammatical tests of validity. The fantasy of the postmodernist's dissemination is partner to the fantasy of the consensus theorist's agreement. At the extremes of the former case we are left with difference and division so pervasive as to be irrelevant; any knower may take up any position in a text. At the extremes of the latter we are enabled to shift our identity across pronouns with the same effect. Both attempt to appropriate difference, to recuperate the demands of the Other simply in virtue of the Other's otherness. The extreme postmodern subject is a resymbolization of Kant's infinitely substitutable subjects who will *will* for others only that which they are willing to *will* for themselves, but without Kant's authoritarian and universal moral imperatives. The communicative agent is a resymbolization of Hegel's dialectical subject whose subjectivity depends on its awareness of the other as other. Unlike Hegel's subject whose subjectivity in the end depends on the becoming of divine reason, the communicative agent's subjectivity participates in the becoming of a kind of divine and absolute grammar. Both readings of the subject are highly rationalistic. These readings may be understood within the framework of psychoanalytic theory.

In the governing narratives of psychoanalysis, the first knowledge is said to be the knowledge of separation, a knowledge coincident with the knowledge of sexual difference. This is obviously a male story, and in many important respects resembles the story of the exile from the garden. The infant experiences itself as continuous with its mother, its body an extension of hers, one flesh. The infant is blissfully unaware of its dependence, its feebleness, the precariousness of its existence, or, like Adam and Eve, of the difference between, even the existence of, good and evil. Its relationship with the mother is symbiotic. When the knowledge of its dependence on the maternal body, which is in fact separate and distinct, and for the boy sexually different, intrudes, the infant experiences rage and sorrow. It knows it knows the evil of separation. And it desires; it desires that which it can never have—union with the maternal body. It knows the difference between pleasure and pain. It desires the unity expressed in the fantasy that Adam and Eve are one flesh. Eve's betrayal of Adam is her bringing to him the knowledge that they are naked. Her desire is his undoing, condemning him to an eternity of desire for prelapsarian ignorance. This is rightly called the fall of *man.* At the moment of the Oedipus Complex, the little boy sees that boys and girls are different, and he is horrified. Out of his terror, he begins to build a moral structure of binary opposites, and a logical structure that excludes the middle. But, that girls lack two things and not just the one most often fixed on is important. Girls lack not only the mark of sexual difference, the phallus, they lack also sexual difference from the mother, and this is the sign of their moral defect. Because women are like their mothers they are more closely confined in the prison house of the body.

In *Cognition and Eros,* Robin Schott describes Augustine's fantasy of prelapsarian sexuality as a state without desire. The prelapsarian state is the natural state, and so it is unnatural for humans to desire. Aquinas displaced desire onto the woman, making woman unnatural, therefore evil. Schott notes that the university originates in the imperatives of the church of the Middle Ages in an atmosphere of extreme asceticism in which knowledge becomes associated with a rejection of the body and a fear of desire.[7] But humans do desire, and that is the curse of humanity. The business of religion and education is to subdue desire by subjugating the body. The business of education becomes a denial of the roots of knowledge in erotic attachment, and separation becomes the foundation and condition of knowledge. Knowledge is shackled to horror.

Loss, frustration, and fear are the conditions of human knowledge in all of our governing narratives. Human consciousness is born in an anguished moment; its history and fate in this tale of origins lead us directly to a kind of wisdom—Stanley Cavell calls it the wisdom of scepticism. Cavell argues that scepticism originates in the very condition of being human. The legacy of philosophy, he argues, is a repression or denial of our knowledge of this condition. Cavell distinguishes two species of scepticism: material-world and other-minds scepticism. For Cavell other-minds scepticism is the real problem, and one not despatched by the solutions which mitigate our anxieties about the material world. Common sense and methodological rules of testing and evidence leave us with good enough knowledge regarding the existence and identity of material objects. At the same time, our optimistic faith in common sense and methodology serve only to repress what Descartes "knew"—we can never *know* the existence of other minds. Descartes was able to intuit his own existence through his consciousness of the act of his own thinking. But Descartes's intuition will never give us access to, knowledge of, *self*-consciousness of, the Other's thinking. As Cavell notes, something is always in the way, something separates us, and that something is the body. The body stands in the way of the penetration of knowledge. In brilliant readings of Shakespeare, Cavell demonstrates that the repression of the failure of knowledge, the sense of lack, is at the heart of human tragedy.[8]

Cavell shows us that the question of other minds, of the Other, is not an epistemological or a methodological problem. I read him as claiming that it is a moral, a psychological, and a political question. It has everything to do with what it means to be a human being dependent on integration into a world of human desire and human care. It has everything to do with trust and dignity. The sceptical, the biblical, and the psychoanalytic tales are all expressions of the same grief and anger and fear—the tragedy of being human. These tales are also uniquely male, expressions exemplary of the male original relation to the lost female object, an object once the source of perfect pleasure. They all report different aspects of male rage and fear.

The hero of all these tales is the autonomous individuated, unitary self. It is the hero of knowledge whose *bildung* is recounted in the metanarrative of the Enlightenment. It will not do to neglect the fact that this hero is sexed. The individuated unitary self is the one, who at the moment of awareness of separation, of individuation, of unitariness, is aware of himself as sexually different from the Other from whom he did not previously experience himself individuated. In these tales, that loss is denied in the peculiarly human device known as making a virtue of necessity. In all of these tales, the moment of separation, the experience of lack and exile, is read as the beginning of knowledge. Loss is thus valorized. Epistemology, psychology, and culture begin in violence and denial. What specifically is denied, and what specifically is the target of violence? The target of violence is the female body—both in psychoanalysis and art and culture. This violence is made possible by the denial of epistemological status to what can in fact be understood as the origin of experience, as the first knowledge—namely that we are connected to and dependent on the Other. The binary logic operative is apparent here, with difference lining up with separation and denial, against sameness lined up with connection. Difference becomes the mark of the individual.

These originary narratives have consequences for education. Our concern with assessment and evaluation, with educational progress says that we expect that we can ask a student, what do you know and how do you know? Certainly the history of the meaning of scholarship is somehow bound up with our asking and answering those questions. But how are such questions meaningful? Our tales of origins require a confession of ignorance, for knowledge is radically impossible. In fact, many of our common sense educational practices betray our suspicion that this is the case. Moreover, those who would argue that education is and ought to be about the development of moral agency, the development of a self which knows good and evil, the difference between them, and is able to act for good, seem to be exhorting us to that which is expressly forbidden human beings, that which is impossible. We might argue that the possibility of mistake implies the possibility of knowledge. This is, of course, Austin's response to scepticism. But we do engage in these speculations, and not simply because we have nothing better to do with our time. That we do, and have done so with some urgency throughout the history of philosophy suggests that the problems raised by these tales of origins cannot be explained away by recourse to method or procedure. Perhaps we need the optimism method promises, just as we need the hope offered by religion and therapy. But optimism is also a denial, a repression, and what is repressed inevitably returns.

Insisting on difference, we betray the persistence of an infantile desire to merge, to return to the garden. We express this desire everywhere in our romance with standards and standardization, our fascination with analogies and homologies, our passion for labeling and grouping, our staging and our sorting. Our conviction that there are only two kinds of persons in the world, male and female, leads to a conviction that we must choose between difference and connection. By denying epistemological status to that first knowledge of connection, our differences become fearsome and burdensome to us. The imperatives of the male drama of selfhood and knowledge demand that that difference be read as simultaneously desirable and invidious. A student with "special educational needs" is not a student anyone wants to be, while the rare student in the 99th percentile is most desirable indeed.

Difference is the mark of the limits and failure of knowledge to enable us to know the Other, to know the Other's knowledge. It is also the mark of the limits of our knowledge of ourselves, dependent as we are for our sense of ourselves on the way that others respond to us. I think Cavell is right in claiming that only our bodies seem to be in the way of our achieving the perfect knowledge of ourselves and others, and that we have this sense of our bodies' intransigence because of our particular romance of knowledge. Nowhere is this uneasy relationship between our bodies and ourselves more obvious than in ascetic practices toward enlightenment. It is apparent in our ordinary ways of talking as when a corpse is designated a *body*.

This inert barrier to enlightenment, the body is also a traitor. Our bodies betray us. Freud reads Dora's gestures to reveal the truth her words disguise; the teacher reads guilt in the cheating student's body. The fantasy of nakedness is an uncanny revelation of the horror of the body. Others' bodies, along with their words, betray us. We can never know for certain when we are being lied to. Teachers can never know for certain that their students know what they are taught. Students can never know what the teacher understands or expects. The knowledge we need is always just out of reach. Insofar as we can, our hunger for a knowledge predicated on the primal tragic experience of difference and separation demands that we school the body out of school.

The body is opaque. It is a trick to deceive the teacher into thinking that an absence is a presence, but the teacher is on to that old trick. The teacher can read our minds even when the eyes in the back of her head are closed. This is her fantasy and ours. The fantasy conceals a desire to rid the classroom of those troublesome bodies; it reveals the existence of the wishful fantasy for a purely legible mind. If trust is essential in the pedagogical relationship, the pedagogical relationship is impossible. We develop strategies and tests to neutralize the overpresent body, and these are substitutes for trust.

The anaesthetics of school buildings and classrooms, the gray and the green, the metal and concrete, discipline the desire for visual pleasure, preparing the eye for the culture's standard of beauty. The twenty-minute lunch in the school cafeteria discipline the appetite for food. The pleasure of rhythm and movement is relegated to recess, a break from the serious business of emotional and intellectual development. Our classroom desks arranged in rows provide a permanent display of the backs of our classmates heads. "Keep your hands off your neighbor." The teacher is the one who sees and knows. The teacher's face and body, though, like the backs of our classmates' heads are inscrutable. What we need to know is just there—out of reach.

Our attempt to exile our bodies from the classroom is a defense against our fear of betrayal. The body can betray in two ways. My body can reveal what I wish to conceal; others' bodies can conceal what I wish them to reveal. In this complex of denial, the texts and papers, the tests and evaluations take on the character of fetishes. The various recommendations of the various reform reports of the 1980s serve a fetishistic function. The fetish permits us to position ourselves at a distance from that which we desire through a process in which we overvalue a substitute for that desire. Longer school days, rigorous testing and evaluation, increased homework, core curricula, basic skills, critical thinking, professionalization, act as fetishes for our repressed anxiety about knowledge and our vain hope that knowledge do more than it can. We can ask ourselves about any of these recommendations what desire they betray and what anxiety they are meant to allay. And we can note that, as is true of all fetishes, these are unsuited to their aim.

In the sceptic's, the Christian's, and the psychoanalyst's tales, knowledge is impossible. In the Christian tale, it is impossible because forbidden—forbidden by an omniscient god jealous of his power. In the sceptic's tale the failure of knowledge is the mark of the human condition. In the psychoanalyst's tale knowledge is a substitute for an obscure and unobtainable, an inscrutable object of desire, but it is a substitute the aim of which, like desire is impossible of satisfaction. These are the tales which result in our postmodern exhaustion. All of these are tales of what stands between human beings—the body and its difference. Education, which aims at the incorporation of each of us into the body politic, struggles to do so against the body's difference and must therefore deny both bodies and differences. And yet only uniqueness, the difference of bodies from others, guarantees identity.

Revolutions in thought have been announced with some regularity in the history of human consciousness. The varieties of postmodernism or post-structuralism enjoying current fashion are invested with revolutionary fervor. My own sense is that far from a revolutionary development, postmodern theories are inevitable heirs to the legacy of the sceptical, biblical, and psychoanalytic schools of interpretation. I am inclined to agree with Habermas that postmodernism is a symptom of exhaustion. It assumes, though disavowing idealist paradigms, a binary logic in which the self is either the Enlightenment hero of knowledge or an endless chain of fictions forged in the Sisyphean labor of interpretation, an infinitely fragmented and displaced series of positions at the sightless windows of the Tower of Babel, now called reverently the TEXT.

The postmodern moment is a further episode in the tale of male development. Unlike earlier episodes in which the hero attempts to subvert the necessity of ignorance imposed by the limits of human knowledge, in this chapter he attempts to make a virtue of it. Like the heroism of his Enlightenment forefathers, this virtue is molded in the crucible of male infantile rage. In all of these narratives of knowledge and its vicissitudes, the first knowledge, the foundation of human consciousness is situated in the cataclysmic event of the Oedipal crisis, whether or not the language deployed is that of psychoanalysis. The foundation of knowledge is separation and difference, an affliction of a soul cast from the presence of things themselves or the maternal body into an absence redolent of nostalgia, a soul imprisoned and limited by its body and senses. This does not mean that women have nothing to learn from such theories, or that we cannot usefully employ them.

The question for feminist educational theorists committed to some sort of emancipatory goal is whether we can employ contemporary theories in our analysis of education without adopting the view of the self of either postmodern or consensus theory. The postmodern self and the self of consensus theory both sustain claims to privilege, even where both embrace goals of emancipation and empowerment. Emancipation, freedom, liberty—these are words we can't avoid in any discussion of education. But, because along each of these routes difference is enslaved, emancipation and empowerment are thwarted. Rationalistic and pragmatic consensus theories, alike, operate through the dominant intellectual mode of assimilation. Opening up schools and curricula to women and to members of oppressed racial and ethnic groups has historically required that all of us become like white men. The stuff of education is taken as given. Participation in speech communities, ideal or the ones we have, requires assimilation to standardized modes of speech. Postmodern theories that reduce us to our rhetorical functions similarly ensnare us in our representations by dominant groups. Just as Freud observed his grandson controlling the mother's absence in the *fort-da* game, our reduction to our images permits our control. The legitimacy of the Other is denied.

Consensus choices insist, in the face of all contrary experience, on our essential sameness. Poststructural choices insist on our difference, but only to deny the importance of our need for connection. Both choices are effects of the infantile fantasy of merging with the mother, a fantasy expressive simultaneously of desire and rejection. Both choices are effects of the arbitrary denial of epistemological status to the infantile experience of being connected to the mother and the assimilation of knowledge to separation.

Understanding the myths of knowledge and knowers constructed in both kinds of theories does enable critical analysis of our educational structures and practices. We embrace these myths to our peril, seductive as each is in its distinctive way. The postmodern self is a weary and often wearying creature. In the contemporary world, however, his refusal of acknowledgment is necessary. He understands that the language games of nuclear deterrence, right to life, are no mere distortions correctible in some ideal democratic speech situation. His often antic criticism, his refusal to settle, expresses the fundamental lie of political optimism and consensus. But the self, asserted as a fiction in some ever-shifting play of language, denies the very material connections that bind human beings together. The self of the consensus theorist is a more attractive creature—one who acknowledges the material fact of human connection. At the same time, connection seems possible in this myth only in assimilative fashion. Having little faith in the efficacy of grammatical rules to keep us honest, I fear this self is as much potential tyrant as the hero of power.

But the hero of knowledge in the governing narratives of consensus always confronts an agony of ignorance and absence. Shoshana Felman argues that ignorance is not an absence, however, but an active resistance to knowledge. She says that ignorance, while the Other of knowledge, is not opposed to knowledge, but is a condition of it, an element in the structure of knowledge itself. Ignorance is that species of forgetting known as repression. Ignorance is an expression of a "desire to ignore." In each of these tales of knowledge, the work of repression entails the ig-norance of the body. For what is repressed is a knowledge that precedes the knowledge that we are separate and different. That knowledge is the knowledge of our connection to and dependence on the female body.[9]

We are different but we are also connected. The fact of connection, the experience and hence the knowledge of connection is the condition of the knowledge that we are separate and different. The repression of this knowledge, the denial of epistemological status to this experience returns, as repressed material inevitably does, in tales of the uncanny and in brutality. The insistence on difference as a lack masks the fear of sameness and it is that fear that is the condition of the will to domination by assimilation. Acknowledgement of the priority of connection makes the play of difference possible. Our knowledge that we are connected can more easily bear the burden of our difference, than the knowledge that we are separate. The knowledge of our connection makes the knowledge of our separation and difference less fearsome.

Both postmodern critics and consensus theorists are influenced by speech act theory. Speech act theory introduces us to the notion of *performative* utterances—utterances that in their execution accomplish an act. The obvious case of a performative is the utterance "I promise to do X," where to speak the promise is to undertake the act of promising. Performatives are often distinguished from *constatives*—utterances having denotative functions only. A search for criteria distinguishing performatives from constatives having proved fruitless, has led some theorists to assert that all utterances are performative, either explicitly or implicitly. According to Austin every speech act carries both meaning and force. The production of meaning is a *locutionary* act; the establishing of interpersonal relationships between speaker and receiver is an *illocutionary* act; and effect on the receiver is a *perlocutionary* act. Austin gives us five categories of speech acts: verdicts, orders, commitments, behaviors (apologizing, e.g.), and expositions.[10]

Poststructuralists tend to emphasize the context of an utterance arguing that changes in the features of the context in which an utterance occurs alters its illocutionary force. The aspect of this claim that fascinates poststructuralists is the boundlessness of context. Any context is always open to further description and any description alters the context. This means that contexts, hence speech acts, are unmasterable. In the language of language games, redescription can always alter the rules of a game or place an utterance in a totally different language game. Where poststructuralism privileges the complication of context in order to accomplish its dissemination of the speaking self, Habermas, among other consensus theorists is equally interested in the components of an utterance that express a speaker's intention and in universalizable, grammatical rules that serve as the court of appeal for establishing the validity of an utterance.

In this context, the pervasiveness of a rhetoric of emancipation and empowerment in educational theory is particularly interesting. Just what are the emancipatory approaches to education at issue in reform controversies and in controversies over the proper theoretical stance? Who is being freed? What is the relationship between emancipator and emancipated? What are the various contexts in which these relationships are drawn? From what and to do what are we to be emancipated or empowered? We may ask what the rhetorical function of emancipation or empowerment is in educational discourse. What does it express and what does it repress? It seems to me clear that the questions of authority, participation, productivity, creativity, and even survival implicated in the goal of emancipation are finally questions of self and community, of persons who exist for and in the representations of others, and for whom others are represented. Who does the speaking is critical. And where.

Contemporary theory has led us to new texts and to new readings of new texts. It has supported the political efforts that result in interrogations of the canon. We can employ these approaches to interpretation in morally instructive ways if only we keep in sight the horizon of our own material specificity—our bodies, as well as our selves. Tales, fictions, biographies, and autobiographies help us to do so because tales are stories of embodiment and particularity. The tale functions in a way that all of the statistics and all of the facts, all of the theories and all of the arguments cannot.

Educational theory seems these days much concerned with power, if the number of titles containing the word "empowerment" is any indication. The call to empowering education is very much a consequence of a psychology of powerlessness. A speech act analysis of the rhetoric of empowerment might reveal to us things we would prefer not to know about ourselves.

The psychology of powerlessness has been often written about—conceptually, theoretically, and empirically. As a particular example of a study of power and powerlessness, and of a powerful use of learning and language, Harriet Jacobs' slave narrative, *Incidents in the Life of a Slave Girl,* gives us a clear picture of the material social, economic, political, and psychological circumstances that required and sustained the institution of slavery.[11] At the same time it is a study in the violence of language and learning. The psychology of powerlessness led Jacobs to deplore her own morality; her selfloathing is an effect of the material distribution of power in a slave-owning society, and of the particular use made of women who are owned. The tale, because of the way its specificity is expressed in dominant ideological categories serves to destabilize the repressive ideology that nourishes the institution of slavery. At the same time, its meaning depends, in a curious way, for its significance in Jacobs' appropriation of certain literary and biblical traditions, even as it exceeds the possibility of representation in those traditions.

At the center of Jacobs' life was her choice to bear two children out of wedlock by succumbing to the advances of a neighboring "good" slaveowner. She chose to do so in order to escape from the sexual persecution of her own owner. The source of her self-castigation is the Christian faith which sustains her understanding of human morality and human relationships. At the same time, her appeals to Christian rhetoric are expressed in terms which compel the Christian reader to take a critical look at the so-called Christianity woven through the fabric of the slaveholder's psychology. She skillfully and perceptively limned the victimization and repression that operated to make the slaveowner's wife, who should have been the slave's ally, complicit in the victimization of other women. In this way, Jacobs forced the reader to consider her own privilege in a slave-holding world and to acknowledge that her privilege exacts extreme costs from her sisters in slavery.

Hers is a peculiarly female story. She said, in fact, that slavery for women was much worse than slavery for men. Slavery is not just slavery. While the degradations that describe and define life under slavery in Jacobs' tale are expressed and analyzed in terms similar to those used by Frederick Douglass, there are critical differences, and these are grounded in sex.

Jacobs was persuaded, against her own inclinations, to tell her story because she saw the history of personal shame as symptomatic of slavery in general. Her degradation at the hands of the family she chose to call "Flint" is not to be read simply as one individual's story. It is potentially the story of all who are owned, bought, and sold by others. This is not to say, however, that stories are interchangeable, nor that any one of us can take the place of Harriet Jacobs. She is no rhetorical function. My reading of her tale is rather an imaginative resymbolization of her story through the conversation that I as reader hold with it. My reading is impossible both without her tale and without the specificities of my own life.

The narrative shuttles skillfully among accounts of personal events, reports of similar circumstances in others' lives, and general moral and political analyses. This motion itself demonstrates that the grievous injuries of slavery are not merely matters of individual suffering, nor is the slave to be read as a statistic in some history. Even her title—*Incidents in the Life of a Slave Girl*—makes this point. These incidents are incidentally events in her own life and necessary incidents in the life of slavery. We move from the facts of a life, to the facts of other lives, to the general and pervasive racism that infects this nation. There is no free soil in the United States, she tells us. The sadness at the end of her story is a mark of the tragic fact that at the moment of her writing, human beings, by virtue of the laws of this land of the free and the brave, may be bought, sold, and owned by others—body, if not soul.

Jacobs begins her journey in the private world of the family, and hers is a journey made in the name of the claims of family. Hers is a double book because it was written by a woman. One of its most obvious themes is that of the division of women from each other by a slaveholding patriarchy. Her tale tells of the sexualization of the slave woman and the idealization and desexualization of the wife. Hers is a tale that reveals the secrets of patriarchy in its concern with speaking and silence. Hers is also a tale of a community of women linked across generations. She describes herself as a grandmother's child.

Incidents is modeled on women's melodramatic fiction, textured with patterns of narration familiar to the nineteenth century reader of women's fiction. It is also familiar to us. She exhorts the reader, much as Jane Eyre does and in similar circumstances. She is alternately sarcastic and ironic. Jacobs appropriates meanings and subverts forms taking the sentimental notions of motherhood and its sanctity in patriarchy and turning them to her own purposes.

The first sentence of the final chapter of *Jane Eyre* is, "Reader, I married him." The final paragraph of Jacobs' narrative begins, "Reader, I am still without a home." In employing the conventions of the romance, she subverts it. At the same time with the doubleness that characterizes the entire narration she asserts the claims of family, of relation, of community.

The melodramatic fiction of the white middle classes is read differently when it is read in company with the slave narrative. For changing relationships and changing contexts destabilize congealed structures of power. This is not a quarrel over texts, their status as objects, or the plausibility of their various interpretations. It is a quarrel over who we are as knowers and what real embodied commitments are required of those who know as members of a social body. Through education we learn who we are; we come face to face with our relations with others; we are initiates into the body politic. We become readers with a history and a future in a company of past and future readers. These are *matters* of the mind.

NOTES

1. Terrence Des Pres, "On Governing Narratives," *Writing into the World: Essays 1973–1987* (New York: Viking, 1991), pp. 249–61.

2. Homer, *The Odyssey,* translated by Robert Fitzgerald (New York: Doubleday and company, 1963), p. 148.

3. Ibid., 156.

4. Barbara Johnson, *A World of Difference* (Johns Hopkins University Press, 1987).

5. Jane Flax, "Postmodernism and Gender Relations in Feminist Theory," *Signs,* 12, no. 4 (Summer 1987): 621–643.

6. For a detailed treatment of the relation between postmodernism and consensus theory, see Christopher Norris, *Derrida* (Cambridge: Harvard University Press, 1987).

7. For a study of the relationship of knowledge to asceticism see, Robin May Schott, *Cognition and Eros: A Critique of the Kantian Paradigm* (Boston: Beacon Press, 1988).

8. Stanley Cavell, *The Claim of Reason* (New York: Oxford University Press, 1979). See also essays in *The Senses of Stanley Cavell,* Richard Fleming and Michael Payne, eds. (Lewisberg: Bucknell University Press, 1989).

9. Shoshana Felman, "Psychoanalysis and Education: Teaching Terminable and Interminable," in Barbara Johnson, ed., *The Pedagogical Imperative: Teaching as a Literary Genre* (New Haven: Yale University Press, 1982), pp. 21–44.

10. Shoshana Felman, *The Literary Speech Act: Don Juan with J. L. Austin, or Seduction in Two languages,* Catherine Porter, trans. (Ithaca: Cornell University Press, 1983).

11. Harriet Jacobs, *Incidents in the Life of a Slave Girl.* Jean Fagin Yellin, ed. (New Haven: Yale University Press, 1988).

26

Turning Tricks

Mary S. Leach

> I am no longer the lining to your coat—your-faithful-understudy.
> Voicing your joys and sorrows, your fears and resentments. You had
> fashioned me into a mirror but I have dipped that mirror into the
> waters of oblivion—that you call life . . . I have washed off your masks
> and makeup, scrubbed away your multicolored projections and
> designs, stripped off your veils and wraps that hid the shame of your
> nudity. I have even had to scrape my woman's flesh clean of the insignia
> and marks you had etched upon it.[1]

> Beyond the horizon you have opened up, she will offer you that in
> which she still lives and that your day has not even imagined.[2]

The valiant words of Luce Irigaray compliment the subject of Jo Anne
Pagano's essay. But, even as her title "Matters of the Mind" struggles to evacuate, precisely, the heterosexist and racist idealism-materialism binary that has
ruled in the generic Western philosophical traditions she so able (bodily)
exposes, it reminds us of the difficulty of our task. And, even as she addresses the "myths of origins" that religion, sceptical idealism, and psychoanalytic
theory engender in an effort to show the different methods by which they
have exiled the body (female), we are continually warned of trickery afoot.
Her dissatisfaction with our past traditions does not deter her in persisting,
however, and she would ask the same from us.

Journeying back to the future is Pagano's method of explaining her title.
She narrates our culture's historical myths of selfhood, always forcing us to

look at the effects of these narratives in what is done to bodies, especially in the containment of the female body, "female Otherness." She persuasively shows what the stories of Christianity, psychoanalytic theory and the most contemporary tales of postmodern thought all have in common, the exile and discipline of the body, with the most horror reserved for the "sight/site of the female." Indeed, Pagano is particularly concerned with the "neat trick" of the latest turn in our intellectual tradition. That is postmodern thought, the go-cart of philosophy, which has, as she sees it, seduced many interested in social change. Pagano believes that the magic act of much of postmodern thought has not been all that "enchanting" in addressing women's embodied specifity. (Male) postmodern theorists particularly trick us in *their* celebration of difference.

Consensus theorists who recognize the mutually constitutive relationship between selfhood and others, as in the case of Habermas, for example, then fail to go on and account for the *significance* of the "essential foreignness of the Other," resulting finally in a difference that makes no difference. It is an old duck/rabbit trick which ultimately serves, given past and current power relations, to andropomorphize the *selves* of women, their sexual specificity, their speaking voice and their writing. Pagano takes care to address the attractions of postmodernism for feminists; its deconstructive method that helps "distance us from received beliefs concerning knowledge, truth, self, and language," its renewal of an impetus (in some hands) of "radical responsibility" and "radical nearness" to the world and to other people, and its anticipatory moment that projects the be/coming of a richly possible future. Still, she concludes, most of it constructs a fantasy of the self like that fantasy of consensus theorists. Both attempt to appropriate difference, to recuperate the desires and demands of the Other with their overly rationalistic sorcery that hides the ghost in their machine—our ultimate differences of the body.

Yet while she focuses much of her attention on the dangers all these theories hold, her position is not merely one of opposition and antagonism but of contiguity and comradeship-at-arms as well. She is in hopes that we like-minded can *use* the extant currents of thought to turn a few tricks of our own. These must be shapechangers which trouble our notions—all of them: classical, biblical, scientific, modernist, postmodernist, and feminist—while making us remember why we cannot want *the* "human" universal. She leaves us asking the question that many of us in education are posing. How can we use all intercultural and multicultural (feminist) theory to construct possible postcolonial, nongeneric, and irredeemably specific, *embodied* figures of reflective subjectivity, consciousness, and humanity—not in the sacred or historical image of the same, but in the self-critical practice of "difference," a practice that re/inscribes and re/vitalizes our connections to each other.

Now, Pagano wisely recognizes the problems of reductiveness that some readers may want to bring to her attention. She acknowledges that the terms she is using are in a sense misleading, suggesting "a unity of thought which simply does not exist." She goes on to make some quick distinctions of her own which would indicate her awareness that any description, especially if it is brief, will oversimplify highly complex bodies of work. This is particularly the case with postmodern thought whose purpose is partly to throw into question (as she wants to) the abstract intellectualized, highly rationalized terms required by any such straightforward monologic descriptions. Postmodern discourse is not monolithic—it is, indeed, an ensemble of *conflicting* discourses.

Pagano also does not try to position her own discourse as outside of, or transcendent to, the received myths of origins. After all, one can almost hear her sigh, "the discourses we have are the discourses we are born into and in which we learned to speak and write, the discourses in which we are schooled." This could explain her use of aspects of psychoanalytic premises even as she criticizes its legacy as a myth. It may be seen by some as ironic but it is no trick. As much as one might want to read her simultaneous use and problematization of this intellectual tradition as one of the "double move," it can as easily signify for her an inevitable bow to the contradictory position from which all outsiders must speak. In that case her grounding in such notions functions more as a rhetorical move that may be seen as making use of available means of persuasion. If this is an adequate characterization of what Pagano is doing she is capitalizing on a revival of rhetoric as an educational tool.

Obviously I'm not using "rhetoric" or "persuasion" in the narrow sense usually employed in the educational master trope of analytic philosophy. What Pagano says is needed in our (too narrow) definitions of reason and authority holds for rhetoric and persuasion as well. Stephen Toulmin has reminded us that *before* the seventeenth century, the diversity of human life resulted in the recognition in philosophy of a diversity of views.[3] These views resulted in an awareness that plurality, ambiguity and the lack of certainty was *no error* but evidence of different kinds of practical knowledge: the "oral, the particular, the local, and the timely. No one questioned the right of rhetoric to stand alongside logic in the canon of philosophy; nor was rhetoric treated as a second-class—and necessarily inferior—field."[4] The setting aside of all questions about argumentation—among particular people in particular situations, dealing with specific, concrete cases "where *varied things were at stake*"—in favor of proofs that could be set down in writing and judged began in the philosophical debate that was started by Decartes.

Resisting the legacy of the canon after Decartes, many feminists are not interested in performing the "trick of certitude" which concentrates on formal analysis of chains of written statements rather than on the circumstantial merits and defects of persuasive discussion.

We know that claiming certitude is a move, not unlike the charges of self-refutation and performative contradiction, preferred by some educational "logicians" who insist on the distinction between "mere" persuasion and "actual, timeless, god-like demonstration."[5] But, this sleight of mind simply allows those who use it to claim the (recent) higher ground, thereby leaving unexamined what persuades reasonable people, including philosophers. It also cleverly hides the "fact" that a scientific or philosophical argument of the demonstrative kind is (merely?) an account of its own argument. Disciplinary philosophers and those they have trained frequently show no such methodological self-consciousness, however, relegating that sort of reflection to metaphilosophy. "*Doing*" philosophy, they proceed to "demonstrate"—in classrooms, at conferences, and in pages of educational journals—the "incoherence" of certain theoretical positions; current picks are relativism, perspectivism, constructivism, and postmodernism.[6] They deal with "fallacies" or other arguments that their methods don't treat by reducing most of human reasoning to an insistence on a *style* of argument that cannot deviate from the "truth" of its premises which they often pick *for* us. The re/casting of an argument so that it becomes logically valid imagines a realm of ideas free of rhetoric—another fantasy of the unfettered mind. Ironically then, this style of argument is allowed to slide by without an argument! All that is left outside the (violence of) reduction is in the realm of rhetoric.

But Pagano argues that women must speak despite our (seemingly) contradictory position. We must speak with certainty without performing the trick of certitude, a position that is often dismissed as "trying to have it both ways." But we are turning that trick, and our turn allows us to keep speaking within the current perception of impasse: it can be described as akin to finding a way to stand on our own shoulders in a world of received tales that has forgotten its own history.

Recognizing that rhetorics of persuasion along with philomathematical "proofs" are *all* arguments, however, does not entail hopping into bed with relativism, that dread figure of chaos. As Barbara Herrnstein Smith points out, the logic that "anything goes" is identical to that of "everything's just as good as everything else." Both depend on taking for granted as *unquestionable* the classic concepts that *are being questioned* [by] the [argument] at hand."[7] Just as she refuses to settle for other intellectual traditions, Pagano refuses the classic measures of absolute Truth—another of Plato's tricks. Indeed, her whole essay shows that women can speak and write even in the midst of such dis/abling methods, theories, ideas, maintained by forgetful but powerful philosophical fathers. She faces these "contradictions", not with self-qualifications, but in a head-on intellectual collision tempered by a knowledge of connection and dependence, a knowledge derived, she believes, from our first connection to a female body.

Writing outside the closures of education's traditional epistemology and philosophy of language, writing that struggles to question the "unquestionability" of inherited ideas such as an objective unmediated reality, or "objective" rightness often turns to different conceptual schemes—traditions which prove more congenial to theoretical innovation. Thus, educational theorists who are engaged in exposing the desire in orthodoxy, frequently make use of tales, fictions, biographies, and autobiographies in attempts to avoid the more "normal" rhetorics of systematic critical analysis which seem only to repeat and sustain our entrapment in the stores of the established orders. And, Pagano finds in Harriet Jacobs and her narrative of slavery a figure of accountability and possible connection for us to turn to our own use. The doubleness of Jacobs' narration—"hers is a double book because it is written by a woman"—is immediately called to our attention. The folds in the tale of Jacobs' journey are recounted. These are the (simultaneously enacted) themes of power and powerlessness, of victimization and resistance, of personal circumstance and the public realm, of speaking and silence, of claims of relation, community, and family within an inhuman, separated system, in a life represented in language but eccentric to it. The logic of noncontradiction necessary to educational analytic philosophical stories makes little sense here. It is in a woman's figure of suffering humanity that is signified—in ambiguity, contradiction, "stolen" symbolism—a possible hope for a better understanding of our connectedness and dependence on one another.

Pagano clearly believes that "newly discovered texts" of this sort, if included in the canon, can have beneficial effects in helping to promote both the desired recognition of difference and connection she sees as crucial to social change. Although this isn't as clear from her writing, it does seem too that the texts she sees as most salutary would be from authors who can be categorized according to race, gender, and ethnicity. Is this because these authors stand in as delegates of a social constituency? If that is so, I wonder if part of this view operates on the assumption that the works they create transparently convey the authentic, unmediated experience of their social identities. Pagano tells us of the generic confusion surrounding the "authentication" of *Incidents*. What she doesn't tell us is what difference she thinks it would make in our "conversation" with the text if the white abolitionist, Lydia Maria Child, proved to be the author. Would the narrative still be as instructive, subversive, appropriating if the imputation of "realness" was removed? These are questions that arise when our literary judgments are grounded in an ideology of authenticity. And, the political stakes are not trivial, for the ethnic (or gendered) claim to its own experience cuts two ways. Henry Louis Gates, Jr. explains it this way:

> We easily become entrapped by what the feminist critic Nancy K. Miller has called "as-a" criticism: where we *always* speak "as-a" white middle-class woman, a person of color, a gay man and so on. And that, too, is a confinement—in the republic of letters as in the larger polity . . . [A] book is a cultural event; authorial identity, mystified or not, can be part of that event. What the ideologues of authenticity cannot come to grips with is that fact and fiction have always exerted a reciprocal effect

> on each other. However truthful you set out to be, your autobiography is
> never unmediated by literary structures of expression.[8]

Pagano does recognize that the narrative of *Incidents* "models" women's
melodramatic fiction of the nineteenth century. What isn't made explicit is
what role that language plays in terms of Jacobs's writing *as a woman*. Is
Jacobs's identity as a slave woman unmediated by the language in which she
expresses it? Pagano leaves me wanting more explanation of her view of the
subject, this "decided self," and its relationship to past and current structures
of discourse.

Working self-consciously outside the plot of Enlightenment Humanism,
Donna Haraway might invite us to read the figure of Harriet Jacobs as that of
a "trickster." In her own imaginative resymbolizing of women's voices of the
past, Haraway's desires, though arrived at and expressed quite differently
echo Pagano's. She too recognizes the need to have feminist figures of
humanity, ecstatic speakers as she calls them, who might "figure the self-con-
tradictory and necessary condition of a nongeneric humanity." She explains:

> I want here to set aside the Enlightenment figures of coherent and mas-
> terful subjectivity, the bearers of rights, holders of property in the self,
> legitimate sons with access to language and the power to represent, sub-
> jects endowed with inner coherence and rational charity, the masters of
> theory, founders of states, and fathers of families, bombs, and scientific
> theories—in short, Man as we have come to know and love him in the
> death-of-the subject critiques.[9]

Haraway chooses Soujourner Truth to represent one Western trickster figure whose (radically nominal) positionality can help us find a route to this
non-generic humanity, "for whom specificity—but emphatically not originality—is the key to connection."[10] For Haraway the female body stands apart
from the historical constructions that render it. She too is aware that the
dominant culture's allowed relations to one's own body (especially if one lives
under the rendering of "woman") are not desirable. But unlike Pagano, who
seems to fearlessly tread over much contested feminist ground in her own
position, Haraway attempts to listen to the material (female) body by relying
on general categories of *inscrutabilities;* by dis/covering discourses where
human meaning fails in an effort to foreground the *failure of language* to fully
capture materiality. In this way she works to both assert the importance of
bodily positionality and refuses to essentialize it. It seems her "weariness"
resides more in impossible modernist tales than in the (admittedly excessive
and extreme forms of social constructionism) of poststructuralist feminist
thought. Thus, she uses its tools in her work to render what might be that
"material onto which we map our constructions"; whatever that "body" *is*
that exists apart from the cultural markings that forms the object of her feminist belief. In her worry about where the body might stand apart from, or at

times against, the representations that encode it at every turn, in her own desire to escape from the commodifications that accompany the body, she looks to trickster figures whose positions allow bodies and identities to be touched upon (yet, not), so that they might be returned to us on *different* terms and in *different* ways.

Wary of real selves as real bodies, her move is to use a term like the "trickster" to evacuate any determinate sense of an original or essential self by which to mark our abused "bodies." She believes one route to escape for the sake of our "bodies," one route to the necessary *precondition* for non-alienated embodiment is the recognition of trickster figures like Sojourner Truth whose "hard name signifies someone who could never be at home, for whom truth was displacement from home."[11] She also appeals to other traditions:

> The Coyote or Trickster, as embodied in Southwest native American accounts, suggests the situation we are in when we give up mastery but keep searching for fidelity, knowing all the while we can be hoodwinked. I think these are useful myths for scientists who might be our allies. Feminist objectivity makes room for surprises and ironies at the heart of all knowledge production; we are not in charge of the world . . . Perhaps our hopes for accountability, for politics, for ecofeminism [which has been most insistent on some version of the world as active subject], turn on revisioning the world as coding trickster with whom we must learn to converse.[12]

Like Haraway, feminist Luce Irigaray is also trying to dis/cover a body that has been so covered over by patriarchal constructions. She chooses yet another route: the more playful, ironic mode of postmodern thought informs her work. While subject to varying interpretations, her writing directly invokes the opacity of objects, especially bodies, that we must learn to see. She speaks of the "opaque barrier that every/body presents to the light."[13] Irigaray leans upon past critiques—Marx and Freud, adding Lacan and Derrida—to (ever contradictorily) give form to a material opacity that women can invest in *for* themselves, without falling back upon the masculine value of *transparent* selves that relate as rivals.

Despite her changes in direction, the purpose of Irigaray's ongoing journey is to write about sexual difference as it has, and has not, been symbolically represented in philosophical discourse. Through ironic intertextual play, *Speculum of the Other Woman,* for instance, shows that the systematic unity and logical coherence of the texts of Plato, Descartes, Kant, Hegel, and Freud rest on a sexualized binary opposition (male/female) which in fantasy and in textual practice reduces the two poles of opposition to one, the "knowing subject" who is masculine and whose narrative voice produces the discourse. In her newer work, based on a close analysis of the language of more recent philosophers, beginning with Nietzsche, and including Heidegger, Levinas, and Derrida, she exemplifies cautious optimism that there may be a way to heal the split between poetry and philosophy—or fiction and theory. This split, which must also be a concern for Pagano, can be healed by a more poetic language "that does not *announce* (demonstrate) the truth but which *makes* the truth, that acts, but not at all in a fiction/theory hierarchy."[14] In her 1991 translated work, Irigaray finds in Nietzsche's prose, for example, a refusal of the authorial and authoritative subject/object opposition in favor of an intertextual *corps-à-corps*.[15] Part of her ironic appropriation and reconsideration of Nietzsche's text in the name, and from the perspecive of, "woman" addresses the broader feminist concern of separatism. In *This Sex Which is not One* she wrote that the "breaking away of women-among-themselves seems strategically necessary, but the staying away will amount finally to the same thing"; a denial, to put it in Pagano's terms, of our connection and dependence.[16]

Pagano's essay and the other works mentioned can be read as journeying toward feminist philosophical positions of difference. All add to a feminist tradition in terms of a web or network rather than of clearly circumscribed truths. They instantiate a feminist dynamic ensemble of *contesting* re/writings of the past, and in doing so articulate social struggles where difference is enscribed. Yet none of these various feminisms' accepts the dualisms which have served to hide our "bodies;" dualisms which have led to a reductive vision of human thought, which devalue the imagination in favor of the pursuit of scientific "truth", defined as the objective, detached, and neutral possession of nature's secrets. Though differently, they all call for new epistemological stands and for a re/founding of female subjectivity (politically) based on the web of social connectedness, communication and community. By taking notions such as embodiment and sexual difference rigorously, Pagano joins in creating new relationships with all of us in education who are (artfully) turning tricks to our own purposes.

NOTES

1. Luce Irigaray, *Marine Lover of Friedrich Nietzsche,* G.C. Gill, Trans. (New York: Columbia University Press, 1991), p. 4.

2. Luce Irigaray quoted in Frances Oppel, "Speaking of Immemorial Waters," in *Nietzsche, Feminism and Political Theory,* Paul Patton, ed. (New York: Allen and Unwin, 1993), p. 88.

3. Stephen Toulmin, *Cosmopolis: The Hidden Agenda of Modernity.* (New York: The Free Press, 1990), p. 28–36.

4. Ibid., 30.

5. See Donald McCloskey, "Platonic Insults: Rhetorical" *Common Knowledge,* 2 no. 2 (Fall 1993): 23–33.

6. See Michael Krause, ed., *Relativism: Interpretation and Confrontation* (South Bend: University of Notre Dame Press, 1989), Larry Laudan, *Science and Relativism: Some Key Controversies in the Philosophy of Science.* (Chicago: University of Chicago Press, 1990).

7. Barbara Herrnstein Smith, "Unloading the Self-Refutation Charge," *Common Knowledge,* 2 no. 2 (Fall 1993): 86. See also, Barbara Herrinstein Smith, *Contingencies of Value: Alternative Perspectives for Critical Theory.* (Cambridge: Harvard University Press, 1988), and Andrea Nye, *Words of Power: A Feminist Reading of the History of Logic.* (New York: Routledge, 1990).

8. Henry Louis Gates, Jr., "'Authenticity,' or the Lesson of Little Tree," *The New York Times Book Review,* November 24, 1991.

9. Donna Haraway, "Ecae Homo, Ain't (Ar'n't) I A Woman, and Inappropriate/d Others: The Human in a Post-Humanist Landscape" in *Feminists Theorize the Political,* Judith Butler and Joan W. Scott, eds. (New York: Routledge, 1992), p. 87.

10. Ibid., 88.

11. Ibid., 92.

12. Donna Haraway, "Situated Knowledges: The Science Question in Feminism and the Privilege of Partial Perspective," *Feminist Studies,* 14 (Fall 1988): 593–596. See also Donna Haraway, *Primate Visions: Gender, Race, and Nature in the World of Modern Science.* (New York: Routledge, 1989).

13. Luce Irigaray, *Speculum of the Other Woman,* G.C. Gill, trans. (Ithaca: Cornell University Press, 1985), p. 193.

14. Irigary, *Marine Lover of Friedrich Nietzsche.*

15. Oppel, "Speaking of Immemorial Waters," p. 92.

16. Luce Irigaray, *This Sex Which Is Not One,* G.C. Gill, trans. (Ithaca: Cornell University Press, 1985), p. 162.

27

Needs, Interests, Growth, and Personal Autonomy: Foucault on Power

James D. Marshall

There is an almost received view that elementary schools today are an improvement upon the elementary schools of the late eighteenth and early nineteenth centuries. A brief reading of Dickens which introduces one to the schools of Creakle and Squeers might be sufficient to persuade us that schools have improved, that we have a more humane approach to schooling, and that we have changed our attitudes towards children. From the last decade of the twentieth century the traditional elementary school appears not merely anachronistic but also almost irrational, because with its authoritarian approach to teaching, and the curriculum, it appeared to be concerned with merely utilitarian ends and social control. More recent liberal views on the importance of the individual, psychological theories of development or growth, demands to respect the needs and interests of children, and more enlightened social and political views have, to a certain extent, penetrated the modern school. Personal autonomy and not social control is now seen as a fundamental aim, if not *the* aim, of modern education (for a critique see Cuypers 1992).

Against a utilitarian, authoritarian, and teacher-directed pedagogy in the traditional elementary school, progressives urged that education should start from the child, from the child's needs and interests and from the child's nature and growth patterns. Progressives rejected the stressing of useful knowledge and emphasised instead the importance of knowledge acquired through discovery and play, and that knowledge was important in its own right. Here the teacher became, after Rousseau, an organiser of learning experiences and not a director, or in Freire's (1972) terms a "banker." Later, the absolute nature of knowledge was to be questioned also, and on both epistemological and cultural grounds. Knowledge of social and ethnic groups became important, not merely as a springboard to further learning, but as promoting the esteem of the child. But this knowledge was important also in raising the esteem of these social and ethnic groups, in promoting regional dialects and minority languages, and in the maintenance of threatened languages. Hence the importance that came to be made of the knowledge that the child brought to the elementary school and of the new ways in which this knowledge could be capitalised upon (Dewey 1938) protested vehemently that the progressive movement lacked a philosophy of education, especially an adequate notion of experience.

Dearden is a good example of a philosopher of education who saw something important in the child-centred movement's notions of needs, interests, and growth. Properly construed these notions are important, he argues, for the development of personal autonomy based upon reason. By this he means first, independence from authorities, and second that of testing the truth of things for oneself, whether by experience or by a critical estimate of the testimony of others, and that of deliberating, forming intentions and choosing shall be in accordance with a scale of values which are self formulated (Dearden 1968, p. 46). Both understanding and choice, or thought and action, are therefore to be independent of authority and based instead upon reason. Dearden and others construe personal autonomy as an ideal, to be aimed at by educators, and to which children are to be enabled to grow.

But are these really reforms, or are they merely *changes* in the forms that social control takes? Are we really more rational and humane than our forbears of a century or so ago? In this essay, I will first briefly summarise a notion of personal autonomy based upon the needs, interests, and growth of the child. Second, I will critique this ideal of personal autonomy from the work of the French philosopher/historian Michel Foucault. In particular, and in relation to the development of personal autonomy, it will be argued that if by personal autonomy there is claimed that there is an *autos* independent of a *nomos* then this is questionable if not mistaken, and if by starting with the child it is claimed that there is any such thing as human nature to start from, then this, also, is questionable. The constitution of the autos by external factors permits us to be governable. Finally, Foucault's notion of governmentality will be used to critique neo-liberal views of the individual which stress personal autonomy and individual choice, and which underlie recent reforms in national education systems (e.g., in Australia, Great Britain, and New

Zealand). The conclusion which will be drawn is that they too involve modern conceptions of governmentality, once again making the notion of personal autonomy problematic, if not illusory.

Starting With the Child

This section briefly develops a notion of personal autonomy which is based upon the philosophy of starting with the needs, interests and growth patterns of the child (refer to Dearden (1966, 1968) for his full account and for Dewey's account of growth (1916, 1938)).

Dearden correctly points out that when statements of needs, other than those of the basic or deficit needs of the child (food, shelter, warmth, . . .) are subjected to scrutiny, it can be seen that they usually depend upon underlying values. Statements of the needs of the child then tend to be systematically ambiguous between statements of fact and value judgements (1968, pp. 14–24).

Nor should statements of need be identified with statements about the wants of the child. Wanting food is not a criterion necessarily of needing food, nor is wanting to watch a particularly violent horror film necessarily a need of the child in the value sense of the term.

Dearden's discussion of the *interests* of the child raises similar problems to those identified in talk of needs. Statements of interests, of what is in a person's interests, are also systematically ambiguous between what a child is actually interested in, and what (s)he *ought* to be interested in (ibid., p. 17).

Dearden's position is then that neither the needs of the child nor the interests of the child can determine on their own the aims of education. However he notes "the real force" of the movement for starting with the child. First, the notions of needs and interests can provide a more meaningful starting point for the learning of basic skills so that they are not taught in mere isolation through drills and exercises. Second, they can provide a base from which "to move outward and onward in educationally valuable directions" (ibid., p. 21). Third, motivation would be improved because individual differences are not ignored and learning thereby improved. Finally this general approach *respects* the child as an individual person having a distinctive point of view and distinctive purposes to pursue. This Dearden concludes is the only moral way for pedagogy to proceed. However, even if needs and interests are suitably construed, and even if they are necessary for a philosophy of starting with the child, they are not sufficient for a philosophy of education.

What is further needed is some notion of growth or development. Here Dearden turns to Dewey's concept of growth. Like many of Dewey's notions, growth depends upon a quasi-biological analogy (Marshall 1984). For Dewey, growth is not to be conceived as being growth towards some end conceived externally to the process of growth but, rather, growth is conceived as an end in itself. As Peters points out, amongst many others, it is therefore difficult to ascertain what the criteria for growth should be (1977). Nor did Dewey's discussions help (e.g., in *Experience and Education*, Dewey 1938). Nevertheless growth then could not just be any form of growth, in any old direction whatsoever. But as many critics of Dewey have asked, in what direction or directions?

In the growth metaphor, when divested of the quasi-biological aspects, there is the notion of the ideal of the development of personal autonomy based upon reason. But whilst Dewey can be interpreted as advocating a form of autonomy based upon reason it is not his notion of autonomy or of reason which Dearden (and others) wish to advocate. The very emphasis by Dearden upon the notion of the personal, and the notions of independence, of testing the truth for 'myself', and of personal deliberation, do not fit easily into Dewey's holistic, shared and communal approaches to meaning and truth. Dearden, who is writing within a traditional liberal framework, sees the notion of personal autonomy identified above as a basic or minimal ideal which gives appropriate recognition to the notions of needs, interests, and growth. Justification of the consideration of the needs and interests of children is to be found in respect for persons and their individual projects, respect for social and cultural groups' values and knowledge, and the potential for harnessing skills to the actual needs and interests of the child which, in turn, should provide good motivation for later moves in educationally desirable directions. Justification for the idea of growth is that what is acceptable in this idea is the ideal of personal autonomy which in itself promotes independence, integrity, truth, and freedom of individual choice and judgement. Growth, in accordance with the defensible needs and interests of the child can be seen then as growth towards a chosen human ideal—personal autonomy.

Fundamental to the notion of the growth of personal autonomy is the very notion of autonomy itself. There are two aspects or components in the concept of autonomy: the *autos* and the *nomos;* or the individual self, and the law or laws which govern the individual self. Autonomy then is concerned with the *autos* or self adopting a *nomos*—laws or principles—independently of the judgements or manipulation of others so that the person is self-governing.

Initially the concept of autonomy was applied in a political rather than in an ethical, or even an educational context. It was city-states that were said to be autonomous, or not, according to their *independence* from more powerful adjoining cities or kingdoms. Plato is usually attributed with extending this notion from city-states to the individual but, arguably, this was improper (Baier 1973).

The subsequent major thrust in education has been to divest the concept of its political overtones and to represent it essentially as an ethical notion (Lankshear 1982). This has led to a masking of the political as if no politics or power is intruding into the "construction" of the autonomous individual.

When reason is further unpacked, and concrete educational proposals are countenanced, it usually turns out that for the young we are talking about inculcation into the disciplines or into forms of thought. How, under such conditions, can creativity, originality and initiative flourish (Lankshear, op. cit.)?

For Foucault, if there were to be any such thing as an autonomous person, in some sense as outlined above, then that person would be the effect of some form of social construction or *constitution*. To understand this we must first understand how Foucault sees the self as being socially constituted. In the terminology adopted above this would be to talk about the *autos*, but for Foucault there is little or no distinction between the *autos* and the *nomos*. In particular there is no self (autos) independent of the behaviour and principles (nomos) that classify or objectify that self as being an individual of a certain kind. Any talk of starting from the needs, interests, and growth patterns of the child to realise the aim of personal autonomy is mistaken for Foucault, insofar as this presupposes any notion of human nature logically prior to the social constitution of the self.

How does he see the self being constituted?

Foucault's Critique of Starting with the Child

Foucault's general answer is that the self is constituted in two ways; first by what can be called technologies of domination and, second, by what can be called technologies of the self. In *Discipline and Punish* Foucault (1979a) had advanced a thesis on the micro-politics of power as exemplified by the application of disciplinary techniques in various institutions but particularly the prison. These are essentially concerned with *how* the self is constituted by others, by "official discourses," and by what Foucault calls "power/knowledge." This thesis is amended later and developed further so that in *The History of Sexuality* (vol. 1, 1980), and in other writings (1983), Foucault looks at how we begin to do this to ourselves, so as to constitute our own identities. These technologies can be called, respectively, technologies of domination and technologies of the self.

Technologies of Domination

Foucault is not interested in Who or What questions about power. His question is *How.* He is interested in the extremities of the political system, at the micro-level, and with what we would normally call the *exercise* of power at these "lowly" levels (Foucault 1976, 1977). Arguably his account of state power is inadequate (Poulantzas 1978, Walzer 1986).

For Foucault power only exists when power relationships come into play—here he is a strict nominalist: power is not something which I can own or claim as only a "relation" of power exists. Power in this sense is to be distinguished from power/knowledge which involves only certain relations of power and a certain kind of knowledge.

Power/knowledge is located within the "deep" regimes of discourse/practice. It is a knowledge which permits statements such as, "children with learning difficulties can be identified within the first year of formalised instruction," to emerge and be legitimated as truth. It is produced by power and in turn induces power. Ian Hacking reads Foucault as asking Kantian type questions about the conditions of knowledge in general (1981). But Foucault's conditions are non-transcendental, and he locates them in socio-historical contexts which he referred to as *epistémès*. If in *The Order of Things* (1973), Foucault's "space" for the identification of these conditions is restricted to language, in *The Archaeology of Knowledge* (Foucault 1972) this "space" has been extended to cover technical and institutional conditions—what he sometimes refers to as discourse/practice. According to Foucault, this depth of knowledge cannot be dissociated from power and is designated therefore as "power/knowledge."

These power relations can cause us to become *subjects,* that is individuals with a certain identity and who can be *subjected?* How does this form of power come into existence? It is in *disciplinary blocks* that power/knowledge was developed and is "exercised" according to knowledge which has itself been the product of the exercise of power. That is power relations come into being because of this knowledge; their very existence in turn has knowledge as its effects. It is a particular type of power *and* knowledge, in which humanistic versions of Man [sic] and the human sciences are deeply embroiled, and it has immense educational implications. This repressive view of power is to be amended in Foucault (1983).

In order for power to be exercised in a disciplinary block a number of conditions must be fulfilled. Essentially these are concerned with the organisation of space, time, and capacities. First individuals are allocated to spaces and second, activities planned for them according to a timetable. The principles here are those of prescribing those activities appropriate to the discipline and establishing set regular rhythms for these activities. Third, activities are broken down into stages so that particular skills, abilities, or capacities can be developed in a given time through constant exercise. Examinations, classifications, promotions, and remedial treatments establish "normal" patterns of expectations. This knowledge developed through the exercise of power is used in the exercise of power to produce what Foucault calls *normalised* individuals. The norms which are established, the examinations and classifications, the promotions, remedial treatments and, where necessary, the disciplinary punishments, become aspects of governance. The examination occupies a key role also in that it lays bare to the individual his identity, or "true" self. In *Discipline and Punish* Foucault places the school firmly in the disciplines (1979a, p. 147).

Technologies of domination then essentially act on the body, and as a result of examination individuals are classified and objectified. But insofar as these objective classifications are adopted and accepted by individuals so also are their selves, their very identities, constructed. Liberal education aims to produce selves who are personally autonomous but any such notion is spurious according to Foucault, because technologies of domination involve the classification of children in certain ways, their normalisation through remedial "treatment", and thereby the construction of needs and interests deemed valuable in the development of personal autonomy. There is certainly no neutral growth or unfolding.

Technologies of the Self

In Volume One of *The History of Sexuality* the key to the technology of the self is the belief that it is possible to tell the truth about one's self (Foucault 1980). According to Foucault the belief that talking to professionals in a confessional manner about the body and its desires can reveal the deepest truths about one's self, has become almost commonplace. These truths are embedded in what Foucault calls sexuality. By telling the truth about one's sexuality, where the deepest truth is embedded in the discourse and discursive practices of sexuality, the individual becomes an object of knowledge both to oneself and to others. In telling the truth one knows oneself and is known to others in a process which is both therapeutic and *controlling*. But if sexuality structures the deepest truths, there are other areas in which we tell the truth. These discourses and the set of discursive practices associated with them are part of what Foucault calls the human sciences: they penetrate and "inform" the professions and their accompanying institutions, such as medicine, psychiatry, psychology, the law, *and* education.

The examination and the confession are the principal technologies for the construction of the self in *The History of Sexuality*, Volume One. These technologies have developed "from" medical models and parallel clinical methods in the nineteenth century. Certain clinical and psychiatric examinations required the subject to speak, and an authority trained in observation and interpretation to determine either the truth of what the subject said, or an underlying "truth" of which the subject may not even have been aware. What was needed for the construction of sexuality as the deepest underlying "truth" about ourselves and of sexuality as a discourse and discursive practice, were the "proper" techniques to elicit and to interpret confessions. But there was a shift from the strict medical clinical model. In that model the patient "confessed" to the doctor as part of the examination and the attempt to classify *objectively* the medical problem which needed correction: in the "new" model the confession and the examination are part of a process of therapeutic construction of the sexuality of subjects so that their discourse is controlled and they become individuals of a certain kind.

In addition in speaking the truth one does not merely describe oneself but one "*makes* it so" because of the performatory feature or function of language. Just as the judge makes the alleged person guilty by a declarative performance of guilt so, also, in speaking about ourselves in the new and refined concepts of the social sciences, do we construct ourselves, our very identities, in those acts of speech. Through the performatory function of speech then we begin to construct ourselves (Foucault acknowledged similarities here with Searle's work on speech acts).

The theme of domination by others is a constant theme in Foucault. The human sciences in classifying and objectifying individuals turn people into (*subjected*) subjects. If the shift in emphasis from "care of one's self" to "know thyself" is bad enough it is a self which is now to be known through the human sciences. To care for one's self in the twentieth century has come to be to fit oneself out, retail, with a set of "truths" which, by being learned, memorized, progressively put into practice, construct a subject with a certain mode of being and a certain visible manner of acting. Foucault believes that this modern self is *not* free because insofar as it is the outcome of the human sciences, political control and not freedom has been the aim.

It should be quite clear then that for Foucault the educational needs and interests of the child reflect values as to what is normal in the disciplinary block of the school. Eventually the child becomes just what the needs and interests classifications began to turn him or her towards—the slow learner, or the scientist, and the manager or the unemployable teenager. These needs and interests, dependent upon the structures of the educational disciplinary block, begin to shape the identity of the child. (Valerie Walkerdine (1984) has an important critique of the notion of the developing child.) In other words how the child develops or grows presupposes the object, the developing child, and because it is presupposed in the very practices and structures of the classroom and the pedagogy, it is hardly surprising that 'it' emerges.

Foucault said often that *Man* is dead. By this he means that "human nature" is a socially constituted entity. Moreover, there is something misconceived, and fundamentally false about this post-Enlightenment conception of Man, according to Foucault. Given that the autonomous person is a leading variant of this conception of Man, he would also deny that there is any such thing as autonomy, insofar as it involved the acceptance of universal laws, be they moral or otherwise (Kant and Barrow as opposed to Dearden and Hare). This is because he does not believe in universal laws or totalising theory. All theory is specific, applicable to localised and specific cases. Here the influences of Bachelard and Canguilhelm are to be seen (Gutting 1989). Just as there is no one history or philosophy of science so there are no universal principles to be used in all cases of independent judgement. In other words, for Foucault, there is no *nomos* to be accepted, if by that is meant there are universal *laws* or a grand totalising theory, to accept.

But if he attacks the *nomos* he also attacks the *autos,* that is the notion of a self which is able, in principle, to accept the *nomos.* This is also socially constituted. The notion of a self able to deliberate upon and accept laws so as to act autonomously as opposed to following laws heteronomously is a fiction, foisted upon the Western world post Kant as the basis for moral action but, for Foucault, in the cause of governmentality.

It is not just that he is objecting to persons accepting the *nomos,* because there is something suspect about the *nomos* that either leads to subjection, or unfreedom but, rather, that accepting the very notion of the *autos,* as being *independent* of the *nomos,* which obscures the fact that the *autos* is socially constituted, leads to unfreedom. It is not then a question of rejecting or negating the laws or *nomos* to be free, but of refusing to enter into any notion of an *autos* which polarises the options in any such manner. Here what he had to say on freeing oneself from sexual repressions is very apposite; sexual freedom was not to be gained à la California by merely rejecting the standard prohibitions.

In summary then the pursuit of the autonomous person involves the "social construction" of something which is destined to fail. From the very outset, the conception involves falsehoods. The particular falsehood to which Foucault objects most is that such a conception implies the possibility of freedom. For Foucault it doesn't because, stripped of its political connotations, it masks the fact that the constitution of such persons is a major political act. Consequently while we believe ourselves to be free, to be acting autonomously, in general, we are not. Instead we have become *governed.*

Governmentality

Foucault coined the term "governmentality" to refer to a domain of research which might also be called "governmental rationality" (1979b). By *governmentality* he meant something like a form of activity designed to guide, or to shape, or to affect, or to change the conduct of some person or persons. Governmentality was to be understood for Foucault both in a wide sense of the government of self and others, and in a narrower sense of self government. The question for governments was how to conduct their conduct so as to secure the security and perpetuity of the state. But according to Foucault the arts of government, or reason of state, have touched us all, so that we are not the free autonomous individuals and choosers of individual projects that the liberal framework (Nozick 1978), and liberal education (Strike 1982), would make us out to be.

Discipline and Punish is concerned with the microphysics of power, with technologies and techniques employing power knowledge at the capillary level. It ignores global issues of state power, and for this "omission" he was criticised by both marxists and liberals (e.g., Walzer 1986). Another criticism was that Foucault had represented society as a network of omnipresent power relations which, in subjugating human beings, seemed to preclude the possibility of meaningful individual freedom. Also rationality is restricted to techniques of power—the techniques of domination and the self—as exemplified in his early discussion of power and knowledge. Overall then he presented in *Discipline and Punish* a grim political scenario in which the grounds for resistance to oppression, even the very possibility of resistance, seem precluded. This amounts to a political philosophy of despair or nihilism.

Foucault's College de France lectures on governmentality were designed to address these issues. The basis of his response was that there was no discontinuity between the micro and the macro but, in trying to make this relationship clear, there was to be no returning to the theory of the state/sovereignty in traditional Hobbesian or Marxist terms. State theory and political philosophy is concerned too much with the state and its institutions, with sovereignty and the legitimation of the state rather than *with practices*.

However Foucault's *how* questions are not directed merely at the actually existing, at the factual domain of practices, or at the domain of the expedient, but they are also concerned with critique, problematisation, the limits of thought about such practices and, thereby for Foucault, with rethinking and inventiveness, at looking and thinking about other possible practices.

The link between micro and macro practices of power is bio-power. *Bio-power* had been introduced in *The History of Sexuality* to designate forms of power which treated people not as individual living beings, but as *subjects* of a population, in which individual sexual behaviour impinged upon population and hence with issues of state policy and power. But as bio-power has addressed itself increasingly towards life, shaping and forming *individuals;* so, also, has it generated a new form of counter-politics. Individuals, so formed, have begun to use that subjectivity as the basis for the formulation of needs and imperatives which are in effect counter political demands. Thus Foucault comes to see that power relations are strategically reversible. This leads to his 1983 reformulation of power in "Afterword" in which, for power relations to exist, the freedom of agents must be presupposed. Power cannot exist if the freedom of the subjects of power is annulled (1983).

Foucault's response to his critics began in 1978, when, throughout Europe a phase of neo-liberalism was commencing. He conceptualises recent neo-liberalism as a version of governmentality and argues that seen in this manner it presents an original and challenging phenomenon to which the Left was ill equipped to respond as it possessed no distinctive art of governing of its own. What was needed from a logic of the Left was a reconceptualisation of individual autonomy along with an assurance of security, for if the welfare state seems to be part of Foucault's target for exercising techniques of subjugation he also recognises its fundamental role in ensuring security for individuals.

Welfare and Education

In New Zealand we have undergone a stunning set of changes in the welfare state and in the education system (in its structure, provision, conceptualisation, and legitimation). There is little doubt that neo-liberal ideas *underlie,* though did not *cause* these changes. (There is no space to discuss this here (see Marshall and Peters 1990, 1991; Peters and Marshall 1992).) What is clear is that the old liberal consensus, and the assumed solidarity of shared community interests and concerns, reflected in the National State Education system, has been shattered. The liberal Left, by which I mean socio-democratic liberalism as exemplified by Rousseau and John Dewey, has had no real response to these changes, either intellectually or in practice, except to repeat the principles and policies of the past. If Foucault is correct, what is needed is an increased vigilance, and an increased imagination and inventiveness, for there is a complex problem space brought into play by these neo-liberal reforms. What is required is a neo-socio-democratic approach to these crises of the welfare state.

Much of the Left and the liberal-left critique of the "reforms", identifies the central theses of the reforms as involving a return to the free market and the commodification of welfare; education, for example, becomes just another economic entity, to be purchased, traded, and traded in for the latest model (or retrained or reskilled). But whereas in the writings of F. A. Hayek the market seems to be a natural phenomenon which needs only the right conditions to function spontaneously, later neo-liberal writers see a need of positive effort by governments to both institute and to sustain it (for example in Germany the *Ordoliberalen* (Gordon 1991, p. 41). According to the *Ordoliberalen* what had to be curbed, in order for the market to function, was the anti-competitive *effects* of society. Hence what was needed were changes in the laws and institutions that impinged upon the market hindering its competitive functioning. Thus conceptualised we have what at best might be described as a government of the social through economic means. That is the domain or area of government activity (Donzelot 1979) that mediates between society and the economy and, for example, cares for those exposed to the ravages of the liberal capitalist economy, is to be structured and controlled by economic means. But, immanent arguably in the later writings of Hayek, and explicit in the writings of the Chicago economist G. C. Becker, there is a move to reconceptualise the social in terms of the economic. Hayek presages this theoretical thrust by arguing that social justice is an empty and vacuous term and that if there is anything which could be called "social justice" that this is the outcome of economic activity. Becker theorises the social in economic terms by a series of extensions of economic theory and the redefining of objects within economic theory.

First there is an extension of the general domain of economics from the study of all behaviours concerning the possible allocation of resources to all behaviours concerning strategic choices between outcomes, means to desired ends and instruments and techniques. In other words it is extended to cover all rational conduct, and finally to *all* conduct, rational or irrational, which is a non-random response to its environment. Thereby economics encompasses the totality of human behaviour (Gordon 1991, p. 43). Given the totality of economic theory then it follows that economic theory would provide a theory for conceptualising and developing policy for the totality of governmental action.

But second in this theory there is a major shift in the objects or individuals of the new theory(ies) from classical economic theory. There is the postulation of a fundamental human faculty of choice. It is not just that human beings are autonomous or that their autonomy can be developed or that it is a duty to exercise autonomy but instead a faculty that sweeps aside or overrides the traditional categories and frameworks of the human sciences.

Autonomy insofar as it postulates a *nomos* and an *autos* permits a considerable amount of social construction in autonomy through the *nomos* or social character of the laws which constitute the *nomos*.

In particular the fundamental concepts of the domains of the human sciences are dispensed with and replaced with categories which reconceptualise the former notions as commodities. Here Foucault critiques Becker's analysis of crime and crime prevention, pointing out that the individuals of criminal and/or penal theory have been replaced by *homo economicus*. Hence there is no place for a psychological criminal type of individual. The criminal becomes a chooser who has chosen a supply of behaviours which society has calculated is not worthwhile tolerating. There is then no overriding category of social order which circumscribes the domain of behaviour. Instead order and criminality become reducible to *a supply of law abiding behaviour,* and *a supply of non law abiding behaviour,* that is, to commodities whose price is determined and calculated by the level of effective social demand. Far from there being absolute notions of acceptable moral and legal behaviour, what is moral or what is legal is seen as the outcome of a calculation of what is worthwhile, economically, for a society to tolerate.

In Hayek and Nozick's neo-liberalism the individual is seen as a person whose behaviour is not to be violated by the activities of government. Nozick sees the individual as possessing a fundamental right to formulate purposes and projects because they have this fundamental and defining faculty. This is a fundamental right which cannot be transgressed according to Nozick.

These new economic theories with another neo-liberal twist—behaviourism—sees *homo economicus* as perpetually responsive to the environment. In which case *homo economicus* is capable of infinite manipulation by the structuring of the environment. It is clear then that the environment can structure the choices of the individual. Hence economic intervention in the social can manipulate the individual, transgressing the fundamental rights of non-violation of the individual, and the individual's self formulated purposes and projects, of earlier liberal thought.

The logical implication is that one's life becomes an enterprise—the enterprise of the self. But it is not the self of classical liberal theory, where the right to formulate one's own purposes and projects was seen as inviolate. It is not just that the insertion of the economic into the social *structures* the choices of the individual but that, also, in behaviouristic fashion it manipulates the individual by penetrating the very notion of the self, structuring the individual's choices, and thereby, insofar as one's life is just the individual economic enterprise, the lives of individuals.

Needs, interests and growth then become contaminated as both needs and interests become constituted by the insertion of the economic into the social. The very *autos* is penetrated by these economic, individualistic, needs and interests, setting growth patterns towards, e.g., freedom from and choice. If the older liberal version of autonomy had some historical justifications, it is clear that these "new" individuals have different needs and interests and that their autonomy is programmatic.

Conclusion

Foucault's critique then is to the effect that personal autonomy in the old fashioned liberal sense of the term is an illusion. Liberal educators such as Dearden, Peters, and Strike, who advocate personal autonomy as a fundamental aim of education do not understand how modern power, through the technologies of domination and the technologies of the self, has produced individuals who are governable. That is, the very concepts which we use to "construct" our identities, even in neo-liberal theory, are such as to make independence and autonomy illusory. Even if modern approaches to governmentality must guarantee the individual, it is an individual whose choices and identity have been constructed. In developing an education whose aim is personal autonomy based upon the needs and interests of the child, we may not have abandoned utilitarian social control at all, but merely changed the forms that it can take. Also, for Foucault, the conjoint beliefs that the human sciences are improving the human condition and that we are progressing are, if not equally illusory, highly problematic. If Foucault is not the first person to make these points, the form and content of his critique are, however, unique.

BIBLIOGRAPHY

Baier, Kurt (1973). "Moral Autonomy as an Aim of Education" in Glenn Langford and D. J. O'Connor, eds. *New Essays in Philosophy of Education*. London: Routledge and Kegan Paul.

Barrow, Robin (1975). *Moral Philosophy for Education*. London: George Allen and Unwin.

Burchell, Graham, Colin Gordon, and Peter Miller, eds. (1991). *The Foucault Effect: Studies in Governmentality*. Chicago: University of Chicago Press.

Cuypers, Stefaan E. (1992). "Is Personal Autonomy the First Aim of Education?" *Journal of Philosophy of Education*, 26(1), 5–17.

Dearden R. F. (1968). *The Philosophy of Primary Education*. London: Routledge and Kegan Paul.

Dewey, John (1916). *Democracy and Education*. New York: The Macmillan Co.

Dewey, John (1938). *Experience and Education*. New York: Kappa Delta Pi.

Donzelot, Jacques (1979). *The Policing of Families*. New York: Pantheon.

Foucault, Michel (1972). *The Archaeology of Knowledge*. London: Tavistock.

———. (1973). *The Order of Things*. New York: Vintage.

———. (1976). "Two Lectures," in *Michel Foucault: Power/Knowledge*. Gordon Colin, ed. Brighton: Harvester Press, 78–107.

———. (1977). "Truth and Power," in *Michel Foucault: Power/Knowledge*. Gordon Colin, ed. Brighton: Harvester Press, 109–133.

———. (1979a). *Discipline and Punish: The Birth of the Prison*. New York: Vintage Press.

———. (1979b). "Governmentality." *Ideology and Consciousness*, 6.

———. (1980). *The History of Sexuality*. Vol. 1, New York: Vintage.

———. (1982). "The Political Technology of Individuals," in Martin, et al.; 145–162.

———. (1983). "Afterword: the subject and power" in Hubert Dreyfus and Paul Rabinow, *Michel Foucault: Beyond Structuralism and Hermeneutics*. Brighton: Harvester Press; p. 206–226.

Freire, Paulo (1972). *Pedagogy of The Oppressed*. Harmondsworth: Penguin.

Gordon, Colin, ed. (1980). *Michel Foucault: Power/Knowledge,* Brighton: Harvester Press.

Gordon, Colin (1991). "Governmental Rationality: An introduction," in (eds.) Burchell, et al., 1–51.

Gutting, Gary (1989). *Michel Foucault's Archaeology of Scientific Reason,* Cambridge: Cambridge University Press.

Hacking, Ian (1981). "The Archaeology of Michel Foucault," *New York Review of Books*, 14 May, 32–37.

Hayek, F.A. (1960). *The Constitution of Liberty*. London: Routledge and Kegan Paul.

Hoy, David Couzens (1986). *Foucault: A Critical Reader*. Oxford: Basil Blackwell.

Lankshear, Colin (1982). *Freedom and Education*. Three Rivers, Ca.: Milton Brookes.

Marshall, J.D. (1984). "John Dewey and Educational research." *Journal of Research and Development in Education*. 17(3): 66–67.

Marshall, James D. and Peters, Michael A. (1990). "The Insertion of New Right Thinking into Education: an example from New Zealand." *Journal of Education Policy,* 5(2): 143–155.

———. (1991). "Educational Reforms and New Right Thinking." *Educational Philosophy and Theory,* 23(2): 46–57.

Martin, L.H., Gutman, H. and Hutton, P.H., *Technologies of the Self*. Amherst: University of Massachusetts Press, 9–15.

Nozick, Robert (1976). *Anarchy, State and Utopia*, Oxford: Blackwell.

Peters, Michael and Marshall, James D. "Education, the New Right and the Crisis of the Welfare State in New Zealand." *Discourse,* 11(1): 77–90.

Peters, R.S. (1977). *John Dewey Revisited*. London: Routledge and Kegan Paul.

Poulantzas, Nicos (1978). *State, Power, Socialism*. London: New Left Books.

Strike, Kenneth (1982). *Educational Policy and the Just Society*. Urbana: University of Illinois Press.

Walkerdine, Valerie (1984). "Developmental Psychology and the Child Centred Pedagogy," in Henriques, J., et al., *Changing the Subject*. London: Methuen, 157–174.

Walzer, Michael (1986). "The Politics of Michel Foucault," in Hoy: 51–68.

28

Putting the Political Back Into Autonomy

James Tooley

Michel Foucault's prose can be rather impenetrable, so it is a relief to find educationalists who are prepared to grapple with it in the hope of finding relevant insights for our work. James Marshall is such an educationalist. He has written a provocative interpretation of Foucault, relevant to recent debates about autonomy and the role of the state in education. However, I think he draws misguided conclusions. Firstly, recent work by philosophers of education on autonomy as an educational ideal is not quite as opposed to Foucault as Marshall implies; however, even these writers *do* fail sufficiently to acknowledge some *political* dimensions of their work, which supports Marshall's criticism. Secondly, Marshall conflates two distinct philosophies under his label of "neo-liberalism"; but Hayek's thought is not susceptible to Marshall's critique. Indeed, Hayek's thinking and Foucault's method converge on a common critique of state intervention in education.

Much of the problem with interpreting Foucault, of course, lies in his understanding of power. In order to make any progress with my response to Marshall, then, I turn to this first.

Foucault on Power

The major insight offered by Foucault, as interpreted by Marshall, is that "the pursuit of the autonomous person involves the 'social construction' of some-

379

thing which is destined to fail. . . . such a conception implies the possibility of freedom. For Foucault it doesn't because, stripped of its political connotations, it masks the fact that the constitution of such persons is a major political act."

But this brings us to difficulties with Foucault's notion of power: for he conflates different types of power, and there are doubts about the efficacy of doing so (see for example Merquior 1985). For Foucault, power is omnipresent, "produced from one moment to the next, at every point, or rather in every relation from one point to another. Power is everywhere; not because it embraces everything, but because it comes from everywhere" ([1978] 1990, p. 93). But, if we are concerned, as Foucault and Marshall are, with domination and lack of freedom, then isn't there a worthwhile difference to be noted between the power exercised *by the state* and other forms of power? If this is conceded, then it has important repercussions for the argument which follows. Let us explore the difference using Foucault's prime example, the examination. Here, Foucault notes, "the superimposition of the power relations and the knowledge relations assumes . . . all its visible brilliance" (quoted in Hoskin 1990, p. 32); examinations function as a relationship of power between those with power (teachers, doctors, employers) to those without (pupils, patients, employees).

Now Foucault dwells on what might be called the "pathology" of examination. But a careful analysis of the historical record reveals that it is only when states get involved that "the examination" becomes pathological. Two examples illustrate this. Compare these two scenarios:

Scenario 1
I voluntarily decide to learn, say, how to solve quadratic equations. I find someone who is voluntarily willing to help; that person, with my voluntary consent, examines my understanding, in a diagnostic way, with a view to helping me perfect my knowledge and skills. Having perfected my skills, I then use them in whatever way I wish.

Scenario 2
The state compels me to attend a school and compels me to learn, say, quadratic equations. I am compelled to take an examination. Without passing the examination, I am forbidden to use the skills acquired.

Surely, to conflate these two situations as being equally oppressive is a gross misrepresentation of power relations?

Under the first scenario, to be sure—perhaps this is a Foucauldian insight?—power relations exist and can be examined (*pace* Foucault, see Merquior 1985, p. 111–12). There is the teacher's power over me, for he or she has the knowledge, skill etc., and I don't, as yet. There will also be the power relations in society which have made the solving of quadratic equations considered important knowledge. But note that all these power relations are far less oppressive than the state relations outlined above—and rather a luxury to be concerned with, if we are concerned with alleviating oppression. Crucially, they are less oppressive because I enter into the learning and examination process *voluntarily*. I don't have to accept that quadratic equations are worth solving; even if I do, I don't have to learn them; even if I learn them, I don't have to submit to the examination of my skills, and so on.

Consider a second example, the examination of the knowledge of the medical practitioner. Again, Foucault emphasises the oppressive nature of "power/knowledge" here. Again, historically, it was only when the state got involved that this circumstance too became oppressive: Foucault observes how the medical examination changed from students passively watching and listening, to where they were actively learning by doing (Hoskin 1990, p. 49). As it stands, this seems as though it could be empowering to those who are supposedly at the butt end of the power-knowledge relationship, the "patients." As Jones notes, rigorous examinations were introduced precisely because of complaints about the standards of medical education (1990). Before examinations became important:

> Examiners usually limited their questions to topics which the candidate had previously specified. They also prompted candidates during orals and ignored the fact that theses had often been written—for a suitable fee—by the students' teachers. In fact it was not until 1760 that the authorities at Montpelier decided it might be a good idea to actually fail some of the medical candidates in order to maintain standards (Ibid., p. 84).

So the examination can empower patients, for they are now in a position to know that their practitioners satisfied some basic requirements of skill and knowledge. Note, again *pace* Foucault, that without the power of the state being involved, a patient doesn't *have* to accept the examination as a *fait accompli*: a patient could still decide to go to an alternative qualification-less practitioner (for reasons of experimentation, or because such a person was cheaper, or whatever); or a patient might still question the usefulness of the qualification; crucially, if medical practitioners depend on patients' patronage for their income, then the patients' reciprocal power is ensured. This isn't theoretical speculation: Green (1985, 1993) documents how working class patients had an extraordinary degree of power over their doctors employed by the Friendly Societies before the state became involved in the power relationship, power in particular to keep charges low, and to dismiss incompetent practitioners.

But it is precisely when the power of the state becomes involved that the pathology of the examination arises. Foucault analyzed in *The History of Sexuality Volume 1* and *Discipline and Punish*, the role of the French state in creating the power of the medical establishment. Similarly, writing from a Foucauldian perspective, Goodson and Dowbiggin note the role of the state in promoting the rise of the powerful psychiatric lobby: "In effect, psychiatry forged *a kind of political settlement with the state* . . . a settlement which bene-fited both parties, but particularly the material self-interests of mental medicine" (1990, p. 111).

Again, Green notes how the medical profession in England "had long resented the dominance of the medical consumer" (Green 1993, p. 98). In alliance with the state, they used the power of the General Medical Council (the body charged by the state with licensing and dismissing medical practi-tioners) to undermine the sources of protection of patients' interests, outlawing competition between practitioners. Next, the medical profession forced through changes to the 1911 National Insurance Act which effectively undermined the mutual aid societies that had effectively ensured power to the working class patients, and gave the organised medical interests greater, and in the end, virtual monopoly power: the 1911 Act, "marked a giant step forward in the emancipation of the medical profession from lay control" (Green 1993, pp. 101–2).

The examination alone could not do this: on its own, the examination had facilitated patients' control over the quality of medical practitioners; coupled with *market* control over the practitioners, the examination gave great power to those who, if Foucault is to be believed, would be powerless. But it was only when the medical profession succeeded in "capturing the state" that these power-relations were distorted, and biased in its favour.

In short, then, even within Foucault's own exemplars, the power of the state must be distinguished from the power of other institutions. It is a seri-ous conflation to fail to separate out these different sorts of power, and not very useful if it is oppression, domination, and exclusion with which we are concerned. As Walzer complains: "Foucault desensitizes his readers to the importance of politics; but politics matters." (Walzer 1986, p. 63). However, if none of this convinces, then we will have to part company in the remainder of this paper. I can accept the Foucauldian insight (if such it is) that we can never get away from power altogether. But this doesn't mean that we can't get away from some types of power which are more oppressive than others.

This distinction between state and other power is crucial in what follows. Let us now turn to the liberal educators' discussions of personal autonomy: do they fall foul of the problems outlined by Marshall?

Liberal Educators, Autonomy and the State

Marshall argues that Dearden, and those writing in a similar vein, is guilty of "a masking of the political as if no politics or power is intruding into the 'construction' of the autonomous individual." Perhaps this is true of Dearden:

but is he representative of later strands of liberal educational thinking about autonomy? Reading Kissack suggests that he is not (1992). Kissack's argument, in brief, is that a *"genealogical educator"* survives Foucault's critique of knowledge and its concomitant power relations of domination, exclusion and oppression. This "genealogical educator" fits in well with the model of the liberal educator as outlined by Pat White (1983). Moreover, the Foucauldian notion of the *"genealogical transgressor"* can be thought of as defining what it is to be autonomous, and this notion fits in rather well with the definition of autonomy as given by John White (1982). Let us go through each of these steps.

The model of the "genealogical educator" put forward by Kissack is of an "interpretative intellectual," whose

> appreciation of the limits of epistemological ambition, her [sic] realiza-
> tion that reason's complicity with power precludes any universalist and
> reconciliatory legislative activity, compels her to adopt an interpretive
> function. (Kissack 1992, p. 168).

The interpretative intellectual can help clarify political conflict by offering contingent explanations: "she attempts to sustain the communicative processes which establish the transient equilibria of political agreement" (p. 169). Now, Kissack says that this intellectual *as educator* can survive the Foucauldian critique of knowledge, for he or she is aware of the status of knowledge, in particular its ambiguous repercussions: knowledge "enables people to organize and structure the world, empowers them as agents within an adverse environment, but, the will to truth as the will to power can also inflict and compound the miseries which the rational exponents of emancipation seek to eradicate" (p. 171). The educator as interpreter teaches the accumulated bodies of knowledge to the next generation, using established pedagogic techniques. However, both knowledge and pedagogy are subjected to scrutiny, along the lines of: "What is this Reason that we use? What are its historical effects? What are its limits, and what are its dangers? How can we exist as rational beings . . . committed to practising a rationality that is unfortunately crisscrossed by intrinsic dangers?" (Foucault quoted, p. 174).

Having constructed this portrait of the "genealogical educator", Kissack then points out that this model fits in well with the model of the "liberal educator" as enunciated by Pat White and John White. The liberal educator "is concerned with the relationship between freedom and reason as it is reflected in the implications of the development of knowledge for the exercise of power. She is 'liberal' because the issue of freedom is a formative and contextualising influence upon her educational projects and practices. . . . As a purveyor of knowledge, the modern educator is sensitive to the political effects of the transmission of knowledge, aware of the exclusionary and oppressive consequences of the formation of knowledge, whose empowering capabilities are acknowledged simultaneously." (p. 171).

Moreover, Kissack then shows that there is a definition of "autonomy" which is also compatible with Foucault's "transgressing genealogist" (p. 172). This is someone who, as *genealogist,* acknowledges the origins of types of knowledge and is aware of its limits and constraints; as *transgressor,* is continually aware that the oppressive, damaging and exclusionary nature of current knowledge can be violated. It is in this recognition that his or her autonomy lies.

But this bears similarities to John White's conception of the liberal educator "initiating" pupils toward autonomy—where autonomy is defined as "an appreciation of the diverse and conflicting possibilities available to the individual, of the limits and constraints imposed by circumstances, and the realisation that rational resolution is often not possible." (p. 160). John White stresses the lack of "any notion of the 'inherent aims of education' structured around a notion of the 'good for man'" (p. 175). Consequently, the liberal educator must allow his or her students to confront the problems of choice, knowing that all sets of criteria for decision are themselves up for grabs. The path towards autonomy consists of attempting to create for oneself a personal and political identity despite the recognition of the uncertainties of knowledge. The liberal educator initiating into autonomy can only help with the student's journey, but cannot point out where it might lead.

So, as argued by Kissack, the work of some contemporary liberal educators fit rather better into Foucault's framework of a form of "autonomy" which is not as illusory as that explored by Marshall. However, Kissack hints at a problem for the Whites—and it is here that the Foucauldian perspective bears fruit. Kissack sees that his portrayal of the liberal educator "emphasizes the necessary exemption of educational institutions from direct and explicit political pressure and prescriptions" (p. 180). But this is in striking contrast to the writings of John White, Pat White, and indeed, virtually every other liberal educationalist one can think of. For most argue, or assume, that their liberal education must be promoted by the state: this is suggested by Marshall, too, in his critique of the neo-liberal position, as we shall see. John White, for example, argues explicitly that it is the role of the state to promote autonomy through, *inter alia* a compulsory national curriculum (White 1990). I have argued at greater length elsewhere against so doing (Tooley 1993). But the most significant objections in the present context are that state involvement in the promotion of autonomy "crowds out" those institutions of civil society which would otherwise be concerned with promoting autonomy—the family, community, religious organisations. Hence, the state involvement in this is paradoxically likely to serve to undermine autonomy rather than promote it. That is, even if it was realistic to expect the state to be involved in supporting the creation of "genealogical transgressors", it would be undesirable to unleash its power in this regard.

So the conclusions here are that, although Marshall is not necessarily correct in showing that all liberal educators fail in appreciating the power/knowledge dimensions of their notion of autonomy, when it comes to conceiving of the role of the state in education, the Foucauldian critique *does* catch them all out. Foucault argues that: "The real political task in a society such as ours is to criticize the working of institutions which appear to be both neutral and independent; violence which has always exercised itself obscurely through them will be unmasked so that we can fight fear" (quoted Ball 1990, p. 7). Liberal educationalists fall into the trap of assuming that state education can be "neutral and independent"—a classic recent example of this can be found in McMurtry (1991) who talks about "independent" education when he means "state" education. Foucault would flinch at this; this has repercussions for our discussion of "neo-liberalism," to which we turn now.

Marshall on "Neo-Liberalism"

Marshall's critique, following Foucault, is that "neo-liberalism" brings about a reconceptualisation of "the social in terms of the economic." This creates a notion of the autonomous individual shorn of any moral considerations; the autonomous individual is "rational economic man," *homo economicus,* whose autonomy is an illusion of commodified choices, rigidly constrained by the economic structures in which the person is found.

Here Marshall reveals a fundamental conflation of different economic theories under the label "neo-liberalism". For Hayek and Becker (Marshall's main examples) are representatives of two fundamentally opposed schools of economic thought, respectively the Austrian and neo-classical schools. Firstly, Marshall's (and Foucault's) criticisms are aimed at *homo economicus:* the neo-classical economists, it is true, do make this behavioral assumption, that people are utility maximisers. But the Austrian economists fundamentally reject such a proposition. Their methodology assumes that individuals consciously act in order to achieve chosen goals. But this does not imply that people are rational actors in the neo-classical sense: People do not have complete or certain knowledge about the range of choices confronting them; their tastes are not identical or given; they do not have consistent or transitive preferences; action takes place through time, the future is not known, so actions may produce unexpected outcomes; people learn from such experiences and errors revealed alter future actions. All this is far removed from the *homo economicus* whom Marshall and Foucault decry (see Reekie 1984).

Again, Marshall complains that the "neo-liberals" seek the extension of economic theory to cover "all behaviours concerning strategic choices between outcomes," so that ultimately economics comes to "encompass the totality of human behaviour." Hayek's assumptions flatly disagree with this. But even for the neo-classicals, this conclusion still might be a little exaggerated: Marshall says that Becker's work on crime and crime prevention leads to order and criminality becoming commodities. But Becker is a positivist. He is making simplifying assumptions about human behaviour to see what follows. At most, order and criminality become "commodities" in the theory; there is no implication that they become this in policy prescriptions.[1]

But even if they did, even if policymakers were misled: then at worse Marshall's criticisms would only apply to the neo-classical economists. Hayek escapes completely. For far from arguing that individual autonomy be reduced to economic rationality, Hayek's view is that individual autonomy is fundamentally important for the protection of liberty; and liberty requires the creation and fostering of voluntary institutions which "serve as proving grounds for intellectual qualities such as seeking the truth and openness to contradiction, moral qualities such as honesty, service and self-sacrifice, and active qualities such as courage and determination" (Green 1993, p. 23).

The common caricature of Hayek as being in favour of *laissez-faire* is not even true: Hayek supports the classical liberal writers, who knew

> that it was not some sort of magic but the evolution of "well-constructed institutions," where the "rules and principles of contending interests and compromised advantages" would be reconciled, that had successfully channelled individual efforts to socially beneficial aims. In fact, their argument was never antistate as such, or anarchistic, which is the logical outcome of the rationalistic laissez faire doctrine; it was an argument that accounted both for the proper functions of the state and for the limits of state action. (Hayek 1960, p. 60)[2]

Marshall is not alone amongst critics of recent reforms to conflate these two distinct philosophies; what is the source of these confusions? Presumably one reason is that both attach importance to "markets". But for Hayek, markets are valuable primarily because of their *epistemic* function: "the market is not primarily an institution that allocates scarce resources to competing ends. Hayek is concerned to show us that neither the resources available in the economy, nor the variety of uses to which they might be put, is known to anyone. The role of the market is to economize on the scarcest resource of all—human knowledge . . . This is knowledge that by its very nature cannot be collected by a central planning board." (Gray 1992, pp. 6–7).

With this background, we can see what an Austrian philosophy of educational provision might look like.[3] Education would certainly not be "just another economic entity, to be purchased, traded, and traded in for the latest model." Education, for Hayek, is to do with moral, social and intellectual development, and, in civil society, these become the province of the whole of the community, parents, relatives, neighbours. Certain dimensions of education, of course, can be bought and sold on the market—books, schooling, computing services. But education itself does not become commodified at all. An Austrian philosophy of educational provision would assess the problems of educational central planning as being much the same as the problems of any other central planning: each unique individual holds different knowledge and skills, and different educational requirements. Information concerning this distribution of knowledge and skills could never be known by any central planning authority. It would also note, because of the tremendous "power that education can have over men's minds," that there were considerable dangers in "placing this power in the hands of any single authority" (Hayek 1960, p. 380). On both these counts the market is an obvious mechanism for distribution of educational opportunities.

Foucault and Hayek: Against State Education

Now we come full circle to Marshall on the liberal educators, for we see how the market in education will facilitate the development of autonomy. There are no state-driven "technologies of domination" and "technologies of the self" operating. Each individual would develop in a unique way, and his or her educational demands would develop iteratively, building on previous educational experiences. The educational "needs and interests" of each unique individual would develop outside of any state-imposed power structures.

Of course, we can agree with Foucault, there will be other "technologies of domination" and "technologies of the self" acting on each individual; but these will not be nearly as insidious as those which are state-imposed. And, these power structures can be much more easily *analyzed in terms of their genealogy,* and, hence, *transgressed* by the individual. For the power structures in which individuals find themselves will be largely of two sorts: firstly in terms of relationships with family, friends, community; secondly, in terms of the knowledge of the society at large. The first type of these power structures, operating as they do on a local level, can be discovered and, if so desired, rejected: we know that people can leave their families and communities behind quite easily. The power structures embedded in the knowledge itself are more diffuse and probably harder to transgress, but even so, if there is no compulsion operating, then the technologies of domination and of the self need not be oppressive: no one has to learn anything, no one has to accept any piece of knowledge or skill as valuable. For sure, there will be benefits to learning certain things, but one can make judgements as to whether to seek these by weighing up their benefits and costs. But, importantly, these benefits and costs are not likely to be in terms of the anti-educational credentialism which we see in today's societies: Hoskin notes, in true Foucauldian fashion, that it is simply the examination that "marks the onset of the . . . credential society" (1990, p. 48). But a careful analysis of the "diploma disease" shows that it is only when *states* get involved in the educational process that credentialism becomes pathological:

"It is not a bad generalisation that the almightiness of the certificate varies in direct proportion to the predominance of the state in the development process." (Dore 1976, p. 74).

Of course, liberal educators will throw up their hands in horror at the idea of markets in education; no doubt they will argue that in markets, there will be lack of equality of opportunity, and that all need initiation into culture before they can make "informed" choices. To the former objection, we can allow that this might bring in the need for a "safety net" in educational provision, a legitimate concern of the state to ensure that no one is too poor to partake of educational opportunities (Tooley 1992). As to the latter, it seems rather farfetched to assume that state involvement, through a compulsory national curriculum for example, will have the result of initiating everyone into the required areas of culture. State compulsion breeds passive and active resistance, imprisoned pupils easily avoid the forced diet of what is supposed to be for the good of their later choices.

So we have Foucault's "transgressing genealogist" and Hayek's philosophy of the market converging on the desirability of markets in educational provision, the opposite of where Marshall saw Foucault's arguments leading. Interestingly however, elsewhere he comes closer to this formulation when he notes that "familiar enough demands from the Left" such as "the redistribution of education, its reorganization, or its cleansing of ideological content" will not satisfy a Foucauldian analysis: "Education," according to Marshall, "because of modern power, must take on a new form in which freedom is not the traditional freedom which is meant to be achieved under the guise of rational autonomy." I suggest that the type of education he is groping towards there is precisely the market model I have outlined. Deinstitutionalised, liberated from the state, the market in education would satisfy his Foucauldian enterprise.

NOTES

1. Friedman stresses that the role of the neo-classical economist is to seek to explain facts and make predictions, not to make realistic assumptions. His example of the billiard play well illustrates this position.

2. So we see that the supposed conflict between Hayek and the *Ordoliberalen*, which Marshall highlights, is imaginary: both seek not markets alone, but also a well-constructed system of law and morals, in order to preserve our freedom.

3. This isn't necessarily Hayek's philosophy of educational provision. Hayek was influenced by Friedman's early discussion of educational provision, in terms of vouchers and compulsion (Friedman 1955). But then Friedman, influenced by West (1970), changed his views (see Friedman and Friedman 1990, pp. 162–3). These later views, doubting the need for compulsion and state funding except in a minority of cases, would seem more compatible with Hayek's position.

BIBLIOGRAPHY

Ball, Stephen J. (1990). "Introducting Monsieur Foucault," in Stephen J Ball, ed. *Foucault and Education: Disciplines and Knowledge.* London: Routledge.

Dore, Ronald (1976). *The Diploma Disease.* London: George Unwin.

Foucault, Michel ([1978] 1990). *The History of Sexuality: Volume 1 An Introduction.* New York: Vintage Books.

Friedman, Milton ([1953], 1984). "The Methodology of Positive Economics," in Daniel M. Hausman, ed. *The Philosophy of Economics: An Anthology.* Cambridge: Cambridge University Press.

Friedman, Milton (1955). "The Role of Government in Education," in Robert A. Solo, ed. *Economics and the Public Interest.* New Brunswick, NJ: Rutgers University Press.

Friedman, Milton and Friedman, Rose (1990). *Free to Choose: A Personal Statement.* Pan Books, London.

Goodson, Ivor and Dowbiggin, Ian (1990). "Docile bodies: Commonalities in the history of psychiatry and schooling," in Stephen J Ball, ed. *Foucault and Education: Disciplines and Knowledge.* London: Routledge.

Gray, John (1992). *The Moral Foundations of Market Institutions.* IEA Health and Welfare Unit, Choice in Welfare No. 10, London.

Green, David G (1985). *Working-Class Patients and the Medical Establishment: Self-help in Britain from the Mid-Nineteenth Century to 1948.* Gower: Aldershot.

Green, David G (1993). *Reinventing Civil Society: The Rediscovery of Welfare Without Politics.* IEA Health and Welfare Unit, Choice in Welfare No. 17, London.

Hayek, F.A. (1960). *The Constitution of Liberty.* London: RKP.

Hoskin, Keith (1990). "Foucault under examination: the crypto-educationalist unmasked," in Stephen J Ball, ed. *Foucault and Education: Disciplines and Knowledge.* London: Routledge.

Jones, Richard (1990). "Educational practices and scientific knowledge," in Stephen J Ball, ed. *Foucault and Education: Disciplines and Knowledge.* London: Routledge.

Kissack, Mike (1992). *Education, Freedom and Reason.* PhD thesis. Johannesburg: University of the Witwatersrand.

Marshall, James D. (1990). "Foucault and educational research," in Stephen J. Ball, ed. *Foucault and Education: Disciplines and Knowledge.* London: Routledge.

Marshall, James D. (1994). "Need, Interests, Growth and Personal Autonomy: Foucualt on Power," in Wendy Kohli, ed. *Critical Conversations in Philosophy of Education.* New York: Routledge.

McMurtry, John (1991). "Education and the Market Model," *Journal of Philosophy of Education* 25(2): 209–217.

Merquior, J.G. (1985). *Foucault.* London: Fontana.

Reekie, W. Duncan (1984). *Markets, Entrepreneurs and Liberty: An Austrian View of Capitalism.* New York: St Martin's Press.

Tooley, James (1992). "Equality of Opportunity Without the State?" *Studies in Philosophy and Education* 12: 153–163.

Tooley, James (1993). *A Market-Led Alternative for the Curriculum: Breaking the Code.* London: Tufnel Press.

Walzer, Michael (1986). "The Politics of Michel Foucault," in *Foucault: A Critical Reader*. David Couzens Hoy, ed. Oxford: Basil Blackwell.

White, John (1982). *The Aims of Education Restated,* London: RKP.

White, John (1990). *Education and the Good Life,* London.

White, Patricia (1983). *Beyond Domination: An Essay in the Political Philosophy of Education*. London: RKP.

West, E.G. (1970). *Education and the State*. London: Institute of Economic Affairs.

Contributors

Kal Alston is Assistant Professor of Educational Policy Studies and Women's Studies at the University of Illinois, Urbana/Champaign. Her research focuses on the cultural representation of teaching and issues of race, gender and sexuality.

René Vincente Arcilla is Assistant Professor of philosophy and education at Teachers College, Columbia University. His writings have explored how questions of pragmatism, particularly those rooted in the work of Richard Rorty, metaphysics, tragedy, and multiculturalism bear on our educational ideas.

Clive Beck is Professor of Philosophy of Education at the Ontario Institute for Studies in Education and the University of Toronto. He has written several books on ethics and moral/values education, the most recent being *Learning to Live the Good Life: Values in Adulthood*.

Philip W. Bennett taught Philosophy at State University of New York at Cortland for seventeen years. His published philosophical writings have focused on the work of Ludwig Wittgenstein. He is now writing a book for more general audiences on living well.

Landon E. Beyer is Associate Professor and Director of Teacher Education in the School of Education at Indiana University. His scholarly writings are interdisciplinary in nature, bringing together curriculum theory, teacher education, social theory and aesthetics. A forthcoming book on *Curriculum Conflict: Social Visions and the Prospect of Democracy*, co-authored with Daniel Liston will be published in 1995.

C.A. Bowers teaches in the area of curriculum theory and environmental studies at Portland State University. In addition to writing articles and books that introduce a cultural and linguistic perspective into the discussion of educational, technological, and environmental issues, he has also published in Deep Ecology journals. His new book, *Educating for an Ecologically Sustainable Culture: Re-Thinking Creativity, Intelligence, Moral Education and Other Orthodoxies in Education* will appear shortly.

Nicholas Burbules is Associate Professor in the Department of Educational Policy Studies, University of Illinois, Urbana/Champaign. He is also current editor of the journal *Educational Theory*. His recent publications include the book, *Dialogue in Teaching: Theory and Practice*.

Suzanne de Castell is Professor of Philosophy of Education at Simon Fraser University in British Columbia. She has published on literacy as well as on educational history, philosophy, and theory. Her current work centers on agency, equity, and representation, including a forthcoming volume with Mary Bryson, *Radical In(ter)ventions: Identity, Politics and Difference/s in Educational Praxis*.

Walter Feinberg is Professor in the Department of Educational Policy Studies, University of Illinois, Urbana/Champaign. He is also Director of the Program for the Study of Cultural Values and Ethics. His latest book, published in 1993, is *Japan and the Pursuit of a New American Identity: Work and Education in a Multicultural Age*.

James M. Giarelli is Associate Professor of Philosophy and Education in the Graduate School of Rutgers University. He has published widely in social philosophy, ethics and educational theory and is co-editor with Peter McClaren of *Critical Thinking and Educational Research*, forthcoming in 1995.

Maxine Greene is Professor of Philosophy and Education Emerita at Teachers College, Columbia University. She has published extensively in Philosophy of Education, education and the arts, and multicultural education. Her most recent book is *The Dialectic of Freedom*.

Kevin Harris holds the Chair in Educational Policy Studies at Macquarie University in Sydney, Australia. He is widely published on topics relating to the social construction of knowledge, the politics of schooling, teacher education, and social and economic aspects of education and schooling. His most recent book is *Teachers: Constructing the Future*.

Wendy Kohli is Associate Professor of Curriculum Studies at Louisiana State University in Baton Rouge. Her published scholarship includes work on critical hermeneutics, critical-feminist pedagogy, and educational theory and practice in the former Soviet Union.

Mary S. Leach is Associate Professor in the Humanistic Foundations program at the Ohio State University. Her scholarship includes work in feminist poststructuralist theory as well as pragmatism and feminism.

James D. Marshall is Foundation Dean of Education at the University of Auckland in New Zealand. He has authored a number of books and monographs, published widely in international journals, and is at present completing manuscripts on Wittgenstein (co-editor) and Foucault.

Jane Roland Martin, Professor of Philosophy Emerita at the University of Massachusetts, Boston, has written numerous articles on the Philosophy of Education, curriculum theory, and feminist philosophy. Her most recent book is *Changing the Educational Landscape.*

Alven Neiman is Associate Dean and Concurrent Associate Professor in the College of Arts and Letters at Notre Dame University. He has written on education in the work of Ludwig Wittgenstein, Alsdair MacIntyre, Richard Rorty, and Saint Augustine.

Nel Noddings is Lee L. Jacks Professor of Child Education at Stanford University. She has published widely in education and ethics and feminist educational philosophy. Her latest book is *Educating for Intelligent Belief and Unbelief.*

Jo Anne Pagano is Associate Professor of Education and Chair of the Education Department at Colgate University. She is the author of *Exiles and Communities: Teaching in the Patriarchal Wilderness.*

D.C. Phillips is Professor of Education and Philosophy at Stanford University. His scholarly interests are centered on philosophy of the social sciences and philosophy of educational research. His most recent books include *The Social Scientist's Bestiary* and *Philosophy, Science and Social Inquiry.*

Madhu Suri Prakash is Associate Professor of Education at the Pennsylvania State University. Her current research interests include multiculturalism, postmodern ecology, ecological literacy, ecofeminism, feminist pedagogy, and ethics and moral education.

David Purpel is Professor of Education at the University of North Carolina, Greensboro. He has edited a number of books on curriculum and moral education and is the author of *The Spiritual Crisis in Education* and (with Svi Shapiro) of the forthcoming *Beyond Excellence in Education and Liberation: A Critique of Public and Professional Educational Discourses.*

Emily Robertson is dual Associate Professor of Education and Philosophy and Chair of the Department of Cultural Foundations Department at Syracuse University. Her primary research interests include analysis of educational aims in relationship to moral, political, and social ideals and to theories of knowledge, particularly the development of capacities for critical reflection and for moral perception and judgment.

Svi Shapiro is Professor and Chair of the Department of Educational Leadership and Cultural Foundations at the University of North Carolina,

Greensboro. He is the author of *Between Capitalism and Democracy: Educational Policy and the Crisis of the Welfare State.*

Harvey Siegel is Professor of Philosophy at the University of Miami. He has published widely in philosophical and educational journals. His most recent book is *Relativism Refuted: A Critique of Contemporary Epistemological Relativism.*

Lynda Stone is Associate Professor of Philosophy of Education at the University of North Carolina, Chapel Hill. She has published works on feminist epistemology and ethics and has edited *The Education Feminism Reader.*

James Tooley studied for his Ph.D. at the Institute of Education, University of London and now works at the University of Oxford, Department of Educational Studies. His current research interest is focused on "enterprise, education, and ethics."

Patricia White is Research Fellow in Philosophy of Education at the Institute of Education, University of London and is currently the Chair of the Philosophy of Education Society of Great Britain. Her published research includes work in the political and ethical aspects of Philosophy of Education, including *Beyond Domination: An Essay in the Political Philosophy of Education.*